THEORIES AND APPLICATIONS
OF COUNSELING

THEORIES AND APPLICATIONS OF COUNSELING

Systems and Techniques of Counseling and Psychotherapy

By

DONALD J. TOSI
STEVEN W. LECLAIR
HERMAN J. PETERS
and
MICHAEL A. MURPHY

The Ohio State University

CHARLES C THOMAS • PUBLISHER
Springfield • Illinois • U. S. A.

Published and Distributed Throughout the World by
CHARLES C THOMAS • PUBLISHER
2600 South First Street
Springfield, Illinois 62794-9265

© *1987 by* CHARLES C THOMAS • PUBLISHER
ISBN 0-398-05345-6
Library of Congress Catalog Card Number: 87-6469

With THOMAS BOOKS *careful attention is given to all details of manufacturing
and design. It is the Publisher's desire to present books that are satisfactory as to their
physical qualities and artistic possibilities and appropriate for their particular use.*
THOMAS BOOKS *will be true to those laws of quality that assure a good name
and good will.*

Printed in the United States of America
Q-R-3

Library of Congress Cataloging in Publication Data
Theories and applications of counseling.

Includes bibliographies and index.
1. Counseling.   2. Psychotherapy.
I. Tosi, Donald J.   [DNLM: 1. Counseling.
2. Psychotherapy.   WM 55 T396]
BF637.C6T48   1987   158'.3   87-6469
ISBN 0-398-05345-6

THIS BOOK is dedicated to Dr. Herman J. Peters. He was a major contributor to the book, and to the profession of counseling as a whole. Dr. Peters was involved with the conceptualization, writing, editing and many meetings so vital to the completion of this project. His thoughts, ideas, and insights into counseling and human behavior have been incorporated in some form throughout the manuscript. It is our regret that he was not able to live to see the completion of this book.

Donald J. Tosi
Steven W. Leclair
Michael A. Murphy

PREFACE

THE PROCESS of counseling and psychotherapy is described by numerous theories giving the impression that each is a complete system. Herink published a book describing 240 different systems and techniques of counseling and psychotherapy — a far cry from Hartman's 36 systems published some years before. The proliferation of theories and techniques of counseling and psychotherapy makes it virtually impossible for a counselor to remain current. With this new wave of counseling approaches that offer counselors a rich and varied menu of possibilities, we decided to include in this text representatives from classical and contemporary systems that have unique qualities and show particular merit for practice.

This text provides a fundamental description of twelve theories of Counseling and Psychotherapy. Each theory is presented so that the reader will be able to grasp the historical and philosophical bases of the approach as well as the principles of assessment, treatment planning and implementation, and evaluation used. To clearly illustrate similarities among the theories, chapters were grouped into Psychodynamic, Existential-Humanistic, Cognitive Behavioral, and Systems and Family Perspectives.

To truly understand the strategies and techniques of counseling and psychotherapy the student must experience them in some way. This was accomplished through the inclusion of case examples. Cases depict the work of counselors and therapists in schools and community settings. Author's comments will accent important shifts and trends for the reader.

The introductory chapter attempts to establish the historical and scientific bases of counseling theory and practice. Such a chapter provides a common ground for the readers to determine more easily the appropriateness of each theory for their own practice. Similarly, the last chapter of the book highlights important issues which currently impact practice in the counseling profession.

Extensive research support will not be presented for each system of counseling within each chapter. Instead, we summarized some of the major reviews of counseling and psychotherapy outcome research across various systems in the final chapter of the book. For example, the work of Smith, Glass, and Miller on meta-analysis of counseling/psychotherapy outcomes by specific orientation is featured.

The Organization of the Text

The major systems of counseling and psychotherapy are organized into four major classifications: Psychodynamic, Existential-Humanistic, Cognitive-Behavioral, and Systems and Family. We endeavored to present each theory clearly and concisely and with sufficient depth. The four classifications and representative systems are:

I. Psychodynamic Perspectives
   a) Edward Bordin's *Ego-Developmental Theory*
   b) Alfred Adler's *Individual Psychology*
   c) Eric Berne's *Transactional Analysis*

II. Existential-Humanistic Perspectives
   a) Carl Rogers' *Person-Centered Counseling*
   b) Fritz Perls' *Gestalt Therapy*
   c) Viktor Frankl's *Logotherapy*

III. Cognitive-Behavioral Perspectives
   a) Carl Thoresen's *Intensive Counseling for Self-Efficacy*
   b) Albert Ellis' *Rational Emotive Therapy*
   c) William Glasser's *Reality Therapy*

IV. Systems & Family Perspectives
   a) Virginia Satir's *Communications and Feeling Approach*
   b) Paul Watzlawick's *Interactional Approach*
   c) Salvador Minuchin's *Structural Family Therapy*

Each theory is organized along two basic dimensions: *foundations and structure* and *applications*. Under the rubric of foundations and structure are: historical foundations; philosophical foundations; social-psychological foundations; the development of the person; concepts of functional and dysfunctional behavior; concepts of behavior change; assessing human functioning; goals and direction of counseling; the counseling process: structuring, facilitating, and terminating; counseling techniques and procedures; and evaluation of counseling outcomes. Case applications reflect a variety of life adjustment problems encountered by practicing counselors that range from career decisions to severe dysfunctional behavior.

CONTENTS

THEORIES AND APPLICATIONS
OF COUNSELING

CHAPTER 1

COUNSELING THEORY: HISTORICAL AND SCIENTIFIC BASES

Introduction

THE COUNSELING profession is gaining wide acceptibility since its more formal recognition in the middle of this century. The scope of the profession covers a range of services to people who need help coping with the demands of the social environment as well as those that are self-imposed.

We live in times of rapid transition. Technology has increased at an exponential rate in this age of the computer while the economy has expanded and contracted numerous times in our life time. Given the presses of social, political and economic change, people seem driven by the need to achieve mastery over themselves and the environment. Several questions may be raised. Has the pace of life accelerated to the point that we no longer comprehend just what it means to be masters of our destiny? Do we have the luxury of time to reflect upon our values and personal philosophy of life? Have we become frantic in our motivations to achieve personal identity? Are we altogether sure about who we are and where we are going? Many people today experience confusion, fear, and self-alienation. But on a more positive note, confusion, fear, and alienation can impel people to find novel and creative solutions to their problems and dilemmas.

The counseling profession's main reason for existence (like other helping professions such as social work, psychiatry, and clinical psychology) is to try to help people make some sense out of the confusion, anxiety, and stresses of our times and to offer, as well, some reasonable solutions and perspectives. Numerous theories of counseling and psychotherapy have come into existence over the years that have impacted on practice. The twelve major theories of counseling and psychotherapy

3

described in this book were chosen because of their popularity and their applicability to the problems of present-day society.

The first chapter is divided into six sections: (1) A definition of counseling; (2) Historical themes influencing the counseling profession; (3) Theory—what is it and what does it do; (4) How a theory is evaluated; (5) Counseling as a systematic scientific, and intuitive process; and (6) Four perspectives on theory in behavioral science.

A DEFINITION OF COUNSELING

Counseling can be defined generally as a relationship between two people, one designated as a counselor (helper) and the other as a client (helpee). This relationship, governed by the laws of learning, has certain characteristics that differentiate it from other relationships. First, the counselor is professionally trained in the applied behavioral sciences. Second, in a collaborative effort with the client, the counselor helps to identify personal, social, or career problem areas; to determinate counseling goals; to implement techniques for behavioral change; and to evaluate the outcomes of counseling. Third, the counselor facilitates the development of a relationship that provides a climate for the client to expand self-awareness, explore possibilities for growth, learn new behavioral skills, and achieve a better understanding of the environment. Characteristics of counseling relationships as we will see are described by numerous theorists with varying emphases.

The focus of counseling, as opposed to remedial psychotherapy, is mainly on individuals who function well but experience some personal difficulties in life adjustment or who want to develop their potential. Counselors do, however, work in settings that require them to deal with severe dysfunctional behavior and health related problems and often do involve themselves in psychotherapy. Psychotherapy usually focuses on personality reconstruction and the remediation of severe dysfunctional behavior. We do, however, recognize that the distinctions between counseling and psychotherapy are often unclear.

Counseling and psychotherapy services are currently offered in diverse settings concerned with helping people deal with life problems. Counselors work in elementary and secondary schools, colleges and universities, mental health and rehabilitation agencies, health care facilities, and in private practice. The general public is becoming increasingly aware that counseling is a vehicle for exploring human potential and promoting better mental and physical health. Moreover, there is growing specialization within the profession. Some specialized applications deal with marital and family problems, divorce adjustment, sexual problems, career development and vocational matters, and vocational rehabilitation.

HISTORICAL THEMES INFLUENCING THE DEVELOPMENT OF THE PROFESSION OF COUNSELING

The history of the counseling profession, like any movement, reflects the sociocultural, political, and economic structure of a given period. A profession, no matter how scientific it may portray itself to be, must be posed against the "Zeitgeist" (spirit of the times). Thus, a brief sketch of some of the historical factors that spawned this profession can add greater perspective to the knowledge of the theories and techniques germane to it.

The profession of counseling psychology was born in 1951 when the Division of Counseling and Guidance of the American Psychological Association became the Division of Counseling Psychology. That same year, the American Personnel and Guidance Association (presently, the American Association of Counseling and Development) was formed. The counseling profession was a product of several streams of influence: the vocational guidance and career development movements, the psychotherapeutic movement, and the community mental health and comprehensive health care movements.

THE VOCATIONAL GUIDANCE AND CAREER DEVELOPMENT MOVEMENTS

The vocational guidance movement was an attempt to improve the vocational adjustment of boys and girls beyond elementary and secondary school. The first vocational guidance program was started in San Francisco in 1885 by George Merrill. In 1898, Jesse B. Davis initiated an educational career counseling program in a Detroit high school. Frank Parsons, a few years later, established and directed the Vocational Bureau of Boston and authored a book titled *Choosing a Vocation* (1909).

In 1913, the National Vocational Guidance Association was founded in Grand Rapids, Michigan. Early developments in vocational education stimulated a number of legislative efforts that furthered the movement. Legislation providing direct support to vocational education, and indirectly benefitting counseling and guidance, were the George-Reed Act (1919), the George-Ellzy Act (1924), the George-Deen Act (1936), and the National Defense Education Act (1958). The National Defense Education Act (NDEA) established funds for the preparation of school counselors and for counselor education training programs. NDEA was expanded in 1964 to prepare elementary and postsecondary school counselors.

Ten years later, Sidney Marland, commissioner of the United States Office of Education, initiated a strong promotion of career education. Counselors who worked in elementary, secondary, and higher education were asked to play major roles in career education and guidance. The need to help people make well informed choices about their work and career stimulated the creation of techniques and procedures to aid in the decision-making process. As early as 1917, tests of mental abilities were developed (Army Alpha and Beta) for screening soldiers in World War I. The Strong Vocational Interest Blank was published in 1927, and in 1939 the Kuder Preference Record for measuring vocational interests was published. Since these earlier times, significant advances have occurred in the identification and measurement of vocational interests.

In the early 1950's, a number of vocational and career development theories were advanced by Ann Roe, David Tiedeman, Donald Super, Eli Ginsburg, and John Holland. These theories attempted to explain the process of vocational and career development and how people formulated their decisions about work. Since that time numerous studies have been conducted on the validity of these theories and on how well they predict vocational and career choice.

THE PSYCHOTHERAPEUTIC MOVEMENT

Counseling for personal and social problems had its beginnings in the early part of the twentieth century with the development of comprehensive theories of personality and of psychotherapy, particularly psychoanalysis. The psychotherapy movement evolved over the course of 80 years and many of its concepts were found to be quite useful for enhancing the personal growth and development of an increasingly wide range of people seen in clinical practice. The contributions of psychodynamic, existential-humanistic, cognitive-behavioral, and family and systems models of psychotherapy of counseling theory and practice are considered in this section.

Psychodynamic Psychotherapy

Sigmund Freud and Joseph Breuer in the classic work, *Studies in Hysteria* (1895), observed that neurotic symptoms involved psychological conflicts and emotional experiences that could be traced to early childhood trauma. They concluded that unconscious forces were largely responsible for many psychological and physical symptoms. Breuer and Freud posited that unconscious forces in the personality can exclude painful feelings from awareness (repression) and prevent the recognition of painful feelings (defenses and resistances). The result was neurotic behavior that stemmed from the interplay of unconscious intrapsychic conflicts and defense mechanisms (dynamics). These fundamental ideas served as the foundation of the psychoanalytic theory of personality.

Freud and Breuer noted that when people became aware of repressed traumatic experiences and were able to verbalize them the symptoms would disappear. For example, Breuer found in working with Anna O, that the cure for "hysteria," a form of neurosis, depended on catharsis ("purging of the soul") as a way to release bottled up emotional energies.

Building on the idea of catharsis, Freud introduced a psychotherapy process characterized by the techniques of *free association, dream analysis, transference,* and *interpretation.* At the same time he developed a more expanded theory of human behavior. Today, psychoanalysis is the most comprehensive theory of personality, psychopathology, and psychotherapy. Many variations in psychoanalytic theory and practice have emerged throughout this century.

Alfred Adler and Carl Jung, two of Freud's closest friends and associates, became disenchanted with the basic tenets of psychoanalysis and formulated psychotherapy systems of their own. Adler rejected the biological interpretation of instincts and unconscious factors that was so fundamental to orthodox psychoanalysis. Adler's "Individual Psychology" gave priority to life style, adaptation to the environment, perception, conscious awareness, and to a practical psychotherapy.

Jung's "Analytic Psychology" acknowledged the creative forces in people. The unconscious for Jung was more than just a reservoir of primitive sexual and aggressive urges but included positive life forces and creative potentials as well.

The Adler and Jung schism from Freudian orthodoxy stimulated others to introduce systems of their own. Otto Rank, a member of Freud's early coterie, originated a social psychological theory of personality placing the *will* at the core. The *will* was the source of integrative power of the personality constituting the active relationship one has with oneself and the world. Rank asserted that the psychotherapy process must concentrate on the individual's active will and that the main "curative agent" or growth promoting force in psychotherapy was the relationship between therapist and patient. Rank's theoretical impact on later existential-humanistic theories of counseling and psychotherapy is very evident.

Wilhelm Reich in the late 1920's proposed a radical theory of personality and psychotherapy. He theorized that the defense mechanisms operate largely through postural or bodily functions. Sexual or libidinal drives are blocked by the body's muscular "armor." Tension builds and must be released through physical manipulation. Current views of psychotherapy emphasizing body awareness, movement exercise and relaxation are based heavily on Reichian concepts.

The 1940's and 50's produced a group known as the "neo-Freudians." The most noteworthy of the group were Karen Horney, Eric Fromm, and Harry Stack Sullivan who all took issue with Freud's emphasis on the biological and instinctual underpinnings of behavior. They challenged the notion of the universality of infantile sexuality and the psychosexual stages of development and believed that environmental factors were more central to the development of the personality.

Karen Horney, in particular, challenged the Freudian tenet that the Oedipal conflict is an inevitable and universally occurring phenomenon. Her postulates on the "tyranny of the shoulds," would influence later cognitive behavior theorists such as Albert Ellis.

Harry S. Sullivan stressed the role of interpersonal relationships in the formation of personality, theorizing that the "self-system" emerged out of the interaction of organism and environment. He noted that language is a powerful tool for shaping social interaction. Sullivan recognized stages in personality formation but saw them as social-psychological rather than psychosexual.

Eric Fromm, with a strong foundation in sociology, embraced many Freudian concepts but framed them in very different ways. He stressed the development of the "self" and the individual's search for meaning within a social context. Human conflict forces one to find meaningful solutions to problems even though one may feel hostile, powerless, and dependent. Psychological difficulties arise because as people move toward freedom they feel alone, insignificant, and helpless. Although his views relate closely to existential philosophy, he readily admits that human problems may result from political, economic, and social inequities.

A psychoanalytic variant that maintained a closer relationship with classical psychoanalytic theory was ego psychology. The more prominent members of this group were Heinz Hartman, David Rapaport, Anna Freud, and Erik Erikson. Ego psychology placed emphasis on the autonomy of the ego. The ego is the organization of cognitive processes which guides and directs behavior and serves as the psychological link to reality. The ego psychologists viewed the development of a healthy ego as a major goal of psychotherapy. Further evolution of psychoanalytic theory and practice was witnessed in the 1950's and 1960's. Edward Bordin, for example, made a substantive contribution to the counseling profession by translating psychoanalytic theory into an ego developmental model of counseling.

Eric Berne, during that same time period, formulated a theory and a system of group therapy called transactional analysis that modified the language of psychoanalysis. A new dynamic theory of personality and psychotherapy resulted that stressed the role of cognitive processes, ego states, and interpersonal transactions. Transactional analysis examined the various levels of ego states that underly interpersonal and intrapersonal transactions.

Berne hypothesized that people play psychological games with one another that are part of a "life script." The object of therapy is to help the participant understand the games and what they symbolize to the individual. Transactional analysis helps people to integrate cognitive, emotional and behavioral states so that they may function with less confusion and dishonesty.

Existential-Humanistic Psychotherapy

Existential psychotherapy is deeply rooted in the philosophies of Heidegger, Sartre, Jaspers and Tillich. These philosophers, all influenced by Husserl's phenomenological analysis of existence, made the understanding of an individual's "being" or "existence" their central concern. The meaning of human existence and human freedom was to replace metaphysics as the major focus of study in philosophy and human behavior.

European psychotherapists Medard Boss and Victor Frankl, and the

American Rollo May, adapted existential philosophy to psychotherapy. Psychotherapy should seek to understand "being" and to "assist" people to explore their "being" and to realize freedom. Existential psychotherapy attempts to capture an attitude toward human existence.

Typically, existential psychotherapists are interested in matters of "existence," "anxiety," "meaning," "death," "self-transcendence," "consciousness," "freedom," "choice," "authenticity," "alienation," and the "here and now." Human beings who are conscious of their being, live in the present, condemned to *meaning*, alone and anxious, and *free* to choose and create their existence. When humans ignore these aspects of existence they may be living inauthentically or in bad faith.

Existential philosophy and psychotherapy oppose strict mechanistic and deterministic theories of personality. Mental illness and psychopathology have little practical value for existentialists. Moreover, existential psychotherapists are not inclined toward highly systematic theories of behavior and behavior change techniques. Diagnostic categories, abstract theory, and the application of formal techniques impede true understanding of human existence. Thus, priority is on the "encounter" between therapist and the client — the concrete, real, and direct experiencing of one another.

Late in the 1930's, Carl Rogers who was influenced by Otto Rank, formulated what is known today as client or person-centered therapy. It was in 1942 that Carl Rogers published *Counseling and Psychotherapy*, giving birth to nondirective counseling, followed by *Client-Centered Therapy* in 1951.

Rogers believes that people are motivated toward self-actualization. The therapeutic relationship is a vehicle through which a person may realize potential for personal growth and creativity. Rogers was among the first psychologists to conduct a significant number of scientific studies on the process and outcome of psychotherapy. Along with Abraham Maslow and Fritz Perls, Rogers was one of the leading exponents of the "human potential" movement. This movement is called the "Third Force" in psychology.

Frederick (Fritz) Perls, founder of Gestalt Therapy, exerted a strong influence on the course of humanistic psychology. His basic theoretical works are *Ego, Hunger and Aggression*, (1947), *Gestalt Therapy*, (1951), and *Gestalt Therapy Verbatim*, (1969). Perls translated many psychoanalytic concepts into an existential-humanistic framework. Human beings mature psychologically when they expand their awareness in the here and now and are willing to accept responsibility for their actions. Perls, like many existential-humanistic theorists, plays down the role of psycho-pathology. He further minimized the role of the unconscious in the treatment of dysfunctional behavior and dramatically altered the techniques of psychotherapy.

Cognitive-Behavioral Psychotherapy

The impact of behavior theory on American psychology is quite evident. John B. Watson, an American, and Ivan Pavlov, a Russian, applied many principles of learning theory to behavioral disorders in the 1930's. During that same time period O. H. Mowrer used classical conditioning for the treatment of bedwetting. A. Salter developed a conditioned reflex therapy in 1949. Dollard and Miller published *Personality and Psychotherapy* (1950), and translated many of the psychoanalytic concepts into the language of behaviorism. B. F. Skinner described psychotherapy in operant conditioning terms. Joseph Wolpe introduced systematic desensitization in *Psychotherapy by Reciprocal Inhibition* (1958), which became one of the most popular and most widely researched behavior therapies.

The 1960's and 1970's ushered in a group of theorists who sought to expand upon behavior therapy through the more formal recognition of the role of cognition in behavior change. Cognitive behavioral approaches to psychotherapy proliferated during this time. Albert Ellis, Albert Bandura, Silvano Arieti, Arnold Lazarus, Aaron Beck, William Glasser, and Carl Thoresen, just to name a few, contributed enormously to the development of cognitive behavior therapy. Carl Thoresen, in particular, translated many of Albert Bandura's social learning concepts into a counseling model that stresses self-efficacy.

Proponents of cognitive behavior therapy generally acknowledge that the individual's belief system is an important factor in motivation and behavior. Most agree that reason, judgment, and thinking cannot be ignored in the management and control of behavior.

Family Therapy

The psychotherapy movement addressed concerns related to individual behavior. During the 1950's and 1960's Gregory Bateson and his associates performed studies on the communication patterns in families of schizophrenic patients. Bateson postulated that a family is a dynamic system of interdependent relationships and that any change in the balance of these relationships can induce or reduce tension. When one member of a family develops psychological symptoms every member is affected. In some way, each family member influences and affects the others.

Bateson suggests that dysfunctional families or individual family members are the result of distorted or disturbed communication. He coined the term "double-bind" to describe a victim in the family who receives contradictory messages. No matter what this person attempts to do in the family, he or she can rarely be successful. The result for the person is confusion, anxiety, frustration, and ineffective coping. Systems and communications approaches to family therapy have been further advanced by Virginia Satir, Jay Haley, and Nathan Ackerman in the 1960's and 1970's, and more recently by Salvador Minuchin and Paul Watzlawick.

THE COMMUNITY MENTAL HEALTH COMPREHENSIVE HEALTH CARE MOVEMENTS

Counseling as a developing profession gained momentum with the enactment of the *Community Mental Health Centers Act* of 1963. The act provided substantial funds for the establishment of comprehensive community mental health centers. Community mental health was conceived to treat psychological problems as well as to prevent them. The intent of this legislation was to provide mental health services to all people. Psychiatric care moved out of hospitals and into the community, thus fostering interdisciplinary models of treatment.

Several assumptions undergirded the Community Mental Health Centers Act. First, because environmental factors influence human behavior, social and community intervention can be effective in modifying behavior as well as society. Second, prevention is a more powerful intervention than remedial or rehabilitative ones in the long term. Third, mental health problems require more than individual psychotherapeutic treatment for their solution. Effective intervention must be comprehensive and include vocational, career, housing, and educational assistance. Fourth, mental health problems are caused in great part by broad-based social stresses such as poverty, racism, and social alienation. Fifth, the treatment of mental health problems should be a collaborative effort between professionals (psychiatrists, social workers, nurses, psychologists, and counselors) and citizens (Resnick, 1982).

The community mental health movement developed largely because of disenchantment with preexisting modes of care for people experiencing emotional problems. Concepts of mental health were changing from a "disease model" toward a "health model." The effectiveness of traditional psychotherapy was seriously challenged with respect to meeting the needs of the poor and correcting the ills of society. Critics of traditional methods of treating people with emotional disorders argued that mental hospitals were more for custodial care than for proper treatment and that the environment of these hospitals promoted and maintained pathology.

President Carter established the Commission on Mental Health in 1978. This commission recommended that Community Mental Health programs extend more service to special groups such as the aged, children, and minorities. The Commission also noted a need for continual support for preventive services.

The concept of holistic or comprehensive health care followed shortly after the community mental health movement. Many specialists who were involved in helping relationships, such as physicians, social workers, clergy, nurses, and counselors began to combine their efforts to offer a total health care package to the consumer.

The notion of comprehensive health was supported by the Health Maintenance Organizations Act which was passed by Congress in 1973. A health maintenance organization (HMO) is a medical plan wherein members pay a fixed yearly cost for health services. The central idea of the HMO is to integrate all health services—inpatient and outpatient—with emphasis on prevention and decreased cost to consumers. Further impetus to this movement was provided in 1979 when the Department of Health and Human Services devised a plan to more than double the number of HMO's by 1988 (Resnik, 1982).

Counselors began to play a greater role in the community mental health and comprehensive health care movements. Counselor training programs, in general, supported the basic philosophies of these movements. Since counselor preparation programs were relatively new on the scene, they were not restricted by years of the traditional domination of medicine.

From the late 1800's to the present, there has been a shift in emphasis from remedial treatment of "sick people" with "psychopathology" to helping people in general realize potentials, modify behavior, and expand self-awareness. There is an increasing trend towards holistic or integrative conceptions of human behavior. Many of the current theoretical systems of counseling and psychotherapy reflect these trends.

The practice of professional counseling with its primary emphasis on helping people achieve richer and fuller lives seems very appropriate in a time when many people desire to maximize their potential and lead more effective lives. Professional counseling is tailored to a broad spectrum of personal, social, educational, work, and health issues.

THEORY—WHAT IS IT AND WHAT DOES IT DO?

A theory is a systematic way of organizing data and information into a set of meaningful relationships: thus, empirical findings (facts) can be placed into some internally consistent framework. Any theory consists of a set of symbols (i.e., semantic mathematical) that code and systematize the storage of information. Kaplan (1964) regards theory as a symbolic construction that represents the symbolic dimension of experience.

Hall and Lindsey (1970) hold that a theory serves three basic functions. First, a theory leads to observation of relevant facts and empirical relationships and to the expansion of a knowledge base. A theory, in order to be scientific, must be comprehensive and verifiable. If it is both comprehensive and verifiable, it generates testable hypotheses and has heuristic value and utility. A second function of a theory allows for the incorporation of empirical facts into a parsimonious and logically consistent framework. Parsimony enhances verification. A third function of theory is that it helps simplify the task of observation by reducing ambiguous and irrelevant facts. A useful theory provides the observer with a set of clear and explicit guidelines about the kinds of data that need to be gathered relative to a particular problem.

How a Theory is Evaluated

How is a theory evaluated? Burton (1974) proposes six criteria. First, a theory must be extensive—"Comprehensive." Second, a theory must be parsimonious—"Specific." Third, a theory must be internally consistent—"Logical." Fourth, a theory must have empirical referents—"Correspond to Fact." Fifth, a theory must be testable—"Researchable." Sixth, a theory must be useful—"Practical." These six criteria can be useful in assessing the validity of each counseling theory described in this text.

Counseling as a Systematic, Scientific, and Intuitive Process

The counseling process is subject to systematic scientific inquiry. It can be said that counseling is an applied behavioral science. Being scientific or systematic implies that one approaches matters in an orderly way. However, in no way does this preclude intuition. A counselors intuition is an important source of information that assists in the development of a more comprehensive understanding of the client.

The applied behavioral sciences are not considered by many as hard sciences like physics and chemistry. Behavioral sciences, however, must eventually approximate the rigor of the so-called hard sciences, but at the same time cannot sacrifice the human element.

FOUR PERSPECTIVES ON THEORY IN BEHAVIORAL SCIENCE

The four broad categories of counseling theory—Psychodynamic, Existential-Humanistic, Cognitive-Behavioral, and Family and Systems are based upon quite different assumptions about the nature of human behavior and how to modify or change it. Some of the differences relative to their scientific orientations will be highlighted in this section so that they may be more easily discerned in subsequent chapters.

The Psychodynamic Perspective

Psychodynamic theory is based largely on clinical data derived inductively from the process of psychotherapy. Recall Freud's psychoanalytic theory emerged from the study of the neuroses. The early Freudians, as well as their modern counterparts, theorize that behavioral symptoms result from the dynamic interplay of intrapsychic-interpersonal forces. Psychoanalysis suggests that any psychic event can be analyzed from at least three points of view—the topographic, the dynamic, and the economic (Greenson, 1967).

The *topographic view* of an intrapsychic event describes the relationship between unconscious and conscious material. A mental operation called primary process directs the unconscious mind while a secondary process directs the conscious mind. The *dynamic view* suggests that behavior is a function of the interaction of three structures—the id (biological), ego (rational), and superego (social). The interplay of these forces and structures must be considered in the constructing of hypotheses concerning drives, ego defenses, conflicts, and symptom formation. *The economic view* explains behavior in terms of the distribution, transformation, and expression of psychic energy. Most psychodynamic formulations suggest that personality develops through various psychosexual and social psychological stages of growth and experience (Greenson, 1967).

The psychodynamic theories covered in this text are Edward Bordin's Ego-developmental Psychology, Alfred Adler's Individual Psychology, and Eric Berne's Transactional Analysis. Bordin and Adler both stress the role of cognition and social factors in human behavior. Berne's transactional analysis redefines and reinterprets many early Freudian concepts within the framework of ego-states, transactions, and games. These systems all represent significant departures from classical psychoanalysis.

The Existential-Humanistic Perspective

Existential-humanistic theories of counseling and psychotherapy are based upon the phenomenological method of analysis and inquiry. This method requires that relationships among variables or facts need to be described before seeking cause and effect relationships. Phenomenologically-oriented behavioral scientists include information and data from the personal and private world of the person, believing that knowing people subjectively is as important as knowing them objectively. Another way of saying this is that the existential-humanistic theorists consider observable objective facts (behavior) as well as subjective facts (perception, feelings, and personal meanings). The theories of counseling and psychotherapy advanced by Viktor Frankl, Fritz Perls, and Carl Rogers hold closely to the phenomenological method of scientific inquiry.

Viktor Frankl (1962) believes that scientific inquiry and counseling technique are secondary to the personal relationship counselors have with clients. Frankl, Perls, and Rogers tend to agree that the counseling relationship itself can be the object of study, as well as the persons who participate in that relationship. Carl Rogers is well known for spearheading a number of empirical investigations into the nature of the counseling relationship.

Rogers, for one, values the concepts that underly the science of human behavior. He and other phenomenologically-minded theorists often do object to the depersonalization and dehumanization of the individual when the scientific method is taken to extremes. Rogers (1967) believes that a true psychological or behavioral science can grow out of the problems encountered in the study of a person's subjective experience and that no true behavioral science can ignore the subjective experience of a human being.

The phenomenological aspects of scientific inquiry are captured effectively by Rogers. He suggests that if one desires to become a scientist, the first step is to immerse oneself in the phenomenon of interest. The more complete the immersion the more likely it is to discover new knowledge, to tolerate ambiguity and contradiction, to value curiosity, and to freely participate in experiencing the phenomenon (Rogers, 1967). It is apparent that Rogers prizes the subjectivity of the scientist and the intuitive dimension of scientific inquiry.

The Cognitive-Behavioral Perspective

Cognitive-behavioral theories of counseling and psychotherapy generally stress the application of the principles of learning and methods and results of experimental behavioral sciences (Ellis, 1978). Scientific methods, according to Thoresen and Coates (1978), contribute to an understanding of the counseling process in at least three ways. First, specific treatments can be derived from research in the experimental sciences. Second, treatments can be tested through experimentation. Third, counseling practices can be evaluated through clinical studies involving a single person.

Carl Thoresen and Albert Ellis both have strong leanings toward the logical and empirical methods of scientific inquiry. William Glasser, while not denying the role of science in the study of counseling and psychotherapy, is more willing to address questions of morality and ethics that are often deemphasized in scientific inquiry. Cognitive-behavioral perspectives on counseling and psychotherapy generally stress scientific rigor in the conceptualization and the measurement of human behavior.

The Systems and Family Perspective

Systems and family theories share the notion that individual behavior can only be understood within the structure of a social system, the primary social system being the family. The family system is the object of systematic inquiry in the theories of Salvador Minuchin, Virginia Satir, and Paul Watzlawick.

Watzlawick, Beavin, and Jackson (1967), in their landmark book, *Pragmatics of Human Communication,* postulate that psychological symptoms develop as a result of dysfunctional communication patterns in family systems. The scientific study of the family involves the observation of interaction sequences between participants and the impact of these on the individual and the system. The family system embodies patterns, rules, and regularities that are predictable and observable.

Present day scientific investigations into family systems tend to be descriptive and exploratory in nature. Minuchin's investigations for instance, attempt to differentiate functional from dysfunctional families (i.e., the "low socioeconomic family," and the "alcoholic"). Most systematic studies of the family investigate communication patterns. Minuchin, a structural family theorist has conducted several outcome and process studies on family therapy. The theories of Minuchin, Satir, and Watzlawick are stated in ways that can potentially translate into testable hypotheses that describe and predict the behavior of families as well as suggest ways of treating them.

REFERENCES

Breuer, J., & Freud, S. (1895). *Studies in hysteria.* London: Hogarth Press.

Burton, A. (1974). *Operational theories of personality.* New York: Brunner/Mazel, Inc.

Dollard, J., & Miller, N. (1950). *Personality and psychotherapy.* New York: McGraw-Hill.

Ellis, A. (1978). The problem of achieving scientific cognitive behavior therapy. *The Counseling Psychologist, 7* (3), 21-23.

Frankl, V. (1962). *Man's search for meaning.* Boston: Beacon Press.

Greenson, R. (1967). *The technique and practice of psychoanalysis* (Vol. J). New York: International Universities Press.

Hall, C., & Lindsey, G. (1970). *Theories of personality* (2nd ed.). New York: John Wiley & Sons, Inc.

Kaplan, A. (1964). *The conduct of inquiry.* San Francisco: Chandler Publishing Co.

Parsons, F. (1909). *Choosing a vocation.* Boston: Houghton Mifflin.

Perls, F. (1947). *Ego, hunger, and aggression.* London: Allen and Unwin.

Perls, F. (1969). *Gestalt therapy verbatim.* Lafayette, CA: Real People Press.

Perls, F., Hefferline, R., & Goodman, P. (1951). *Gestalt therapy.* New York: Julian Press.

Resnik, H. (1982). The counseling psychologist in community mental health centers and health maintenance organizations — Do we belong? *The counseling psychologist, 10* (2), 53-60.

Rogers, C. (1942). *Counseling and psychotherapy: Newer concepts in practice.* Boston: Houghton Mifflin.

Rogers, C. (1951). *Client-centered therapy: Its current practice, implications, and theory.* Boston: Houghton Mifflin.

Rogers, C. (1967). Some thoughts regarding the current presuppositions of the behavioral sciences. In W. Coulson & C. Rogers (Eds.), *Man and the science man.* Columbus, OH: Charles Merrill.

Thoresen, C., & Coates, T. (1978). What does it mean to be a behavior therapist? *The Counseling Psychologist. 7* (3), 3-20.

Watzlawick, P., Beavin, J., & Jackson, D. (1967). *Pragmatics of human communication — A study of international patterns, pathologies, and paradoxes.* Palo Alto: W.W. Norton Co., Inc.

Wolpe, J. (1958). *Psychotherapy by reciprocal inhibition.* Palo Alto: Stanford University Press.

Additional References

Bandura, A. (1977). *Social learning theory.* Englewood Cliffs, N.J.: Prentice Hall.

Belkin, G. (1984). *Introduction to counseling* (2nd ed.). Dubuque, Iowa: William C. Brown Publishers.

Gurman, A., & Kniskern, D. (Eds.) (1981). *Handbook of family therapy.* New York: Brunner/Mazel.

Kazoin, A. (1968). *History of behavior modification: Experimental foundations of experimental research.* Baltimore: Univ. Park Press.

Korchin, S. (1976). *Modern clinical psychology.* New York: Basic Books.

Kuhn, T.J. (1976). *The structure of scientific revolutions* (2nd ed.). Chicago: Univ. of Chicago Press.

Monroe, R. (1955). *Schools of psychoanalytic thought.* New York: Holt, Rinehart, and Winston.

Osipow, S., Walsh, W.B., & Tosi, D. (1984). *A survey of counseling methods,* (rev. ed.). Homewood, IL: Dorsey Press.

Salter, A. (1949). *Conditioned reflex therapy.* New York: Creating Age.

Whiteley, J.M. (Ed.). (1980). *The history of counseling psychology.* Monteray, CA: Brooks Cole.

PART I

PSYCHODYNAMIC PERSPECTIVES

PART ONE presents three psychodynamic perspectives on counseling. This section describes the psychodynamic theories of Alfred Adler, Edward Bordin, and Eric Berne. Psychodynamic perspectives on counseling trace their origins to Sigmund Freud and the development of psychoanalytic theory. Recall that Freud hypothesized that an organism's psychological functioning is an attempt to satisfy biological needs, drives, and instincts. The motivation for observable behavior is, in great measure, determined by unconscious impulses that are frequently aggressive or sexual in nature. Freud observed that a person's psychobiological needs were in frequent conflict with the environment and were sources of anxiety. The experience of inner conflict gave rise to defense mechanisms or psychological maneuvers designed to avoid anxiety.

Alfred Adler objected to Freud's heavy emphasis on sexual or biological drives and turned his attention to the sociological influence of the family and to an individual's psychological makeup. Edward Bordin, in more recent years, has translated the psychoanalytic position into a counseling framework that stresses the operation of the ego. Eric Berne also has borrowed heavily from psychoanalytic theory to develop hypotheses regarding ego states, games, and social transactions.

Adler, with his social orientation, proposed that individuals perceive organ inferiority and compensate with superior strivings. These strivings concomitantly form attitudes, perceptions, and beliefs about the self and the environment. Cognitive organization (a cognitive map) provides a structure in which one can cope and seek goals. The life style is the socioteleological manner in which the individual approaches the life tasks. Adler's Individual Psychology places much emphasis on conscious

21

decisions, secondary gains, and reinforcers for symptoms or organ deficiencies. Freud's psychoanalytic theory focused primarily on the organism while Adler turned to the milieu as a person's primary source of
social interest and gratification.

Edward Bordin operationalized psychoanalytic theory and synthesized ego psychological concepts to formulate an ego developmental
theory of counseling. Bordin's concepts of self-actualization show a strik-
ing similarity to those of Carl Rogers. The ego developmental theory
holds that unconscious regressive impulses or drives may emerge upon
the experiencing of a developmental task. People complete one set of developmental tasks and move on to the next stage of development. The
transition, resolution or inability to complete developmental tasks is the
focus of Bordin's theory of counseling. Bordin asserts that self-actualization is a function of the successful completion of a developmental task.

Bordin emphasizes the importance of cognitive, emotive and behavioral integration. His soft-deterministic view sees change occurring in
one system and then effecting another interdependent system. Therefore, Bordin in the analytic tradition attempts to increase awareness of
the unconscious regressive emotions, thoughts, and conflicts.

Eric Berne, trained in the psychoanalytic model, underwent psychoanalysis himself. During the course of analysis, he became interested
in the neurobiological mechanisms of ego states. Later, he shifted his attention to ego states and social transactions. Berne's theory, similar to
Adler's, considers sociological exchanges as important to personality development and human functioning. The life script of transactional analysis is similar to the Adlerian notion of "life style" in that each involves a
specific behavioral repertoire and both are determined to a great extent
consciously. The life script evolves from cultural and familial myths and
symbols and is influenced by parents through their communication of
behavioral "shoulds."

In social transactions, Berne shows that people follow stereotyped or
rigid ways of behaving. People ritualize certain social transactions into
games. Some parallels between Freudian theory and Berneian theory
may be drawn. For instance, the parent, adult, and child (ego states) are
somewhat analogous to Freud's superego, ego, and id. Similarly, games
may speak as defense mechanisms in that people repeat previous behavior patterns to cope with anxiety.

Bordin, Adler, and Berne believe in the importance of the relationship in the counseling process. Additionally, each adds new dimensions
to counseling theory. Adler, for instance, introduced the idea of treating

families in counseling. Berne believed that group transactional analysis was an appropriate adjunct to individual sessions. Bordin saw the relevance of vocational and personality inventories in counseling, believing that test information could be a significant tool to foster client understanding. The psychodynamic views of Bordin, Adler, and Berne all tend to look at how people function in society, and all recognize the role of cognition in their theories of counseling and behavior change. Through self understanding or cognitive reorientation, these theorists believe people can become more self-determining.

CHAPTER 2

EDWARD BORDIN'S
EGO DEVELOPMENTAL THEORY:
A PSYCHODYNAMIC VIEW OF COUNSELING

FOUNDATIONS AND STRUCTURE

Historical Foundations

EDWARD BORDIN (1913-   ) was educated at Temple University and The Ohio State University where he was granted a Ph.D. degree in psychology in 1942. After completing his Doctoral studies, Bordin joined the staff of the counseling center at the University of Minnesota. In 1946 he accepted a position at Washington State University, and remained there for two years. Two years later Bordin began his long association with the University of Michigan as Chief of the Counseling Division in the Bureau of Psychological Services.

Bordin, early in his career, formulated a psychodynamic view of counseling. In 1955 he wrote *Psychological Counseling*. Bordin's more current interests in diverse theoretical approaches and the process of counseling and psychotherapy are reflected in *Research Strategies in Psychotherapy*, published in 1974. Presently, Bordin's theory of counseling is of an ego developmental variety based on a synthesis of psychodynamic, behavioral, developmental, and cognitive theories.

The ego developmental model in the psychoanalytic tradition gives full consideration to past experiences and their central role in motivating present behavior. However, Bordin essentially sees the counseling process as contributing to personality development by appealing to the cognitive functions of the ego.

Bordin (1955) sees a distinct difference in counseling interventions

25

between clinical populations and more normally functioning individuals who experience acute developmental problems. Psychoanalysis is a long-term reconstructive therapy focusing on modifying personality structure. Bordin believes that this classical analytical model may not be appropriate with people who have relatively well-integrated personalities. He sees the major focus of the ego developmental counselor as working with people who are experiencing emotional conflicts about developmental tasks within various life stages. Emotional difficulties may arise relative to career decisions, interpersonal relationships and because of intrapsychic conflict (Bordin, 1955 & 1965). Bordin's ego developmental counseling model, stressing insight into the experiential pattern of life and the strengthening of the ego, is designed to attend to the problems and conflicts stemming from the process of human development.

Bordin integrated Freudian, Rankian, and Eriksonian notions into his theoretical model. From Freud, he incorporated the notions of impulse management, ego strength, resistance, and the mechanisms of defense. He found the Rankian concepts of conflict, frustration, and ego gratification to be quite useful to his own dynamic perspective. And finally, from Erikson, Bordin saw the value of the developmental stages of the life cycle.

Philosophical Foundations

Bordin (1955a) believes that human behavior operates in accordance with the laws of nature and of cause and effect. He values a more realistic as opposed to idealistic view of human nature. Bordin assumes that the accumulation of knowledge via scientific observation will lead to a more rational understanding of people.

Bordin embraces centralism or a soft deterministic view of behavior, but does admit that human behavior is greatly influenced by unconscious "drives" and "needs" of people. Bordin also realizes people have the potential to understand the unconscious processes, to direct their behavior and to achieve life goals. Bordin (1979) and Lansford and Bordin (1983) adopt a Neo-Freudian position that suggests a more integrated conception of mind and body.

Bordin (1955) places a priority on the use of reason and insight in the control of behavior. Evidence of the effective use of reason and logical thinking suggests a strong ego system that can postpone immediate gratification, tolerate tension, and is oriented to reality. Bordin recognizes that in some cases unconscious conflicts, desires, and impulses may cloud human reason. For that reason alone, unconscious processes and the way they operate need to be understood (Bordin, Nachmann & Segal, 1963).

In a manner which is consistent with the humanistic tradition, Bordin posits that people have a drive to self-actualize. However, when they encounter blocks to development they may experience intense anxiety and regress to more primitive levels of functioning. Regression involves the use of defenses and behaviors appropriate to prior stages of development. Bordin notes that regression and other defense mechanisms serve to fragment the personality, thus making it impossible for one to self-actualize.

Counseling, according to Bordin (1955a), is for people who are well integrated and who experience conflict or anxiety relative to the tasks of a particular developmental stage. Counseling is differentiated from psychotherapy as it is time-limited and focused on specific developmental concerns. Psychotherapy is a process to accomplish personality reconstruction. Bordin sees counseling similar to education in that information or some remediation may be necessary for people to more fully understand their current behavior or inner motivations and drives.

Social-Psychological Foundations

Social-psychological concepts in Bordin's theory are based on the neo-analytic theories of Otto Rank, Eric Fromm, Karen Horney, and Harry Stack Sullivan, all of whom operated from a strong social-psychological foundation. In Bordin's formulations, the social environment is stressed as a major influencing force in the development of personality.

Counseling is a structured social interaction through which the counselor assumes a role that facilitates the personality development of the client. The client is assisted in making decisions and gaining necessary insights into the self for optimal functioning within a particular developmental stage. The primary goal of the counselor is to help the client increase understanding of both interpersonal and intrapersonal obstacles which may inhibit ego development and effective coping in the environment. The counselor's ability to be sensitive to the complexity of the person's dynamics contributes to a more positive counseling process and outcome (Bordin, 1979). People derive a sense of well-being from the successful mastery of developmental tasks.

Emotional problems, from the dynamic framework, arise when a social situation is perceived as a threat to the individual and when the person's ability to cope with such a threat is minimal. Successful coping depends on maturity and the integrative forces of the ego. Bordin (1955a) believes that maturity and integration are relatively synonymous concepts that imply a balance of meeting internal drives, impulses, and social demands.

A person's interaction with the environment may be so negative that ego deficiencies may emerge. These ego deficiencies may inhibit effective ways of coping with development tasks and social situations. The counseling relationship is a more positive environment that facilitates maturation and personality integration in the sense that it contributes to the formation of a healthy ego. In a counseling relationship, people are encouraged to confront situations associated with frustration, anxiety, and personal conflict in a climate characterized by warmth, understanding, and support.

The Development of the Person

Ego developmental counseling rests on five major assumptions regarding personality functioning. These assumptions are based heavily on neo-psychoanalytic theory (Bordin, 1955, 1965).

The first assumption is that behavior is related to an inner core of attitudes, emotions, and impulses. The inner core of the personality is an enduring and stable aspect of ego functioning. Modification of core attitudes, emotions, and impulses can result in behavioral change.

A second assumption is that the individual's basic impulses, drives, and satisfactions are expressed and managed by a rational ego. Bordin (1955a) believes that behavior must be understood within a psychodynamic framework, because such a framework addresses the complexities of personality development. To comprehend personality, it is critical to learn how the inner core is expressed through the rational ego. The individual's expression of inner drives has a direct relationship with success in coping with developmental tasks.

A third assumption is that ego development occurs through stages over the life span of the individual. Stages of development postulated by Erikson are: trust-mistrust (infancy), autonomy-shame and doubt (toddlerhood), initiative-guilt (pre-school), industry-inferiority (elementary school), identity role diffusion (adolescence), intimacy-isolation (young adulthood), generativity-stagnation (adulthood), and integrity-despair (late adulthood). Table 2-1 provides a description of Erikson's

Table 2-1

THE DEVELOPMENTAL STAGES OF ERIK ERIKSON, EXEMPLARY DEVELOPMENTAL TASKS AND PROBABLE OUTCOMES

STAGE	EXEMPLARY DEVELOPMENTAL TASKS	PROBABLE OUTCOMES
I. Trust vs. Mistrust (Infancy)	Discovering that the environment is nurturing and predictable. Developing the feeling of being cared for by others.	Capacity for intimate contact. Viewing the world realistically and positively.
II. Autonomy vs. Shame and Doubt (Toddlerhood)	Cultivating a like for one's own body. Learning to control bodily functions. Learning self-control of impulses.	Self-control. Self-esteem. Integration of conflicting emotions (love-hate).
III. Initiative vs. Guilt (Pre-school)	Initiating a variety of new tasks in new environments. Experiencing the impact of one's behavior on the environment.	Mastery of self and environment. Greater control of impulses. Maximized self-expression.
IV. Industry vs. Inferiority (Elementary school)	Satisfaction in accomplishments at school and play. Gaining recognition from others. Relating to new people.	Extension of ego-boundaries. Gaining of self-esteem through work and achievement.
V. Identity vs. Role Confusion (Adolescence)	Distinguishing oneself from others. Knowing one's mind.	Self-affirmation. Self-acceptance.
VI. Intimacy vs. Self-Absorption (Young Adulthood)	Formation of love relationships. Exploration of sexuality. Marriage.	Personal satisfaction. Freedom of emotional expression. Ability to cooperate and share.
VII. Generativity vs. Stagnation (Adulthood)	Developing a career. Cultivation of intellectual and aesthetic interests. Having a family.	Creativity. Productivity. Impact on environment. A philosophy of life. Self-actualization.
VIII. Integrity vs. Despair (Late Adulthood)	Accepting that life ends. Consideration of meaning in life. Retirement.	Personality integration. Expanded self-awareness and self-acceptance. Wisdom.

developmental stages, tasks, and outcomes. Ego development is a function of the level of mastery achieved at each stage. Extreme frustration at any stage may result in adjustment problems, personal conflict and regression.

A fourth assumption is that personality evolves largely out of the integration of conflicting tendencies (dependence and independence). A person may desire to act out and behave independently of others, but may experience a strong conflicting emotion to depend on others. One may experience ambivalence or inner conflict when attempting to strive for independence. Ambivalence occurs when both regressive and actualizing tendencies are simultaneously experienced. Ambivalence is a core emotion that translates into an ineffective coping behavior (Bordin 1965).

A fifth assumption is that ego development presupposes that the concepts of resistance and transference are basic to human behavior. Transference suggests that people's positive or negative feelings toward others may have their origins in significant past relationships. Resistance occurs when there is a threat to the ego. Threat is aroused when people become increasingly aware of unconscious impulses that are primarily sexual and aggressive in nature. Thus, people may avoid or refuse to deal with conflict between conscious and unconscious desires.

To protect themselves against overwhelming anxiety people may use a variety of defense mechanisms (rationalization, displacement, isolation, repression, and suppression). The rational ego learns to organize and integrate both acceptable and unacceptable impulses. If an impulse is not expressed because of psychological blocking (defenses) or environmental blocking (rules), frustration results and tension builds. A strong rational ego leads to effective management of impulses and to the mastery of life tasks.

Environmental factors play a significant role in shaping the personality. Bordin believes that a child's early environment plays a crucial role in development. Early parental and family relationships serve as a foundation for the structure of the ego. In the ego developmental view, cognitive functions in human beings are extensions of the rational ego, and are quite necessary for the effective control of behavior.

Concepts of Functional and Dysfunctional Behavior

Six ego functions are involved in effective human behavior. A fully functional ego implies that people: (1) have insight and understanding

Table 2-2

THE MAJOR DEFENSE MECHANISMS OF THE EGO

REPRESSION

The process of keeping out of consciousness unacceptable impulses of a sexual or aggressive nature. For instance, a son may hate his father but is unaware of the feeling. The feeling of hatred may return in disguised form (i.e. hatred toward authorities).

REACTION FORMATION

A defense related to repression. As repressed material enters consciousness it is transformed into an opposite feeling or emotion. For example, excessive hate becomes love.

ISOLATION

The separation of an idea or thought from an emotion that usually accompanies it. For example, a person may have an image of a very traumatic emotional experience without being aware of the emotion.

UNDOING

This unconscious defense involves compulsive rituals of atonement or expiation for the commission of unacceptable acts or engaging in unacceptable ideations.

PROJECTION

The process of ascribing subjective meanings to an objective event. For example, a person who blames another for his/her own mistake (scapegoating).

DISPLACEMENT

The process of transferring an emotion from its original object to another object. For instance, a young child may transfer hate of a parent to a younger sibling.

RATIONALIZATION

Rationalization means to justify ones thoughts, or actions in an attempt to make them appear reasonable — when in fact they are not.

TRANSFERENCE

The projection of positive feelings (positive transference) or negative feelings (negative transference) onto the counselor or therapist who represents a significant person of the past.

INTROJECTION

The incorporation into the ego-structure of the idea or symbolic representation of an object (usually a person) as one perceives the object to be. The person may then treat the object representation or the object in reality.

Table 2-2 (Continued)

IDENTIFICATION	When a person introjects an object and then proceeds to think, feel, and act like the object. This is the defensive mechanism in an unconscious process.
SUBLIMATION	The modification of an instinctual urge so that it conforms to societal expectations and norms. Sublimation is a way of substituting one activity for another in a socially acceptable fashion (i.e., substituting love of God for the love of a man or woman). There is some debate as to whether sublimation can be classified as an ego-defense since it involves an effective channeling of impulses.

into the forces that motivate behavior (psychological, sociological, biological); (2) find acceptable ways to channel their impulses; (3) delay immediate gratification; (4) integrate past experiences into more adaptable modes of behavior; (5) make rational decisions about life's choices and (6) relate meaningfully to others.

People who exhibit dysfunctional behaviors more often: (1) lack insight; (2) experience fragmentation in their thoughts and feelings; (3) have difficulty delaying immediate gratification for long-term goals; (4) make choices based on unconscious needs and (5) have more difficulty establishing meaningful relationships (Bordin, 1974).

The degree to which ego development is impaired indicates the level of difficulty people have coping with developmental tasks such as choosing a career, relating to others, and achieving one's goals (Bordin, 1974). A strong ego is a well-differentiated one which implies that the person is more insightful, more effectively participates in life tasks, and is able to minimize anxiety. An undifferentiated ego is an infantile ego (helpless at birth) and is often ineffective with respect to adapting itself to the environment.

An effective person is one who exhibits maturity, self-understanding, and a strong personal identity. With timely mastery of developmental tasks, the person matures and develops a strong personal identity through a process called individuation. Individuation is the process of forming and specializing one's individual nature, while remaining cognizant of the environment and one's place in it. The fully developed individual is less defensive, less confused, relatively free from conflict, and personally effective in the environment (Bordin, 1974).

Concepts of Behavior Change

Bordin (1979) believes that meaningful behavior change occurs through a cognitive process in which the rational ego learns to integrate conflicting emotions into a more healthy ego structure. For this to occur, a person needs to explore core emotions and experiences.

Bordin's (1955a) theory of behavior change in the context of a counseling relationship, is based on four dimensions. The first is the *ambiguity dimension,* referring to the lack of structure in the counseling relationship. Essentially, the counselor remains relatively detached and unclear to the client (Bordin, 1955b). Successful management of the ambiguity dimension by the counselor may facilitate behavior change. Ambiguity encourages transference which is essential to a better understanding of the client's motives, impulses and needs. Ambiguity tends to contribute to the therapeutic relationship because it sets the stage for later interpretations of transference necessary for insight and understanding of core emotions.

The second dimension contributing to behavior change is the *personal dimension,* that is, the counselor's personal style and approach to counseling. The tone of the counseling relationship is influenced by how the counselor relates to people in general. The personal dimension suggests that the counselor's personality contributes to therapeutic change (Bordin, 1968). The personal dimension is directly related to the third dimension of *warmth.*

Acceptance, genuineness, and responsivity define the warmth dimension. The qualities of spontaneity, commitment, and effort suggest that the counselor is involved heavily in the work of counseling.

The fourth dimension is the *cognitive-conative balance.* Changes in human behavior need to occur in these two basic categories. The cognitive dimension is somewhat analogous to the ego and super-ego and the conative dimension to the id (affect).

Counseling is a cognitively-oriented, problem-solving process in which a balance in the cognitive and conative dimensions must be achieved. When a person becomes more insightful into unconscious drives, motivations, and impulses (fundamentally a cognitive effort), meaningful behavior is more likely to occur. The restructuring and reorganizing of core cognitive and emotional domains enhance maturation. Furthermore, the rational integration of conflicting thoughts and emotions tends to lessen anxiety, strengthen the ego, and increase the possibility for more effective functioning in the environment.

Assessment of Human Functioning

The Use of Tests in Counseling

Bordin (1955) believes that psychological tests and inventories can be employed by counselors to assess the cognitive abilities, interests, personality traits, and self-perceptions of their clients. Testing serves many important functions in counseling, one of which is to encourage self-exploration (Bordin, 1955a).

Since the client participates in the testing process there is a high degree of ego involvement. The client's participation in the interpretation of test results can facilitate insight. While Bordin suggests that the process of selecting tests be a cooperative effort shared by the client and the counselor, the counselor does the major share of test selection.

Bordin (1955a) hypothesizes that clients can deal most effectively with their own feelings and attitudes when they participate actively in the assessment process. The interpretation of tests can contribute to the understanding of the personal conflict, their origins and resolutions. Test data as well as clinical observations contribute to the formulation of meaningful diagnostic hypotheses.

The Diagnostic Constructs

Bordin asserts that the diagnostic concepts help counselors understand the needs and personality dynamics of the client. Diagnosis is an attempt to categorize behaviors so they may be more effectively explored in counseling. Valid decisions about the focus of counseling are more likely to be made when the behavioral characteristics, core emotions, and thoughts associated with maladaptive functioning are differentiated.

Bordin postulates five diagnostic constructs — *choice anxiety, self-conflict, dependence, lack of information,* and *lack of assurance.* Knowledge of these constructs may help the counselor identify the coping styles and ego-functioning of various individuals as well as the motivational forces that underlie behavior.

Choice Anxiety. When a person is faced with conflicting alternatives regarding a personal, social, or career decision, choice anxiety may result. Choice anxiety impairs the functioning of the rational ego. Choice anxiety is generally high when individuals are confronted with developmental tasks. Choice often implies commitment to implementing decisions. Once decisions are implemented, anxiety often is reduced, allowing for more effective ego functioning.

Self Conflict. Bordin (1955a, 1979, & 1983) notes that people often have life experiences that conflict with their self-perceptions (i.e., lying, cheating, stealing). Such experiences may be threatening, increase anxiety, and activate defenses. When a person's behavior is not consistent with core thoughts and feelings about the behavior, the behavior becomes isolated from the ego. An example of this is an introverted, shy man who fears asking a woman for a date, and therefore, avoids the woman. The experience may raise anxiety and thus increase conflict about the action. The resolution of self-conflict begins when the person is willing to explore some of the unconscious motivations underlying the conflict. Expanded awareness into the nature of the conflict is necessary for the ultimate strengthening of the ego.

Dependence. Excessive dependence reflects anxiety and low-ego strength in meeting the developmental tasks of life. Excessive reliance on parents or others to solve problems or to meet life tasks is a manifestation of dependency. People who participate in counseling often resist taking the responsibility for change, thereby projecting dependency attitudes onto the counselor. Fear, anxiety, and helplessness are usually the core emotions that foster dependence in people.

With greater insight into the self-defeating emotional aspects of dependency, people can minimize a significant barrier to personal independence and responsibility. Psychodynamic counselors encourage experiences that strengthen the ego. As the ego develops, personality integration and self-responsibility increase. Decision-making and problem-solving become less anxiety arousing and more self-fulfilling.

Lack of Information. Often people do accept responsibility for their own decisions, but may lack information that could lead to more intelligent ones. People who lack experiences or self-knowledge are more likely to hold a less accurate picture of their strengths and weaknesses. For example, individuals who have insufficient information about the occupational world may have difficulty evaluating their goals and aspirations. People who lack knowledge of appropriate social behavior, often feel insecure and ineffective in social situations.

Lack of Assurance. Many people require excessive amounts of assurance for the decisions or commitments they have made. According to Bordin (1955a & 1979), these individuals look toward counseling for such reassurance. The counselor needs to be aware of the dynamics that may initiate and reinforce a lack of confidence and assurance and can do so through the clarification and interpretation of feelings. The counselor can help minimize anxiety, direct attention to ego enhancing activities, and help the client crystallize choices and direction.

Diagnostic constructs help clarify the dynamic behavioral patterns associated with ego strengths and weaknesses. Assessment of human functioning, from Bordin's perspective, is an attempt to recognize core emotional themes, and how these change with the individual over time (dynamics). Diagnostic constructs and test information are vehicles through which the goals, directions, and foci of counseling may be discovered.

Goals and Directions of Counseling

The goals of Bordin's psychodynamic counseling center largely on minimizing anxiety and conflict and developing insight into core dynamics. An effective counseling relationship fosters personality integration through the development of a strong ego structure. Expanded self-awareness of significant core emotions permits the ego to execute its function more efficiently, thereby permitting a greater mastery over the environment.

Bordin (1963) believes that vocational and career choices play a major role in ego development and functioning. People select the type of work that provides intrinsic gratification, or a mode for the ego to express drives, impulses, needs, wishes, and desires. Bordin notes that each growth stage in ego development provides a basis for understanding vocational selections.

The goals of ego developmental counseling, according to Bordin (1979), are more extensive than in behavioral therapy. Understanding the nature of conflict and anxiety as well as making wise choices contribute to an integrated ego structure. A well-developed ego enables one to master tasks more effectively through all stages of development.

The Counseling Process: Structuring, Facilitating, and Terminating

The counseling relationship is a working alliance between the client and counselor (Bordin, 1979 & 1983). The concept of the working alliance suggests a collaborative effort. A therapeutic alliance is made to structure a relationship which focuses on certain problems, decisions, and goals.

The working alliance is task-oriented. The counselor interprets, clarifies, and reflects the client's core emotions and thoughts. The client's role in the working alliance is to reflect on experiences, explore conflicts, and associate core emotions and thoughts with behavior.

A therapeutic bond develops in psychodynamic counseling (Bordin, 1979 & 1983). The bond may vary over time depending upon the background of the client and the type and intensity of the client's concerns. If a client is simply seeking occupational information, the bond formed between that person and the counselor will be different from one where the client is experiencing intense social anxiety. The bond between the client and counselor is supportive and enables the counselor to confront a client's resistance, defenses, and transference. Bordin (1983) asserts that the therapeutic working alliance may be *built* and *repaired*, suggesting that the mutual agreement, task, and bond are flexible and modifiable in the counseling relationship.

Bordin (1955) believes that the initial interview frequently contains the most accurate representation of a person's conflict. In the first session the client may manifest anxiety about the problem or the counseling process itself. The counselor tries to structure the session so that the client can reduce enough anxiety to articulate meaningful concerns. The counselor does this by varying the ambiguity dimension. Defensive clients, for instance, may require more ambiguity to increase self-disclosure. In the initial sessions, the ground work is laid for a working alliance which reflects the strength of the counseling relationship over time (Bordin, 1979 & 1983).

Since the counselor is frequently working with relatively well-adjusted and integrated individuals, psychodynamic counseling is most often time limited. Such people are more likely to learn, gain insight, and alter their behavioral patterns in short-term counseling.

As the working alliance develops, the client displays a greater capacity to experience and express conflicting emotions and unacceptable impulses. The counselor does not hesitate to encourage a rational understanding of the core emotions that influence dysfunctional behavior.

The intermediate and final stages of counseling are characterized by a deeper exploration of unconscious processes and their relationship to current behavior and future goals (Bordin, 1955). In effect, the client becomes more aware of conflicts, impulses, resistances, and defenses. The counselor further facilitates the client's modification or reorganization of the cognitive and emotional aspects of conflict with the intent of achieving a more integrated ego structure. Individual goal-directed behavior may result with a greater understanding of motivational influences which previously may have impeded the client from attaining specified goals.

Ego developmental counseling is generally time-limited. Thus, when termination is near, a client may show a strong dependency on the counselor and engage in regressive behavior. The counselor interprets and clarifies these behaviors for the client.

The final stage of counseling is attained when clients exhibit more insightful and reflective thinking about their inner experiences. They show a greater commitment to rational decision-making and have a greater understanding of how unconscious processes operate in their lives. They have worked through many of the resistances and ego defenses that made ego functioning more difficult.

Counseling Techniques and Procedures

The counseling techniques and procedures in Bordin's system are designed to enhance the ego functioning of the client via insight and problem-solving. The "working through" of ego defenses, conflict, transference, ambivalence, and anxiety occur through the techniques of *clarification* and *interpretation*. Recall, however, that a good working alliance is required for the technique to have maximum impact (Bordin, 1979 & 1983). As the working alliance becomes strengthened, interpretation can be used more extensively. Clarification and simple restatement are usually employed in the early states of the relationship.

Clarification

The counselor uses clarification to simplify complex personality dynamics. Through clarification the client begins to associate feelings with maladaptive behavioral patterns to arrive at a more accurate cognitive perspective. As the dynamic picture becomes clarified, the client has less need to use defense mechanisms. The counselor must be sensitive to the client's defenses such that an overemphasis on gaining insight does not reinforce intellectual defenses. Clarification may be viewed as an initial stage of interpretation.

Interpretation

Interpretation is a technique that is designed to uncover the significance and meaning of a client's behavior. Interpretation implies seeking information which lies beyond the surface of manifest thoughts, feelings, and emotions. In effect, the counselor uses interpretation to piece together bits of information that seem fragmented to the client.

One interpretive technique is *comparison*, used when two behaviors, thoughts or emotions are dissimilar. For instance, one person may approach authority figures differently than another. The dynamic pattern may be clearly seen when the comparison of the two behavioral approaches is made. The counselor may also compare a present day experience with prior developmental tasks to highlight the client's ego strength or weaknesses. The technique of comparison can help integrate fragmented behavioral patterns to achieve a more organized rational ego.

Wish-Defense

Wish-defense, another form of interpretation, refers to the wish-fulfillment aspects of a psychological conflict. For example, a client may avoid (defense) or project a career decision on the counselor (wish). The client transfers decision-making to the counselor, perhaps as he or she would to a parental figure. The counselor then must confront the defense mechanism by clarifying and interpreting how it enables the client to avoid taking action.

Bordin (1974) believes that interpretations need to be phrased as tentative hypotheses which the client can either accept or reject. The counselor must be sensitive to client readiness for interpretative statements. Interpretations need to be timely and are most effective once the client has established a good working alliance with the counselor. Interpretation employed without a sound working alliance often increases resistance or encourages transference. Premature interpretation can arouse anxiety and defensiveness in the client and may lead to early termination.

Before using the powerful techniques of interpretation, the counselor may use *support* or *reassurance* to minimize client anxiety. Another very important point to consider is that the counselor should encourage clients to make their own interpretations through the formulation of tentative hypotheses that are tested against experience. It is essential that certain conclusions become apparent to the client after meaningful bits of information are put together.

The counselor should be aware of how the four basic dimensions (ambiguity, cognitive-conative, warmth, and personal) operate when implementing techniques. For example, if the client excessively intellectualizes problems (cognitive), then the counselor will need to focus on the affective element (conative) in an interpretation. The ambiguity, warmth and personal dimensions may be managed by the counselor to increase the effectiveness of interpretation. Transference is encouraged when the counselor's personality is more ambiguous to the client. Therapeutically, it is the interpretation of the transference relationship that fosters meaningful insight into client behavior and the nature of resistances and defenses.

Evaluation of Counseling Outcomes

Psychodynamic counseling, from Bordin's perspective, seeks to help people acquire an understanding of the core emotions which motivate current behavior. Bordin (1979) views psychodynamic counseling as being quite different from other therapeutic approaches (i.e., behavioral approaches focusing on learning specific skills). Bordin's approach emphasizes personality interpretation and ego development. Psychodynamic goals are more broadly conceived and attend to the core conflicts, emotions, and motivations which all contribute to the maintenance of anxiety and defenses. The centralist position held by Bordin suggests changes in core processes resulting in the modification of interrelated systems.

The measurement and assessment of psychodynamic goals is as complicated as the criteria are broad. Bordin (1955) does not specifically address the issue of formal evaluation of counseling outcomes. The counselor and client may subjectively evaluate outcomes in the areas of anxiety, use of defenses and general ego functioning.

Similar to many other ego psychologists, Bordin is more interested in the process of counseling than in its outcome. This is due, in part, to his belief that process and outcome eventually are the same. People who gain insight and alter core emotions become more accepting of their strengths and limitations. Anxieties and defenses are minimized as the ego develops and activates its potentials. Bordin claims that the people who undergo psychodynamic counseling tend to appraise their value as human beings more realistically. They are more likely to be self-determined and tend to make more rational decisions about developmental tasks. Since the core processes become more clearly understood, regressive tendencies such as resistance and dependency are minimized in favor of a more productive approach to life.

COUNSELING APPLICATION

An application of Bordin's theory of counseling in an educational setting is described in this section. The case concerns a student who blocks on examinations. This case explores the anxiety and fears associated with her perceptions, and underlying conflicts.

Psychodynamic Counseling in a High School Setting

Myra B., an 18-year-old high school student, entered counseling because she blocked on examinations. She was preparing to take the Scholastic Aptitude Test (SAT) and was worried about performing poorly on the examination. Myra carried a 3.8 high school G.P.A., was well liked, but had a very negative view of herself. Myra was physically attractive but very shy socially. Excerpts of the first session follow.

Myra: I don't know what is wrong with me. I can't take these kinds of examinations. My mind stops working. (Pause).

Counselor: Uh-huh. Could you tell me more?

Myra: No, not really! I have no idea why this happens to me.

Counselor: No idea at all?

Myra: No.

Counselor: Could it be some fear you have?

Myra: Yes! Maybe. But I am not sure. I am never sure about things like this (isolation of affect).

Counselor: Uh-huh. (The counselor, taking a very easy, casual approach and sensing Myra's feelings, encouraged her to express her emotions.) I sense you are holding back tears.

Myra: I am not sure of myself (Myra began to cry).

Counselor: How long have you felt this way?

Myra: Forever. Ever since I was a child. I worried constantly about doing well.

Counselor: Uh-huh. (Pause).

Myra: Why do I feel this way?

Counselor: I wonder why too.

Myra: Why can't you tell me that—why I am here! (Myra expressed frustration with the counselor—an example of negative transference.)

Counselor: Could it be that the answer to your question may reside within you?

The counselor leads Myra to look within herself for answers to personal questions. The counselor does not take this responsibility. Myra shows signs of dependency and transfers her dependency and frustration onto the counselor. She does this by trying to force the counselor to provide answers that will reduce her anxiety. Myra's anxiety and dependency serve as major obstacles to effective coping, self-acceptance, and personal independence.

Myra's dependency most likely is an underlying dynamic that gave rise to her symptoms. The counselor from the psychodynamic framework, tries to help Myra develop insight through exploring the nature of her dependency as well as more effective coping patterns. As the session continues, the counselor assists Myra to clarify her perceptions of the problem.

Counselor: It seems to me that you hesitate to look toward yourself for explanations.

Myra: When I do I block.

Counselor: You block?

Myra: Yes. I can't seem to see anything inside me. I think I am afraid of something.

Counselor: So then it is much easier to rely on others for an explanation or for some understanding.

Myra: Yes, thank God for my parents. They both have good judgment. I defer to them all the time. They are both so successful people and so rational. They can't figure out why I break down and cry so often when I have so much.

Counselor: Uh-huh. Let's pursue that, OK?

Myra: If it wasn't for my parents I would be nothing. I owe them everything.

Counselor: You must have a great deal to prove to them and to yourself.

Myra: Yes. I've respected and admired my parents for years.

Counselor: I see. I sense you want their approval or perhaps even fear you might lose it.

The counselor encourages Myra to explore her feelings about her parents. She moved from discussing blocking in examinations to blocking when she tries to consider her real feelings about matters. The counselor offered an interpretation of Myra's feelings of respect for her parents when he said "I sense you want their approval or perhaps even fear you might lose it."

Myra: I'm feeling tense right at this moment. I can't think anymore. I want to leave. May I leave now?

Counselor: What *would* you like to do?

Myra: I want to leave. (At this point, Myra starts sobbing.)

The counselor pauses. Myra continues to cry. The counselor assures her that it is quite appropriate for her to express her feelings. Myra became composed and then smiled at the counselor.

Myra: I hope you don't think I am awful.

Counselor: (Remained silent.)

Myra: You do think I am awful, don't you? (Myra shows irritation with the counselor.)

Myra for the most part exhibited positive transference toward the counselor in the first few sessions. But there were moments, however, when Myra displayed frustration and irritation with the counselor. This was especially the case when the counselor was ambiguous and did not offer clear cut answers.

The session continued in about the same way for several appointments. Myra became quite frustrated and irritable with the counselor. She was afraid, however, that the counselor would drop her and expressed this fear in the seventh session. Myra also became aware in herself of a significant degree of anger and resentment, but could not identify either the source or object of her feelings. The counselor, realizing that Myra was not ready to explore the deeper aspects of her feelings encouraged her to project them onto him (encouraged transference).

Myra: I don't think you are helping me. I'm getting frustrated with this whole thing. I originally came to you because I had problems taking tests.

Counselor: Are you upset with me?

Myra: Yes, and now I am more confused than ever before . . . I had a dream that frightened me to death. I dreamed my head was made of glass and I banged it against our patio wall and it shattered all over . . .

Counselor: Were you by yourself in the dream?

Myra: (Myra seemed startled.) No. My parents were watching me.

Counselor: Uh-huh.

Myra: They just stood there. They were stunned; couldn't help me. I was out of control. I awoke in a panic.

Counselor: Did you regain your composure?

Myra: Eventually.

Counselor: It never ceases to amaze me how people can find ways of handling their feelings. (The counselor reinforces Myra's ability to cope.) Have you been able to connect your dream with some of the feelings that have bothered you lately? (The counselor encourages Myra to interpret for herself the significance of the experience.)

Myra: I think there is a lot of rage within me and I just don't know whether I can control it.

Counselor: Do you think that has something to do with blocking?

Myra: I never thought of it that way. It could be. I'm really afraid to explore that part of my personality. Rage is so unacceptable—being out of control is so out of character for me. I wasn't brought up that way.

Myra is beginning to achieve a certain degree of insight into the relationships between feelings of anxiety, rage, and blocking on exams and in other situations. Myra's insight and expression of feelings produced a significant reduction in tension (cartharsis). The counselor encouraged Myra to continue expressing her feelings over the next several sessions.

In the 10th session Myra is more able to express her feelings and understand her blocking.

Myra: I never thought there was this part of me.

Counselor: Can you clarify that a bit?

Myra: My anger. I see it—it continues to disturb me—but I don't block as much anymore. In a way I feel out of control but more in control at the

Counselor:　　　　　same time. These bad feelings of mine have developed over a long period of time, haven't they?

Counselor:　I think you have some ideas about that question.

Myra:　　　Maybe I do—

Counselor:　Could you share these?

At this juncture, Myra was able to achieve greater understanding into the role past experiences played in her current feelings. In ego developmental counseling, the counselor is concerned with developmental processes that facilitate or inhibit maturation.

In this counseling sequence with Myra, the counselor used the ambiguity dimension quite effectively. Myra was able to (1) transfer both positive and negative feelings onto the counselor; (2) to achieve some insight into the nature of her problem of blocking on exams; (3) to explore her feelings without relying totally on the counselor; and (4) to achieve a reduction of her symptoms of anxiety.

Critical Comments

Psychodynamic counseling is a therapeutic approach for working with relatively well-integrated individuals. It is based on an "ego" psychology as opposed to an "id" psychology. Bordin stresses an understanding of core dynamic motives which maintain anxiety and defenses, and the role of the ego in managing behavior. The strengthening of the rational ego's faculties is the ultimate goal of ego developmental counseling. Bordin's theoretical approach is derived from psychoanalytic theory, but he has incorporated ideas from learning theory and humanistic models.

Bordin distinguishes counseling from psychotherapy. Bordin has effectively translated psychoanalytic theory and practice into a set of concepts that are easily applied to the majority of people. He believes that a time-limited psychodynamic counseling provides the impetus for ego development especially with people who are relatively effective in their lives. Bordin does, however, recommend long-term counseling if the need arises. As Patterson (1980) points out, it is sometimes difficult for the counselor to assess when an emotional conflict may best be worked with using counseling or psychotherapy. In recent years, Bordin's distinction between counseling and psychotherapy has been modified (Bordin, 1979 & 1983).

Bordin's theory of counseling also recognizes the significance of educational and career development. His views integrate analytic concepts and use them in the career selection process. Bordin's comprehensive treatment of vocational and career development may be useful for counselors interested in vocational rehabilitation, job training, career development, and education.

Bordin's ego development system does not preclude the use of tests and information in counseling. Tests are means of gathering more information about an individual's strengths and weaknesses and can be used to assist the client in the exploration of alternative actions. Bordin is aware that test interpretation may bring deeper emotional conflicts to the surface. For the client, testing is a valuable experience in self-observation and self-exploration.

Bordin's theory of human functioning and behavioral change may be lacking in specificity. The attempt to simplify rather complex psychoanalytic concepts does not appear to be too successful. For example, one wonders how the diagnostic categories are operationalized in actual practice and about the extent to which they shed light on interpersonal and intrapersonal dynamics.

Bordin's system of counseling has generated little research. However, support for a psychodynamic system of counseling may be found in the more recent meta-analysis of psychotherapy outcomes. This research is further discussed in Chapter 14.

We believe the most significant problem in the system is related to the concepts and the criteria for behavioral change. Bordin's psychodynamic counseling model is based upon the assumption that a modification of the inner core of personality results in overt behavioral change. However, the inner core is largely subjective, unconscious, and difficult to measure and to assess in relatively short-term counseling.

Overall, ego developmental counseling provides a moderately comprehensive framework for understanding human functioning and dealing with human behavior. Special consideration is given to the working alliance between the counselor and client. The major strength of Bordin's theory is the emphasis he places on the therapeutic relationship, its process, and its ultimate contribution to ego development.

REFERENCES

Bordin, E.S. (1955a). *Psychological counseling.* New York: Appleton-Century-Crofts, Inc.

Bordin, E.S. (1955b). Ambiguity as a therapeutic variable. *Journal of Consulting Psychology, 19,* 9-15.

Bordin, E.S., Nachmann, B., & Segal, S.J. (1963). An articulate framework for vocational development. *Journal of Counseling Psychology, 10,* 107-118.

Bordin, E.S. (1965). The ambivalent quest for independence. *Journal of Counseling Psychology, 12,* 339-345.

Bordin, E.S. (1966a). Free association: An experimental analogue of the psychoanalytic situation. In L.A. Gottschalk and A.H. Auerback (Eds.), *Methods of research in psychotherapy,* (pp. 189-208). New York: Appleton-Century-Crofts.

Bordin, E.S. (1966b). Personality and free association. *Journal of Consulting Psychology, 30,* 30-38.

Bordin, E.S. (1968). The personality of the therapist as an influence in psychotherapy. In M.J. Feldman (Ed.), *Studies in psychotherapy and behavioral change: Research in individual psychotherapy.* Buffalo Studies Vol. IV. Buffalo: State University of New York at Buffalo.

Bordin, E.S. (1974). *Research strategies in psychotherapy.* New York: John Wiley & Sons.

Bordin, E.S. (1979). The generalizability of the psychoanalytic concept of the working alliance. *Psychotherapy: Theory, research and practice, 16,* 252-260.

Bordin, E.S. (1983). A working alliance based model of supervision. *The Counseling Psychologist, 11,* 35-42.

Lansford, E. & Bordin, E.S. (1983). A research note on the relation between the free association and experiencing scales. *Journal of Consulting and Clinical Psychology, 51,* 367-369.

Patterson, C.H. (1980). *Theories of counseling and psychotherapy,* (3rd ed.). New York: Harper & Row Publishers.

CHAPTER 3

ALFRED ADLER'S
INDIVIDUAL PSYCHOLOGY

FOUNDATIONS AND STRUCTURE

Historical Foundations

ALFRED ADLER was born in a suburb of Vienna in 1870. Although he was the son of Hungarian-Jewish parents, his cultural heritage never played a particularly strong role in his life. He was the second son and third child in the family, a position which later proved to be quite important in the development of his theories. At an early age, Adler suffered from rickets and pneumonia, contributing to the early development of a keen interest in becoming a physician. Although he was an active and fairly talented child, he did not feel his childhood was a particularly happy one (Bottome, 1957).

Adler earned his M.D. degree from the University of Vienna in 1895. Although he was originally trained as an ophthamologist, he first opened a general practice in a lower socioeconomic neighborhood in the city. He was fascinated by the fact that many performers from a nearby carnival (acrobats and other physically skillful performers) had often compensated from a weakness or physical trauma in childhood. The early experiences he had in this practice contributed to his ideas on organ inferiority and social interest.

In 1902, Freud invited Adler to join one of his ongoing discussion groups dealing with psychoanalysis (later evolving into the International Psychoanalytic Association). This was an influential union for Adler, for during the time of this relationship his ideas began to solidify and become more integrated. In 1917, he published his first major work *Study of Organ Inferiority and Its Psychical Compensation,* a book dominated by the physical nature of his theories at that time. Contrary to some beliefs, Adler was a colleague of Freud, not a student, and their ideas were often in conflict. Even though Adler was made the first president of the Vienna Psychoanalytic group in 1910, he and Freud finally reached a point where their ideas appeared to be incompatible and, in 1911, they broke from contact. In 1912, a large number of supporters accompanied Adler and joined with him to form the Society for Individual Psychology.

Even though the concept of social interest had been developing throughout Adler's early work, it entered the center of his formulations following World War I. He had spent two years as a physician near the Russian front and had later worked in a military hospital in Vienna. During this experience he was able to gain first-hand knowledge of the ravages of war which expanded his awareness of a variety of social issues. After this time, a shift to a very strong sense of social responsibility and caring flavored his theories and writings.

One way that Adler could see to activate this social responsibility notion was to develop and attach Individual Psychology Clinics to each of the State Schools in Vienna. These were the beginning of child guidance clinics and between 1921 and 1934 Adler and his students met with so much success in running these centers that the delinquency rate in the city was noticeably diminished (Rychlak, 1981).

During the 1920's and 1930's Adler expanded his techniques to include the first work on group methods and family therapy. He spent considerable time traveling to other countries, speaking and demonstrating his techniques to educators, social workers, and other professionals. After the change in governments in Austria in 1934, he fled Europe and lived in New York with his wife. He died on a European speaking tour in 1937 at age 67.

Many of Adler's ideas have been incorporated into other frameworks, often without suitable acknowledgement (Ansbacher and Ansbacher, 1964; Mosak, 1979). Ellis (1973) eloquently summarized Adler's work and identifies him as the father of modern psychotherapy. He states:

- Adler founded ego psychology.
- He stimulated the humanistic psychology movement.
- He called his system psychotherapy and formulated the theory of individuation.
- He stressed a holistic view of people.

Ellis reasons that many psychotherapists who have been called neo-Freudians should more correctly be called neo-Adlerians.

Today, Adlerian training programs can be found in many countries, but their principle home is in the United States. This approach's strong concentration on reeducation instead of "cure," outreach instead of professional immobility, and a democratic counseling style instead of one which is professionally dominated is attractive to many counselors who enjoy playing a dynamic yet supportive role in personal and community development.

Philosophical Foundations

Individual psychology is based heavily on the tenets of philosophical Stoicism and the assumptions of Kant and Nietzsche. Often, many of the philosophical aspects of Adlerian theory must be placed within a societal or cultural context in order to be fully understood. Adler's concept of social interest (the willingness to work for the common good) is also central to all aspects of his theory.

Influenced by the Stoics, Adler developed the idea that people have goals and values which evolve into a directed life plan. Stoic philosophy assumes that the people pursue their life plans through rational logical decision-making. Adler was also influenced by the neo-Kantian Hans Vaihinger's "as if" philosophy. This philosophical tenet suggests that people are motivated by fictitious goals which have no basis in reality yet contribute an orderliness to life. Stoicism and the fictitious "as if" concept lead Adler (1956) to propose that people are motivated by future goals, rather than past experiences. This concept of being "drawn" (in contrast to the Freudian deterministic style of being "pushed") is the foundation of Adler's teleological design of life games and the life style.

Individual psychology reflects a few themes that are directly related to Kantian philosophy (Mosak, 1979). Adler borrowed from Kant to create his idea of categorical imperative which suggests that people have explicit belief systems and ideas about what their life and the world should be. The second Kantian theme that Adlerian theory draws upon is related to his concept of private logic. Adler's theory of personality development is cognitive and assumes that people make choices about their life course based on their own experiences. The rationale or motive for a decision on life course is not objectively or clearly seen, rather it is subjective, individualized, and private. Overcoming, a concept seen in much of Adler's early work, also is related to Kantian philosophy. This stance proposes that one overcomes difficulties and weaknesses (typically physical) simply because they exist. At one time, Adler called overcoming "the fundamental law of life" (Adler, 1964b, p. 71).

Nietzsche's philosophical system suggested the concept of "will to power." Adlerian theory encompasses the concept of power, and also attends to the normal strivings for competence. Nietzsche was concerned with the concept of superman-like strivings with people; however, Adler expanded the will to include feelings and attitudes of competence, equality, and social interest (Mosak, 1979).

Adler's theory is holistic and suggests a view of people as complete organisms, with no separation between mind and body. He has indicated that the mind and body are related through something he calls the *law of movement* (Adler, 1964b). All animals have the capacity to identify either a threat or a goal and are able to move to reach the desired end state. He therefore links movement with motivation and says that both physical and psychic movements are made based upon set structures which become that organism's typical patterns of responding. The mind and body enact these patterns in a unified manner, reflecting what is referred to as the personalty.

The behavior emitted by an organism based upon the set patterns is purposefully selected to assist in reaching a goal. Based upon the concepts of categorical imperative and private logic discussed earlier, Adler sees behavior as a function of each person's subjective perception of events. The meaning that is attributed to a situation by a specific person will provide the context for that individual's behavior. "Reality," therefore, is based upon an individual's perceptions and not necessarily upon a universally accepted ideal.

Adler's theory is a subjective, forward-moving, goal-oriented, holistic approach that pays particular attention to the development of individualized set patterns of behavior. The goals people develop often concentrate on personal competence, equality, and social acceptance.

Social-Psychological Foundations

Adler's early work was largely based upon a medical model and was reflected well in his first book, *Study on Organ Inferiority* (1917). The thesis he proposed was that people are typically born with at least one potentially weak organ. Stress from everyday activities, if dealt with ineffectively, can eventually lead that organ to break down. The organism, in order to avoid this breakdown, will try to overcome the danger by trying much harder to succeed (overcompensate). In time, he made a shift in his thinking from a solely organic explanation to one which acknowledged the influence of social and psychological components. In his later writings, he proposed that all people are born with feelings of inferiority and incompleteness and they spend their whole life trying to make gains to reach above their present level of functioning. These feelings of inferiority are generalized to a variety of functions and behaviors, thereby extending beyond a specific organ or physical function. This concept of *social inferiority* is central to one's goal-oriented motivation.

Out of the feelings of inferiority grows the one human drive that Adler acknowledges—the drive of *superiority*. As his ideas evolved, he challenged Freud's emphasis on sexuality as one of the prime behavioral motivators and replaced sexuality with aggression, seeing humans as aggressive animals who have learned to rely on this aggression for their survival. The contact he had with many clients simply did not reinforce this concept so he began to view motivation from a power-powerlessness perspective. Eventually, he concluded that people just wish to feel superior, regardless of their present state. Adler treats superiority as the prime mover in life, a personal perception that serves as an eventual explanation for why one does what one does.

In addition to experiencing feelings of inferiority and the drive of superiority, Adler believes that people do have other mental mechanisms which serve to either shape or help define the direction of behaviors. One mental mechanism which has been briefly discussed in relation to social inferiority is the concept of *compensation* (or overcompensation). Adler referred to the extreme forms as safeguarding tendencies, where the person will insulate those aspects which are perceived to be inferior either by building them up or by avoiding situations where they must be used. Another mental mechanism noted by Adler is the *protest*, or the tendency for people to cognitively and behaviorally concentrate on an issue to the exclusion of others because they may feel unprepared to reach the desired goal. *Identification* was described by Adler (1954) as the empathy one person feels for another, derived from a social consciousness.

Identification is related to another social-psychological concept in Adler's theory, that of *social interest*. Actually, the ability to identify or be empathic with others is a component of the more universal trait of social interest which is actually an innate interest in other human beings. Adler looked at this almost as instinctual, just needing human contact to activate it. The feelings of inferiority which are common to all people form a bond which facilitates the development of social interest.

Maturity is judged by how well a person is able to set aside self-centered goals and cooperate with others for the common good. In referring to social interest, Adler said, "It means striving for a form of community which must be thought of as everlasting, as it could be thought of if mankind had reached the goal of perfection" (Ansbacher and Ansbacher, 1964, 34-35).

In Individual Psychology, the personality is a forward-moving dynamic process which provides set patterns of behavior called the *life style*. This life style is the prescribed method each individual develops to reach the goal of superiority. The life style involves both the energy provided by internal mechanisms and the presses from the environment which may aid or detract the person with respect to goals. Of the two forces, the internal mechanisms are far more important in Adlerian thought.

Among the more important internal mechanisms is *private logic,* or the unique expectations and ways of thinking all people develop in response to their own idiosyncratic perceptions of their life and the environment. Dinkmeyer, Pew, and Dinkmeyer (1979) identify a hierarchy of goals related to the private logic including the distant goals of the life style and short-term goals which may be timely or situational. These authors say while the long-term goals provide the "substance of the life style," each person has the power to proact and react in the present. Another aspect of the private logic is the hidden reason which is a major facet of each individual's decision-making process that is functioning below the threshold of one's awareness.

A second aspect of the life style is called the *life plan* (in later writings, Adler referred to this concept as the *prototype.*) Dinkmeyer, Pew, and Dinkmeyer (1979) identify the life plan as a specific map children lay down to prepare them for living. During the first five to six years of life, children face real and fictionalized successes and difficulties which teach them to feel and respond in very specific ways in response to certain stimuli. The patterns that one develops through a repetition of these coping response sets typically form a very solid base for all future transactions. The life plan later develops into the life style, the overall orchestral theme behind each person's life.

During childhood, each person develops *fictional goals* which are the ideals of superiority and social belongingness. While the past may set the stage for the life style, these futuristic aims determine what actions will be taken and how. In practice, these goals are typically unattainable, often involving requirements of perfection or complete consistency (always or never). In most cases, the personality is consciously aware of these goals and much day-to-day behavior is enacted because of them. The meaning of daily occurrences is often derived by filtering it through the fictional goal, thus gaining perspective and continuity.

Four types of life styles have been identified by Rychlak (1981). The first is the *"ruler"* (dominant) lifestyle which concentrates on directing and planning for others. A second type is the *"getter"* who is constantly looking for a provider to take care of their needs, however slight they may be. The *"avoider"* describes the third type, a person who withdraws from others, especially in situations where one's feelings of inferiority are reinforced. The fourth type is the *"socially useful"* person, someone who tries to be actively and caringly involved with others in time of need. These types certainly do not represent an exhaustive list of all possible life styles but do represent a few examples of commonly found behavioral sets.

Both the family and cultural contexts play important roles in Adler's theory. He did not feel, however, that an individual's behavior is a product of the environment but, rather, one must actualize the inherent need of social interest individually. In Adlerian thought, the personality is shaped by the family and the environment, especially with regards to the family *constellation*. Adler (1964b) saw birth order, the size of the family, the sex and age of siblings, the relationships between family members, and individual personality characteristics of members as comprising crucial variables a child must deal with in gaining membership to this first group. The manner in which the child approaches this task and the roles and functions one learns to accept help to shape the life plan and eventual life style.

The Development of the Person

It has already been proposed that Adler sees people as unique individuals who are always in a state of movement toward the fictionalized goals of the life style. In this section, the concept of uniqueness is discussed within a developmental framework as is the process people encounter in the establishment and implementation of a life style.

From an Adlerian perspective, the actual number of factors which are potentially influential in the human development process is unestimable. Certainly, genetic factors play a role in shaping the developmental process whether they are physically or cognitively related. Adler saw social interest as an "automatic" (or hereditary) trait common to all people and the way each person enacts this need is individually determined based upon other genetic and environmental factors.

Adler (1968) did believe in an informal stage process (which he referred to as epochs), but this sequencing process lacked the strict nature of Freud's psychosexual stages. For Adler, the developmental stages were more fluid and typically unassociated with critical periods of personality development. While he did acknowledge that certain developmental tasks are often associated with levels of growth, the teleological and forward-moving nature of his theory would suggest that future projections are more important to deal with than incompletely processed tasks from the past.

The Family Structure

The influence of family structure and forces is probably the most important factor in Adler's developmental perspective for it is within this social milieu that the child will develop private logic, the life plan, and methods to enact the principle of social interest. Birth order has received a considerable amount of research and practical attention by Adlerian counselors. Dinkmeyer, Pew, and Dinkmeyer (1979) argue that much of the research done in this area has not conceptualized birth order as a dynamic, individualized experience, the meaning of which being dependent upon the perceptions of the child. Birth order is actually a psychological concept and not limited to the chronological order of family membership. The reader should keep this limitation in mind when reading the next few paragraphs regarding the beliefs about birth order.

In a multiple child family, the first (oldest) child is often put in a position of authority, acting as an extension of parental authority (Adler, 1964a). The probability is greater for first children to develop a conventional outlook on life because of their early experiences in a grown-up world and the responsibility they either experienced or perceived themselves as having. An only child has the advantage of growing up in an adult world and receiving the undivided attention of parents, but does not experience the sense of responsibility that a first child may.

Second children are most likely to feel that a challenge is placed on them because of their position in the family constellation. They often may feel inferior to the older child simply because of the competence older children will achieve due to the growth process. This feeling may make the urge to overcome inferiority even stronger, thereby increasing the competitive nature. The very strong drive to succeed which may develop causes the second-born to be somewhat less attentive to authority and conventional ways.

The last (youngest) child in a family often is put in a position of either needing to compete with and become superior to all other siblings or accept the likelihood of being pampered as the baby in the family (in a similar manner to the first child but, in this case, there is competition for attention.) Pampering often leads to the development of selfishness, expecting all things to come easily and handily.

Since birth order is a psychological concept, focusing on each individual's perceptions of the order and relative position of the other members, a counselor must assess individual characteristics which may shape these perceptions. Traits such as sex of siblings, stability of family membership, and occurrence of long-term illness or disability all may enter into the process of determining relative position.

Another family-related concept involved in the developmental process is the family constellation, briefly discussed as a social-psychological aspect of Adler's theory. The developing life plan is shaped by all of the diverse aspects of the constellation. Not only are people put into a position within the family group by the other members, but they also actively try to find their own niche as well. This family constellation exerts considerable influence upon individual development by providing the context within which the person tests reality and tries out new behaviors.

The Family Constellation

The family constellation involves all the family values and attitudes which lead to an overall family atmosphere. Dewey (in Nikelly, 1971) listed many types of family atmospheres including authoritarian (rigidity and strong values for children to be obedient), suppressive (limitations placed upon certain behaviors, especially those related to the expression of thoughts and feelings), martyrdom (a tendency to suffer nobly and honorably, receiving considerable reinforcement from the family to do so), overprotective (the parents create an atmosphere where the children do not learn responsibility for their behavior), high standards (an atmosphere where the children simply cannot live up to standards set by parents), and materialistic (a concentration on succeeding in material gains with little emphasis on enhancing the social interest needs). The important component of this concept is the fact that the family atmosphere is a set of *shared* values and a child's inability to follow through with "appropriate" behaviors or disagreement with the basic assumptions will add to that individual's difficulty in learning how to negotiate and join a group later in life.

The Life Style

The development of the life style is, in part, shaped by heredity, early experiences in the family, the family constellation, and the child's unique perceptions of these characteristics and events. The life style is never completely developed, rather, it is a dynamic process which is constantly being modified and adapted in order to remain functional in the environment. We have already discussed the private logic (the thinking processes which shape each person's view of reality), the life plan (the prototype or map which is developed very early in life in response to successes and difficulties), and the fictional goal (the ideal state all people identify for themselves). The activities that shape the development of the life style (and operationalize private logic, the life plan, and fictional goals) are work, society, and sex. Adler (1956) views these three factors of life as challenges to which each person becomes committed. In many cases, the life style is broad or flexible enough to successfully deal with most of life's problems. In others, however, the life style may be so constricting that it does not offer an adequate framework within which the person can succeed even in basic activities.

During the initial development of the life style, children make convictions about themselves and reality. These convictions are confirmed by subsequent experiences, whether or not outside reality actually would back up this validation. The perceptual mechanisms of the individual are designed to validate the experience in a way which maintains the personal point of view. Mosak (1979) divided life style convictions into the following four groups:

- The Self-Concept — Beliefs of personal identity
- The Self-Ideal — Attitudes and beliefs of what the person should be
- The Weltbild — Pictures of the world — attitudes about reality
- The Ethical — Convictions and beliefs of what is "right" and "wrong"

Discrepancies may exist among these convictions, potentially leading to confusion in the life style.

Adler (1930) has said that no one epoch of development or a single situation can change a person. He does recognize, however, that adolescence, early adulthood, and later years all force the individual to harmonize individual, family, and societal goals. It is during adulthood that many of the idiosyncracies of the life style first become evident through and individual's reactions to various tasks.

Concepts of Functional and Dysfunctional Behavior

Functional behavior, in Adlerian terms, is behavior which will enable an individual to satisfactorily cope with the three problem areas of life: work, society, and sex. In each of these three areas, one can see the strong social aspect of his theory where everyone's true ability is operationalized in situations which bring them in contact with others. A "functional" person is one who puts social interest ahead of self interest and achieves goals through the use of creative power and a will to cooperate (changing the context of Neitzsche's will to power). This person feels a sense of belongingness and openly and actively contributes to the group. The life style should be specific enough to provide a base and direction for the behavior yet broad enough to accommodate a variety of life tasks and situations. Dysfunctional behavior may be a result of any aspect of the life style which does not allow for satisfactory transactions in work, society, or sex.

Problems may arise from a variety of different sources, but most difficulties can eventually be traced back to either the development of ineffective goal structures or the implementation of methods which are reaching inefficiently for those goals. The development of a "number-one priority" occurs within the first few years of life and can include the need for comfort, pleasing others, control, or superiority (Schoenaker and Schoenaker, 1976). After the development of this priority, all future components of the life style are designed around this single need. While no priority is in and of itself a negative trait, difficulties arise when behaviors designed to accommodate this need do not allow for the needs of social interest and belongingness to survive.

In Adlerian thought, feelings of inferiority are universal. When people no longer just *feel* inferior and begin to *act* as if they were inferior, Adler refers to this as a inferiority complex. It becomes an open demonstration of the goal contained in the life style (in this case, a goal of weakness in the face of life tasks.) Rychlak (1981) indicates that the whole notion of "complex" is one of the few times that Adler identified specific traits within the personality. Other complexes noted by Rychlak include the power complex (a dominating goal), the Oedipus complex (a dependency goal due to overpampering), the leader complex (high ambition leading to a persistence regardless of competence), and a spectator complex (a goal of interest but non-participation). Complexes may vary greatly due to the wide variations in life style.

Adler said that the basic distinction between "normal" people and those who have neurotic symptoms is the way they have designed their life style. Often the neurotic lives, what Adler (1968) called the "life lie," where the world has been simplistically divided into opposites and the person plays one side against the other. These processes are unconscious, yet neurotic people will live closer to their fictitious views of reality than do people without these tendencies. Despite this consistency, the goals are not met, few tasks are performed well, and neurotics continue to create situations where their fictional goals can be validated. The more serious pathology of psychosis is seen by Adler (1964b) as a complete failure in work, society, and sex. The fictional goals become a complete system into which they enter, thus requiring high levels of care. All examples of psychopathology (alchoholism, antisocial behavior, depression, etc.) are also related to life styles which are set up in such a way that they lead people to behave ineffectively in attaining their fictional goals.

Dysfunctional behavior, therefore, is a function of both the structure and dynamics of the life style. Family atmosphere, parenting styles, socioeconomic factors, and hereditary factors may all contribute to the development of life difficulties.

Concepts of Behavior Change

Since Adlerian theory sees the primary problems people face as mistaken life styles, the change process concentrates on removing blockages to growth and reeducating clients so that they are able to move in new, more effective directions. More specifically, the counselor must first help clients change their view of reality (the cognitive map) and develop a belief that it is possible for them to live free from the life lie they had developed for themselves. The counselor must then help the client develop a more efficient capacity for social interest and learn how to put it into practice.

Underlying all of the Adlerian counseling strategies and techniques is an implicit assumption that all behavior is purposeful and directed at the future (not ruled by the past). In contrast to many other theories, Adlerian thought does not assume that a client is helpless in the face of past experiences. Rather, it is assumed that all behavior outside or inside of the counseling relationship can be interpreted as signs of the overall life plan and therefore have a distinct meaning and diagnostic utility. The counselor shows to clients the reality of their behavior by helping them to become aware of the motives and purposes of actions.

Once people become more aware of the purpose of their behaviors, they are put in the position of being active coparticipants in the counseling process (Adler, 1964b). While the responsibility for the outcome of counseling is in part related to the client-counselor relationship, it is also dependent upon the clients' ability and willingness to introspect and gain insights about their private logic and fictional goals.

Understanding the life style is the first task in the Adlerian counselor-client relationship. The client's position and role in the family along with the family values, expectations, and attitudes may suggest how the life plan was determined. The experiences, conditions, and demands that have increased inferior feelings facilitate both understanding and the goal of superiority (Adler, 1964b). Adler suggested that once the plan is disclosed, the life style may become more free to change.

The notions of faith, hope, and love are key facilitative elements in the process of individual behavior change (Adler, 1964b). Faith acknowledges the individual's capability to understand the life style and learn behaviors of social interest. Adler (1956), a humanist, stated that the individual has the desire to "become" and this reflects the faith to cope with existence. The Adlerian counselor also encourages the sense of hope that people can overcome their faulty teleological goal. Hope is a component of the therapeutic underpinning of counseling and suggests that the individual is capable of behavior change. Love, the third therapeutic element, suggests that the Adlerian counselor cares deeply and is committed to the individual's welfare and best interest.

Assessment of Human Functioning

The assessment phase in Adlerian counseling is crucial to the effectiveness of the relationship because of the individualized nature of life style and problem development. Mosak and Dreikurs (1973) indicate that the assessment process has two purposes: understanding the dynamics of the life style and identifying how the life style affects current behavior in day-to-day life tasks. Since all behaviors are purposeful, everything that clients say and do from the very first moment they enter the room is noted by the counselor. At the very beginning, the counselor is identifying potential patterns which will lead to insight regarding the life style.

Typically, a counselor will first concentrate on gaining information about the present functioning of the client. Dinkmeyer, Pew, and Dinkmeyer (1979) discuss a few of the areas where information may be helpful.

They say that social relationships, work, sexuality, the self-concept, and goals can be investigated, concentrating on not only the facts and figures but also the feelings the clients have toward each of the areas and their participation in them.

In order to gain an understanding of early processes which may have helped to shape the development of the life style, the counselor gains information on the family constellation and dynamics, early recollections, and basic mistakes in perceiving themselves in the world. This information is then integrated into a picture involving relationships, perceptions, and assets which is shared with the client for validation and/or revision. The *life style analysis* helps the counselor to better understand the client and also helps develop trust in the relationship by making the client feel understood.

Information about the *family constellation* can be gained through the use of a questionnaire or interview format. The information derived includes the psychological position of the client in the family, the perceived relationships between siblings and between the client and the parents, characteristics of family members, and other influential forces within the family. The information gathered is very specific, with the counselor being careful to gain as many of the precise perceptions of the client as possible. It is more important for the information given to be truthful from the client's perceptions than consistent with "objective reality."

Family dynamics and atmosphere are other important informational areas which often add even more to shaping a life style than the family constellation does. Again, this information can be identified with the use of a questionnaire or an interview but the counselor may reach less success than with the family constellation information. The ambiguous nature of values and attitudes makes it difficult to measure these concepts in a reliable manner. Therefore, it is important for the counselor to be aware of these values and attitudes being played out in both day-to-day behaviors and the counseling relationship itself.

An *early recollection* is a specific incident which is recalled by clients from their early childhood. Recollections are not broad summaries of a life phase or a relationship, they are direct memories of situations and events of the past. From these it is possible to assess the cognitive orientation and operations of clients. Adlerians assert that from the early recollections counselors can draw many of the attitudes, beliefs, and values which have shaped the dynamics of the life style. These recollections remain because they remind the client of those instances which justify their present life style. The counselor listens to not only the content of the recollection but also to the process the client uses to recall it. Both the content and process of gaining early recollections is indicative of the purposeful nature of client behavior and of the goals they have chosen to live by.

From the information gained from plotting the family constellation, discovering the family dynamics, and identifying early recollections, the counselor can uncover the life style's *basic mistakes*. Basic mistakes are cognitive maneuvers which teleologically direct the life style, leading the person to draw erroneous conclusions about life. The private logic may shift a person's orientation to life in such a way that social interest is minimized and a need for superiority over others is increased. Mosak (1979) identified the following classification scheme of basic mistakes:

- Overgeneralization from one event to all people, places, or things
- Excessively demanding need for security
- Misperception of self and reality demands
- Minimization of one's abilities and self-worth
- Faulty values serving self-interest and excessively minimizing social interest

The last major assessment area focused on by Adlerian counselors is a listing of recognized client assets. The counselor will be able to observe many other assets but is most interested in those which clients themselves identify and acknowledge.

Throughout the counseling process, the assessment procedure continues to identify the structure and dynamics of the life style, concentrating on the consistency among the various modalities of behavior and expression. When a direct observation is made that may either validate or falsify the initial analysis, it is shared with the client in order to enhance that individual's capacity for self-study. Assessment in Adlerian counseling is an on-going process, continually being tested and reformed into new patterns.

Goals and Directions of Counseling

As has been mentioned before, a person who is behaving in a functional manner is one who is able to satisfactorally cope with the three problems of life: work, society, and sex. The general goal of Adlerian counseling is that people will gain the self-knowledge, skills, and motivation to succeed in their quest to gain personal competence by developing (or redeveloping) effective life styles which will enable them to move in a positive direction, thereby satisfying their own needs through cooperation with and caring for others. The following are a few examples of specific goal areas in the human development process:

- *Social interest.* Individual needs are satisfied in cooperation with others, and people are committed to meaningful interpersonal relationships.
- *Individuation.* People are aware of their unique strengths and assets that may be used to meet personal and social interest.
- *Creative power.* People have the power to draw upon their own assets and internal resources so that they may achieve their goals.
- *Life style development.* The life style is based upon social interest, minimizes basic mistakes, and acknowledges feelings of inferiority without increasing the strivings for superiority.
- *Courage.* Life challenges are approached with minimum of anxiety and increased levels of enhancing, positive attitudes.
- *Freedom to choose.* People make realistic choices about their life style and accept the responsibility for these decisions.
- *Cognitive organization.* People base their ideas and behaviors on reality and their assets, not on "life lies."
- *Free will.* People determine their own life style goals, providing direction and motivation for their actions.

Dinkmeyer, Pew, and Dinkmeyer (1979) identify four specific goals of the counseling process itself (which reflect the four stages of intervention.) They say, (1) the establishment of an empathic relationship, (2) helping clients understand the dynamics which determine their life style, (3) helping clients reach insightful conclusions regarding any nonfunctional life style dynamics, and (4) helping clients assess alternatives to their present situation and commit to change, are goals involved in engaging the client in the counseling process.

The Counseling Process:
Structuring, Facilitating, and Terminating

The Adlerian counseling relationship is characterized by openness, trust, and equality. It is a "calm scientific process" which is essentially collaborative and consultative. Since the medical model was abandoned by Adler, the counselor works with the client less from a power position and more from that of an educator. The client takes an active part in the learning process, assuming much of the responsibility for the outcome of the relationship.

Adlerian counselors are aware of their own feelings, perceptual processes, values and attitudes. It is important for them to express their openness in experiencing clients from the client's perspective without imposing their own value structure on the counseling process. Adler (1963) felt that the most effective counselors are those who can "see with the other person's eyes, hear with his ears, and feel with his heart: one must identify with him" (p. 162).

The counseling process to be discussed in this section coincides with the goals of counseling as outlined by Dinkmeyer, Pew, and Dinkmeyer (1979). The first step is to *develop an empathic, open and trusting relationship.* During this phase, the counselor and client determine what the focus of the relationship will be and agree upon responsibilities for each member. Counselors must share their own agendas as well as elicit from clients any goals and expectations they have about the counseling process. The purpose of this is to have both participants arrive at a tentative agreement about the goals and process of counseling so that a common framework can be established.

The relationship is a method of communicating the message that the client is a worthwhile person who can learn to take responsibility for thoughts, feelings, and behaviors. The counselor encourages clients to explore themselves in a trusting, open environment and cooperate with the counselor's requests and suggestions. Adler doesn't really speak of transference in the Freudian sense, but he does acknowledge the development of strong client feelings for the counselor. This is quite simply explained as a positive sign of the development and use of social interest.

Once the relationship has been established and the initial goals have been identified, the counseling process moves into its second phase: *helping the clients understand the structure and dynamics of the life style.* The assessment process has already been discussed in some detail in a previous section, but it is important to explore how this information is presented to the client.

The life style summary is discussed with the client in an easily understandable manner so that the client is able to recognize patterns and analyze the dynamics with the counselor. It is important to remember that the life style will be played out even in the client's analysis, so sensitivity will be needed to differentiate objectivity from symptomatic behavior. As the life style is analyzed, a plan for future counseling emerges. Involving the client in this process offers the opportunity to mutually develop the structure and direction of the counseling process.

Throughout the counseling process, the client is being confronted with components of the life style, either being played out in the counseling relationship or outside in society. With increased knowledge of the dynamics of the life style, the client will occasionally gain insights into the reason for their behaviors. This is the third step in the Adlerian counseling process, *helping clients reach insightful conclusions about non-functional life style dynamics*. This insight is a crucial step for Adler who once said, "The cure can only be effected by intellectual means, by the patient's growing insight into his mistake, by the development of his social feeling" (Adler, 1964b, p. 181). Through the concept of holism, a change in the cognitions will lead to changes in other systems.

Insight can be gained through a variety of means (including self-study and a seemingly "out-of-the-blue" *aha* experience), but the most common and probably the most powerful method is direct interpretation. This is different than the Freudian use of interpretation which concentrated on the cause of behaviors. Instead, Adlerian counselors tentatively interpret the movement, purpose, and use of behaviors in relation to the ineffective fictionalized goals. Adler (1964a) indicated that interpretation is effective when it is "so clear that the patient knows and feels his own experience in it instantly" (p. 74).

The last phase of Adlerian counseling is called *helping clients assess alternatives and commit to change,* also known as *reorientation.* In this phase, the counselor helps to reorient the clients' cognitive map thereby assisting them in the task of facing and overcoming life's challenges. This is a reeducation process where the Adlerian counselor helps the client develop skills and actively reinforces attitudes, beliefs, and expectations which are based on reality and the client's assets. The counselor encourages clients to take risks and try out new behaviors so they will have the opportunity to act in a more personally satisfying, socially constructive manner.

Counseling Techniques and Procedures

Among the major techniques in Adlerian counseling are life style assessment, the taking of early recollections, and interpretation; procedures which have already been discussed in previous sections. Also discussed have been the techniques and procedures used in developing an effective client-counselor relationship, a task Adlerian counselors regard very highly. In addition to the relationship development and assessment techniques already discussed there are a variety of additional strategies that may be used in the insight and reorientation phases of the counseling process. In this section, the authors describe a few of these techniques but do not arrange them in any particular order due to the individualized nature of Adlerian counseling in operation.

Specific Techniques

Acting "As If." Clients may often begin statements with the phrase, "If only I could . . ." In these cases, the counselor may suggest that the client should act out the "as if" behavior for a specified period of time, forcing them to try out a new role. The tactic may show clients that they actually can be successful with these new behaviors, thereby reorienting their cognitive map and modifying the life style.

Avoiding Tar Baby (Allen, 1971). The counselor only acknowledges and reinforces those behaviors and thoughts that enhance the growth and development of the client. The "traps" that clients use to fit the counselor into their reality (tar babies) are avoided.

Catching Oneself. The counselor teaches clients how to monitor their behaviors and stop themselves when they are about to perform the behaviors they would like to change. The counselor may suggest avoiding or modifying the "hot" situation or help clients use more effective behaviors in place of the dysfunctional ones.

Dream Analysis. An Adlerian counselor uses dream analysis to gain information about the client's goal structure (Adler believed that dreams are the clearest representation of the life goals.) Adler felt that dream analysis may, in some instances, be an efficient way to gain information, but certainly not the only way. Anything that can be gained from dreams can be observed in day-to-day activities.

Imagery and Symbolization. The counselor may suggest an image to the client which is symbolic of the fictional goals. The technique may involve using a picture, a phrase, a word, or even a sound; anything that will conjure up a symbolic representation of the life goals. The client can use this as a way of putting the present situation into perspective or as a simple reminder of their goal.

Paradoxical Intention. The counselor encourages clients to maintain and, in some cases, increase their problem behaviors. What this does is make clients become all the more aware of their behaviors by magnifying their consequences. The prescription also takes away any power clients have gained in maintaining their behaviors. Given this change in perspective, clients often give the behaviors up since they have lost their potency.

Pushbutton Technique (Mosak, 1979). The counselor asks clients to close their eyes and think of incidents from their past that bring up various emotions. As they do this they are told to attend to their feelings. In this way, Adlerian counselors teach clients that emotions can be created by thoughts, therefore people actively choose how they feel.

Removing a Behavior's Payoff. Dinkmeyer, Pew, and Dinkmeyer (1979) refer to this technique as "spitting in the client's soup." The counselor acknowledges the purpose of a dysfunctional behavior, making it less interesting and useless to the client. For example, when parents point out to their son that his tendency to "eat like a pig" is done just to anger them and they acknowledge that he is old enough to monitor his own eating habits from now on, the effect of his behavior loses much of its punch.

Task Setting. Adlerian counselors set tasks at levels which will ensure client success. Clients are asked to perform this "homework" and then discuss it with the counselor during the next session. The goals of each task are specific, attainable, time-limited, and typically focus on a behavior designed to heighten social interest.

Adlerian counselors acknowledge the fact that factors may exist below the threshold of awareness that influence current functioning. Most of the techniques are direct, behavioral, and are designed to increase the level of recognition one has for these processes. Adlerian techniques also promote clients to become involved with activities which will enhance both social and self interest.

Evaluation of Counseling Outcomes

Adlerian counselors work with both developmental and remedial issues in two-person therapeutic relationships, family counseling relationships, group counseling modes, and in childhood guidance and educational centers. This amply illustrates the comprehensive nature of this approach as well as its range of practical application.

The theoretical formulations which provide the basis for Adlerian counseling methods are logical and have been empirically validated through the years. While there may be obvious inconsistencies in the way different practitioners will operationalize Adler's theory, most difficulties come either from idiosyncratic interpretations or placing an emphasis on only one phase in the development of the theory.

The ability to clearly and efficiently evaluate the outcome of counseling services is essential for followers of a theoretical approach to document its worth. In the case of Adlerian counseling, however, there have been comparatively few examples of empirical, nomothetic evaluation studies (Mosak, 1979). In the past, most research undertakings relied upon case-study methods and other types of idiographic procedures. Because of the Adlerian's reliance on the individual nature of the person, coupled with the idiosyncratic structure of insight, most counselors probably feel that large-group, comparative studies may not represent the full breadth and depth of the approach. Studying individual change is seen as the only way to truly understand either the process or outcome of the counseling relationship. Therefore, while the research methods used by Adlerian counselors may be somewhat different from those used by clinicians representing other theoretical approaches, they still represent valid and effective procedures.

COUNSELING APPLICATION

Adlerian Counseling in an Educational Setting

Bob is 13 years old and attends a large urban high school. He is well-liked and is known for his humor and wit. He writes for the school newspaper and his sense of humor is communicated through his short stories. Recently, however, his use of humor has merged with anger and he has become very disruptive. He is becoming known as the class clown, and Bob's teachers feel that his behaviors seriously distract the class. He has many friends but he has periods of moodiness, tending to withdraw at times.

Bob has a strong interest in athletic activities and is extremely knowledgeable about the details regarding current sporting events. He has tried out for several sports teams, always either quitting or being cut from the squad. The withdrawal and depression which follow the times of his involvement in athletic activities has stopped. He has historically been a A−/B+ student, but recently his grades have dropped to a C− average.

Bob's father is a distribution manager for an automobile parts and supply store. His mother is a homemaker and has artistic interests in painting. Bob has an older brother, an A student in the 12th grade, who is an excellent athlete. He is regarded by their father as a "model" son. The younger daughter is in the 6th grade and is also athletically inclined, taking gymnastics lessons and competing in local meets. Both

Bob's father and mother make a fuss over the achievements and accomplishments of the older son and their daughter. The father regards Bob as athletically clumsy.

Bob was referred to the school counselor when his teachers noted a substantial decrease in the quality of his academic work coupled with an increase in acting out behaviors. This is the first session with the counselor.

Counselor:	Hi, Bob. Have a seat.
Bob:	Mrs. Jones sent me here.
Counselor:	Your teachers have been concerned about your behaviors in class and say you have been having problems. What is the problem as you see it?
Bob:	Well, (pause) I was cut from the basketball team two weeks ago, my brother made it and was elected team captain. I feel depressed and angry about it. (with sarcasm) He's Dad's delight!
Counselor:	You seem to feel jealous toward your brother. You feel he receives a lot of attention from your father.
Bob:	Yeah, he gets all the glory . . . all the attention. He and Dad keep talking about college and scholarships. Mom follows my sister to all those gymnastic meets, and I get cut from every team I try out for. I'm the *wimp* in the family.
Counselor:	Even the weak and powerless receive attention in our society. People feel sorry for them. It looks like you'd really like to receive attention from your family and friends because of athletic accomplishments. When you don't get the attention you want, you seek it through other means . . . What would it mean to you if you were to be a basketball star?
Bob:	I'd finally get some of the recognition I deserve. My Dad and Mom would watch what I did and tell me how good I was. I'd be the talk of the school. Everybody would want to know how well I did or played! I'd show 'em.
Counselor:	I think most people like attention, they like to be noticed, acknowledged and recognized. This is natural for most people who want to be involved with other people. Bob, what do you do when your teachers, friends, and parents don't pay enormous attention to you?
Bob:	(sarcastically) They pay attention all right!
Counselor:	How do you get them to pay attention?
Bob:	Well, in class, sometimes I don't do anything . . . I just sit back and wait. Then I make funny statements and jokes about the teacher or what we're doing. The other students think it's great, they laugh and the teacher gets mad.
Counselor:	And then?
Bob:	The teachers get on my case and they say that I'm not like my brother. They think this will change me!
Counselor:	To be like your brother? (Bob nods) You appear to have some power here. First, you get to be the "goof off" in class so you get the negative attention of people telling you you're no good . . . or at least not as good

as your brother. Then, when people try to help you, you do the opposite. In disturbing others you get attention; I think you see that you are not a helpless "wimp," as you call yourself. There is strength in your so-called weakness.

Bob: Well . . . I guess so.

At this point, the counselor reinforces the fact that Bob has power in the classroom and then shifts the focus of discussion on the generalization of this to his involvement with family and friends. The counselor focuses on behavior of social interest with Bob.

Counselor: How do you get the attention you want at home?

Bob: I make jokes about what my Dad and brother do. I exaggerate the mistakes they make and I point out how funny their mistakes are. I think it's funny, but they get kind of mad and ignore me. I tell them I'm only kidding.

Counselor: You tend to disguise your anger by making jokes. Your humor seems to further alienate you from your brother and father. This doesn't seem to be working quite the way you'd like it to.

Bob: It doesn't hurt them . . . They don't care what I do . . .

Counselor: This is just the point. You want attention, but your way of getting attention defeats your goals and increases the distance between your father and brother. Perhaps your humor is a compensation to feel superior to your brother. This attention you want is at the expense of getting along with your family. You seem to think that by viewing yourself as superior, you will have the power to control these relationships.

Bob: I don't know why I think I have to be better than everyone. I am just afraid they won't like me the way I am!

Counselor: It looks like you try to compensate for your feelings of being a "wimp" by trying to be a star. I think you might consider more desirable ways of getting attention and achieving your goals.

Bob: Well . . . I agree . . . I'm just getting in more trouble with *everybody*. I guess I'm not sure what my goals are: All I think about is becoming a star.

At this point, Bob is gaining an understanding of his attempt to compensate for his weaknesses through superiority over others. The counselor in future sessions focuses on redefining Bob's goals in relationships and his own assets and strengths. The following exchange takes place five sessions later.

Bob: I haven't cracked any jokes at all in class or made fun of my brother and sister. Things are going great. I think it's best for me to stay out of the athletic area. Mrs. Forsythe, the faculty advisor on the school newspaper, said I did a great job on a short story. I'm probably the best writer in school, the best in a few years.

Counselor: I think that it is beneficial to be involved in rewarding activities that fit

	into your life style. Do you think that you need to be superior to others in the area of writing?
Bob:	Yeah . . . I want to get a story published in a magazine. To do that you have to be better than others.
Counselor:	What will happen if you get the story published?
Bob:	Mrs. Forsythe will commend me and my parents will realize I am somebody.
Counselor:	So you want everyone to see how great you are rather than simply feeling a true sense of accomplishment for yourself, right?
Bob:	I see what you mean, I guess I still want more attention and recognition for what I do.

Bob continues to become aware of his own needs to compensate to attain superiority. The goal of counseling with this client is to feel internally regarded for his efforts and maintain social interest through relationships with peers and family members.

Critical Comments

Individual Psychology has been characterized in this chapter as a subjective, teleological, holistic approach used for individual education and development. The philosophical basis for counseling is a moralistic one, laden with very strong "pro-society" values. Since development is a very unique event and based upon one's perceptions of reality, the counseling approach is highly individualized and places the responsibility for change on the client's shoulders. Above all, however, Adlerian counseling is practical, attempting to help clients change their set patterns of behavior.

Adler's perspective has been often called "more than just one of the many popular approaches to counseling and psychotherapy." Raymond Corsini, after his own introduction to Adler's theories and concepts, said "I soon discovered that Individual Psychology filled a void, giving me an understanding of human nature which was superior to that of all other systems, and which gave me a philosophy of life . . ." (Manaster and Corsini, 1982, p. 257). The comprehensive nature of Adler's ideas has been very appealing to people who wish to integrate the depth of philosophy with the accountability of science. While the approach may not be fully comprehensive, leaving some rather significant gaps in the explanation of the change process, the authors do feel that Adler offered an elegant perspective to explain individual development and behavior.

One criticism of Adlerian counseling is the strong moralistic nature of the theory. Adler believed that a person's character is defined only within a social context, or, how that person affects others. "Rights" and "wrongs" do exist in his framework, all related to how an individual's behavior contributes to the community. It is the counselor's responsibility to point out where behaviors are not useful and suggest a change in that part of the life style (in many cases the consequences of a behavior will lead to its elimination without intervention). A counselor should have the ability to identify these socially ineffective behavioral patterns, be willing to point them out and be ready to help the client identify more acceptable alternatives. While a counselor takes responsibility for structuring the relationship and leading the assessment process, it is essential for the client to be an active participant, taking full responsibility for behavioral change.

A cornerstone of Adlerian theory is its concentration on teleological principles in both the development and resolution of problem behaviors. On the one hand, this perspective may seem to be more straight-forward and usable than the complex nature of Freud's determinism but, on the other hand, the seemingly simple goal structure of Individual Psychology is difficult to describe and very complicated to efficiently operationalize. While teleology may be an expedient theoretical model to use in explaining developmental concepts, the idea that all behaviors are purposeful and related to one's life plan may at times become somewhat unwieldly. What is often seen by the untrained, outside onlooker as simple applications of very obvious principles, is actually the orchestration of a very complex web of interrelated behavioral patterns.

The individualized nature of Adler's theoretical perspective is both a strength and a weakness. The strength lies in the acknowledgement that each person is unique and behaves in an idiosyncratic manner based upon a singular life style. The Adlerian counselor fully acknowledges this concept and enters into the relationship with the belief that the counseling experience will be a different one each time. Despite this very positive frame of reference, it is also very difficult (if not impossible) to predict a person's behavior because of the complexity of the life style. Therefore, while the valuable concept of individuality is stressed throughout the Adlerian counseling approach, this same concept may result in an ambiguous context within which the counselor must work.

Despite criticisms of either the theory or the counseling approach, Adler's legacy is truly a great one. He was the first psychotherapist to include one's perceptions of the social context as a major contributor to the development of the personality. He also was the first of his contemporaries to focus on counseling as development and education in contrast to the remedial nature of the medical-disease model. This is probably one of Adler's most meaningful contributions and has helped counselors, psychologists, social workers, and physicians to see themselves, in at least a part of their professional lives, as educators.

REFERENCES

Adler, A. (1917). *Study of organ inferiority and its psychical compensation.* New York: Nervous and Mental Disease Publishing Co.

Adler, A. (1930). *The education of children.* London: George Allen & Unwin, Ltd.

Adler, A. (1954). *Understanding human nature.* New York: Fawcett World Library.

Adler, A. (1956). *The individual psychology of Alfred Adler.* In H.L. Ansbacher & R.R. Ansbacher (Eds.). New York: Basic Books.

Adler, A. (1963). *The problem child.* New York: Capricorn.

Adler, A. (1964a). *Problems of neurosis.* New York: Capricorn.

Adler, A. (1964b). *Social interest: A challenge to mankind.* New York: Capricorn.

Adler, A. (1968). *The practice and theory of individual psychology.* Totowa, NJ: Littlefield, Adams & Co.

Allen, T. (1971). Adlerian interview strategies for behavior change. *The Counseling Psychologist, 3,* 40-48.

Ansbacher, H.L., & Ansbacher, R.R. (1964). *Superiority and social interest.* Evanston, IL: Northwestern University Press.

Bottome, P. (1957). *Alfred Adler: A portrait from life.* New York: The Vanguard Press.

Dinkmeyer, D.C., Pew, W.L., & Dinkmeyer, D.C., Jr. (1979). *Adlerian counseling and psychotherapy.* Monterey, CA: Brooks/Cole.

Ellis, A. (1973). *Humanistic psychotherapy.* New York: McGraw-Hill.

Manaster, G.J., & Corsini, R.J. (1982). *Individual Psychology.* Itaska, IL: F.E. Peacock.

Mosak, H.H. (1979). Adlerian psychotherapy. In R.J. Corsini (Ed.), *Current psychotherapies.* Itaska, IL: F.E. Peacock.

Mosak, H.H. & Dreikurs, R. (1973). Adlerian psychotherapy. In R.J. Corsini (Ed.), *Current psychotherapies.* Itaska, IL: F.E. Peacock.

Nikelly, A.G. (Ed.). (1971). *Techniques for behavior change.* Springfield, IL: Charles C Thomas.

Rychlak, J.F. (1981). *Introduction to personality and psychotherapy* (2nd ed.). Boston: Houghton Mifflin.

Schoenaker, T., & Schoenaker, T. (1976). *Adlerian social therapy.* St. Paul, MN: Green Bough Publications.

CHAPTER 4

ERIC BERNE'S
TRANSACTIONAL ANALYSIS

FOUNDATIONS AND STRUCTURE

Historical Foundations

TRANSACTIONAL ANALYSIS (TA) is a contractual and interactional counseling procedure developed by Eric Berne, M.D. (1919-1970). Both the theory and techniques of counseling are eclectic, having been influenced by a variety of psychological and sociological perspectives. Transactional Analysis presents a comprehensive theory of personality functioning based on the active dynamic functioning of parent, adult, and child ego states in a culturally influenced, yet individually determined life plan called the life script.

The originator of transactional analysis, Eric Berne, was trained in psychoanalysis and entered analysis himself with Erik Erikson. Based upon his analytic experiences, he became interested in the concept of ego states, a major focus of his later writings. Berne began to lay the foundation for his comprehensive theory in the mid 1950's, culminating in the publication of *Transactional Analysis in Psychotherapy* (1961), the first formal text outlining and describing the approach.

Initially, TA was designed to be used in groups as an adjunct to psychoanalytic sessions for his patients. Berne soon formalized the TA theory and began implementing the conceptual approach in his individual sessions. Berne found that his clients readily learned the concepts and were able to apply them to their counseling experiences. The foundations for TA are based on the influence of psychoanalysis, communications theory, and small group behavior. The influence of psychoanalysis lead to an interest in ego psychology and intact structures of past ego states (Dusay and Dusay, 1979). Berne borrowed from communication theory the idea that people communicate in both overt and covert messages and behaviors are largely related to the meanings attributed to these messages. Theorizing that social transactions were related to ego states, Berne hypothesized that group TA would increase the effectiveness of insight, minimize ritualized behaviors, and enhance the appropriateness of communication patterns.

Many researchers and theorists influenced Berne's work including Penfield and Roberts (1959) and Chandler and Hartman (1960) who confirmed his belief in a neurological basis for ego states (which Berne believed could be *stimulated* and *activated* by social stimuli), Spitz (1945) who suggested the importance of physical and emotional attention to ego development (related to the concept of *strokes*), and Abraham's (1948) early work on character types (leading to the development of *transactional games* and *life scripts*). Berne's own research on intuition led him to believe that insight can be reached via nonlogical means through a spontaneous perceptual evaluation of an event, person, place, or thing.

Berne integrated his own clinical experience with theory and research to form a dynamic system of ego psychology which explains personality functioning and outlines a transactional counseling approach. The process is quite educational in nature, with counselors relying on homework assignments designed to help clients reach a fuller understanding of behavioral patterns and life scripts. Clients are eventually taught to analyze their own transactions and identify their own and other's ego states.

Philosophical Foundations

The philosophical foundations of TA are based on the assumption that people use reason in choosing their own destiny and existence. Berne asserts that people make decisions about their existence based on their experiences. He draws heavily from the Kantian philosophical tenet which states that people use spontaneous and authentic *reason* to make decisions and plan their own lives. Berne sees the adult ego state as responsible for this form of reasoning, providing the person with a capacity to make rational decisions and to become involved in authentic relationships.

Berne assumed that people are ultimately responsible for their own life decisions. In counseling, clients take responsibility and ownership for their problems and must take constructive action toward the resolution of their difficulties. An assumption is made that clients are capable of actively interpreting their own ego states.

The philosophical tripart concepts of Hegelian logic are rooted in TA theory (Brady, 1980). The triadic notions of thesis, antithesis, and synthesis are associated with ego states and life scripts. Thesis refers to an idea or action, antithesis suggests a counter idea, and synthesis refers to the resolution of these opposing forces and emergence of a new idea or action. The existence of these triadic concepts suggests the need for integrated ego states. TA counselors see people who have integrated ego states as capable of resolving their conflicts and existential decisions.

From his training in psychoanalysis and medicine, Berne developed a scientific attitude. He postulates that the ego states of the parent, adult, and child are empirically observable. This position contrasts with Freud who stated that the id, ego, and superego are not directly observable elements. A scientific position is evident in Berne's counseling theory, where one finds a parsimonious explanation of behavior and a demystification of the treatment of problems in human existence. Counseling is analygous to education with a primary goal of understanding ego states and learning genuine and authentic ways of interacting with others.

Transactional analysis relies heavily upon the complex cognitive operations of the brain. Berne's research into intuition lead him to conclude that images, intuition, and insight are capabilities that people possess. Integration of the ego states leads to the expression of intuition, creativity, and insight. Berne (1949) found that the higher thought processes of intuition and empirical logic increase creative efforts. According to Berne, insight into one's own problems is also a function of the ego states.

Social-Psychological Foundations

There are two major components in the social-psychological foundations of TA, the structural aspects of the transactional processes. While the authors will separate these two concepts and discuss them individually in this section, it must be kept in mind that TA views personal functioning as a result of the integration of these elements.

Structural Aspects

Berne (1961), identified and described three distinct structural aspects of TA, constructs he referred to as ego states. The *exteropsyche* or *parent* (P) ego state includes the identification and introjection of values, attitudes, and images of the biological parents (Dusay and Dusay, 1979). Typically, the parent ego state is either nurturing or critical in form. A second ego state is the *neopsyche* or *adult* (A), representative of rational, realistic, and logical processes. The adult is concerned with processing information and making sense out of data in the person's life. The third ego state, the *archaeopsyche* or *child* (C), is seen in the form of either a free child (uninhibited and spontaneous) or an adapted child (the conforming and rebellious nature of an individual). These ego states, according to Berne (1966), are dynamic and activated by either external or internal stimuli. Each state is observable and consists of a stereotypic emotional-behavioral repertoire.

The ego states may be diagrammed to depict functional or dysfunctional behavioral patterns. Berne (1964) believed that drawings provide valuable educational and therapeutic models for both the client and counselor. Symbols of the functional ego states are presented below.

P — Parent or exteropsyche

A — Adult or neopsyche

C — Child or archaeopsyche

The healthy individual may also be depicted or symbolized by an egogram, a graphic illustration of the relative levels of intensity afforded to each of the ego states—critical parent (CP), nurturing parent (NP), adult (A), free child (FC), and adapted child (AC) (Dusay, 1972).

Egogram

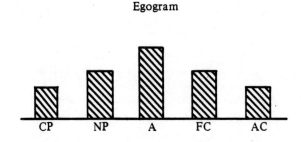

Based upon learning and early experiences with biological parents, the levels of ego states (as depicted on the parents egogram) may vary greatly from person to person. The functioning of each ego state or the inhibition of certain ego states will determine the type of symptom or maladaptive behavior an individual experiences.

A structural analysis of ego states may reveal a vast range of functioning from dysfunctional ego boundaries to functional and active processes. In TA theory, the intrapsychic relationships between ego states may include (Berne, 1977):

- *Mutual isolation* — The ego states are fragmented, thereby increasing inner confusion and psychological distress.
- *Conflict* — The uneven or ineffective functioning of the ego states leads to greater tension, anxiety and neurotic symptoms.
- *Contamination* — One ego state permeates the boundaries of another leading to significant disturbance as in schizophrenic or psychotic functioning.
- *Invasion* — One ego state interferes with the processes of another resulting in severe personal and social conflict.
- *Predominance* — One ego state dominates all others as in a workaholic (adult ego dominance) or a severely regressed individual (child ego state).
- *Cooperation* — The ego states operate efficiently to minimize conflict and anxiety and increase constructive individual action.

The structural aspects of personality functioning are formed by early parental and environmental forces which influence how people meet their early developmental needs.

Transactional Processes

Berne (1964) believes that as people interact the ego states of each individual are activated and stimulated. Dusay and Dusay (1979) describe three rules of communication occurring in transactions.

- Communication may proceed indefinitely when an ego state of one individual relates to the same ego state in another.
- A transaction is "crossed" when two people communicate with each other using different ego states (i.e., adult to parent or parent to child). In these instances, the transaction is ineffective and soon discontinues.
- Behavior is explained not only by the social transaction but also is determined by the psychological meaning of the message to each of the communicators.

According to TA theory, the social level of communication is overt, yet may lack the predictability that one may gain from the covert, psychological meaning of a message. It is this ulterior message that may offer more information concerning the type and direction of an individual's behavioral response.

In social transactions people may become involved in *games*, or stereotyped ways of behaving. Berne (1964) states that there are three specific levels of games. In the first level, no one is physically hurt and the game is socially acceptable. A second degree game typically results in an aggressive act towards another. The third degree game is serious and results in such things as physical injury to another, complicated divorce, or severe social and personal conflict. Berne indicates as the degree of game playing becomes more serious, the payoffs for each player become higher. Berne (1977) states that games are superficial ways of relating and, in part, express an ulterior motive.

Games according to Berne (1964), become self-reinforcing once they are a part of a person's behavioral repertoire. They became the "easy" way to respond in marital, family, social, and business relationships. In order to change these games and learn new responses, people must understand their ego state's ulterior motive in the transaction. Exploring the game increases understanding of both the ego states and the transaction, and creates an opportunity for more authentic ways of relating.

The Development of the Person

Berne first used TA as an adjunctive group therapy for his patients undergoing psychoanalysis. For this reason, the initial emphasis of the counseling style and the underlying theory of human development was on adults (Berne, 1961). More recently, others have begun to use TA with children, adolescents, and the elderly, and a more comprehensive picture of the human development process has evolved.

Berne was very interested in the work of Spitz with institutionalized children and the comparative psychology of Harry Harlow. The findings of these researchers underscore Berne's theory of human development and his concepts of social interaction. The TA theory of development suggests that people meet psychological and physical needs through either receiving strokes or satisfying needs. A *stroke* is a physical or emotional form of recognition that meets a psychological need. Putting oneself in a position which will lead to strokes is a primary behavioral motivator. Hunger can be viewed either as structure hunger, a person's need to organize meaningful activity, or transactional hunger, a need to relate to and interact with others.

Berne's psychoanalytic training led him to conclude that early experiences with one's biological parents may reinforce or inhibit the development of the different ego states. Children learn parental attitudes, values, and norms, and incorporate these into the ego state structure. These influences may be direct, as in the case of beliefs that parents communicate to the children, or indirect through injunctions (behaviors that symbolize parental values and norms). The social-psychological make-up of the individual is influenced by these experiences, leading to the development of a behavioral pattern called the *life script* (Dusay and Dusay, 1979). The life script is demonstrated in personal-social interactions and is determined largely by conscious decisions. The life script, a fully psychological profile, is reinforced, maintained, and acted on throughout the life span.

Games and *pastimes* are social transactions which are derived directly from the life script and provide evidence of its structure (Berne, 1972). Certain ego states are activated, excessively repeated, and generalized in social situations. The games ritualize a person's social transactions and most often result in negative social consequences. Games are superficial and unauthentic ways of meeting stimulus hunger needs yet they do result in personal-social rewards (Berne, 1964). Pastimes, on the other hand, are simply ways of ritualizing social transactions, and ways of passing time. A pastime does not contain an ulterior motive, it is simply a well-structured and well-organized social transaction designed to minimize anxiety and risk. The pastime is not authentic, and maintains social distance (Berne, 1977). If used frequently, pastimes do run the risk of eventually leading to games.

Transactional analysis implicitly attends to cognitive development and operations in describing the role of ego images and intuition. This line of thought suggests that conscious activity plays a role in ego development. An image is sensorial as well as psychological, and may be associated with anxiety and tension (Berne, 1955). The image forms a basic attitude about the self and others, and forms the basis for the life script. Images have a lasting impact on ego functioning and are learned in the early environment. The ego image is a conscious symbol of the person's identity and how the life script may be enacted.

According to Berne (1977) the development of the life script is more strongly related to conscious factors than unconscious processes. Ego states are activated by both ongoing social transactions and internal stimuli. Ego state functioning may represent past experiences and the possibility for current social interaction.

TA theory assumes that people have a tendency toward effective personal and social functioning. This tendency (the drive *vis medicartix naturae*) represents a person's need to enhance both physical and psychological well being (Berne, 1966). One's need to seek help, the desire to understand oneself more fully, and the tendency to potentiate one's abilities are suggested in this drive.

Concepts of Functional and Dysfunctional Behavior

People are functioning well when their ego states are balanced and they are able to draw upon the ego state which is most appropriate for the specific social transaction (Berne, 1966). The ego states should be spontaneous, able to meet here and now needs, and also postpone gratification when necessary. As stated earlier, all people desire stroking in order to meet attention and recognition needs (Dusay and Dusay, 1979).

Early parenting and childhood experiences have symbolic meaning which shape the child's behavior and ego states. In early childhood a person seeks recognition regardless of the consequences. Berne (1961) hypothesized that the frequency and intensity of stroking is related to the behavioral patterns the person employs. For example, if in early childhood the person is deprived of attention and stroking, this will most likely lead to some maladaptive behavior. The pattern of parental stroking is therefore important to the development of both the ego states and the life script (Dusay and Dusay, 1979).

People develop views of themselves in relation to others based on the evaluation of the ego image (Berne, 1964). In TA, these views are expressed in polarities and are called *life positions*. Berne identifies the following four life positions: (1) I'm OK, you're OK; (2) I'm OK, you're not OK; (3) I'm not OK, you're OK; and (4) I'm not OK, you're not OK. These positions reflect the degree of perceived functional or dysfunctional behavior in self and others. The first position suggests the person is perceiving the world in a functional, well-integrated manner. The second projects dysfunction on others while the third position introjects dysfunction on the self. The final position reflects dysfunction in both self and others, typically reflecting a self-destructive attitude.

As mentioned before, scripts are developed based upon observation, modeling, symbolic-cognitive processes, and the messages communicated to the child by the parents. Berne (1972) indicates there are five requirements for a script:

• Results from messages communicated by parents.

- Increases maladaptive personal and social responses.
- Leads to existential decision about self and life.
- Results in success or failure.
- Results in maladaptive social transactions.

The inflexibility and stereotypic nature of life scripts in general may often lead to maladaptive behaviors.

Recall that games are a variation of the life script, occurring at both a social and psychological level. At a psychological level, an ulterior message is communicated, leading to payoffs and rewards. The people involved in a game are frequently unaware of the ulterior motive. In fact, when people are often involved in games they frequently deny and are unaware of their own ulterior motives. For this reason, Berne (1964) states that ulterior motives are, at least in part, unconscious.

Game transactions may increase the potential for the individual to "blow up," "have a free depression," or have self-reinforcing emotional consequence Berne calls a "racket." In essence, the game strategy becomes a neurotic maladaptive behavioral response and since games are repetitive and rewarding, people collect or remember their losses. The losses, to Berne (1964), become what he calls "trading stamps." These trading stamps are often used and manipulated to gain rewards, thereby developing a "racket" which may be rich in payoffs for the individual.

The net effect of games (scripts and rackets) is dysfunctional behavior which decreases the possibility for more intimate relationships among people. Inherent in transactional analysis is the notion that people have the potential to function with minimal disturbance and reliance on games and scripts. Berne (1977) asserts that people have capabilities and unconscious desires to behave and respond to others in reasonably realistic and spontaneous ways. He feels that people have the capacity to examine scripts and games and can minimize the effects of those self-defeating processes.

Concepts of Behavior Change

The first steps of TA counseling are essentially educational. The TA counselor teaches about the structural aspects of personality, the ego states. Berne suggests that people may reach an adequate understanding of the system in about ten sessions. The counselor may suggest outside work assignments which can include reading TA educational and self-help materials. The educational emphasis in the process of analyzing ego states may increase individual awareness and integration. The understanding of the ego states may decrease the client's anxiety, enhance awareness, and encourage the recognition of material to be processed in later counseling sessions.

Gradually, behavioral changes become the focus of counseling. The counselor examines how the dynamic interplay of ego states has maintained life-long behavioral tendencies. Berne indicates that throughout the course of any day there is a multiplicity of transactions, each one maintained by subtle social reinforcers.

The counselor then focuses attention on the maladaptive patterns of games. Importantly, the TA counselor attends to the ego states involved in the game. Since games most often exist as a function of anxiety, it is important for the counselor to identify the cause of the anxiety and the client's individual reaction to it. Rackets, a variation of the game, often have a strong affective component as well, therefore awareness and insight into the feelings associated with a racket can minimize its self-defeating effects.

The TA counselor uses contracts with the client designed to maintain an awareness and focus on games and social rituals. The contract also minimizes game playing by the client and counselor in the relationship itself. In the relationship, the counselor is an active educator and also a very sensitive listener, concentrating on the client's tendency to act out the life script in the session. When this occurs, the counselor may actively interrupt and identify game playing or enactment of the life script. This increases the client's awareness of the self-defeating nature of the game or script. Concomitantly, more authentic and intimate ways of relating are explored and encouraged. The here and now attitude of a TA counselor reinforces constructive action first and analysis of self-defeating affect.

Despite Berne's psychoanalytic training, TA does not embrace the analytic view of insight. A TA counselor feels that insight is derived from direct experience in life and in counseling. Active, experiential learning plays an essential role in the counseling process, with clients being encouraged to test out new behaviors in social settings. Berne (1949) does place an important emphasis on the intuitive processes. The child ego state is more uninhibited than either the parent or adult ego states in terms of accepting new ideas and exploring ways of approaching personal-social situations. When the adult and parental ego states are integrated with the child's intuitive processes, then creative efforts are more likely. Through the counseling process, the receptive adult ego state is integrated with the child state, producing a more effective, spontaneous capacity for decision-making and problem-solving.

The TA theory and techniques of behavioral change were not fully addressed by Berne. The assumption is made that a sensitive and intuitive counselor will be able to provide an adequate TA framework within which the client can change. Berne is humanistic and assumes that the counseling transaction is important to client growth, but he never really delineates how this change is to occur. On the surface, at least, TA emphasizes a counseling relationship which concentrates on helping clients become aware of and minimize dysfunctional respone patterns and learn new behavioral repertoires.

Assessment of Human Functioning

Berne does not embrace the traditional role of assessment and testing in TA theory and counseling. Counselors may use tests in counseling to help develop tentative hypotheses about the ego states, but these are all explored during the counseling sessions. Studies designed to assess outcomes of TA have relied on personality inventories, problem checklists, and symptom checklists in order to assess change in behavior and personality.

In practice, TA uses *ego diagrams, ego grams,* and *script matrices* to assess how the ego states are operating and to assess the overall functioning of the person. The ego diagrams illustrate the structure dynamics of the ego states while ego grams assess the relative strength and quantity of time spent in these ego states. Script matrices may be used to analyze the role of ego states in transactions. TA assessment techniques provide data on what ego states operate most frequently and how the ego states are activated socially. The procedures may provide therapeutic direction for the counseling sessions but of paramount importance is the educational value that clients derive from these assessment procedures.

A script checklist has been developed by Berne (1972) to assess the functioning of the ego states. The counselor may choose to use the entire checklist (if developmentally appropriate) or may select questions which may be asked during counseling. These questions may stimulate the awareness of material about the ego states, allowing the TA counselor to observe when ego states are activated.

Following Berne's philosophical foundation of empiricism, TA is based upon the assumption that the ego states are observable, measurable, and quantifiable. The ego gram fills the role of assessing ego functioning, but the TA counselor typically extends and integrated the notion of assessment into the counseling process by actively testing hypotheses directly with the client. The counselor, because of TA's empirical foundation, may analyze, question, or confront a game, script, or transaction, thereby maintaining an active involvement in the assessment process.

Goals and Directions of Counseling

Berne's philosophical view is based on a phenomenological humanistic model. Functional people, according to Berne (1977), behave authentically in relationships with others and meet their psychological and emotional needs in a realistic manner. Implied in the TA theory of personality is the notion of responsibility for one's self (Berne, 1961). People take ownership of their emotions, thoughts, and behaviors. Following Berne's philosophical assumptions, it is assumed that people can make decisions based upon an integration of their needs and a realistic perception of their environment.

TA facilitates the structural integration of the ego states so that individuals may draw from the strengths of the various ego states to make decisions, solve problems, and creatively engage in life tasks. Effective ego boundaries and differentiation occur in functional people.

Transactionally, people who function well make conscious decisions to minimize games, rackets, and social rituals which maintain disturbing relationships. TA's goals are for people to examine their games, explore their socially manipulative nature, and learn to communicate more responsively and authentically.

TA counselors believe that the direction and primary goal for counseling is to clearly examine both the structural and transactional nature of life scripts. For this reason, in the initial session, the counselor may ask the question, "Will you let me cure you?" (Berne, 1972). This statement implies that the role of the counselor is to intervene therapeutically to minimize game behavior and restructure the life scripts. Berne (1972) eloquently stated that people see counselors not so that they will develop personally but to learn how to live more comfortably with the disturbing condition they have. Therefore, TA counselors are sensitive when games are manipulating the counseling process. Intuitive counselors, if manipulated, may become more aware of the game and disclose their role in it, leading to a decrease in game behavior and domination of life scripts.

The Counseling Process:
Structuring, Facilitating, and Terminating

The TA theory of personality suggests that problems are maintained by games and social rituals and the purpose of counseling is to minimize these behavioral patterns, thereby freeing the individual to respond more effectively. During all phases of counseling, the TA counselor is an active listener who attends and responds to the client's verbal and nonverbal communication. The TA counseling relationship is contractual, as the client and counselor mutually agree on a desired task (Dusay and Dusay, 1979). The counselor may intervene with techniques directed at increasing the client's awareness of games and redirecting the life script.

During the initial stage of counseling the TA counselor teaches the client TA theory and the structural aspects of ego states. Clients learn about the dynamic nature of ego states, how ego states are formed, and the ways that their own ego states are activated and stimulated. Homework facilitates the learning of TA theory of personality and helps clients become aware of the concepts of games, scripts, rackets, trading stamps, and payoffs.

Once the client has learned the TA system, counseling can begin to focus on the transactional nature of the client's behavior and how the ego states operate in the social environment. Moving from the structural stage to the transactional stage of counseling facilitates a gradual shift to the social-psychological tendencies of the person.

Game analysis occurs in the intermediate stage of the counseling process. The TA counselor explores a game when clients' verbal behavior is incongruent with their nonverbal behavior. For example, the counselor may notice that people smile or laugh when they report engaging in self-defeating behaviors like fighting, drinking or other similar processes. Berne suggests that psychodrama, role playing, or other here and now techniques may be used to explore the game strategy as well as to teach alternatives which may be more personally and socially rewarding.

Script analysis, though addressed in the intermediate stage of counseling, is of interest to the counselor from the outset of the relationship. Scripts are quite varied and can be based on characters in theatrical dramas, myths, folk tales, and movies (Berne, 1972). They are mostly conscious and represent cultural and parental attitudes which have been reinforced since early childhood or adolescence. For redirection of behavior to take place, it is necessary to confront the content of the script and help the client become aware of its relationship to the ego states.

Role playing, psychodrama, and guided imagery are employed to direct attention to the determinants of the life script.

TA counselors are aware that clients may consciously or unconsciously regress toward the end of the counseling relationship. They must be aware of client regression in order to identify areas which may need further stabilization. The counseling process is successfully completed when the client is able to take responsibility for their behavior and the ego states have become sufficiently integrated.

Counseling Techniques and Procedures

The theoretical description and understanding of personality functioning, scripts, and games is well addressed in TA theory. Berne himself did not develop a variety of explicit techniques but many of his colleagues and students have advanced the development of procedures based on TA foundations (Dusay, 1981). Berne asserted that counseling is not a ritualistic experience, but an individualized and creative experience designed to reverse scripts, minimize games, and stabilize ego states.

Educational-Learning Techniques

Techniques such as bibliotherapy or homework with TA materials may effectively teach the principles of personality functioning and build the foundation for behavior change. Therefore, homework may efficiently increase the learning of the TA concepts and systems. The use of educational diagrams of ego states or transactions may help clarify behavioral responses and also stimulate behavior patterns free of games or scripts. TA counselors stress the importance of learning behaviors which are free of scripts and games. Awareness or insight into self-defeating scripts and games may lead to an opportunity to learn behaviors that are ego-enhancing.

Redirective Techniques Focused on Integrative Functioning

Script and game analysis are intervention approaches that TA counselors often employ in counseling and are directed at integrating the behavioral, cognitive, affective, and physiological domains of human functioning (Erskine, 1980). The TA theory of behavior change views counseling as an environment in which people may *actively* explore and direct their functioning in an ego-enhancing manner. This is contrary to the psychoanalytic *passivity* of the analyst and the associative processes of therapy and counseling.

Berne draws an analogy between the theatre and the therapeutic environment. He suggests that people enact their script, drama, and games in counseling. Either the counselor or the client may become the director and recreate and analyze situations. The counseling environment becomes a safe arena or stage for either the client or counselor to redirect behavior. Redirection of scripts and games facilitates awareness and learning while improving integrative functioning.

Role playing, a behavioral intervention, is a procedure in which the client may experiment with new behaviors in the counseling environment. The technique teaches new responses to the client, thereby minimizing the tendency to rely on stereotyped behaviors. TA counselors may note that appropriate behaviors arouse anxiety and the counselor may desensitize or deprogram injunctions.

A technique similar to role playing is the *empty chair technique,* where dialogues and transactions with people outside of the counseling relationship are reenacted and processed. This procedure allows the counselor and client to achieve a greater understanding of the activated ego states and games. Awareness and clarification of emotional problems are more likely to occur, increasing the probability of more rewarding behaviors.

Guided imagery is a cognitive technique which directs the client's attention to the early decisions regarding life scripts. This procedure may also be used to focus on events in which parental injunctions were introduced. The client is taught to deeply relax and the counselor then guides the client's thoughts and images to experiences that are relevant. This procedure is suggestive and passive compared to the directive activities of the other techniques. Following the guided imagery procedure the client can discuss the material and process events which are significant and relevant to behavioral change.

TA intervention is relevant and tends to integrate cognitive, affective, behavioral, and physical learning experiences. Whether emphasizing game analysis or script analysis, the dialogue between client and counselor is focused on understanding and integrating ego states.

Evaluation of Counseling Outcomes

Berne (1964) suggests that individuals who have undergone TA tend to confront their own game playing and become more spontaneous in social transactions. Games and pastimes are minimized and more purposeful social interactions take their place. In essence, people confront themselves within the larger context of society and are directed by their sense of need and their drives. They are thereby able to potentiate their own personal and social resources. In addition, the structural boundaries of the ego states are strengthened by TA and the functioning of the parent, adult, and child is more integrated and complementary. This allows people to be creatively involved in social relationships and derive a great sense of personal satisfaction.

TA theory implies that the life script is reversable (Berne, 1972). In this case, the individual has an increased capacity to adapt to social relations, no longer relying on a predetermined fixed role. People who function well tend to behave in a more personally rewarding manner, consciously making effective decisions about problems in their lives. The role of unconscious factors is sufficiently reduced, making cognitive functioning more reality-based.

As has been discussed at length in this chapter, Berne believes that the parent, adult, and child ego states are all empirically observable and measurable elements. It follows, then, that the scripts, games, and rackets that an individual may have developed are observable, behavioral components of human functioning. If these two statements are accepted as true, then the outcome of TA is both measurable and varifiable. It appears, however, that changes in overt behavior may not provide adequate evidence that changes have occurred in such broad conceptual areas as "life scripts" and "ego states." A considerable explanatory gap exists in the relationship between counseling outcome and the underlying social-psychological assumptions and foundations of TA theory.

COUNSELING APPLICATION

A case will be presented to illustrate the use or educational and redirection techniques. The case was chosen because of the nature of the problem and the client and counselor interaction.

TA in a College Counseling Center

Stan is a freshman at a large state university. He was a C+ student in a large metropolitan high school and decided to go on to the university because many of his friends would be there. His high school counselor recommended options which may have been more in line with his abilities such as junior college or a technical school, but Stan didn't want to listen to the advice. Since the death of his mother when Stan was 10, he looked forward to the day when he would get a college degree and make the family proud of him. So off he went to the university, not sure why he wanted to go there and completely undecided about a choice of academic major.

During his first semester, Stan began experiencing adjustment problems. He had a difficult time keeping up on assignments. Stan met with his psychology instructor on several occasions to discuss his classwork and test grades. During these appointments, Stan mentioned the problems he was having in his other classes. The instructor referred him to the university counseling center.

The initial dialogue between the counselor and Stan is as follows:

Stan: I'm having a lot of problems here. My grades are low, and I don't think I fit in. My Dad thinks I should be an engineer, but I can't cut the math. In a way, I feel like packing my bags and going home.

Counselor: Do you have plans on what you would do at home?

Stan: No, but I know my Dad will say, "I told you so."

Counselor: How do you mean, "I told you so?"

Stan: Well . . . he will say, "I said you should have gone to a technical school."

Counselor: And how would you respond in this transaction?

Stan: Probably that I'm not living up to his expectations.

Counselor: You seem to feel depressed after this type of transaction.

Stan: Yeah, humiliated (loudly). He thinks I can do better. I'm letting him down.

Counselor: When you let your father down you get a free depression. That is, when you transact with your father, he is frustrated because he wants to help you; you become depressed because you let him down. It sounds like a *game* or a typical pattern you have with your father. You have a racket going—meaning you get a free depression for not living up to your father's expectations.

Stan: I'll never live up to his expectations.

Counselor: You may not, but your game appears to be maintained because of the payoffs.

Stan: What do you mean?

Counselor: Well, you have a strong tendency to live up to his expectations. Each of you ends up with bad feelings—your father's frustrated—you're depressed. Your payoff is a fairly strong motivator; you get a free depression.

Stan: I never thought of myself this way before.

Counselor: You may want to learn more about your transactions with your father and others. *I'm OK, You're OK* is a book designed to help people identify how they typically behave in social situations. I think that this would be a beneficial way to learn about transactional analysis. This book also teaches people new ideas about how the child, adult, and parent parts of themselves can function more effectively.

Stan: I see. That sounds interesting.

The counselor quickly pointed out the game transaction between Stan and his father. The counselor also suggested homework Stan could do to learn about TA and more appropriate ways to interact with people. In the first session, Stan continued to talk about situations at the university which were problematic. The counselor contracted to work with Stan on this game transaction.

Stan continued to see the counselor for the duration of the quarter. We pick up the dialogue during the sixth session. Stan reported that he did some reading in *I'm OK, You're OK*.

Stan:	I've been thinking about my life. I think my parents wanted me to be successful at everything. It gets awfully frustrating when I don't live up to my father's expectations.
Counselor:	You appear to be following the success story life script. You must be achieving, confident and successful in everything you do.
Stan:	When I had problems it was hard to talk about them. I had to be a macho man — like my Dad.
Counselor:	Yes, you feel your need to conquer the world; be a macho man and don't let anyone know when you're hurting.
Stan:	You're damn right (with emotion).
Counselor:	You *always* maintain a macho man image and when things don't go right, you become depressed, sulk alone, and withdraw from others.
Stan:	Yeah. That's what I do. Damn, its frustrating as hell (his fist clenched).
Counselor:	Yes it is, because you're *always* maintaining this script of being a macho man. I think it might be a good idea to analyze this script as you experience intense frustration and rage with it. By analyzing the script, I think you can decide on your life plan. This will minimize your frustration and rage and perhaps allow you to function more effectively in relationships.
Stan:	I'll do it if you think it will help!
Counselor:	What are you telling me about yourself.
Stan:	I want to know if this will really work.
Counselor:	It appears that you're wanting to play a game.
Stan:	(Smiling) I guess I want you to tell me this will really help.
Counselor:	You want a guarantee of success and if it doesn't work you get a free depression. I think this will require work and learning on your part. Do you want to work on this script?
Stan:	Yeah. I'll try.

Stan's script of the young success story is self-defeating, leading to frustration and expectations of conquering the world. Note that when the counselor referred to Stan's script he used the word "always," because of the strong tendency to play out the script. An "always" script (Dusay & Dusay, 1979) means that Stan repeatedly experiences intense frustration. The counselor was also aware that Stan was enacting a game in the session. The counselor confronted this behavior which, in turn, increased the overall awareness of the game. Thus, Stan took more responsibility and contracted to work on script analysis. Through greater understanding and analysis the existing script may be minimized and reconstructed. Stan can then gradually over time exchange the script for more functional personal and social behaviors.

Critical Comments

Berne's theoretical framework for understanding the social-psychological determinants of behavior and personality functioning is comprehensive and based on research and clinical experience. According to Berne (1977), counselors require theoretical constructs to understand observable behavior. Therefore, counselors are able to encourage and reinforce more genuine and authentic transactions. TA fully considers the social and psychological underpinnings of behavior. Berne's theoretical descriptions of ego states and his astute observations of transactions among people provide a dynamic understanding of intrapersonal and interpersonal functioning.

TA theoreticians have pointed out certain critical limitations of the approach. Dusay (1981) asserts that Berne's theory of personality development and functioning via games and scripts accurately describes human functioning; however, the TA concepts of behavioral change are left incomplete. Berne did not develop a theory-based technique for script and game reversal. Counselors who desire to implement TA may borrow from Gestalt counseling, psychodrama, and cognitive approaches to redirect the script. Berne's lack of clarity in delineating a model for behavioral change or specific behavioral change is a serious limitation of the theory.

Criticism of TA theory has also been directed at the lack of humanistic motivation constructs of functional behavior (Dusay, 1981). Growth and motivational concepts are not fully embraced by Berne. This may be related to TA's lack of behavioral change constructs. Berne (1961) does assume that people have a drive, *vis medicatrix naturae,* which is related to both physical and psychological well being. This motivational drive is integrated with the concepts of ego states, games, and scripts but is not yet fully developed.

The operationalization and measurement of ego systems in TA is questionable. Berne indicated that the activation of one ego state implied a stronger intensity and energy level as compared with the other ego states. A consistently high frequency and intensity of one ego state may eventually lead that state to capture most of the person's existence. While this may be theoretically sound, it is difficult to empirically validate this in light of the complex interacting nature of the life script and ego states.

Berne's theoretical work is original in that games and scripts have added a fresh perspective to the study of human functioning. His observations of ego states and social transactions are certainly signficant contributions to the field of ego psychology. While TA has been excessively popularized, and gaps in the conceptual framework do exist, it is rich in both the theoretical and practical descriptions of human behavior and transactions.

REFERENCES

Abraham, K. (1948). Selected papers. London: Hogarth Press.

Berne, E. (1949). The nature of intuition. *Psychiatric Quarterly, 23,* 203-226.

Berne, E. (1955). Intuition IV. Primal images and primal judgment. *Psychiatric Quarterly, 29,* 634.

Berne, E. (1961). *Transactional analysis in psychotherapy.* New York: Grove Press.

Berne, E. (1964). *Games people play.* New York: Grove Press.

Berne, E. (1966). *Principles of group treatment.* New York: Oxford University Press.

Berne, E. (1972). *What do you say after you say hello?* New York: Grove Press.

Berne, E. (1977). *Intuition and ego states.* San Francisco: Harper & Row.

Brady, F.N. (1980). Philosophical links to TA: Hegel and the concepts of the adult ego states. *Transactional Analysis Journal, 10,* 155-258.

Chandler, A., & Hartman, M. (1960). Lysergic acid diethylamid (LSD-25) as a facilitating agent in psychotherapy. *A.M.A. Archives of General Psychiatry, 2,* 286-299.

Dusay, J.M. (1972). Ego grams and the constancy hypothesis. *Transactional Analysis Journal, 2,* 37-41.

Dusay, J.M., & Dusay, K.M. (1979). Transactional Analysis. In *Current Psychotherapies* (2nd ed.). R.J. Corsini (Ed.), (pp. 374-428). Itasca: Peacock Publishers, Inc.

Dusay, J.M. (1981). Eric Berne: Contributions and limitations. *Transactional Analysis Journal, 11,* 41-45.

Erskine, R.G. (1980). Script Cure: Behavioral, intrapsychic and physiological. *Transactional Analysis Journal, 10,* 102-106.

Penfield, W., & Roberts, L. (1959). *Speech and brain mechanisms.* Princeton: Princeton University Press.

Spitz, R. (1945). Hospitalism: Genesis of psychiatric conditions in early childhood. *Psychoanalytic Study of the Child, 1,* 53.

PART II

EXISTENTIAL-HUMANISTIC
PERSPECTIVES

THE THEORIES of Carl Rogers, Frederick (Fritz) Perls, and Viktor Frankl are presented in this section. These systems attempt to capture the human themes of authenticity, genuineness, and being and becoming self-actualized. The theories of Rogers, Perls, and Frankl trace some of their basic tenets to the philosophies of Husserl, Nietzsche, Sartre, and Tillich.

Existential and humanistic orientations share a phenomenological approach to counseling. This holistic view recognizes the interrelatedness and interdependence of the environment and psychological structures of humans. But, more importantly, existential-humanistic theorists see people being directed by consciousness, engaged in meta-cognition, or "thinking about thinking." Existential and humanistic theorists stress awareness, perception, and insight. Their aim is to orient people so that behavioral repertoires and attitudes correspond more closely to value systems and self-perceptions.

Existential-humanistic theory values an individual's subjective report of life experience. The counselor cultivates a relationship in which personal experiences can be explored more fully. The semantic exchange and the relationship are believed to be of paramount importance to the existential-humanistic counselor. The concern is not with theoretical or abstract notions that label and intellectualize experience, but with the encounter and the experience of one another in the here and now. Downplaying psychopathological constructs, existential-humanistic counselors turn their attention to existence, experience, awareness, meaning, growth, and the creative efforts of people. For these reasons, personal responsibility for existence and experience is encouraged so that a person becomes more fully functioning.

Carl Rogers' Person-Centered counseling was developed, in part, from his reactions to Psychoanalysis and Behaviorism. Through personal as well as clinical experience, Rogers concluded that the therapeutic environment was the key to successful counseling. He hypothesized that if people perceive warmth, genuineness, and empathy in the counselor, that a healthy climate would encourage one's tendency to self-actualize.

Rogers, a scientist as well as a theoretician and practitioner, tested out many of his hypotheses. His research on the counseling relationship and outcomes was innovative.

Viktor Frankl, representing the existential view, was initially trained as a psychoanalyst. His clinical experiences, philosophical inclinations and observations of world-wide conditions led him to formulate logotherapy. His ideas gave consideration to a person's philosophical and spiritual needs. The highest value or experience for Frankl was the experience of God. Human experiences such as suffering, death and personal sacrifice as well as more positive aspects of existence were means to discover meaning and purpose to life.

People are motivated primarily by their will to meaning. Following an existential-humanistic tenet, Frankl holds that no matter how an individual suffers or whatever adverse environmental conditions exist, people have the responsibility to determine their own destiny.

Fritz Perls, also trained in psychoanalysis, founded the system of Gestalt psychotherapy which is based heavily on phenomenology and existentialism. Perls also sees the therapeutic relationship as an encounter in which two or more people meet to experience one another. Perls theorizes that there are layers of human behavior. Gestalt therapy tries to penetrate through the superficial layer to the deepest explosive layer which is the core of human functioning. Defenses, distortions, and misperceptions are pushed aside so that awareness of experience in the here and now may emerge. At the explosive layer of existence people can act on their inner promptings, and become spontaneous and authentic. Perls believes that people need to question their own questions, dreams, and behaviors and that they are capable of understanding their own motivations and intentions. It is through the accurate and nondistorted perceptions of reality that people may become aware of and experience their being.

Consciousness of self is vital to effective human functioning. The existential-humanistic theorists believe that human actions may be incongruent, discordant, or meaningless with respect to values, perceptions, or beliefs. Therefore, individuals may perceive discrepancies between how they act and how they would like to act.

Existential-humanistic theories of counseling and behavior change highlight several factors. Human beings are responsible for actions and perceptions of reality, and they direct their own fate and destiny. Ultimately, the individual is responsible for constructive or self-defeating behaviors. Through the counseling relationship persons may learn to accept responsibility for choice and decision, and ultimately accept themselves.

CHAPTER 5

CARL ROGERS'
PERSON-CENTERED COUNSELING

FOUNDATIONS AND STRUCTURE

Historical Foundations

CARL R. ROGERS (1902-1987) was educated at the University of Wisconsin, Union Theological Seminary, and Columbia University's Teachers College. His education and training has contributed to a humanistic-phenomenological orientation to philosophy, psychology, and education. Rogers' Protestant work ethic and theological studies have undoubtedly pervaded his beliefs in personal freedom and self-determination. The concepts of progressive education, evinced by John Dewey and William H. Kilpatrick, made a major impact on Roger's ideas of theory, practice, and research in counseling and psychotherapy. Goodwin Watson, a progressive educator at Columbia, advised Rogers to consider the study of clinical psychology.

Rogers' early work as a clinical psychologist focused on the delivery of services to disturbed children, parents, and families. Before Rogers conceived of a client-centered approach to counseling, he followed a fairly traditional clinical model that included gathering data, formulating a diagnosis, interpreting behavior, making suggestions, and reinforcing client behavior. The distance and objectivity expected of counselors contributed to Rogers' dissatisfaction with the directive-authoritarian clinical model of psychotherapy that was prevalent in those days. He observed that the best thereapeutic results often occurred when the atmosphere of counseling was virtually nonthreatening to the client.

Rogers, reflecting on personal experiences as a practicing psychologist in Rochester, New York, found inspiration in the views of Otto

Rank and Jesse Taft. Rank had developed notions on relationship therapy and Taft emphasized the freedom and sense of internal control people have over their destiny. As a result, Rogers wrote *The Clinical Treatment of the Problem Child* in 1939. Traditional counseling approaches were addressed in this work, but greater consideration was given to the importance of the counselor-client relationship, itself a major vehicle through which psychological growth is achieved.

Rogers began experimenting with a dramatically different approach to counseling. He listened carefully to clients as they expressed concerns about life, and followed their lead instead of his own. He noted that people were able to explore themselves more fully and less defensively when he made an attempt to be more empathetic and understanding. Gradually, Rogers moved away from directive counseling and focused on the characteristics necessary to foster a warm, supportive and growth-producing relationship.

Rogers' views soon were formalized into a nondirective model of counseling. To note his departure from the more objective and directive therapies, Rogers' novel therapeutic ideas were published in *Counseling and Psychotherapy* (1942) and *Client-Centered Therapy* (1951). Rogers' theoretical views were further refined and expanded upon in *On Becoming a Person* (1961) and *Carl Rogers On Personal Power* (1977). More recently Rogers' assumptions of growth and learning have been focused on the relationship of teacher and student. These conditions of the teaching relationship are expressed in *Freedom To Learn for the 80's* (1983).

As a scientist as well as a theoretician, Rogers began a series of research studies on his ideas at The Ohio State University, between 1940 and 1950. His work continued at the University of Chicago and the University of Wisconsin where he conducted research on the therapeutic relationship and its impact on schizophrenics. Rogers completed his career as a resident Fellow at the Center for Studies of the Person in La Jolla, California.

Philosophical Foundations

Client or person-centered counseling is a system that rests on a basic trust in human beings. Rogers believes that individuals have resources for self-understanding and have the ability to offer their perceptions of themselves and direct their own behavior. These potentials or abilities can be developed more fully in a climate characterized by freedom, understanding, and respect.

Counseling is not just a set of methods, but a philosophy of living and developing relationships (Rogers, 1980). The person-centered philosophy assumes that people are inherently good, fundamentally rational, trustworthy, and capable of realizing their potentials. Rogers believes that within every organism there is constructive movement toward personal growth and self-actualization. This tendency may be frustrated as a result of a social environment that poses obstacles or barriers to the natural inclinations of human beings. Rogers believes that all people are able to redirect their movement toward the constructive fulfillment of potentials in spite of social constraints.

Rogers' philosophy of counseling is a synthesis of Protestant theology, pragmatism, and idealism. Rogers has a fundamental belief in the psychological integrity of human beings (Rogers, 1942). He believes that the individual is fully responsible for choosing personal goals and directions. The theological idealism in Rogers' theoretical framework can be observed in his emphasis on self-determination regardless of biological or sociological factors that may frustrate such attempts.

Rogers' orientation blends humanistic, existential, and pragmatic values. He trusts an individual's innate tendency to behave rationally, constructively, and to self-actualize. Rogers' existential perspective is similar to Frankl's in that people may experience loss, anxiety, or psychosis, but are capable of creatively coping, directing their lives, and discovering personal meaning. The pragmatic influences upon Rogers have helped him to extend his focus beyond reason alone, to a trust in human experience and a strong interest in scientific inquiry.

Rogers, in the phenomenological tradition, values his own subjective experiences as a source of data and inspiration for his person-centered approach. Persons who are in the process of developing their full potentials are able to live subjectively and to accept that aspect of self (Rogers, 1961). He further notes that when people move in self-selected directions, they chose responsibly and experience life more fully.

Social-Psychological Foundations

The principle social-psychological concepts in person-centered counseling are the *organism,* the *phenomenal field,* and the *self.* The *organism* is the total individual while the *phenomenal field* represents the sum total of a person's experience. The *self* is the differentiated portions of the phenomenal field, constituted of conscious perceptions of the "I" or "me" (Hall and Lindsey, 1970).

The *organism* reacts to the *phenomenal field* for the satisfaction of its needs. Its primary motive is to maintain and actualize itself. The organism has the capacity to symbolize experiences or deny them symbolization. Symbolized experiences become conscious while experiences not symbolized become unconscious (Hall and Lindsey, 1970).

The *phenomenal field* consists of all conscious and unconscious experiences. Experience consists of all the functions of the organism — cognitive, affective, sensory, physiological, and behavioral motoric. The organism reacts to the phenomenal field as it is experienced and perceived. Reality for the person is the perceptual field, therefore it is a personal and subjective experience. External conditions are relevant to the extent they are symbolized, experienced, and perceived by the person. This does not imply that there is no objective reality. Rogers (1951) believes that the individual must test perceptions of the world against the world as it is.

The *self-concept* (organized conscious perceptions of the "I" or "me") is an organized gestalt of self-referent thoughts (Rogers, 1959). The self develops out of constant interaction with the environment. In so doing, the self incorporates values of significant others and may misperceive or distort them. The organism strives for balance and consistency by rejecting experiences that are inconsistent with the self-structure. Rogers (1959) refers to the *self as process*. He views the self as a dynamic and changing construct that is modified through experience. Four other social-psychological dimensions are of importance in Rogers' theory. These are *organismic valuing,* the *concept of congruence,* and *actualizing tendency,* and the *conditions of worth.*

Organismic Valuing

The organism's valuing system is ultimately responsible for self-acceptance and personal growth. Rogers (1951) asserts that values may be categorized as *operative, conceived,* and *objective.* Operative values involve a simple behavioral choice. For example, a person chooses an occupation that is consistent with the self-concept. Conceived values are more complex and reflect the cognitive symbolic activity of the person. An example of this case is the situation where a person may value aesthetic experiences over monetary rewards. Objective values are those which a person believes to be preferable. This implies that some activities may be objectively desirable, yet subjectively threatening and tension provoking. A person's valuing system is experiential, occurring over the life span and contributing to the development of the self-concept.

Values may be introjected and internalized as a result of the person's experiences with significant others. Valuing is differential or *extensional* when the person engages in experiences and activities that are self-enhancing. Trust in one's own organismic experiences begins when valuing is extensional. Extensional valuing leads to spontaneity and self-actualization. *Intensional* valuing suggests that one has an idea of what one desires, but refuses to act. Constructive action is inhibited with an increase in defensive behavior and a decrease in trust in self. The valuing system shuts off its own tendencies to actualize.

The Concept of Congruence

Congruence may be defined as the matching of experience, awareness, and communication. When an individual's actual experiences are inconsistent with the self-concept, a state of incongruence results. For example, a person who says, "I love all people," but at the same time rejects certain minority groups, is said to be incongruent. To the extent that organismic experiences and valuing are congruent with the self concept, the person is integrated. Incongruence often leads to conflict and fragmentation of the self.

The Actualizing Tendency

Rogers (1951) posits the existence of an innate motive for human beings to actualize their potentials. This motive leads to purposeful and rational attempts for the organism to satisfy its needs and become what it is capable of being. Human beings, therefore, have a tendency to actualize themselves, to *become* their potentials.

Rogers (1961) equates the actualizing tendency with the directional trend evident in all human life. The directional trend includes the urge to expand, develop, mature, and to activate all the capacities of the self. The actualization tendency exists in all people even though its expression may be denied or buried in the unconscious. The proper conditions must exist in the social environment in order for one to release and express this tendency. Since self-actualization is the motivational force for creativity, when significant experiences are denied, the creative tendencies become blocked or self-defeating.

An organism actualizes itself within the parameters of heredity. This forward movement or self-expansion is an ongoing process throughout the life span. Self-actualization can be inhibited if a person cannot discriminate between self-enhancing and self-defeating ways of behaving.

Awareness of how one symbolizes experience becomes an integral part of the actualizing process. When people know what they are choosing, they are better able to move forward in their development (see Figures 5-1 and 5-2).

Conditions of Worth: The Need for Positive Regard and Self-Regard

Learning how to identify and express one's emotions occurs through interpersonal transactions. In the early stages of human development, people learn to differentiate themselves from the environment and also note differences in the way others respond to them. The social responses of others have a major effect on positive and negative affect. When responses from others are characterized by respect, warmth, liking, and acceptance, these are likely to be experienced positively by the person. Such positive responses are categorized as positive regard, a need of all human organisms. If a person is not regarded positively by others, ambivalent affect and negative self-perceptions often result. Essentially, people apply the values of others to themselves as if they were their own. More will be said of the conditions of worth in the next section — The Development of the Person.

To summarize, Rogers is noted for his self-theory of personality. The self-concept is a key social-psychological dimension, symbolizing the person's picture or view of existence. The real self constitutes actual perceptions of existence while the ideal self refers to how one would like to be. A healthy self-concept develops when the person is able to integrate the real and ideal concepts of self. Self-esteem results when people regard their behaviors, thoughts, and feelings as worthwhile or meaningful in relation to others.

Rogers believes conditions of self-worth arise from experiences with significant others. Family members or peers tend to conditionally regard the behavior of a given person, therefore, the person is conditionally accepted. Over time, the individual internalizes conditions of worth which become incorporated into the self-concept. If significant others have unconditionally accepted the person then that individual will have a high self-regard. If the internalized conditions of worth are based on arbitrary beliefs, however, this may lead to negative self-regard and a poorly developed self-concept.

Rogers hypothesizes that the self is formed through perception, values, and experiences. Self-esteem and self-regard are positive when the individual engages in activities which are congruent with the self. Incongruent experiences are threatening and arouse the person's defenses, often leading to denial or distortion of experiences.

The Development of the Person

Rogers' theory of human development proposes that the phenomenal field and self-concept are congruent among people who are functioning well. Congruence implies optimally adaptive behaviors wherein the person's subjective value system matches the awareness and experiences of the self. This leads to self-awareness, continuing personal development, and minimization of stress and anxiety.

Rogers asserts that people are innately motivated to self-actualize. Infants are able to perceive, experience and organize events in their lives at a simple primitive level. The social environment has a significant effect on these early perceptual processes. The infant does have an inherent tendency to value experiences as positive or negative. The valuing system has the power to reinforce self-actualization or detract from it.

As development continues throughout childhood, adolescence, and adulthood, the person gradually integrates experiences into the self-concept. If experiences are perceived and valued as negative (or inconsistent with the self-concept), then maladjustment occurs. Rogers (1961) holds that people have diverse experiences which they value, some of which are congruent with the self-concept, while others may be frustrating, disappointing, and incongruent. Self-esteem is derived from the organization and integration of these experiences into the self-concept.

Rogers emphasizes that people relate to significant others and experience positive or negative regard from them. These conditions of worth or regard from others are incorporated into the structure of the self-concept. An example of this is when a child engages in behavior of self-interest but is negatively valued or reinforced by the parents. In cases such as this, the child may inhibit self-enhancing actions and avoid potentially meaningful life experiences. The conditions of worth are introjected into the self, and the child consequently learns that certain behavior or aspects of the self are unacceptable. Figures 5-1 and 5-2 illustrate the process of the innate sequence of behavior and the learning of self-conflict respectively.

Rogers' (1951) theory of personality development consists of a generalized set of statements derived from clinical experiences. He outlines a theory of human development in a set of propositions or hypotheses

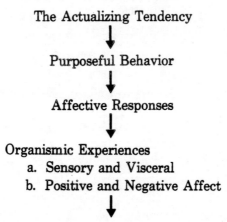

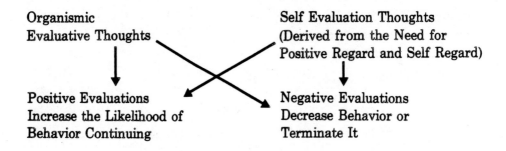

Adapted from Ford and Urban (1965)

Figure 5-1. The innate sequence of behavior.

which are scientifically testable. Person-centered theory of human development considers the organism, the phenomenological field, and the self-concept. Several major propositions are as follows (Rogers 1951):

- Individuals exist in a changing world of experience and the individual is the primary organizer of experience.
- The organism reacts to the field as it is experienced and perceived, the perceptual field is, for the individual, "reality" or the environment.
- The organism responds as an organized whole to this phenomenal field.

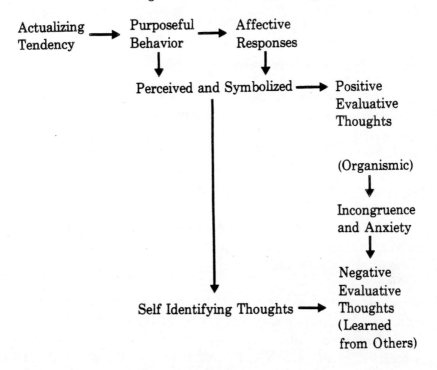

Adapted from Ford and Urban (1965)

Figure 5-2. The learning of self-conflict.

- The organism's primary motivation is for self-actualization.
- Behavior is basically the goal-directed attempt of the organism to satisfy its needs as perceived and experienced in the environment.
- Emotion accompanies and, in general, facilitates goal-directed behaviors, emotion relates to the seeking versus the consummatory aspects of behavior. The intensity of emotion is related to the perceived significance of the behavior of the organism.
- The best perspective for understanding behavior is from the internal frame of reference of the individual.
- Every experience is organized in the perceptual field and is gradually integrated in the self concept.
- The organism interacts with the environment and evaluates interactions with others which contributes to the structure of self as an organized structure.
- The values attached to experiences are a part of the self-structure

and in some instances are values introjected or taken over from others.

- Experiences are either: (a) perceived, integrated, and organized into some aspect of the self, (b) ignored because there is no perceived relationship to the self-structure, and/or (c) denied or distorted because the experience is inconsistent with the structure of the self.
- Most behavior is consistent with the concept of self.
- Behavior may be brought about by experiences and needs which may not have been symbolized. Behavior may be inconsistent with the structure of the self.
- Psychological maladjustment exists when the person denies awareness of significant experiences. Consequently, experiences are not symbolized into the self-concept. Thus, there is a basic psychological tension.
- Psychological adjustment exists when experience is assimilated on a symbolic level into a consistent relationship with the self-concept.
- An experience which is incongruent with the self concept may be perceived as a threat. The more often threat is perceived, the more rigid and inflexible the self-concept becomes.
- Under certain conditions, as in client-centered counseling, absence of threat to the self-structure is minimized. Experiences which are inconsistent may be examined and the self-concept is revised to assimilate the incongruent experiences.
- When the person perceives and examines experiences, the self is revised to assimilate congruent experiences.
- When the person perceives and accepts into the self-concept sensory and visceral experiences, then the person is more understanding and accepting of self and others.
- As experiences in the phenomenal field are integrated with the self-concept, the value system is clarified resulting in spontaneous goal-directed behavior.

Concepts of Functional and Dysfunctional Behavior

According to Rogers (1951), maladaptive behavior occurs when large discrepancies exist between an individual's perceptions of self and the ideal self (how the person would like to be). Such perceptions are often distorted and contribute to a fragmented self-structure characterized by tension and anxiety. Distorted self-perceptions and the fear and anxiety often associated with them tend to inhibit self-enhancing goal directed behavior (Rogers, 1959).

Rogers' basic assumption that people have the inherent motivation and capacity to actualize their potentialities, suggests that they are able to transcend biological, psychological, or social determinants of behavior if they are aware of themselves. Awareness of self and experiences is a prerequisite for self-determination.

Incongruence between perceptions of self and reality increases the likelihood that a person may experience severe organistic anxiety (see Figures 5-1 and 5-2). One may defend against anxiety by denying objective reality and distorting experiences so they are inconsistent with the self. Defenses against anxiety inhibit the tendency to actualize. If the self-concept is severely disorganized then a person may avoid thought of those experiences or actions that are truly desired. The organization of the self-structure becomes rigid and inflexible, a process that Rogers and Meador (1979) refer to as intensionality, implying that the person perceives experiences as threatening and conditional.

Rogers proposes that human beings function more effectively when they are self-directing and are able to mobilize their inner resources or potentials. A psychologically healthy person is spontaneous, desires experiences that are fulfilling to the ideal self, and does not deny reality. Psychological adjustment implies that an adaptive person's perceptions of self are consistent with experiences. Moreover, fully functioning persons have a high level of positive regard for themselves (self-esteem). They continually seek experiences which enhance the self, leading to greater self-acceptance. As the ideal self and the real self converge, the tendency toward self-actualization is more likely to be expressed behaviorally.

Concepts of Behavioral Change

People enter counseling when they are in a state of incongruence (i.e., limited awareness) that is experienced as psychological tension. Excessive tension, anxiety, and incongruence undermine the self-actualization tendency (Rogers, 1951). The counseling relationship is a vital, therapeutic environment in which people can explore their potentials and move toward self-acceptance.

Conditions for Behavioral Change

Four therapeutic conditions are essential to facilitate changes in behavior. These are *accurate empathy, genuineness or congruence, acceptance,* and *respect.* These four conditions represent counselor variables that are analogous to the conditions of worth described earlier. When the counselor offers these four "facilitative conditions" to a significant degree, the stage is set for constructive behavior change. However, it is necessary that clients eventually perceive these attitudes in the counselor.

Rogers (1961) defines empathy as sensing, perceiving, and responding to the internal frame of reference of another. Accurate empathy is a process wherein a counselor attempts to fully comprehend the innermost thoughts and feelings of a person within that person's phenomenal field of experience. Empathy in this respect means comprehensive understanding of a behavioral sequence (thought, feeling, behavior, situation) in the phenomenal field.

Rogers (1959) differentiates empathy from identification. Empathy has an "as if" condition associated with it. One can sense and perceive the feelings of another without losing the recognition that it is "as if" one had those feelings. If this quality is lost, the result is identification.

Respect is an attitude of nonpossessive caring for another person and a recognition of their being, leading to an attitude of *acceptance*. Acceptance implies that the counselor does not ascribe negative values to the behavior and personality of the client. The client is prized as a person with dignity and worth no matter how the client behaves. Acceptance involves a deep respect for human existence on the part of the counselor and a willingness to communicate this to the client.

Congruence as we have already seen suggests that the counselor's experiences are available to awareness and can be communicated accurately. Thus, the counselor can function in a real or genuine way in a counseling relationship. This "realness" means that the counselor is free to respond to others without the restrictions of defenses and fears. Congruence implies a willingess to be known as well as an openness to experience. A perfect state of congruence is not attainable, but Rogers believes that human beings are capable of achieving higher levels of it with time and experience.

Rogers (1942) in his very early writings proposed a sequence of behavior change consisting of twelve steps: (1) The person has felt a need for help; (2) The counseling situation is defined; (3) The counselor encourages the person to freely verbalize thoughts and feelings; (4) The counselor unconditionally accepts, attends to, and clarifies the meaning of negative thoughts and emotional states; (5) The person is able to symbolize negative emotions as well as positive ones; (6) The counselor clarifies positive emotions; (7) Greater congruence in the person is noted; (8) The person considers alternative actions; (9) The person initiates constructive actions; (10) Constructive action is followed by more accurate discriminations and symbolizations of situations, thoughts, feelings, and behavior; (11) Positive feelings and behavior become integrated into the self-structure; and (12) The person feels a decreasing need for counseling.

Rogers (1977) maintains that the person's self-concept is enhanced as the core conditions are more deeply experienced. This in turn fosters a decrease in psychological defenses and anxiety and a greater degree of self-acceptance. Overt behavior change in person-centered counseling is acknowledged as a significant aspect of the process, but it is not the central focus. Personal growth implies a more complex reorganization of the self-structure so that the inner potentials of the person are actualized. Assumed in this definition of growth is willingness to engage in new behaviors and experiences.

Awareness of Experience and the Self in Behavior Change

Distortion of perception and self-denial tends to limit awareness and leads to a fragmented or poorly organized self-concept. Rogers assumes that awareness allows the person to see new relationships within the self and environment. Awareness impacts on the person's entire self-system. Awareness is a process that is not episodic; it can continue to expand throughout the life span. Awareness and self-exploration have a mutually reinforcing effect. One stimulates the other as both unacceptable and acceptable emotions, thoughts, and behaviors are ultimately owned by the person, and a higher level of congruence is achieved. This results in more constructive and responsible behavior.

Reflection of the Human Experience

When the core conditions are perceived, the person becomes more open to inner as well as external conflicts associated with the self. The person then may reflect on these experiences, that is, step away from them and view them more objectively. Rogers assumes that people are fully capable of self-reflection, a process that helps to reinforce and expand awareness. Reflection, as will be discussed later, is a major technique counselors use to facilitate behavior change.

Assessment of Human Functioning

Rogers (1951) believes that a comprehensive psychological evaluation of people is not necessary to the counseling process. He feels so strongly about it that he has asserted that traditional assessment may significantly deter from the counseling process. The time and effort committed to assessment could be more successfully directed at building a solid therapeutic relationship.

Rogers' approach to assessment centers on the quality of the relationship and the subjective experiences of the counselor and client in the "here and now." The counselor attends and listens carefully to the inconsistencies or incongruencies in the client's awareness, experience, and communication. Rather than relying on traditional diagnostic formulations, Rogers' assessment procedures consider the presence or absence of facilitative conditions offered by the counselor (empathy, congruence, genuineness, and respect). The perception of these conditions by the client determines the degree of self-awareness, self-exploration, and constructive actions ultimately taken by the client.

Rogers and Rablen (1958) formulated a *Process Scale* to evaluate how a person experiences and benefits from counseling. The scales assess how one functions relative to personal constructs, acceptance of feelings, expression of personal meaning, perception of relationships, and experiencing in the "here and now." The scale consists of seven stages, ranging from the person being defensive, mistrustful, and unaware of feelings to a high level of personal functioning indicative of "here and now" experiencing and congruency. Theoretically, as the person gains awareness and integrates incongruent experiences into the self-structure, the self-concept becomes strengthened.

The person-centered counselor relies on direct experience in counseling and follows and responds to the client's lead. The counselor formulates hypotheses about incongruencies in awareness, experience, and communication. For example, when a client says, "I am confused about my goals and life," or "I want a better relationship with my boyfriend, but I am not sure if he will approve of me," it provides important information about discrepancies between the real and ideal self. These clinical hypotheses are tested through the counselor's reflections and clarifications of the client's emotional themes related to ongoing functioning and experience. The counselor tries to assess the extent to which incongruencies impact on the self-concept, emotions, and behavior.

Rogers believes that people have the ability to assess what they have personally gained from an experience. Most importantly, they have a sense that they are able to determine a great part of their personal, social, and career development.

Goals and Directions of Counseling

Person-centered counseling is aimed primarily at helping persons achieve more independence in determining the directions of their lives, so that they may more effectively cope with present and future problems (Rogers, 1942). The counselor works, at the onset of counseling, toward helping the client discover directions for growth. No person is free of conflict and every client can cultivate a more mature understanding of conflict and how it can hinder creative problem-solving.

Rogers (1961) conceives counseling goals as directions. The person moves away from facades; moves away from shoulds; moves away from meeting expectations; moves away from pleasing others; moves toward self-direction; moves toward a "being" process; moves toward being complex; moves toward openness to experience; moves toward acceptance of self and others; and moves toward trust of self.

Rogers (1961) believes that people who successfully experience the counseling process move *toward* being what they actually are and move *away from* being what they are not. They cultivate a deeper sensitivity to human experience, an expanded self-awareness, and a greater commitment to self-actualization.

The successful client is one who becomes more congruent and is able to achieve an integration of the "real self" and the "ideal self." Moreover, there is less reliance on others, with one's focus of control shifting from others to the individual. Therefore, the person achieves greater maturity and a higher level of creative expression. By moving away from rigid cultural expectations and the pressures of social conformity, a person is more apt to choose values and engage in behaviors that are more congruent with the self-concept. There is no guarantee that the choices made will be wise ones, but the person is more likely to benefit from mistakes. Finally, the person comes to know and understand that the actualization of existing possibilities is an internally-directed process.

The Counseling Process:
Initiating, Facilitating, Terminating

Perhaps more than any other theorist described in this text, Rogers espouses a process conception of counseling. Rogers (1961) believes that the quality of the relationship between the counselor and client is the essence of the counseling process. When the client perceives that he/she is understood empathically, and accepted as a human being, then behavior change is possible.

The process of counseling for Rogers is a "moment to moment" set of experiences, whereby, one thought, feeling, psychological response, or behavior leads to another one and builds upon the other. It is a "dynamic" experience that permits one to expand self-awareness through the exploration of new possibilities.

Rogers likens the process of counseling to a changing "Gestalt" consisting of seven dimensions of experience. Rogers and Wood (1974) describe these dimensions on a continuum ranging from low to high levels of therapeutic experience.

- **Change in the Relationship to Feelings.** In the earliest stage of counseling, the client does not recognize or own personal feelings. Feelings and thoughts are isolated from one another. The client exists in a state of "incongruence" (i.e., "I have a strong desire to scream." "This is not like me." "I don't know why I feel this way.") In later stages, the client knows his/her thoughts and feelings and is able to communicate them accurately.

- **Change in the Manner of Experience.** The client gives consideration to experiencing and trusting deep feelings. The client becomes less fearful of owning negative thoughts, feelings, and behaviors. There is a greater desire to acknowledge and experience a feeling as part of the self. The client increasingly recognizes and confronts disparities between the real and ideal self (i.e., "I have this feeling, but shouldn't have.")

- **Change in Personal Constructs.** This refers to the way a client construes personal experience. Initially, personal constructs or systems of understanding the self and the world were rigid and dogmatic (i.e., "I can't do anything right." "I must be perfect." "I am no good." "People hate me.") As the client confronts personal constructs, they become less rigidly construed. The client is better able to reflect upon personal beliefs and question their validity. ("Maybe I am not a louse." "I do have this feeling, and maybe it's not so bad." "I can't really say for sure that people hate me.") At the highest level of this experience, the client can view personal constructs as tentative, not inevitably attached to an experience.

- **Change in Self-Communication.** Initially, clients tend to talk about external conditions that affect them. There is an unwillingness to discuss the "self." ("My son has been a major problem for his teachers." "If it wasn't for my boss, I wouldn't be in this fix.") Self-communication becomes more therapeutic and growth enhancing when the individual begins to refer to the complexity of being. The person loses consciousness of self as object. The "I" emerges into the perceptual field. Individuals are aware of their subjectivity and unique ways of experiencing being (i.e., "The real truth of the matter is that I do lie at times").

- **Change in Relationship to Problems.** On the change continuum, clients do not have a full awareness of how their problems impact on them. During the course of counseling, people come to see that their difficulties arise from within rather than from without. There is the recognition that problem feelings are in relation to others. Of great import is the awareness that out of problem feelings may come more constructive actions, if they are accepted.

- **Change in Interpersonal Relations.** In the course of counseling, the client experiences a move toward interpersonal intimacy. The client moves away from being afraid of close personal contact. Gradually the client learns that it is safe to risk expressing true feelings. The client finds the courage to behave more openly inside of the counseling relationship, as well as outside it.

- **The Upper End of Experience.** In this final stage of experience the person expresses feelings with immediacy and richness of detail. Experience is interpreted and understood in the "here and now." The self is the subjective experience of the moment. The person is more congruent, achieves a greater integration of negative and positive experiences, and is able to communicate more effectively. The person becomes "more fully functioning."

A person-centered counselor believes that when an optimum environment exists, then people are free to learn. In this situation, people will suspend their critical attitudes, experience themselves more fully, and consider more constructive actions.

During each counseling session, the client assumes the responsibility for exploring incongruent experiences and communicating them more openly. This person learns the value of personal freedom, and that the many impulses and behaviors that may diverge from social mores may be fully expressed in counseling.

As the counseling relationship unfolds, a client begins to explore experiences which had been previously denied from awareness. The client learns to accept the symptoms, experiences, or behaviors which eventually become more accurately symbolized or construed by the person and gradually integrated into the self-concept. The counselor does not pressure the client for it is assumed that each person will confront one's own personal issues.

Person-centered counseling terminates when there is evidence that the client is successfully engaging in extensional behaviors and self-regulatory actions. As counseling terminates, a person more accurately perceives the self and is able to integrate incongruent experiences within the self. Anxiety and psychological tension are minimized and the person further realizes that actualization or growth is not a simple utopian process, but one requiring work, attention, effort, commitment, and self-sacrifice.

The counseling process may be nearing the final stages when:

- The person experiences greater self-regard;
- Psychological defenses are minimized;
- The person becomes aware of incongruities in experiences and minimizes them;
- The person assumes greater responsibility for his or her value system;
- The person is able to experience genuine feeling without being afraid of losing the counselor's respect;
- The person attains a more realistic view of the self because of the decrease in defensiveness;
- The real and ideal self move closer together;
- The person views others more realistically and is more accepting of self and others (Rogers, 1961).

Counseling Techniques and Procedures

The person-centered orientation to counseling stresses process rather than technique. However, Rogers employs procedures that are integrated into "core conditions" in the sense that they serve to operationalize them. The major techniques of person-centered counseling are focusing, clarification, and reflection of feeling. The techniques are the communication bridges between "Counselor-offered core conditions" and "Client self-awareness, self-exploration, and self-acceptance."

Focusing

Focusing permits the counselor to direct the client's attention to significant cognitive, emotional, behavioral, and situational elements of the phenomenal field. This technique serves several purposes. Focusing facilitates client awareness of incongruent states and significant experiential states. Focusing also allows the client to grasp the concrete, immediate and changing feeling states in the counseling process. Experiential focusing permits the client to direct attention to conscious as well as preconscious personal meanings (Gendlin, 1962).

Gendlin (1978) postulates that focusing consists of six movements. These are:

- **Clearing a Space**—Refers to the identification of problem feelings. Problem feelings are viewed objectively—at a distance.
- **Felt Sense of the Problem**—Involves the specification of the most pressing problem area and sensing the problem is experienced relative to the whole self-system.
- **Finding a Handle**—Suggests the discovery of a word or image that symbolizes the problem feeling, thought, or behavior. This is a labeling of feelings and meanings.
- **Resonating**—Is a validating procedure that poses the "felt sense" against the "label." The confirmation of an appropriate "label" for the "felt sense" is experienced by the body.
- **Asking**—Refers to an inquiry into the meaning of the felt sense or need. The inquiry is passive rather than active. No answer is deliberately sought. Asking is analogous to "reflective questioning." ("I wonder if I am feeling good or bad about this or that.")
- **Receiving**—Is based on a trust of the body's reactions or shifts (feelings, thoughts, behavior). Bodily reactions are experienced—not evaluated—merely attended to.

Clarification and Reflection of Feeling

The "technical vehicles" through which experiential focusing is accomplished are *clarification* and *reflection of feeling*. Clarification narrows the phenomenal field so that the awareness of emotional meanings becomes more apparent to the client. Through clarification of personal meanings, the subjective world of the client can become more objective. The counselor essentially restates the thoughts and feelings of the client so that clearer perceptions of the self and environment emerge. It should be emphasized that focusing and restatement follow the client's leads.

Reflection. Perhaps the most powerful technique the person-centered counselor uses, captures the subjective experiences of the client in such a way that the client is better able to perceive the counselor's acceptance and empathic understanding. Reflection is more than just mirroring the

client's personal meanings. Reflection encourages a deeper self-exploration of feelings and meanings.

In summary, the counseling techniques of reflection, clarification
and restatement, and focusing help bring the inconsistencies of the
person's experiences into awareness, encouraging self-exploration and
self-disclosure. Rogers believes that the perceived relationship and the
psychological environment for counseling are critical factors for client
progress. These factors are perhaps more important to the counseling
process and outcome than the actual techniques implemented. Techniques are of value to the extent that they assist in the restructuring of
the self-concept via expanded awareness and depth of self-exploration.

Evaluation of Counseling Outcomes

Rogers' theory stimulated a plethora of research into the process and
outcomes of counseling. These investigations were systematic, quite
well-executed, and consistent with self-theory.

Recall that one goal of person-centered counseling is to help a person
integrate the "real" and "ideal" self. Theoretically, person-centered counseling results in: (1) a decrease in the discrepancy between the perceived
self (real) and the valued self (ideal); and (2) this decrease in discrepancy
is related to movement or growth in counseling (Rogers, 1961).

To measure changes in self-concept, Rogers and his associates used a
"Q" technique consisting of one hundred self descriptive items placed on
cards. The aim was to include the widest range of ways individuals could
perceive themselves (i.e., "I am sexually attractive," "I hate myself," "I
am really upset," "I feel very calm"). The person is asked to sort the cards
into nine piles, ranging from most unlike me to those most like me. The
number of cards in each pile were (1, 4, 11, 21, 26, 21, 11, 4, 1). When
the sorting of cards was completed, the person is asked to sort the cards
once more. This time the person was to describe "the person he or she
would like to be."

The various sortings were then correlated. Correlations could be obtained between the self precounseling and the self postcounseling and
between the real and ideal self. High correlations show little discrepancy
or change. Low correlations indicate higher discrepancies and change
(Rogers, 1961).

Research on the process of counseling was also undertaken. Scales
were developed by Barrett-Lennard, and Charles Truax and Robert
Carkhuff to assess the "core conditions" of empathy, respect (then called

unconditional positive regard), congruence and acceptance. These measured conditions were then related to the depth of client exploration and to outcomes (and measured by judges ratings and psychological inventories). In general, studies on the effect of "facilitative" or core conditions indicate that when they are offered to a great degree and are perceived by the client, positive outcomes are more likely.

Rogers (1961), summarizing research on the process of counseling, notes that a counseling relationship characterized by high levels of accurate empathy, congruence, respect, and acceptance offered by the counselor will have a high probability of producing desirable change in the client. This assertion of Rogers continues to gain considerable research support to date.

Rogers has a strong commitment to the scientific study of human behavior in general, and counseling in particular. To advance the body of knowledge about the counseling process, Rogers (1961) asserts that investigators must be willing to place their most passionate beliefs and convictions to the objective test of empirical research. Rogers also notes that the study of the counseling process and its outcomes has not resulted in a "sterile abstraction" of the human condition.

COUNSELING APPLICATION

The case presented illustrates the process and technique of person-centered counseling. This case concerns Bill, a practicing attorney, who suffered from physical symptoms of stress, and expressed dissatisfaction in his life. He would prefer to intellectualize his concerns, rather than explore the nature of them. He was initially fearful and defensive, but as the therapeutic relationship developed, the conditions favorable for self-awareness followed.

Person-Centered Counseling in a Medical Setting

Bill was examined by his family doctor for general bodily complaints and neck pain. A physical examination yielded negative results and he was referred to a neurologist for a neurological work up. Again, the results were negative. The neurologist discussed with Bill the possibility that his complaints were stress-related.

Bill is 35 years old, he is married and has two children, one three and the other two. His law practice has not developed as he expected. Bill's wife does not work, but has considered working full-time to supplement their income. Bill has expressed dissatisfaction with his career but does not know what other career to pursue. Bill is frequently irritable and annoyed with minor frustrations. After the initial introductions, the counselor and Bill begin to talk about his problems.

Bill: Well, I don't know what you can do for me, but my wife and doctor think you can help.
Counselor: Uh-huh.
Bill: I think they think my symptoms are psychosomatic or I am a *hypochondriac.* (Emphasizing the latter.)
Counselor: I see.
Bill: Well . . . what do you think?
Counselor: I get the feeling you would like me to define and label you as this or that.
Bill: If I knew why I had this pain . . . I could deal with it.
Counselor: Somehow if you could understand yourself and your pain you might be more able to cope.
Bill: Damn. It's just been so frustrating. I've been angry over minor things . . . Little things just tic me off.
Counselor: I sense your frustration. Minor things so often seem like major things when your life isn't what you want it to be.
Bill: Yes. I can't stop dwelling on the negative parts of my life.
Counselor: It seems that you only see the more negative aspects of yourself.
Bill: Yeah . . . I get to feeling down a lot, because I'm not sure what career I want. I'm not happy being a lawyer . . . it's just not working out, but I don't want to lose what I have now for a risky new career.
Counselor: Change is risky business, but you don't want to give up what you have gained.
Bill: I do give up in the face of frustration. I feel embarrassed and inadequate when I give up.
Counselor: Are you not living up to certain expectations?
Bill: Yeah . . . I feel depressed when I don't bring enough money home. My wife wants to work, but I won't let her.
Counselor: Somehow you feel a loss of self-esteem and pride.
Bill: I feel inadequate and pressured to do something.
Counselor: But at the same time you just don't know what to do.
Bill: That sums it up.

Bill was moderately defensive during the initial session. He wanted a diagnosis or label for his symptoms. Notice the incongruence between his "self" and "experience." He wants to be in a successful career, but his self-perceptions are that he is inadequate and incompetent. The result is frustration, fear, and anger.

As the session progressed, Bill focused more on his feelings and moved away from his intellectualized approach to life. The counselor responded to Bill's feelings in the "here and now" context and didn't rush or probe or question him about other areas of his life. Notice that Bill was initially defensive, started talking about "things," and then expressed a specific situation he was concerned about.

Bill remained somewhat apprehensive about counseling even though he began to communicate feelings of deep insecurity about his job and spouse's desire to work. Bill still complained of fatigue and neck pain. He openly expressed resentment. The counselor uses a focusing technique to help Bill expand awareness of an incongruent state.

The Fourth Session

Bill: I still feel physically awful.

Counselor: Bill, let's see if you can step back a bit from your pain—looking at it from a distance (clearing a space), then try to sense how the pain affects your whole being (felt sense of the problem). Could you concentrate on your pain from a distance, and perhaps label it in some way?

Bill: Yes. (Bill closes his eyes, pauses a minute or so) *Weakness* comes to mind.

Counselor: Does this label accurately reflect the experience of pain? (Resonating.)

Bill: Yes, I think so.

Counselor: Could you ask or inquire into the meaning of your pain? (Asking.)

Bill: That's rough.

Counselor: Try. But don't force anything.

Bill: (After three minutes Bill reported very deep feelings associated with pain and fatigue as well as negative thoughts about himself.) I am feeling very weak, helpless, indecisive, like I have no value at all as a person. I see that along with my pain—as though my body is telling me something—I feel. Yet, I don't want to believe that.

Counselor: You don't need to evaluate the experience. Just try to capture it and what it means to you (Receiving).

The focusing experience helped Bill to visualize and experience states of incongruity and their effect on his self-concept. Bill became aware of feelings that he was not enough of a man if his wife worked to partially support the family. He also connected pain and physical weakness with "psychological impotence."

In later sessions, Bill showed signs of becoming more congruent. He could more easily experience negative feelings, be aware of them, and communicate them to the counselor.

The Eighth Session

Bill: My pain has gotten better, but one day it was terrible.

Counselor: Hmm.

Bill: The only thing that happened was that my wife was hired as a bank

teller. She has excellent possibilities for advancement. The damned
economy is so bad that I bet she will be laid off shortly.

Counselor: That means something to you — your value and self-esteem. I sense you
are upset.

Bill: I feel bad that I feel this way. It's so confusing.

Counselor: You want to feel positive, but you can't.

Bill: I get so frustrated and angry with myself . . . I think it is one reason I
have this pain.

Counselor: You mean that these feelings are a source of confusion, and that pain
tends to interfere with your own goals and directions.

Bill: Yeah, blaming her for my own frustrations really doesn't get me anywhere. Maybe I need to be more realistic about matters.

Counselor: Uh-huh.

Bill: When I started my law practice I immediately assumed that it would
not go . . . though I never told my wife this. This damned feeling of
weakness, of impotence, it does find its way into my body.

Counselor: Perhaps it does. But, do these feelings need to blind you to other resources?

The counselor following Bill's lead reflected feelings that enabled Bill
to bring into his awareness aspects of the self that were previously denied
and distorted. The process of self-awareness is sometimes painfully slow.
Bill began to open himself to many of the inner resources that he previously denied. When he made connections between negative thoughts,
feelings, and bodily states, he eventually noticed a reduction in physical
symptoms. He also moved away from the idea that he was personally im-
potent. Self-awareness is of paramount importance in person-centered
counseling. Distortion or denial of experience limits awareness and
leads to a fragmented or poorly organized self-concept. Awareness allows the person to see new relationships with the self and environment.
Person-centered counseling asserts that awareness is a process that allows the person to organize perceptions and experiences in a more self-
enhancing manner. Therefore, awareness occurs bit by bit, and as it
increases, the person's self-concept becomes more organized and
strengthened. Bill became more aware of incongruent experiences.
Thus, he could not only own unacceptable emotions, thoughts, and behaviors, but could minimize their influence over him.

Critical Comments

Carl Rogers' person-centered theory of counseling must be regarded
as one that is rich in "conceptualization" and "practicality." Rogers offers:
(1) a general theory of personality; (2) a theory of behavior change; and

(3) a theory of counseling. Starting with some basic assumptions of human nature, Rogers developed a "self-theory" of personality in which he describes innate as well as learned sequences of behavior. Self-theory translates into a set of propositions regarding the social-psychological conditions necessary to facilitate the development of a fully functioning person as well as those conditions that inhibit that process. Self-theory also generates a number of internally consistent hypotheses regarding the nature of the counseling relationship as a vehicle to foster personality change.

There is a logical consistency between person-centered theory, practice, and research. While remaining true to a phenomenological and humanistic philosophy, Rogers, as a behavioral scientist, relies on facts derived from research as well as those gained from personal experience. He has studied counseling outcomes, but his most substantive research contributions are in the investigations of the counseling process. Moreover, Rogers has been willing to expand and refine his theoretical views in light of new insights gained from research as well as from personal experience. Over the course of four decades, Rogers' theories of counseling and human behavior have stimulated a great deal of research.

A criticism of Rogers' self-theory is that his "phenomenological perspective" does not address the significance of unconscious processes in determining the content of consciousness and choice. For example, he plays down the use of "defense mechanisms" that may account for maintaining and reinforcing "incongruent states" or the bridging of the gap between "conscious" and "unconscious" processes. Concepts such as "organismic experience" and "accurate empathy" are so subjective in nature that they do prove to be a problem for researchers as well as counselors to operationalize.

In Rogers' earlier writings he proposed that the facilitative or core conditions were necessary and sufficient for behavior change to occur in counseling. Rogers has been challenged on this point by many critics. Research findings seem to suggest that these core conditions do operate in counseling and when they are offered at a high level, positive outcomes are more likely to result. It would be naive to assume that Rogers believes that the facilitative conditions impact in some magical way on the client or that they are sufficient in and of themselves. Rogers is careful to discuss these conditions in relative terms and is quite explicit about how they do operate in counseling.

Idealistic assumptions about human nature pervade Rogers' theory. Many of these assumptions are not necessarily easy to test empirically or to justify on logical grounds. Major questions do arise. Is the nature of humans basically good? If so, what evidence is this assertion based upon? Is there an innate motive for self-actualization? If so, where is the proof? A problem here arises because Rogers has greatly deemphasized the biological bases of human behavior in his writings.

We question why Rogers flatly rejects diagnostic constructs as having little or no value to counselors. Has he not made an error of exclusion? While diagnostic categories may not always lead to appropriate choice of a treatment, they may be very helpful to counselors in gaining some perspective on self-destructive behavior and counseling directions. Would it not be useful to the counselor to be able to discriminate among people who's symptoms of depression are due to "organic brain syndromes," versus the experience of a significant loss? While Rogers' views force people out of "sterile clinical thinking," they may at the same time force people into risking "theoretical naivete."

It has been our experience to date, that counselors who practice "person-centered" counseling are relatively open to techniques from other schools of thought. Many employ procedures from Gestalt, Rational-Emotive, and Behavioral approaches to deal with a variety of specific client concerns (assertiveness, phobias, and marital conflicts). Many counselors feel comfortable with "technical eclecticism" while subscribing to a humanistic philosophy and theory of behavior.

Person-centered theory, currently serves as a humanistic foundation for some models of "holistic health care." "Holistic health" attempts to integrate humanistic philosophy and the practices of counseling and medicine. Rogers undoubtedly had a profound influence on what today is referred to as the human potential movement.

In his later years, Rogers extended his humanistic theory to concerns beyond one to one or group counseling relationships. His ideas have found their way into the field of education, business, industry, and theology. Rogers' ideas seem very applicable to any endeavors that require solutions to human problems.

REFERENCES

Ford, D.M., & Urban, H.B. (1965). *Systems of psychotherapy.* New York: Wiley.

Gendlin, E.T. (1962). *Experiencing and the creation of learning.* New York: The Free Press of Glencoe, Division of MacMillan Co.

Gendlin, E.T. (1978). *Focusing.* New York: Everest House.

Hall, C.S., & Lindsey, G. (1970). *Theories of personality.* New York: John Wiley and Sons, Inc.

Rogers, C.R. (1939). *The clinical treatment of the problem child.* Boston: Houghton-Mifflin.

Rogers, C.R. (1942). *Counseling and psychotherapy.* Boston: Houghton-Mifflin.

Rogers, C.R. (1951). *Client-centered therapy.* Boston: Houghton-Mifflin.

Rogers, C.R. (1959). A Theory of Therapy, Personality, and Interpersonal Relationships, as Developed in the Client-Centered Framework. In S. Koch (Ed.) *Psychology: A Study of a Science, Vol. III. Formulations of the person and the social context.* (pp. 186-256). New York: McGraw-Hill.

Rogers, C.R. (1961). *On becoming a person.* Boston: Houghton-Mifflin.

Rogers, C.R. (Ed.) (1967). *The therapeutic relationship and its impact: A study of psychotherapy with schizophrenics.* With E.T. Gendlin, D.J. Kisler, and C. Louax. Madison: University of Wisconsin Press.

Rogers, C.R. (1970). *Carl Rogers on encounter groups.* New York: Harper & Row.

Rogers, C.R. (1977). *Carl Rogers on personal power.* New York: Delacorte.

Rogers, C.R. (1983). *Freedom to learn for the 80's.* Columbus: C. Merrill.

Rogers, C.R. & Meador, B.D. (1979). Person-centered therapy. In Corsini, R.J. (Ed.), 2nd Ed. *Current Psychotherapies* (pp. 131-184). Itasca: R.E. Peacock Publishers, Inc.

Rogers, C.R. & Rablin, R.A. (1958). *A scale of process in psychotherapy.* Unpublished manuscript. University of Wisconsin, Madison. (Available from the Center for Studies of the Person, LaJolla, California.)

Rogers, C.R. & Wood, J.K. (1974). Client center therapy: Carl Rogers. In A. Burton (Ed.) *Operational theories of personality* (pp. 211-258). New York: Brunner/Masel.

CHAPTER 6

FRITZ PERLS' GESTALT THERAPY

FOUNDATIONS AND STRUCTURE

Historical Foundations

A LARGE PART of the historical sketch of Gestalt Therapy follows the personal and professional development of one individual, Frederick (Fritz) Perls (1894-1970), its originator, its impetus, and its guide. It would be impossible to integrate into one chapter all of the different approaches which now make up Gestalt Therapy; so, for the purposes of this text, the ideas outlined by Perls will constitute the basis of the presentation. Other perspectives will be offered from time to time in order to more clearly describe selected concepts.

Fritz Perls was born into a middle-class family in Berlin, Germany in 1893. After serving in the German Army during World War I, he completed his medical degree at Frederich Wilhelm University in Berlin in 1921. He trained at the Psychoanalytic Institutes of Berlin, Frankfurt, and Vienna. It was in Frankfurt that he met Lore Posner, whom he later married. When he was in training, his own psychoanalysis was with Karen Horney and Wilhelm Reich (among others), both of whom influenced him greatly and became key figures in the development of his theories.

In 1933 he fled Nazi Germany to Amsterdam with his wife and two-year-old daughter. After a year fraught with frustration Perls and his family moved to South Africa where he was able to establish a practice as a psychiatrist. They stayed there for twelve years, during which time he wrote his first book, *Ego, Hunger and Aggression* (1947). In this text he integrated the principles of Gestalt psychology with personality development and psychotherapy. Perls became more and more concerned about the racist trends in South Africa and moved to the United States in 1946.

In his first years in the United States, Perls practiced as a psychoanalyst in New York, affiliating with the William Alonson White Institute. Difficulties between him and Laura (who had changed her name in the U.S.) led them to separate in 1950. In the subsequent five years, Perls moved to a variety of locations trying to find acceptance for his newly developed Gestalt Therapy. His recent book with the same title (co-authored with Ralph Hefferline and Paul Goodman) was published in 1951 but there seemed to be a slow acceptance of his ideas. From 1950 to 1955 he lived in at least five different cities, conducted workshops wherever he could, and established Gestalt institutes in New York and Cleveland. For the decade between 1955 and 1964 he consulted and established a private practice in Los Angeles. In 1964 Perls moved to the Esalen Institute in Big Sur, California where he truly developed his image and following. It was at this time that Gestalt Therapy was first recognized as a new form of psychotherapy. In 1969 he moved to Vancouver, British Columbia and developed the Gestalt Institute of Canada. In 1970, at the age of 76, when he was in the midst of carrying out professional training seminars, writing two books, and planning new targets for his Gestalt Therapy, he died in Chicago of a heart attack.

Perls did not develop his ideas in a vacuum. He was influenced by many in his own personal and professional development. His psychoanalytic training and practice certainly impacted the manner in which he approached his theory. While he rejected many of the basic tenets of psychoanalysis, he still acknowledged the importance of insight as well as the importance of working with dreams and dream-like states (although what he did with them was quite different from analysts). The importance of spontaneity and human involvement was learned from Karen Horney, his first analyst. From another analyst, Wilhelm Reich, Perls became aware of the importance of attending to the body as a part of the gestalt. Kurt Goldstein introduced Perls to Gestalt psychology, to the writings of Wertheimer and Kohler, particularly sensitizing him to the concept of holism. The influence of Jung brought him a realization of the importance of opposites in life. Laura Perls probably had more influence upon Perls than any other single person. She is often seen as the cofounder of Gestalt Therapy, but her contributions have been somewhat obscured due to their close relationship for 25 years.

Philosophical Foundations

Gestalt Therapy is an existentially-based approach to counseling which accepts the notion that the individual always functions as a part of the environmental field. Perls' thinking became quite interactionist in later years and in *The Gestalt Approach and Eye Witness to Therapy* (1973) he said: "The study of the way the human being functions in his environment is the study of what goes on at the contact boundary between the individual and his environment. It is at this boundary that the psychological events take place" (p. 17). In the Gestalt approach the content of counseling is actually promoting and teaching clients how to attend to the *process* of what occurs at this boundary, thereby helping them become more aware of their experience.

Van De Riet, Korb, and Gorrell (1980) have outlined the major philosophical assumptions associated with Gestalt counseling. The counselor first assumes that everything existing in the world is a process. Despite an object's substance or form, it is made up of atomic particles which are all in a constantly moving and changing process. Far beyond the atomic level, a Gestalt therapist recognizes that all things exist in relation to other things. The process of this relationship defines what that object is and gives it meaning. While many objects appear to be static, this only leads to the conclusion that their relationship with other events or objects may be stable for the time being, subject to change when either they change or their environment changes.

The second assumption made by Gestalt counselors is that existence alone is enough of a reason for an organism to change, adapt, and maintain. This premise is the foundation of existentialism, a basis for much of Gestalt counseling. The concrete nature of the world is known to people only by their perceptions of it. An individual's world view is that person's definition of reality, therefore reality may mean different things to different people, depending upon their frame of reference and experiences.

Since reality is defined by the individual, then the order, meaning, and structure of one's experience flow from that definition. Perls sees us all choosing what we will do and how we will behave in relation to some set of environmental stimuli. Since we have a choice, we also have the responsibility for making that choice an effective one. While there do exist certain world views which are consistently accepted, each person will see things through an experience which is unique, and since this experience is a process, the world view must always be changing.

The fourth aspect of a Gestalt counselor's philosophical foundation is related to the nature of knowledge production and communication. Pure knowledge does not exist in Gestalt Therapy because of the individualized nature of the world view. Perls (1973) indicated that meaning is created by the figure and foreground (perception) posed against the background (reality). Knowledge is present-centered awareness, and it is irreducible as an experience. The person "knows" by accepting stimuli through the senses and creates meaning by filtering these stimuli through inner experiences.

The last point made by Van De Riet, Korb, and Gorrell is that the Gestalt counselor does not accept any inherent "rightness" or "wrongness" in situations. Moral and ethical viewpoints are societal and are individualized by all people through their experience. "Rights" and "wrongs" exist, but only within the context of the environment.

Gestalt counselors accept the premise that all people maintain a unique existence in a reality of their own making, with no "rights" or "wrongs" independent of their and society's view of that reality. In this existence, all that is experienced is a process about which one gains knowledge by a responsible, present-centered awareness. In order to summarize the philosophical framework of this approach, we will list eight assumptions made by Passons (1975) about the Gestalt nature of persons:

- Each person is an interrelated, interdependent whole made up of physical, emotional, cognitive, and perceptual parts.
- People exist as a part of their environment and cannot be understood outside of it.
- People are proactive to internal and external stimuli in their world.
- Each person can be aware of the sensations, perceptions, thoughts, and feelings which make up the whole.
- Through awareness, people can choose behavior in a responsible fashion.
- People can live effectively through their own assets.
- People can only experience the present. The past and future are both experienced in the now.
- People exist in their experience, they are neither basically good nor bad.

Social-Psychological Foundations

Gestalt psychology, initially developed to explain perception through intrapersonal organizational processes and the relationship among elements making up the stimulus, serves as a basis for much of Gestalt

Therapy. While it is beyond the scope of this work to offer an explanation of the complexities of Gestalt theory, the authors will present a short discussion of its basic tenets. Koffka (1935) discussed the major organizational laws in Gestalt theory: proximity, similarity, continuity, common fate, and closure. Proximity refers to the tendency for people to group elements if they are spatially or temporally close to each other. A grouping tendency based upon commonalities in function or in physical make-up is called similarity. The law of continuity indicates that the direction of a set of elements will determine the direction of the next element in the sequence. The law of closure says that incomplete figures will be experienced as wholes and the law of common fate indicates that objects which move or change together are seen as a single unit.

Gestalt theory also accents the importance of figure-ground relationships, or the process of experiencing an object within its environmental context. The ability to sense that object and perceive the meaning attributed to it is directly related to how effectively the figure (object) is differentiated from the ground (environment). In Gestalt psychology, the world is perceived in synthesized wholes so the individual parts, while they do have properties which enable them to be sensed, must be perceived within the context of their environment. These concepts of organization, figure-ground, and holism are central to Gestalt Therapy. In the next pages these concepts and others will be applied to intra- and interpersonal functioning to form the basis for our discussion of the counseling approach.

People are essentially physical organisms who experience basic needs which must be met for survival. When deficiencies exist, the organism acts in a manner designed to restore the balance. Perls (1947) indicated that this principle, which he referred to as *organismic self-regulation,* illustrates the organism's continuous striving for an equilibrium between its needs and their satisfaction. This concept is not limited to purely physical needs. People regulate their actions in order to maintain a comfortable equilibrium in all areas of their lives. In a later work, Perls (1973) referred to this concept as *homeostasis.*

In order to sense their own needs and enact the homeostatic processes, people must be aware of their internal processes, the external environment, and the interaction between the two. This *present-centered awareness* is a focal point of much Gestalt Therapy because Perls believed that each person must be able to gather and synthesize information in order to act in a responsible, authentic manner. Awareness is knowledge of individual needs coupled with the ability to satisfy those needs. The point at which the individual makes contact with the environment is called the *contact boundary.* This is an essential concept to growth in Gestalt Therapy, because it is at this point that the organism expends energy in order to transact with the environment. Without contact, nothing different from the self is encountered, therefore there is no possibility for growth.

According to Perls, Hefferline and Goodman (1951), the personality serves as the ground in the figure-ground relationship of experiencing. While the incoming sensations of a stimulus make up the figure, these sensations are perceived against a background made up of prior living, unfinished business, and the flow of present experience (Polster and Polster, 1973). In other words, each figure is processed through a ground which includes: (1) all of the biological and learned characteristics forming the individual; (2) experiences which have yet to reach closure; and (3) all other processes which are occurring simultaneously in the now.

The process of *symbolization* involves the organism's propensity to transform undifferentiated figures into meaningful patterns. These symbolizations serve the purpose of representing sensory stimuli to the organism in understandable terms. The representations are often developed in the form of *polarities,* opposite views of concepts which exist to establish boundaries of experiencing. Polarities are typically based upon an evaluative model and are portrayed in a dualistic manner such as warm-cold, good-bad, love-hate, important-unimportant, and me-not me. The importance of polarities can be seen as the individual develops a consistent method of relating to the world. Difficulties occur when behavior becomes too predictable and the individual no longer acts in a spontaneous manner.

In identifying specific parts of the person, Perls et al. (1951) noted that the aspect of the organism which makes growth-producing contact with the environment is called the *self.* They described the self as the portion of the person which "is aware and orients, aggresses and manipulates, and feels emotionally the appropriateness of environment and organism . . . It is the organism-as-a-whole in contact with the environment that is aware, manipulates, feels" (p. 373-374). The self is the immediate experience of a situation in which the organism is acting in a spontaneous, present-centered manner.

The *ego,* on the other hand, is the mobilization of actions which are directed at satisfying the organism's needs and wants. The ego integrates the functioning of the whole organism toward the most urgent needs and identifies with the contacts which are seen as necessary to meet them.

Ego functioning may be based upon false assumptions concerning either the organism or the environment, leading to limited awareness and ineffective behaviors. In these cases, the ego identifies with specific parts of the self and disregards or alienates itself from others. Ego boundaries are set up to protect the gestalts which have been developed and identified as parts of the self. While ego boundaries serve the important purpose of maintaining a sense of self and meaning, the state of self-actualization leaves no purpose for the boundaries because homeostasis takes over completely. This is a rather unique occurrence, however, and most people who experience a state of complete organismic self-regulation do not remain in that condition for long.

The Development of the Person

Gestalt counselors define the developmental process in terms of the person-environment interaction as they do with all aspects of human existence. From the beginning of life people interact with the environment in order to meet their needs. When a need arises the contact is made and satisfaction is reached through a process of assimilation. The resulting state of balance lasts only a short while as another need soon is experienced and the process begins anew. Perls (1969) said, "Life is practically nothing but an infinite number of unfinished situations — incomplete gestalts. No sooner have we finished one situation than another develops" (p. 15).

The contacts that people learn to make become gestalts, holistic processes which are developed to meet individual needs. If the organismic needs are met and the gestalts are flexible enough to adapt to changing needs and a changing environment, then growth occurs. If however, the gestalts which are formed do not meet the needs of the individual and are rigid and inflexible, then an unclear figure-ground relationship is formed leading to growth problems. The portion of the person that initiates and develops adaptive contacts with the environment is called the self. Perls et al. (1951) called the self "the contact-boundary at work; its activity is forming figures and grounds" (p. 235). The self, therefore, is not only responsible for the adjustments, it *is* the point of interaction between the organism and the environment.

Perls placed maturation at the center of his concept of development, referring to it as "the transcendence from environmental support to self-support" (1969, p. 28). Even though mature people accept the responsibility for their own support, complete self-sufficiency is not the goal of maturation, because the process occurs within the social system and involves other people. Mature people are responsible for their own actions, needs, and expectations and not those of others. In discussing responsibility, Perls (1969) said, "I am not in this world to live up to other people's expectations, nor do I feel that the world must live up to mine" (p. 30). Mature people also accept their unique potential (an acceptance of who and what one is) and portray themselves to the world in a congruent, authentic manner.

During the development process each individual is faced with the task of leaving familiar stages of growth and moving on to new, untried territory. Each new experience mobilizes different parts of the self, thereby actualizing those elements which had previously been out of awareness. When the change is too great, too fast, or too unorganized, the organism feels anxiety, an emotional reaction the the incomplete gestalt encountered in the experience. While anxiety is often at the root of problems, it is a very commonly occurring aspect of the developmental process for everyone. It is "the gap between the now and the later. Whenever you leave the sure basis of the now and become preoccupied with the future, you experience anxiety" (Perls, 1969, p. 30).

Individual development is seen as a continuous process which does not flow through distinct, ordered stages. A person continually assimilates experiences and new aspects of the self are discovered throughout the growth process. Gestalts which are found to be no longer functional are replaced in order to maintain growth and meet individual needs.

Concepts of Functional and Dysfunctional Behavior

An effectively functioning individual is characterized by present-centered, holistic behavior which is directed at satisfying needs identified through an active awareness of both internal and external processes. Functional behavior is the ability to form new gestalts and replace old ones when the organism must adapt to new need structures or new environmental pressures. People learn to accept and depend upon themselves, what they *are* without significant influence from the past or projections into the future. While anxiety does occur as a result of the developmental process when contact is made with unfamiliar environmental stimuli, this is natural and the functional person will adapt alone or with the assistance of others. Functionality is based upon a person's willingness and ability to be responsible for his actions within the social context.

Sources of Psychological Discomfort

Problems occur when the person-environment interaction somehow becomes out-of-balance, blocking the "I" from naturally functioning in a homeostatic manner. One of the main sources of psychological discomfort for most people is *unfinished business,* or incomplete gestalts which require significant amounts of energy to maintain. The natural need of the organism is to complete gestalts, and when a situation arises where the person avoids closure, then the energy which should be allotted to other life tasks is taken up by this experience. The anxiety caused by this situation becomes chronic, possibly reaching a point where the specific cause of the tension has become buried. Whether the organism is aware of the unfinished business or not, these unresolved situations keep influencing the ability of the organism to function effectively in its environment.

A second type of problem formation occurs when a person experiences the results of disturbances in the ego boundary, that portion of the self which identifies with gestalts leading to the satisfaction of needs and alienates away from those that do not. Perls et al. (1951) identified four mechanisms which block awareness and lead to psychological distress and impeded growth. The first of these, called *introjection,* is defined by Perls (1947) as "preserving the structure of things taken in, whilst the organism requires their destruction" (p. 129). Ideally, the result of the person-environment interaction is a discriminating selection of those environmental stimuli which can help promote growth. In some cases the organism accepts ideas, attitudes, and other data from the environment without thoroughly discriminating between those bits and pieces that are needed from those that are not. When a person introjects, that individual extends the boundary of what is "I" to the point where it may cause a loss of identity and the tendency to accept responsibility for actions outside of the self. *Projection* is related to the positioning of ego boundaries as well but, in this case, they are pulled in a little too much toward the person, thereby eliminating those portions of the individual which are in conflict with introjected thoughts, attitudes, and values. This results in the person seeing the environment as responsible for actions which originate internally. When no boundaries exist at all (both parts and whole and figure and ground are indistinguishable from one another) the individual is said to be in a state of *confluence.* While this is a natural state for newborn infants and is common when people reach states of extreme concentration or ecstasy, it is pathological if experienced as a chronic condition by adults. Individuals are unable to distinguish themselves from others and the world around them so actions are without meaning. The last boundary disturbance is called *retroflection,* defined by Perls (1947) as "some function which originally is directed from the individual toward the world, changes its direction and is bent back toward the originator" (p. 119-120). People who retroflect treat themselves as they want to treat others. Energy is directed inward as a substitute for the environment, leading to a split in the person's awareness and experience of both the self and the environment.

A neurotic's defenses are characterized by extreme forms of introjection, projection, confluence, and retroflection. The confusion between the self and the environment is central to each of these mechanisms. Perls (1969) discussed five layers of neurosis, each delineating a process of person-environment interaction. The first, or *cliché layer,* includes the superficial, token behaviors dictated by societal or cultural proprieties. Under this layer one finds the *role-playing layer* where the individual follows those expectations of a given role and hides the real self. This layer is synthetic in nature yet very real to the individual. It is in the role-playing layer that one finds the top-dog/under-dog conflict, the internal battle between the righteous, domineering top-dog which tries to control through intimidation and threat and the insecure under-dog which makes its control attempt by placating and procrastinating. If this layer is removed, if the familiar roles are taken away, the *impasse layer* is reached. An impasse can be described as a feeling of being stuck or lost in nothingness. The reference points supplied by the roles have been taken away and the organism only has itself to depend upon. The *implosive/explosive* layer is next, where the organism feels the "fear of feeling" and goes beyond it by accepting it. Once this fear is accepted, the organism explodes into joy, orgasm, grief, or anger. Getting beyond the implosive/explosive layer enables the person to transcend learned responses to the world and experience the *authentic self,* the inner core.

Psychological distress is ultimately related to the organism's awareness of internal and external processes. This difficulty may be the result of selective attention or inattention, ineffective ego boundaries, misrepresented figures, or poor environmental contacts. The severity of the problem is dependent upon the degree to which the organism is aware of itself and its surroundings. In the next section, the authors will present a discussion of the process Gestalt counselors use to change these problem areas.

Concepts of Behavior Change

As has already been discussed in the section on developmental process, change is a natural phenomenon from a Gestalt counseling perspective. Without change in reaction to interactions with the environment, there would be no growth. When a person faces a new situation or one which causes anxiety, certain adaptations must be made based upon a functional assessment of the need and the identification and utilization of available environmental resources. For some, this is a normal task but for others it may be seen as an insurmountable problem which will impede their actions in other areas as well. In the latter cases, a change either within the person or in the environment is necessary to initiate or restore effective functioning. The process of change involves helping the individual focus on the self and allow the change to occur without all of the resistance developed by expectations and worry.

The actual process of change in Gestalt counseling is paradoxical in nature (Beisser, 1970). The presenting problem is not the focus of intervention. Rather, the counselor tries to identify what underlying processes are maintaining the psychological distress relative to the situation. The problem, then, is not the situation, it is the reaction to the situation by the individual. This reaction is an incomplete gestalt and becomes the focus of counseling. The counselor does not encourage the client to talk *about* the problem. The focus is on experiencing whatever is necessary to facilitate the closure of the gestalt. The counselor facilitates the client's opportunity to experience *what he is, here and now*. This awareness is essential for change to occur. As Perls (1969) said, "With full awareness you become aware of this organismic self-regulation, you can let the organism take over without interfering, without interrupting; we can rely on the wisdom of the organism . . ." (p. 16-17).

Therapeutic change, then, is a process which allows the individual to encounter incomplete gestalts in a safe environment and allow the organism's natural adaptation ability to perform. Perls had a considerable amount of faith in the organism and felt that change would occur if the person could be put in touch with "the obvious."

Assessment of Human Functioning

Traditional diagnosis does not play a strong role in Gestalt counseling, because most standard diagnostic techniques are not based upon the here-and-now. Since this counseling approach is experiential, any assessment that is done is performed as a part of the present-centered process of promoting contacts between the person and the environment. Fagan (1970) says that the counselor is first and foremost a "receiver and constructor of patterns." She refers to the "assessment" process in Gestalt counseling as *patterning*. This involves the identification and creation of a picture which reflects an integration of the person's present functioning. The picture which is developed does not reflect a medical model which is designed to reach a certain label and develop treatment strategies based on that label. Rather, the assessment is designed to identify the unique patterns which are leading *this person* to difficulty. It is the counselor's role to recognize and point out repeated patterns to the client. The more aware the counselor is of the interrelationships of cognitive, perceptual, physical, and emotional processes making up the individual, the more effective the counseling relationship will be as a learning experience for the client.

The assessment process is continuous, as the counselor is constantly evaluating the reactions of the client to the developmental steps taken in the sessions. A monitoring of splits in attention and awareness is maintained throughout the relationship. As difficulties are observed and the crux of the problems is identified, then techniques will be chosen which reflect the background of the counselor and the relationship existing between the counselor and client. Therefore, as opposed to gaining large amounts of information through formal history-taking or psychometric measurement, the Gestalt counselor gains information from the present-centered process of interacting with the client. The point of intersection, the contact-boundary, is the portion of the individual that is observed, making internal elements important only in the client's reaction to them in the present.

Goals and Directions of Counseling

The major goal of Gestalt counselors reflects their view of the maturational process. The counselor sets the stage whereby clients can assume responsibility for themselves, rather than acting in the world based upon a set of external expectations. The shift from environmental support to self-support is essential to maintain the possibility for individual growth. This process is achieved by helping the person to integrate the cognitive, perceptual, physical, and emotional process into a total organismic existence in the world. The integration is facilitated by enlarging the awareness of internal and external events so that natural functioning can take over.

Perls (1969) said, "Now there is no such thing as total integration. Integration is never completed; maturation is never completed. It's an ongoing process for ever and ever . . . There's always something to be integrated; always something to be learned" (p. 64). The awareness of this concept and the ability to endure unwanted, bothersome emotions is a minor goal in Gestalt Therapy. Perfection does not exist in human existence so the fully-functioning individual must be able to deal with the problems which develop from typical life events.

Integration, awareness, and acceptance of who one *is* rather than who one would like to be are the three components to the goal of healthy growth in Gestalt Therapy. Since the setting is in the natural environment and all interactions are performed in the *now,* clients get the opportunity to work on their development, learn about themselves, and try out new behaviors all in the "real world." The process of reaching this goal is not a simple task; it requires considerable energy to focus and approach areas which often have considerable anxiety associated with them. The next section presents a discussion of the process of counseling and the role played by the counselor in this process.

The Counseling Process: Structuring, Facilitating and Terminating

It is a difficult task to describe the process of Gestalt counseling because the basis of gestalt counseling is process. Perls (1969) states that the "two legs upon which Gestalt Therapy walks [are] "now and how" (p. 44). A present-centered awareness of the process of interacting with the environment is the focus of therapy. The client is forced to face *how* his problems are enacted in the *now.*

Steps in Gestalt Therapy

Van De Riet, Korb, and Gorrell (1980) delineate specific steps in the Gestalt Therapy process. The first task of the counselor is to set the stage so that the client can *express inner experiences* to be objectively observed by both the client and the counselor. The counselor's role is to point out observations which may have some importance to be validated by the client. These authors indicate that therapeutic intervention can take place only when the inner experiences have become overt expressions.

The second step in the counseling process is called *differentiation.* The assumption is made that overt problems indicate internal conflict which can only be resolved when the opposing forces involved are separated.

The self has become fragmented and intervention is necessary to help the client recognize these previously disowned portions of the self. The interventions, referred to by Perls et al. (1951) as "experiments," are created by counselors out of their own experience, awareness, and learning. Perls (1973), in describing this portion of the therapeutic process, said, "In therapy, then we have to reestablish the neurotic's capacity to discriminate. We have to help him discover what is himself and what is not himself; what fulfills him and what thwarts him. We have to guide him towards integration" (p. 43).

Affirmation, the third stage of Gestalt counseling, involves the recognition and acceptance of the parts of the self discovered during the differentiation stage. It is not a positive acceptance of these phenomena; the client is encouraged to simply acknowledge those parts which have heretofore been hidden. This affirmation is done regardless of the inconsistency of elements, thoughts, feelings, and beliefs. It is an acceptance of what *is*, not what *should be*. Along with the recognition of these elements, comes the realization that only "I" am responsible for my behaviors and my reactions to them.

When personal awareness has been mobilized and previously unknown elements have been affirmed, the client is free to choose those behaviors which "fit" the situation as opposed to continuing dysfunctional styles. When the conflicting energies are differentiated and affirmed a calmness occurs which serves as the signal of a completed gestalt. Counseling is over when the client has reached this state of self-satisfaction and has the ability to accept even those things in life which do not progress in a comfortable manner. While problems may still exist (as they do for everyone), these problems do not seem to devastate the individual and can be approached in a manner free from dysfunctional ties to the past or future.

Therapist's Role

The counselor is a highly active, process-oriented, person who is a suggestor rather than a director. By this it is meant that rather than an expert model of intervention, an experiential model is used where the counselor is involved with the client in a very human relationship. In this relationship, the counselor suggests ways that the client can expand awareness. It is imperative that the counselor be very aware of his/her own internal processes and in touch with the client-counselor contact boundary. Various roles for gestalt counselors have been presented in the literature. Fagan (1970) wrote that the counselor's major tasks are patterning, control, potency, humanness, and commitment. Others include such roles as working through an impasse with the client (helping the client concentrate on *how* he/she is stuck), providing "safe emergencies" so that the client can learn how to face and deal with frustrating events, and helping the client become aware of the obvious (the overt experiences which are out of the client's awareness.)

To some degree the process of Gestalt counseling has a direction leading to some generalized goals. That direction is individualized, however as are the specific techniques used in the encounter. To some, the process may appear as an "anything goes" experience but, in actuality, the interventions are developed in reaction to the processes encountered among clients. More discussion of specific techniques used in a Gestalt approach will be presented in the following section.

Counseling Techniques and Procedures

An attempt at identifying all of the possible techniques used in a Gestalt approach would be an impossible task. This is due to the individualized, creative nature of the interventions, chosen and developed for *this* client, in *this* environment, by *this* counselor. The techniques in Gestalt counseling can be differentiated into two groups: those related to increasing the client's awareness of personal experiences and those related to the development of self-support through responsible behavioral choices. The counselor concentrates on the "I" and tries to promote both awareness and responsibility with techniques involving every possible part and/or function of experiencing.

Most of Gestalt counseling takes place in groups, either in a formal therapy-type group or in a more informal workshop style, characteristic of the way Perls himself worked. The group approach still reinforces the encounter as being between the counselor and client directly, but the remaining members become a sounding board, sometimes in the background and sometimes as a very necessary portion of the foreground. One very important benefit of group counseling is vicarious learning. Many clients who are not actively involved in the present encounter learn from their own experience in reaction to someone else.

Rules and Games

Levitsky and Perls (1970) presented a discussion of the "rules and games" of Gestalt counseling. They referred to the rules as ways they have found to be effective in "unifying thought with feeling." The rules include a constant concentration on the "now," concrete acknowledgement of the sender and receiver in communication, an acceptance of "I" language, concentrating on present experiences in awareness, and the use of genuine rather than hypocritical questions (which can most often be reworded into statements.) The games which were noted by these authors include the following:

Games of Dialogue. Clients are asked to create a dialogue between two parts of themselves which are in conflict. The top-dog is asked to talk with the under-dog, the "good guy" is asked to talk with the troublemaker, the male is asked to talk with the female, etc. The purpose of this exercise is to help the client experience the different elements which exist internally, acknowledge their existence, and integrate them into awareness. Some call this technique "the empty chair" which is also used to help the client try out new behaviors in a safe environment.

Making the Rounds. The client is asked to express a thought or feeling toward each of the other group members in order to learn how to express inner experiences in a more articulate fashion. The client may be asked to express these experiences through voice, touch, or any other communication style.

I Take Responsibility. The client is asked to follow each statement with a phrase denoting personal responsibility. This is intended to make clients aware of the impact of their statements and behaviors and help them to accept personal responsibility for them.

I Have a Secret. The client is asked to think of a shameful or embarrassing secret and imagine how others would react. This exercise makes the client aware of feelings of guilt and importance attached to the internal experience of the secret.

Playing the Projection. The client is told to play the feeling that person has projected onto others. This leads to the awareness that the feelings may be a part of the self that the client has been disowning.

Reversals. In Gestalt counseling, overt behavior is often seen as the opposite of inner impulses. In order to make the clients aware of both poles of the behavior, they are asked to play the reverse and experience it.

The Rhythm of Contact and Withdrawal. A Gestalt counselor recognizes the importance of polarities in individual functioning. In order to restore energy a period of rest is needed. A natural need is to withdraw from the contact of the group from time to time. The client is asked to fantasize about a very comfortable experience and to share the feelings related to it. Soon, the counselor asks the client to come back to the group and join in again.

Rehearsal. Much of our behavior is rehearsed in our own inner experience. In order to promote the clients' awareness of the type and degree of this rehearsal, the counselor asks them to share with the group their internal practice.

Exaggeration. When a person's movements, verbalizations, or other behaviors are seen as important yet outside of the client's awareness, the counselor will ask that individual to repeat it, exaggerate it, or emphasize it in another way in order to accent its meaning.

May I Lend You a Sentence? When counselors conclude that a particular message is implied by something that clients either say or do, they can offer the client a sentence to try out. Clients, as active participants, explore their feelings toward the experience of saying the sentence and possibly become aware of previously unidentified feelings or thoughts.

Other techniques used in Gestalt counseling include working with dreams, where the counselor structures an experience for the client to act out roles and objects in the dream in the present and deal with unfinished situations; working with fantasy which, in a similar manner to working with dreams, is designed to facilitate the encounter between what is and what the client thinks "will be"; and here-and-now awareness exercises designed to assist the client in becoming more aware of feelings, cognitions, perceptions, and sensations.

All of these techniques are used by gestalt counselors with each professional's own imprint on the specific content and process of the intervention. Levitsky and Perls (1970) noted the vast range of possible techniques when they said: "True to its heritage in Gestalt psychology, the essence of Gestalt Therapy is in the perspective with which it views human life processes. Seen in this light, any particular set of techniques such as our presently used rules and games will be regarded merely as convenient means—useful tools for our purposes but without sacrosanct qualities" (p. 140).

Evaluation of Counseling Outcomes

The purpose of Gestalt counseling is to promote client's ability to solve their own problems, rather than deal directly with those problems in the sessions. At the end of the counseling process, clients will hopefully be in the position of either being able to solve current problems and minimize future problems without assistance or realize when outside help is necessary and feel comfortable seeking it. As mentioned previously, the specific goals of counseling are maturation, awareness, acceptance, and integration. While these are certainly appropriate processes to strive for, they do not lend themselves to efficient evaluation.

The evaluation of Gestalt counseling can follow along with the stages as outlined by Van De Riet, Korb, and Gorrell (1980). In the expression stage, clients become aware of their present experiences and share them with the counselor and any other members of the group. Once the feelings are allowed to surface, the counselor encourages each client to differentiate those feelings through experimentation. In this phase the counselor is observing the ability of clients to clarify, express, and separate the parts of the self which emerge. Once the differentiation has occurred, the counselor sets the stage for clients to experience the differentiation, eventually coming to the realization that these feelings are all a part of the same inner experience. Clients thus affirm the experience and are ready to make effective behavioral choices based upon the awareness of the various internal elements. With continued practice of the new behaviors coupled with the awareness of their effect upon the environment, the person integrates these previously undiscovered internal elements into the self. Throughout the stages of counseling the counselor attends to the behaviors of the client in an on-going evaluation process. Since there are no specific outcome goals involved in this style, the evaluation process is continuous as the counselor remains aware of both his or her own internal processes as well as the counselor-client contact-boundary. This dual awareness is the dialectic of counseling, attending to the self, the client, and the interaction all within the Gestalt theoretical framework.

One critique of Gestalt counseling which relates to outcome evaluation is the possibility that a person who has learned to be much more self-supportive and in touch with inner experiences will tend to lose interest and excitement toward life due to the way much of society operates (Shepherd, 1970). The pretentiousness and destructiveness of society at large may be quite unappealing to these people, causing them to be somewhat unadjusted to work effectively within this context. In these cases, the very things we look for among "successful" clients, self-sufficiency and inner-directedness, may be liabilities if taken to the extreme. While this critique may hold some validity, it is doubtful that individuals will experience Gestalt counseling in a vacuum, and people who are truly functioning well will be able to adapt to the environment even more effectively with their new levels of awareness.

COUNSELING APPLICATION

In this section the authors will present an illustrative case showing Gestalt counseling in practice. The case was chosen because the issues are largely developmental in nature and are therefore quite appropriate for a Gestalt intervention. The authors will offer comments after the case presentation in order to describe the process and accent the experiences of both the client and counselor.

Gestalt Counseling in a Mental Health Setting

Carla is seeking counseling services at a community mental health center due to increasing depression and feelings of disinterest in life events. She has been a high achiever all of her life and has earned a rather influential position in a medium-sized corporation as well as the respect of friends and coworkers. At this point, she is confused and worried about the depression because, as far as she is concerned, all should be going well. The counselor is seeing her on an individual basis for this, the first session.

Carla: Well, maybe I should tell you why I am here.

Counselor: I'd like you to stop for a minute and settle in. Feel yourself and this place and then begin when you feel ready.

Carla: (Pauses for a while, looks at the counselor, takes a deep breath) For the past few months I have been really down. Things that were enjoyable in the past, like my job and my family, are just not interesting to me now. Something has to change or I don't think I can take it any longer. (Begins to cry softly)

Counselor: Allow those feelings to come.

Carla: (Holds back tears) I don't do this very often . . . cry, I mean. I don't know what's coming over me. (Begins to cry again)

Counselor: Yes, allow yourself to feel. (Seeing blocked feelings in the client)

Carla: (Loudly) I get so upset with myself! This makes me so damn mad! Here I am, bright, successful, talented and it just isn't enough!

Counselor: It isn't enough for whom?

Carla: I don't know. I guess for me.

Counselor: So you have the notion that whatever you do it is never enough.

Carla: I guess I'm just a perfectionist.

Counselor: And you feel frustrated by that idea that you have in your head.

Carla: Yes! I just can't get rid of it.

Counselor: Say that again, Carla.

Carla: I can't get rid of it.

Counselor: Say it again, but this time change the "can't" to "won't."

Carla: (Slowly) I won't get rid of it.

Counselor: How do you feel about your statement?

Carla:	It makes me frustrated.
Counselor:	Why don't you say, "I am frustrated."
Carla:	I am frustrated by my perfectionism. I really am. I know that I can control it if I really want to but for some reason I just don't.
Counselor:	What blocks you from doing this, Carla?
Carla:	I guess I tell myself that I need to accomplish everything even though sometimes I forget my family and other important things. That's so frustrating!
Counselor:	It sounds like one side of you is working and achieving, but there's another part that would like to slow down a little.
Carla:	It does sound like that, doesn't it.
Counselor:	Let's do something with this. Can you become this quieter side?
Carla:	What do you mean?
Counselor:	I'd like you to carry on a conversation between your high achieving side and your quieter side. Let them meet each other.
Carla:	I'm not sure how to start.
Counselor:	One side of you would like to slow down a little, right?
Carla:	Right.
Counselor:	Well, start with that side telling the other how she feels.
Carla-1:	O.K. You know, I'm getting real tired of the way you are always pushing, pushing, pushing. Sometimes it's as if you're a machine. You just don't know when to stop.
Counselor:	Now respond back to this side with the other.
Carla-2:	Well, I may be pushing hard, but if I didn't you'd hold me back and I'd never get anywhere. If you had your way, I'd still be back in my first job plodding along.
Carla-1:	That sounds pretty good to me. At least I could take time to enjoy things then.
Carla-2:	You sound just like Dad, always taking the easy route.
Carla-1:	Maybe you could have learned something from him, he was certainly happy during his life. He knew when to slow down.
Carla-2:	But it's different for me. I can't . . . *won't* be like him.
Counselor:	Carla, I'd like you to switch now and talk to your father here in this chair. (Points to an empty chair)
Carla:	Dad, I don't want to be like you were but I'm not happy like this. I don't know how to stop.
Counselor:	(Pointing to the chair) Now go over and be your father.
Carla/Father:	What do you want to stop, Carla?
Carla:	I just want to be happy. I want to get out of this rat race, that's all.
Carla/Father:	Come now Carla, you know what you have to do to stop.
Carla:	No I don't! You always said that! I could never please you!
Counselor:	(As father) So you decided to be more successful than I was. So I would be impressed and love you.
Carla:	(Sobbing) Yes! Yes! But it didn't work! You died before I could ever show you what I could do! I never got a chance to make you proud of me.
Counselor:	I'd like you to be still for a moment, Carla. Let yourself experience what has just happened.

Carla:	(Still crying softly, sitting quietly for a few moments) I never really thought about that before. I've been trying to please my father all along but I never really had to.
Counselor:	How do you feel right now?
Carla:	Very light. Like a weight has been lifted off from me. I feel good, like I can afford to relax a little.

In this session the counselor first reinforced the client's expression of feelings in the safe environment. When she had successfully begun to experience her feelings in the now the counselor tried to help her become more aware of these feelings as they represented different aspects of her inner experience. The counselor encouraged her to personalize her statements, question her beliefs, and own her feelings. The game of dialogue was used to help Carla become in touch with the internal conflict between the side of herself that promoted achievement and the part that was tired of her efforts. This experiment uncovered the unfinished business between Carla and her father, which was approached in this session through talking to her father. The counselor interjected into the conversation as the father to offer an observation. While closure was reached for this exchange, more work will be done on attaining closure in Carla's relationship with her father. The process has started, however, and the counselor will continue to help Carla become more aware of her inner experiences and move toward self-sufficiency.

This example was presented to show the reader Gestalt counseling in action. Regardless of the number of transcripts read or the number of films observed, counselors in training cannot truly grasp the process of Gestalt counseling unless they themselves are involved in the process. Gestalt is the most experiential of all counseling styles and observation, while beneficial on a cognitive basis, does not allow other aspects of the person to experience the full process.

Critical Comments

Gestalt counseling has been developed from a rather broad base of existential, phenomenological, behavioral, psychoanalytic, and systems perspectives. It is a very difficult form of counseling theory to describe simply because of its individualized nature. Not only is the intervention process individualized to adapt to specific clients (as is true with most forms of counseling) but counselors also must integrate and practice the Gestalt approach in their own individualized style. Therefore, a discussion of the actual process of Gestalt counseling would be a discussion of how *this counselor* works with *this client* in *this situation*. Much of the ambiguity many practitioners have faced as they have tried to learn about Gestalt counseling may have resulted from this predicament.

From a Gestalt point of view, people develop problems because they have lost contact with their inner self, the "I" which has the capacity to self-regulate and adapt to both environmental changes and changes in need structures. What has happened in these cases is the formation of barriers which impede normal growth and development. The purpose of counseling is to remove these barriers and assist clients in becoming more aware of their own ability to make accommodations to the environment in order to be both aware of and satisfy previously unmet needs.

Shepherd (1970), a Gestalt counselor herself, notes certain limitations of the approach. She says that the skills, training, and experience needed to effectively function as a Gestalt counselor are significant. This approach is not a "technique-oriented" style of counseling. Indeed, the counselor's personal attributes are constantly tested. The job of maintaining a present-centeredness while attending to the theoretical ramifications of actions, feelings, thoughts, and perceptions can be a monumental task. In contrast with other schools of thought, there are no prescribed background requirements in Gestalt training programs. The major institutes certainly attend to the quality of the training experience, but many people have enrolled in a "Gestalt weekend" and later called themselves "Gestaltists."

Another criticism offered by Shepherd cites evidence which indicates that a Gestalt approach is most effective with a person who is restrained, constricted, inhibited and looks toward society for support rather than focusing inward. More severely disturbed people (including those with impulse control problems such as sociopaths) are usually not helped by this approach as they often incorporate many of the experiences into presently existing roles of behavior.

The activity level of the counselor is another area that Shepherd notes as a possible difficulty. Depending upon the counselor's level of training and experience, the use of techniques may be well spaced and appropriately timed or, in other cases, they may be excessive leading to increased dependence upon the "system" rather than the goal of self-sufficiency. Even for experienced counselors, a major task is to constantly be aware of both the individual and group dynamics so people who tend to be dependent will not be reinforced for this behavior.

Other criticisms of Gestalt counseling include its unclear procedure, the general lack of a research base, the overemphasis on the here and now, and its general reliance on a group modality. While these may be valid when one looks at Gestalt therapy as developed and practiced by Perls, it may not be as valid today. Recently, there has been more acceptance of Gestalt techniques which are used within a variety of eclectic frameworks. Fewer people are practicing a specific type of counseling, preferring to borrow from a variety of approaches in order to integrate what will work best in their setting with their clients. Gestalt approaches are widely used to accent the awareness of the here and now and assist in integrating different parts of the self. It is quite common to see new counseling students learning and practicing Gestalt techniques in a pre-practicum laboratory class. These may be very effective if the counselor learns to use them as a part of an integrated approach rather than as simply some bits and pieces in a counselor's "bag of tricks."

Perls felt that his approach was ultimately practical. Gestalt counseling was not designed to help people change reality, it was designed so individuals can become more aware of the existing reality. Its purpose was to help the organism do what it does best, gain internal and external feedback and self-regulate. He said, ". . . all I can do is possibly to help people to recognize themselves, to function better, to enjoy life more, to feel — and this is very important — to feel more real. What more do you want? Life is not violins and roses" (1970, p. 33).

REFERENCES

Beisser, A.R. (1970). The paradoxical theory of change. In J. Fagan & I.L. Shepherd (Eds.), *Gestalt therapy now* (pp. 77-80). Palo Alto, CA: Science and Behavior Books.

Fagan, J. (1970). The tasks of the therapist. In J. Fagan & I.L. Shepherd (Eds.), *Gestalt therapy now* (pp. 88-106). Palo Alto, CA: Science and Behavior Books.

Koffka, K. (1935). *Principles of gestalt psychology.* New York: Harcourt, Brace and World.

Levitsky, A., & Perls, F. (1970). The rules and games of gestalt therapy. In J. Fagan & I.L. Shepherd (Eds.), *Gestalt therapy now* (pp. 140-149). Palo Alto, CA: Science and Behavior Books.

Passons, W.R. (1975). *Gestalt approaches in counseling.* New York: Holt, Rinehart, and Winston.

Perls, F. (1947). *Ego, hunger and aggression.* London: Allen and Unwin.

Perls, F., Hefferline, R.F., & Goodman, P. (1951). *Gestalt therapy.* New York: Julian Press.

Perls, F.S. (1969). *Gestalt therapy verbatim.* Moab, Utah: Real People Press.

Perls, F. (1973). *The gestalt approach and eye witness to therapy.* Palo Alto, CA: Science and Behavior Books.

Polster, E., & Polster, M. (1973). *Gestalt therapy integrated.* New York: Brunner/Mazel.

Shepherd, I.L. (1970). Limitations and cautions in the gestalt approach. In J. Fagan & I.L. Shepherd (Eds.), *Gestalt therapy now* (pp. 234-238). Palo Alto, CA: Science and Behavior Books.
Van De Riet, V., Korb, M.P., & Gorrell, J.J. (1980). *Gestalt therapy: An introduction.* New York: Pergamon Press.

CHAPTER 7

VIKTOR FRANKL'S LOGOTHERAPY

FOUNDATIONS AND STRUCTURE

Historical Foundations

VIKTOR E. FRANKL was educated at the University of Vienna, where he received his M.D. degree in 1930 and a Ph.D. in 1949. From 1930 to 1938, Frankl was associated with the Neuropsychiatric Clinic at the University and specialized in neurology and psychiatry. In 1946 he was appointed chair of the Department of Neurology at the Poliklinik hospital in Vienna. One year later, Frankl was appointed Assistant Professor of Psychiatry and Neurology at the University of Vienna and in 1955 became University Professor. Frankl's academic interests ultimately shifted to existential philosophy and its implications for the teaching and practice of psychology.

Frankl did demonstrate a precocious interest in psychoanalytic theory and existential philosophy throughout his early years. In 1921, at the age of 16, he reported experiencing a spiritual experience while reading Freud's *Beyond the Pleasure Principle*. Three years later, at age 19, his first article was published at Freud's personal invitation in the *International Journal of Psychoanalysis*. Frankl became part of the Freudian "inner circle" with Alfred Adler, Otto Rank, Carl Jung, and others. He became quite disenchanted with the narrowness of the present day psychiatric orientation to human issues and found more meaning in the philosophical writings of Heidegger, Jaspers, and Husserl.

Frankl devised the idea for the Youth Advisement Centers in Vienna for distressed youth. It was here that he developed the fundamentals of logotherapy. At the center, he observed hopelessness, confusion, and depression in young adults. While working with adolescent patients, Frankl concluded that existential suffering pervaded all age groups, cultures, and societies. Given the significant social unrest in Europe and worldwide depression, Frankl saw the prevalence of rootlessness and subsequent despair among the youth of Europe between the two world wars. He further realized the limitations of the psychiatric-medical model and psychoanalysis to deal with such concerns. It was from his patients that he gained clinical insight into the existential conditions of human existence.

Frankl found through the psychotherapeutic process and through personal experience that a sense of purpose and meaning was the main concern of people — not money or external rewards. Some people saw no meaning anywhere in their lives, leaving them with an emptiness that was unbearable. This existential suffering often resulted in feelings of despair.

The term *Logotherapy*, from the Greek *Logos* (meaning), first appeared in Frankl's writings in 1938. Frankl has developed an entire counseling approach based on the core assumption that meaning in daily living is the crux of existence. Frankl (1973) believes that when people find meaning in their life conditions and circumstances they are spiritually active. The spiritual aspect of people refers to the energy, direction, and commitment for living. This is not a theological inclination of people but a cognitive understanding and feeling for life.

By 1942, the members of a "third Viennese school" (the others being the Freudians and the Adlerians) were exploring the individual's search for, or lack of, meaning. However, Frankl and his family were swept into the Nazi wave of terrorism and war. Frankl himself experienced the degradation of the human spirit and personality in the Nazi concentration camps.

Frankl's personal experience in the concentration camp led him to conclude that, even under the most extreme environmental conditions, people can choose to direct their lives. For example, people can have meaning and spirituality in their lives when they are confronted with painful experiences or significant social pressures. Suffering severe and significant hardship may increase spirituality and meaning.

Frankl lost members of his immediate and extended family to the gas chambers. These experiences reinforced Frankl's notions of existential theory and philosophy. Frankl was impressed by people's will to meaning and a desire to maintain their spirituality in order to transcend physical and emotional trauma. The existential philosophical foundation of

Frankl's theory is seen in his theory of human functioning and his concepts of behavior change.

Philosophical Foundations

Logotherapy is based on existential philosophy. Existentialism centers upon the subjective aspects of being human. Abstract explanations of behavior are idealistic and philosophical terms are not as important as what one does and what one experiences in the moment.

Logotherapy and existentialism share the notion of the singular uniqueness of each individual. Each person is ultimately responsible for determining life values, directions, and behaviors. Frankl stresses a spiritual commitment to life, goals and tasks. What people give to life and how they meet the tasks and challenges of life determine meaning.

Frankl (1973) holds that having a sense of personal meaning is inherently human. Each person views life quite unlike any other and acknowledges a responsibility to create their own identity or essence. Self-observation and reflection are vitally important to personal understanding and the creation of meaning. The "will to meaning," the existential strength of the human spirit, enables one to understand the human condition and draw from the experiential resources to meet life tasks.

Societal and cultural forces may inhibit or repress the will to meaning. People may feel unchallenged, purposeless, and unfulfilled, resulting in emptiness and a poor sense of identity. Frankl (1959 & 1967) describes this emptiness as the *existential vacuum*. The difficulty in assigning meaning or determining the purpose of life is existential frustration. Excessive conformity to rules and social rituals reflects attempts to cope with existential frustration. Meaningless activities serve the temporary purpose of filling the existential vacuum and may ritualistically structure the emptiness of life.

Frankl (1963) believes that people who search for an abstract meaning to life will be frustrated and unrewarded. He suggests that people derive meaning from life through personal values and experience. There are three types of values: creative, experiential and attitudinal. *Creative values* facilitate problem solving and intellectual processes that contribute to task achievement. The fact that people are committed to tasks, goals and existence is the *experiential value*. The third value is *attitudinal* and is responsible for how people confront their existence. The range of a person's attitudes towards existence may extend from simple conformity to social norms all the way to an active confrontation for their existence.

Because of the contemporary human condition, individuals may experience confusion over their values, directions, and goals. Questions about personal freedom and responsibility may arise. Freedom is experienced, according to Frankl (1978), by accepting instinctual needs, their inherited disposition, and the environment. Personal freedom is the result of a deep responsibility to life yet may be anxiety-provoking and tend to increase a person's avoidance of freedom. Frankl asserts that personal freedom is a required commitment to life.

Frankl's own experience in a concentration camp reinforced the existential notion that people have the freedom to choose their destiny even when suffering extreme adversity. Freedom carries responsibility. People's actions and choices do impact on significant others and society. The meaning derived from the human experience occurs through involvement with others, and true freedom exists in the context of community and society (Frankl, 1967).

Social-Psychological Foundations

Logotherapy recognizes strong sociological-psychological processes in human functioning. Frankl (1967) asserts that the environment (including other people) provides a situational context in which the individual is forced to respond. The person, at any moment, may choose the meaning of a social experience.

Frankl (1963) believes that it is an error to think that human instincts are the sole determining factor of behavior (a falsehood he calls pandeterminism). In Logotherapy, human beings are seen as primarily self-determining, choosing their responses to environmental conditions. Whether environmental conditions are pleasurable or intolerable, the individual's personal values ultimately determine the meaning of existence.

Sociocultural forces may collectively reinforce conformity and inhibit human spontaneity (Frankl, 1959). Group social-psychological pressures may emerge as a collective neurosis, characterized by four distinct symptoms: an ever-present boredom with life tasks and work; a fatalistic view of one's existence and destiny; conformity to societal values, rules, or rituals; and a collective fanaticism.

Collective neurosis leads to the fear of taking responsibility for one's existence coupled with an escape from freedom (Frankl, 1967). The Collective neurosis encourages idealism and symbolism designed to maintain cultural norms, rules and standards. As a result, people may come to doubt their existence, lack meaning, feel purposeless, and conform to social demands.

Problems with one's existence contribute to existential neurosis — the existential vacuum. The existential vacuum manifests itself through experiential deficits in the daily functioning of a person. Existential frustration or the frustration of the will to meaning is the key determinant to the existential neurosis.

Logotherapy differs from other counseling orientations in what it regards as the fundamental motivational force. Freudian psychoanalysts posit the pleasure principle and Adlerians focus on a will to power and the principle of inferiority. Logotherapists give priority to the search for the *meaning* of existence and the search to fulfill this meaning.

Will to Meaning

According to Frankl (1963), the will to meaning is a tendency or fundamental social-psychological motivation in behavior. A striving for human meaning in daily activities or tasks is the major contributing factor to the essence of existence. The fundamental ideas of the will to meaning set forth by Frankl are:

- All reality has meaning (*logos*).
- Meaning is specific and changes from person to person and moment to moment.
- Individuals are unique, and each life contains a series of unique "assignments" to be discovered and responded to.
- Personal meaning is derived from the search for one's specific "assignments" and the response to them.
- Happiness, contentment and peace of mind are incidental to the search for meaning.

The achievement of life goals is a by-product of one's commitment and involvement with one's existence and life tasks. The person's search for meaning is what makes humans different from other living organisms (Frankl, 1963).

The Noetic Model

Logotherapy gives full consideration to the cognitive and intellectual processes of human functioning. Frankl (1967) uses the word *noetic* (from the Greek word *noos*), which means "knowing by the intellect." The noetic realm includes knowing through direct experience and through self-evident knowledge. This process is not an abstract or an intellectualized understanding of life, but a knowing that one's existence is a conscious effort to be responsible and free. Implied in the noetic realm is commitment to present tasks. The noetic model does not deny the subconscious, for people may truly be unaware of their freedom and responsibility and the meaning of existence.

Recall, *logos* means "meaning," but it also refers to the spirituality of existence. Frankl asserts that the spiritual and noetic dimensions of human existence transcend the social-psychological functioning of people. However, Frankl (1969) views people as holistic integrations of spirituality, mind, and body.

The Development of the Person

Logotherapy is not founded on a comprehensive theory of personality development. Based upon the philosophical considerations of existentialism, Frankl (1973) supports the idea that people choose the type of person they want to be. Therefore, people have singularly unique personalities, traits, and dispositions with the primary motivation for the will to meaning.

Developmentally, Frankl (1973) observes that adolescents, after puberty, begin to question the meaning in their lives. He does acknowledge that this questioning process certainly has implications for personality development; however, Frankl does not posit stages in any specific developmental tasks. Within the limitations of any personality dispositions or traits, Frankl believes that people have opportunity to make decisions and choices about their development and life course.

Frankl observed, in the concentration camp, that some camp guards would exhibit sadistic tendencies while others would risk their lives for an opportunity to help others. He concluded that people have an inherent ability to make a conscious choice about an event or situation which has personal meaning.

Personality development is seen as secondary to the primary motivation of the will to meaning, a construct which is shaped by person values. Frankl does admit that values may be taught to people through social exchanges. If taught excessively ritualistic values, then people tend to develop personality styles which conform to the rules of society. To rid themselves of the constraints of societal values, people may shift their attention to the development of their own unique set of values.

According to Frankl (1967) all people possess creative, experiential, and attitudinal values, and choose to implement them in their daily lives.

When people experience excessive hardship and distress, their attitudinal values can shape how they confront the condition of their existence. People may focus on misery, as many concentration camp prisoners did, and give up all hope for life. On the other hand, people may choose to cope, and commit themselves to survival and existence. So often Frankl observed people looking into the future to understand what meaningful tasks await their efforts. Even through the most miserable human conditions, people can appreciate the unique beauties of life and value of existence. The creative values of people bring effort, concentration, and attention to the specific task of one's existence.

The most fully developed or integrated personality, according to Frankl (1978), is one that actualizes existential values. Self-actualization is not the purpose or goal of life; it is secondary to existence. Self-fulfillment or actualization is not a reward to be sought in life in and of itself, rather, it tends to occur through great personal sacrifice, responsibility, and commitment to one's goals and tasks.

Frankl's theory of human development is predicated on the assumption that people function more effectively in the present once they are committed to life assignments for the future. This is in contradistinction to the Freudian concept of personality functioning which is based on early childhood experiences.

Concepts of Functional and Dysfunctional Behavior

Historically, Frankl recognized that when people were confused or frustrated with their lives they looked to the theologians for answers. Spirituality, according to Frankl, may have theological implications in that human beings experience the greatest meaning for their belief in a deity. Frankl (1967) acknowledges the temporal existence of human beings and recognizes that if life were infinite, motivation to actualize one's values or attend to the daily activities of living would be meaningless. For Frankl, death provides meaning to life. The end of life or the knowledge that life is not infinite forces people to search for meaning in the tasks of life.

A person's search for meaning is the surest sign of being uniquely human. Even if this search is frustrated, it cannot be considered a sign of disease or pathology. Frankl believes that in most cases it is spiritual distress, not a pathological syndrome or disorder, that is important.

Concepts of adaptive and maladaptive behavior may be described from the theoretical framework and philosophy of logotherapy. The concepts of functional and dysfunctional behavior as outlined below are taken from Frankl (1969, 1978). These concepts take into account a person's existential resources and experiences. Table 7-1 provides examples of functional and dysfunctional behavior.

Table 7-1
FUNCTIONAL AND DYSFUNCTIONAL BEHAVIOR

Functional	Dysfunctional
• People are free to choose their fate and destiny.	• Life is controlled by society and external forces. Conformity or personal confusion is a symptom of existential neurosis.
• Under extreme environmental hardship people decide their attitude and spirituality. Suffering has existential meaning.	• Despair and depression occur as a result of experiencing no meaning in suffering, love and work.
• Human existence is uncertain. People may trust in their values to actualize and see the total life.	• Uncertainty and a lack of meaning may create value and existential conflicts. Tension, anxiety and guilt may be a result of the conflict.
• People have the existential resources to respond to the present situation. Past experiences or instincts do not fully determine present or future functioning.	• People respond to present situations based on past experiences.
• People derive meaning and self-fulfillment from involvement and commitment to assignments, tasks and people.	• The meaning of existence comes through others and the acquisition of material things.
• Human beings are significantly unique and each individual is responsible and free.	• People should conform to political ideals and institutional ideals.
• Love for another human is the highest expression of commitment to another person or life.	• People find fulfillment and motivation through monetary rewards.
• The contemplation of death gives meaning to life.	• Death is meaningless and is to be feared at all costs.
• People have existential resources to draw upon to meet present and future tasks.	• People need to be provided with most resources to cope with existence.
• Labels and abstractions provide little meaning in life. The concreteness of one's existence provides a context to respond within.	• People need to abstract, label and intellectualize their existence.

An understanding of the spiritual or noetic dimension of Frankl's existential viewpoint is essential to a full comprehension of human functioning. The noetic dimension is a higher order blueprint of the self, what existentialists call the "I" in the "I-Thou" relationship. Frankl asserts that this dimension of the personality was not fully acknowledged in psychoanalytic theory. The noetic realm, while being mostly the result of the conscious domain, is the creative force of artistic expression, humor, and faith. The noetic realm is experienced by the person as the conscious and intuitive voice which, if listened to and acted upon, can guide the individual to a more constructive and authentic existence. Frankl (1967) strongly asserts that the future is not determined by maladaptive responses to past situations because each person has the inner resources to transcend previous social-psychological influences.

Concepts of Behavior Change

Frustration and personal crises lead to a sense of purposelessness and a lack of meaning among human beings. Spirituality is questioned and people may become confused about the purpose of life. Logotherapy attempts to strengthen the philosophical or spiritual aspect of human functioning and encourages people to take more responsibility for themselves and ultimately gain greater personal freedom.

When people suffer psychologically, they turn inward in an attempt to discover their own resources. Frustration and anxiety are often the result of this action because, in an attempt to find solutions, people often focus on symptoms or a perceived personal inadequacy. Frankl (1963) refers to this as *hyper-reflection* because the individual is overly aware and sensitive about personal issues. On the other hand, *hyper-intention* is excessive attention concentrated on a task, leading to great anxiety in the process of trying to complete it. Logotherapy attempts to turn attention away from these self-defeating processes to more spiritually rewarding aspects of the experiences. *De-reflection,* a logotherapy technique to be discussed more fully later in the chapter, deemphasizes hyper-reflection or hyper-intention processes and encourages more constructive personal action.

Frankl believes that the therapeutic relationship is essential to promoting behavior change because it provides a person with the opportunity to explore spiritual and existential frustrations. Through the expansion of awareness, people can explore the lack of meaning in their lives and take responsibility to work on goals. Change in behavior or attitudes occurs when a person is willing to make personal sacrifices to achieve a goal. Personal freedom results when the individual has become deeply committed to goals and learns to draw upon existential resources to achieve them.

To effect meaningful changes in attitudes and behavior, logotherapy appeals to the *conscious processes*. It is Frankl's belief that these conscious processes distinguish human beings from other living creatures. It is through this higher order of cognitive activity that people can redirect behavioral patterns and change their attitudes about themselves and life. Frankl (1963) believes that given any physically or psychologically disabling condition, a spiritual perspective must be gained in order to approach successfully the adaptation process.

The logotherapeutic counselor attempts to encourage constructive behavior change by focusing on significant life tasks and goals. Consciousness or awareness is increased with the de-reflection technique. Awareness has a spiritual implication, in that the individual learns to reflect on those experiential and existential resources that foster involvement with goals, people, and tasks. The individual begins to acquire a spiritual commitment to life's goals.

Assessment of Human Functioning

The three factors in an emotional disturbance, according to Frankl (1973) are physiological, social-psychological, and spiritual. A clinical assessment of the individual should reflect the nature and the weight of each factor in the person's life and its relative contribution to dysfunctional behavior. Frankl's existential approach to assessment is characterized by a psychological and spiritual holism.

Frankl (1967) assumes that psychological problems arise because of existential conflict. People become confused, depressed, or anxious, because they are in conflict with their values and sense of meaninglessness and purposelessness in their lives (constituting an existential crisis). Therefore, a counselor's task is to assess not only social-psychological domains, but spiritual and physiological ones as well. Psychological symptoms are to be understood in an existential context. Frankl (1967) believes that in any pathological syndrome or disorder, existential issues and resources must be fully addressed. Whether the person is psychotic, neurotic or normal, human values and the "will to meaning" in life need to be confronted.

Comprehending the Spiritual Domain

The spiritual domain is characterized by an existential struggle (an essentially healthy process). For instance, boredom, meaninglessness, tension, and frustration can be desirable experiences when they lead to a deeper exploration of values and the will to meaning. Issues of responsibility and freedom are reflected in spiritual distress.

Understanding the Psychological Domain

Psychological conflicts such as neuroses involve both spiritual and physiological difficulties. When a person experiences intense anxiety regarding existence and death issues, a neurosis may result. According to Frankl (1967), neurotic symptoms arise when people undergo traumatic situations that arouse anxiety and guilt. The experience of intense anxiety leads to confusion and the inability to actualize values.

Frankl (1967) believes that the existential crises underlie the more neurotic disturbances. The counselor's task is to direct the client's focus to existential resources and values in order to minimize anxiety and frustration. Ultimately, the client must consider values and tasks which provide meaning to existence. The client then needs to consider how attitudinal values shape the self and learn to accept personal responsibility.

Frankl (1973) formulated two diagnostic concepts which can be categorized as a part of the psychological domain of human functioning. The first, noogenic neuroses, arise out of value conflicts. Existential frustration results from the loss of meaning and a feeling of incompleteness and emptiness attributable to one's existence. Noogenic neuroses is the difficulty people have maintaining spirituality in their existence.

The collective neurosis, the second diagnostic construct, describes people who sacrifice individuality, values, and freedom for social conformity. People abandon their identity to conform to sociocultural values. Under these circumstances, people choose group doctrines and rituals and give up their freedom. Counselors may recognize the collective neurotic themes in people when a new societal idea or value is introduced.

The Physiological (Physical) Domain—
Melancholia and Schizophrenia

Melancholia and schizophrenia fall under the physiological domain as the disorders that inolve more extensive biochemical changes. Intervention is aimed at stabilizing biochemical processes as well as encouraging spiritual and psychological growth. Frankl (1967) recognizes that these disorders have a biological as well as psychological dimension with specific symptoms. Each diagnosis, however, may be considered from an existential logotherapeutic perspective.

Melancholia, characterized by depressive or manic symptoms, involves an existential fear of the future. For the depressive client there is anxiety about the self in tasks and commitments as well as *prediction* of future catastrophe. People who experience depression feel anxious, inadequate, or insufficient. The depressive person shirks and avoids the realities of life, becoming confused about identity. The manic individual also has a fear of the future but engages in excessive planning. These people are in constant fear over the failure of their plans, resulting in frustration over purpose and compulsive ritualistic attempts at self-fulfillment.

Frankl (1967) suggests that people with schizophrenic symptoms are prone to passivity in their existence. He based this observation on his experience with schizophrenic patients who exhibit extreme inner confusion and lack direction and commitment to life. He believes that schizophrenics view themselves as objects, therefore lacking identification with themselves. They feel a sense of abandonment or nonexistence of the ego.

The physiological domain of human functioning is but one aspect of human existence. The attitudinal value towards life is perhaps even more important to the process of gaining a sense of self and meaning and, the most difficult to attain.

Goals and Directions of Counseling

Frankl (1967) asserts that a primary direction in life is to heal or strengthen the health of the soul. In a manner which is very different from the theological view of saving the soul, Frankl (1963) refers to the health of the soul as a spiritual excitement and commitment to life. The soul represents the desire to transcend a simple survival of life and reach a point where the person takes full responsibility for work, love and meaning.

The goals and direction of logotherapy are summarized as follows (Frankl, 1963, 1967):

- A person can move toward accepting any given environment or condition and respond or act according to personal values and existential resources.
- A person can implement decisions or commitments that will bring meaning, develop personal values, and/or encourage the development of individual attitudes.
- A person can learn to trust the conscience as an intuitive learning guide for direction in life.
- A person can minimize hyper-intention by attending to and centering on one's difficulties.

- A person can accept freedom.
- A person can actualize values (creative, experiential, attitudinal) and minimize conflict. Actualization may not lead to total pleasure and comfort but may provide more meaning and purposefulness to life.
- A person can understand the singularity and uniqueness of existence in a community.
- A person can accept the fact of temporal existence and focus on tasks, assignments and work in the "here and now."
- A person can accept suffering and frustration in existence while deriving meaning from significant tasks and people.
- A person can achieve mature love, which is the highest expression of the worth and singularity of another human being.
- A person can transcend difficulties and frustrations with the use of existential and experiential resources.
- A person can accept the self while acknowledging environmental restrictions.

In summary, the goals of logotherapy are based on an optimistic rather than a pessimistic existential philosophy. This optimistic existential attitude recognizes the spiritual domain through the acknowledgement of each person's search for meaning and the underlying process of actualization . . . a commitment to work, to be free, and to sacrifice.

The Counseling Process:
Structuring, Facilitating, and Terminating

Recall that Frankl postulates that human functioning has three primary domains: the spiritual, the psychological, and the physiological. The counseling relationship is structured to attend to each of these domains. Through the process of counseling, a person reaches a greater commitment to responsibility through focusing on a philosophical reconsideration of personal attitudes, values, and morals.

Responsibility for one's actions and existence is encouraged in the initial counseling sessions. The counselor fosters a therapeutic environment in which the philosophical concerns, values, and concrete problems may be explored, rather than reinforcing a focus on the abstractions and intellectualizations that may often blind people to the realities of life. In the initial sessions, the counselor tries to cultivate an environment conducive to existential analysis. The counselor expresses a positive regard for the client, acknowledges the existential crises, and encourages insight into the meaning of the client's existence. Early on, the counselor directs the client's focus toward future goals and explores the client's level of personal commitment. While acknowledging the client's suffering, the counselor directs the client's efforts toward the conscious discovery of freedom and choice. Frankl (1967) notes that some people may have an unconscious desire to maintain their symptoms in order to avoid the uncertainty of personal responsibility and freedom. For this reason, the techniques of *de-reflection* and *paradoxical intention* are used to expand the client's awareness of the meaning of symptoms and behavior.

In the intermediate stage of counseling, the counselor directs attention to specific tasks assigned to the client. The spiritual dimension of existence begins to surface and is explored more fully. The client is encouraged to explore more deeply the attitudes, values, and cognitive styles which serve as existential resources needed to accomplish important life tasks. The focus of counseling moves another step into the dimension of responsibility for work, for love, for tasks, and for meaning of existence.

In the intermediate stages of counseling, the client experiences the existential frustration involved in behaving more responsibly and authentically. The counselor attends to value dilemmas because, so often, the client is confused about how to identify and actualize values. The client may also stubbornly cling to values that are socially or culturally conforming as the counselor tries to encourage the development of more effective values and foster a belief in the singularity and uniqueness of the individual.

The final stages of the counseling relationship are characterized by the client gaining a deeper appreciation of the search for meaning and an understanding of their own existence (Frankl, 1973). The client exhibits a stronger personal identity, freedom, and the increased ability to influence personal destiny. This person is more spontaneous and is able to acknowledge personal resources.

The process of existential counseling is a concrete experience within which people can attend to the discovery of personal responsibility and become aware of the singularity and temporality of existence. The counseling relationship is a context in which people may come to appreciate themselves more fully and to affirm their values.

Counseling Techniques and Procedures

The counseling experience for Frankl is one where individuals may examine and restructure their philosophical ideas and attitudes about existence. While it is a very concrete experience, it is also philosophical in the sense that people become actively involved in gaining perspective on their experience.

While a supportive counseling relationship is of significant importance, as it is in most counseling approaches, a philosophical restructuring of current behaviors and values also needs to occur. The techniques involved in the restructuring process give full consideration to the conscious processes, creative values, commitments, faith, intuition, humor, self-observation, and self-reflection. The two major techniques employed by Frankl are de-reflection and paradoxical intention.

De-Reflection and the Philosophical Consideration of Meaning

De-reflection is used when a person is excessively preoccupied with a disruptive living pattern. The idea is for the counseling process to direct attention away from the problem and toward the client's own resources. The use of de-reflection is based on the philosophic belief that people have a capacity for self-awareness and the ability to find resources within themselves to facilitate change.

According to the logotherapy model (Frankl, 1975a), meaning exists in any life situation, including the negative aspects of human existence such as suffering, guilt and anxiety. The assumption is also made that death can be turned into something more positive. The counselor is forced to accept an individual's suffering and sacrifice as part of existence, while attention is shifted to work, love, personal goals and commitment to meaning. The counselor and client need to accept the limitations of environmental conditions and existential frustration, but must continue to work collaboratively on goals and tasks relevant to existence.

De-reflection is used to deal with hyper-intention and hyper-reflection. Recall that hyper-reflection occurs when people ruminate and worry about anticipated situations, events, or experiences with people. For example, a student may worry about receiving a low grade in a school subject and begins to ruminate that future grades will also be low. De-reflection may help the student turn attention to the process of learning and help that person focus on the educational tasks constituting that process. De-reflection moves the attention away from a neurotic process to an existentially constructive one where attention is shifted from past experiences and future anticipations to the immediate experiences and specific tasks to be completed.

Paradoxical Intention as a Principle Logotherapeutic Technique

Frankl observed that people become more frustrated and anxious about people, places, and things than one may reasonably expect given the situation. When taken to extremes, this becomes a pathological experience that represents a paradox in existence. The will or intention to commit an act (i.e., assertiveness) is present but intense anxiety is experienced as well, and the will to meaningful action is constricted or inhibited. Frankl (1967) found that when he encouraged the neurotic behavior or had the client imagine the experience, the client's awareness was altered and the symptom was minimized. In essence, Frankl prescribed the neurotic behavior and helped the client become more aware of the paradoxical nature of this behavior through exaggerating it. Paradoxical intention may allow the client to laugh at the ritualistic and psychologically ineffective behaviors which are usually sources of frustration and anxiety.

Paradoxical intention fundamentally deals with the anticipatory anxiety experienced by people who suffer with phobias and obsessive-compulsive symptoms. When a person holds an irrational fear to the extent of being immobilized, it is called a phobia. The avoidance of the feared object tends to reinforce anxiety. With encouragement and support, the counselor prescribes the symptom, and in essence says, "it's okay to have the symptom." The counselor helps the individual form a new attitude about the phobia which says, "Don't fight it, participate in it." When the client observes that nothing happens after a behavior has been emitted, the anxiety begins to wane. The counselor's major concern is not with the symptomatic behavior, but with the person's attitude toward the symptom.

To summarize, the techniques of de-reflection and paradoxical intention show people how to philosophically examine meaningful values in their lives. These techniques concentrate on concrete thoughts, feelings and situations and may enhance a person's existence by helping them to see the paradox of life.

Evaluation of Counseling Outcomes

Frankl suggests that people can transcend biological and psychological conditions through a transformation of their spirituality (Frankl,

1963). This philosophical position suggests that when people undergo logotherapy they derive the most benefit when they take the responsibility to create their own destiny. Personal freedom is attained when people become spiritually committed to life.

For Frankl, successful counseling outcomes are attained when a person accepts the fact of existence and discovers that intellectualizations and abstractions are meaningless and may even lead to a greater sense of confusion and boredom. People begin to have a greater appreciation of their own existential resources and draw more freely upon them throughout the life cycle.

Frankl would also suggest that a person who experiences logotherapy is more able to accept the paradoxes of life realistically and with humor. A person can derive meaning from even the most mundane experiences of life. Life becomes significant because it exists and the person wants to give something to it.

The evaluation of counseling processes and outcomes in logotherapy is more of a subjective matter than an objective one. In their phenomenological orientation, logotherapists believe it is the individual's subjective appraisal of psychological gain that is important. Logotherapists are not as concerned with specific change in behaviors or adjustment to the environment as they are with changes in attitudes and philosophy of life.

COUNSELING APPLICATION

The case presented demonstrates Frankl's logotherapy approach in a university setting with a young adult who is anxious and confused over his identity. Notice the counselor focuses on the concrete philosophical consideration of meaning, existence and experiential resources that may actualize values.

Logotherapy in a University Setting

William is twenty-seven. For the past five years he has been excessively anxious and complained of deep feelings of loneliness and despair. He attempted suicide a year ago when he felt he had completely lost his identity and no longer had any real sense of "who he was." William is a professor of music and serves on the faculty at a major eastern university. He sought counseling from a well-known existential counselor who was associated with the university. The dialogue takes up in the initial session, and exemplifies the existential encounter.

Counselor: What is bothering you, William?

William: I am depressed, lonely and confused. I really don't know.

Counselor: Can you tell me more?

William: Sometimes I dream at night about the meaninglessness of my life. I see myself on my knees begging others for solutions to my problems. I see myself as a prisoner in my own body. I want someone to free me from anxiety. When I awaken I feel life is pointless. Why is it that others enjoy their lives? Why am I suffering?

Counselor: You give those questions a great deal of thought.

William: Yes! But I am still crippled by doubts and fear.

Counselor: What do you do when this happens to you? (The counselor directs William's thoughts to his existential resources.)

William: I play my violin. I enjoy the works of the great composers. I think I identify with their personalities—the depth and creativity of their personalities. Most of them—Bach, Mozart, Beethoven—show profound sensitivity to the meaning of human existence. They are able to express this meaning universally.

Counselor: There seems to be something in their creative work that you believe in, but somehow you are not able to capture that creativity for yourself.

William: That's right.

Counselor: The great composers, artists and writers seem to be able to bridge the gap between universal values and meaning and an individual's personal meanings. Sometimes we need to rely on and trust the vision of people greater than ourselves in our search for meaning. Perhaps this implies an emotional rather than an intellectual trust. Let me ask you a question about Beethoven's Ninth Symphony. Does not the music move you first to tears and then later to a feeling of exhileration? Are you then able in those moments to touch your being?

William: I never quite considered it in that light.

Counselor: Isn't it conceivable that at such moments, when you experience the aesthetic quality of the music, you encounter some *meaning* in your own life? At such moments intellectual questions seem irrelevant—abstractions are unnecessary. What is meaningful is the moment of existence. It is the experience or *being in the moment* that is of value.

William: Yes, but I can't seem to capture that momentary experience of being you talk about. I do at times feel a relationship to God.

Counselor: Perhaps it is in this way that you are able to feel close to something ultimate.

William: How do I eliminate the experience of emptiness? Why is there a void in my life? In spite of what I know intellectually, why do I feel alienated from people?

Counselor: Perhaps the great people with whom you identify are merely abstractions—ideals. You might consider reading the writings of Nietzsche, Sartre, and Camus.

William: Why?

Counselor:	Some of these writers have agonized over man, concerning the same matters you have explored. There is some danger in this in that you may overintellectualize — put distance between your problems and yourself. However, you *may* achieve a certain intellectual honesty in that you may come to understand your personal problems as an essential aspect of the human condition. Perhaps you may become united with the community of suffering humanity who have too suffered from the experience of the basic meaninglessness of existence. Consider one point — patience. Can you consider the possibility of identifying a final resolution of your dilemma?
William:	Am I mentally ill or not?
Counselor:	Are you asking for a psychiatric label — another abstraction? Your personal difficulties are common to humans, especially those who are most sensitive.
William:	I don't mind suffering so much, but I can't figure it out. I am immobilized — frustrated.
Counselor:	Let me say that your search for meaning in life is not pathological. It is your prerogative. People of your age constantly challenge themselves and the meaning life has for them. Consider your questioning as evidence of your very existence. In a sense, your will to meaning justifies your underlying faith in meaning.
William:	Perhaps I have ignored very basic resources within me. I must think about this more.

The encounter between the counselor and client in this sequence is characteristic of the existential approach. William complained of a lack of meaning in his life and confusion over his identity. He wondered whether he was mentally ill because of symptoms of depression, loneliness, and anxiety. It was apparent that he was looking for something outside himself for a sense of meaning (the music of the masters, a psychiatric label). The counselor helped him focus on concrete aspects of existence ("momentary feelings," "questions of being") and facilitated his move away from intellectualizations and abstractions. The counselor also encouraged William to read books written by existential philosophers — Sartre, Camus, Nietzsche. These writers also had struggles with the meaning of life similar to William's.

Later counseling sessions follow a similar pattern. The counselor directs William to attend to the facts of his existence as evidenced by very concrete, even mundane experiences of daily life and to see the value of existence — the fact of existence. William still wanted intellectual answers to existential questions. The counselor, however, directed him to become more conscious of his own personal, experiential resources.

Critical Comments

The aim of Frankl's logotherapy is to enhance the meaning of existence through spiritual or philosophical insight. The spiritual aspects of human functioning are not negated or down-played in this approach to counseling. Frankl believes that to have a belief in God may be the highest form of meaning in human existence. A belief in God can add a spiritual content to suffering and even terminal illness. Frankl (1963) asserts that the task of logotherapy is to heal the soul while the task of religion is to save the soul. Spirituality, according to Frankl (1975b) is a human's conscious effort to take responsibility for this endeavor.

Frankl's emphasis on spirituality may seem a bit too theological or idealistic for some. While he talks of the concrete aspects of human existence as being most important, he seems to contradict himself by invoking highly abstract and symbolic concepts. De-reflection and paradoxical intention, the principle techniques of logotherapy, are not necessarily based on existentialism. The shifting of the focus of attention from maladaptive behaviors to adaptive behaviors is common to most theories of counseling and behavioral change.

Something should be said of Frankl's concept of self-actualization. Some prominent humanistic theorists such as Carl Rogers suggest that self-actualization is a by-product of the process of working, maintaining relationships, and suffering. This is an important distinction between Frankl and Rogers. Frankl's concept of self-actualization is based more on the completion of concrete tasks. Through the involvement in tasks, people discover the will to meaning and feel a greater sense of purpose for their existence. Self-actualization for Frankl emerges out of concrete actions, as opposed to existing as an innate motive force as suggested by Rogers.

Logotherapy seems to have its greatest value in cases where the major client concern has to do with the meaning of life. The approach is quite sensitive to human value issues and conflicts; however, for many people, the approach may be too philosophical and spiritual.

Logotherapy would be appealing to counselors with strong theological leanings and those who subscribe to a Judeo-Christian existential philosophy. Counselors who embrace a brand of existential philosophy similar to Sartre and Camus would have difficulty with Frankl's spiritualistic themes.

Existential philosophy usually embraces a phenomenological approach to inquiry and research. Frankl, unlike Carl Rogers, appears reluctant to translate philosophical concepts into social psychological ones. Frankl's existential therapy may lack practical value and as a result prove to be a problem for many practical counselors.

We would have to conclude that most concepts in Frankl's theory of counseling are meta-psychological in nature. This may be fine for philosophically inclined counselors, but not for more pragmatic counselors. On a positive note, Frankl's view of people is fundamentally a positive one. His writings are provocative in that they force people to consider questions of individual freedom, responsibility, and the power of the will.

REFERENCES

Frankl, V.E. (1958). On Logotherapy and Existential Analysis. *American Journal of Psychoanalysis, 18,* 28-37.

Frankl, V.E. (1959). Logotherapy and the Collective Neurosis. In J. Masserman & J.L. Moreno (Eds.), *Progress in Psychotherapy,* Vol. 4 (pp. 262-264). New York: Grune & Stratton.

Frankl, V.E. (1963). *Man's Search for Meaning: An Introduction to Logotherapy.* New York: Washington Square Press.

Frankl, V.E. (1967). *Psychotherapy and Existentialism: Selected Papers on Logotherapy.* New York: Washington Square Press.

Frankl, V.E. (1969). *The Will to Meaning: Foundations and Applications of Logotherapy.* New York: New American Library.

Frankl, V.E. (1973). *The Doctor and the Soul: From Psychotherapy to Logotherapy* (2nd ed.). New York: Vintage.

Frankl, V.E. (1975a). Paradoxical Intention and De-Reflection. *Psychotherapy: Theory, Research, and Practice, 12,* 226-237.

Frankl, V.E. (1975b). *The Unconscious God: Psychotherapy and Theology.* New York: Simon and Schuster.

Frankl, V.E. (1978). *The Unheard Cry for Meaning and Psychotherapy and Humanism.* New York: Simon & Schuster.

PART III

COGNITIVE-BEHAVIORAL PERSPECTIVES

THREE COGNITIVE-BEHAVIORAL theories of counseling are described in this section, yet these models vary in theory and practice. Because most behavior theories of counseling presently incorporate the notion of cognition or rationality, we have titled this section Cognitive-Behavioral Perspectives. Some might argue that we may have taken a little liberty here by placing William Glasser's Reality Therapy under the same rubric as Albert Ellis' Rational Emotive Therapy, and Carl Thoresen's Intensive Counseling for Self-Efficacy. However, all three systems assign a heavy weight to the role of cognition and rationality in the control of behavior. Given the common themes of *reality orientation* and *cognitive control* over the emotions and behavior, these systems do show marked differences. The intent of this section is to highlight differences in theory and application while at the same time expositing many of the similarities of the systems.

Carl Thoresen's Intensive Self-Efficacy theory of counseling, an emerging system, is based on Albert Bandura's Social-Learning Theory. Thoresen, more so than Ellis and Glasser, operates within a rigorous scientific framework that defines counseling as an experimental process. Thoresen very carefully operationalizes the concepts of counseling and behavior change so they are more easily observed and measured. Counseling is a very systematic and scientific endeavor that requires the counselor to continuously assess through intensive single case research designs the effectiveness of a particular counseling technique.

Thoresen employs a wide assortment of behavioral techniques but prefers those procedures that promote self-control and self-managed behavior change. He is partial to the methods developed by Bandura that promote self-efficacy. Thoresen, more so than Ellis and Glasser, has made substantive contributions to vocational and career counseling. At the same time, his theory has been applied to personal, social, and health problems. Scientific rigor, the cornerstone of Carl Thoresen's theory of counseling, is balanced by humanistic themes.

Albert Ellis refers to rational emotive therapy as an "elegant" cognitive behavior therapy. The rationale-emotive counseling process, similarly to the others described here, is primarily a reeducative one. Ellis believes that human beings are most effective when they learn to reason their way through the experiences of life. More so than the others, Ellis gives greater attention to the role of reason and language in behavior change. Relying quite heavily on the logical empiricism of Bertrand Russell and the general semantics of Alfred Korsybski, Ellis notes that the structure of language largely defines the way people think, experience emotions and behave.

Ellis acknowledges the role biological factors play in explaining human behavior. He asserts that humans have biological predispositions to behave irrationally as well as rationally. More so than Thoresen and Glasser, Ellis credits much of his theory of human behavior and counseling to many of the great philosophers such as Barvch Spinoza, Bertrand Russell, and Marcus Aurelius.

Ellis, like the others, does not believe that counseling need be limited to the interview room. Counseling is ultimately effective when it results in significant changes in the clients' thinking, feeling, and behaving in the real world. The work of the counselor, as well as the client, is quite demanding. Ellis has written extensively on demystifying the counseling process, and as the other theorists, has vigorously challenged psychoanalytic theory and many of the theories of personality and counseling that are not rooted firmly in scientific method.

William Glasser's reality therapy, a practical system of counseling, is based on learning principles and educational programming. Reality therapy has found its way into schools, correctional institutions, social agencies, and pastoral counseling settings. Glasser's theory is particularly useful to people who believe that moral issues are at the core of most emotional and behavioral problems. As we shall see, Glasser's system of reality therapy has advanced since its inception in 1962. The more recent theoretical innovations will be highlighted.

CHAPTER 8

CARL THORESEN'S
INTENSIVE COUNSELING
FOR SELF-EFFICACY

FOUNDATIONS AND STRUCTURE

Historical Foundations

CARL THORESEN (1933-   ) received his Bachelor of Arts Degree in History at the University of California at Berkeley in 1955. He completed an M.A. in Counseling and Administration at Stanford in 1960, and in 1964 he attained a Ph.D. in Counseling Psychology. After a brief period at Michigan State University, Thoresen returned to Stanford where he is currently Professor of Education.

While a student at Stanford, Carl Thoresen was influenced by Albert Bandura (social learning) and John Krumboltz (operant learning). He has authored, coauthored, and edited several books on counseling and psychotherapy including *Behavior Modification in Education* (1973); *Behavioral Counseling: Cases and Techniques* (1969) (with John Krumboltz); *Behavioral Self-Control* (1974); *Self-Control: Power to the Person* (1974) (with Mike Mahoney); *The Behavior Therapist* (1980) (with Thomas Coates).

Thoresen is past president of the American Educational Research Association: The American Psychological Association — Division of Counseling Psychology, served on numerous editorial boards, and is active in numerous professional organizations. Thoresen has made extensive contributions to theory and research in the field of counseling. His most current interests are in the application of behavioral techniques to health and medical problems.

Philosophical Foundations

Thoresen, similar to other theoreticians discussed in this section, is fundamentally an empiricist. His philosophy of behavioral science is based on logical positivism pervasive in American and British philosophy and science. Thoresen has little to say about the nature of existence; humans are seen as neither good nor bad. Moreover, he rejects many of the so-called All Encompassing Theories of Personality, such as psychoanalysis. Consequently, he downplays meta-physical and abstract explanations of human behavior as he focuses on what is concrete and observable. Thoresen can best be described as a behavioral scientist with a strong practical orientation. Therefore, to understand his notions of human behavior, one must know something of his philosophy of science and research methodology.

Dissatisfaction had arisen over time with psychoanalysis and other traditional forms of psychotherapy mainly because of their limited practical value. Thoresen and Coates (1978), note that behavior theory and therapy evolved as the need was seen for more precision in the study of human personality and behavior change. The rigorous application of the scientific method became the hallmark of behavior therapy.

In a strict sense, behavior therapy has been associated with Watson's behaviorism. Watson suggested that mental events are virtually irrelevant to the understanding of human behavior, because they cannot be studied scientifically. Later, B.F. Skinner reinforced this notion. Thoresen and Coates (1978), however, note that few behaviorists today would make the bold and far reaching claims of Watson and Skinner.

Thoresen believes that the scientific process is an experimental enterprise designed to facilitate the understanding of nature. A science of human behavior is permeated by doubt and demands that ideas and explanations about phenomena, at some point, be put to critical tests (Thoresen and Coates, 1978).

While not entirely rejecting the notion that people are influenced by external conditions, Thoresen believes that people are both producer and product of the environment. Each person has the potential for altering the course of his or her life by modifying the many factors that influence personal action. Thoresen posits a strong humanism—in effect a behavioral humanism. He points to the importance of personal responsibility, capability, and efficacy. Thoresen and Coates (1978) even go so far as incorporating some existential elements into their thinking about behaviorism. "I am what I do." "I can learn to do things differently." "We are responsible for what we experience."

Thoresen's behavioral humanism "views counseling as science. Good counseling is the practice of good science." However, Thoresen and Coates warn that the hard-earned progress of a behavioral scientific approach may be stymied by three insideous forces: theoretical orthodoxy, rigid methodology, and convenience.

Thoresen's behavioral orientation maintains a high degree of flexibility, yet at the same time it does not sacrifice scientific rigor. Perhaps more than any other theoretical position presented in this book, his is marked by the scientific method. He views counseling as an experimental approach to the individual client and the counselor as an applied behavioral scientist.

Thoresen argues for the scientific spirit in counseling theory, research, and practice. A scientific attitude forces those involved in the practice, research and theory development of counseling to challenge, to question or to try to refute favored techniques and models. Science forces one to doubt very basic ideas and assumptions relative to the phenomenon under investigation.

Thoresen challenges those who believe that the counseling and psychotherapy process is not researchable and should not be researched because it destroys the delicate nature of the process. The methods of counseling should be acceptable only if they withstand the empirical test. Thoresen's view, once again, does not preclude a humanistic attitude toward the scientific process. He does not take scientific objectivity to the extreme nor does he deny the human factor in the scientific enterprise. Theories of counseling are useful when they are explicit, flexible, and able to guide the search for more potent interventions and new applications. New theories should be embraced cautiously, never blindly. Moreover, Thoresen attacks eclecticism because these models avoid formal theoretical propositions, thus making them difficult to test (Thoresen, 1973a).

Philosophically, Thoresen's position can be summed up as behavioral humanism—a radical departure from Watsonian behaviorism. Thoresen's scientific orientation is a rational one in that it does not exclude facts simply due to a restricted methodology. A major contribution of Thoresen and his associates lies in the area of expanding and refining the methods of scientific inquiry into the counseling process.

Social-Psychological Foundations

The social-psychological foundations of Thoresen's theory of counseling are rooted in the cognitive social learning theory of Albert Bandura.

Bandura (1977) proposes that behavioral change strategies are effective to the extent that a client comes to believe that certain newly acquired behavior can result in positive outcomes. People believe that they can become more assertive, they can reduce blood pressure, they can relax, they can monitor their actions, and they can modify their thinking. Expectations of personal efficacy determine whether people will initiate constructive action and the effort they will expend. The self-efficacy model suggests that when people have high efficacy expectations, they will more likely have positive outcomes expectations and initiate the behaviors necessary to produce these desirable outcomes.

The Cognitive Social Learning model provides a framework for understanding the interdependent and reciprocal influences of behavioral, environmental, cognitive, and physiological factors in human functioning. No single factor is the sole influence of behavior. All must be considered relative to one another (Thoresen, Telch, and Eagleston, 1981).

Thoresen and Coates (1978) propose that much more than simple sequences of behaviors are learned. People learn ways of (1) structuring their thoughts about the physical world, (2) retrieving information from memory, (3) relating one thought to another, and (4) enacting complex sequences of action. Two variables that influence human actions, *competence* and *performance*, are distinguished.

Competencies refer to what people can do. People learn to generate complex behavior patterns through direct experience, by observing others, and through imitation. Competencies also include learning about social rules, the structure of the physical world, and about self and others. Also included are various cognitive activities such as transformations performed on information, methods through which behavior is committed to memory, and sequences of behavior retrieved in specific situations (Thoresen and Coates, 1978).

Performances refer to what people do in specific situations. People generate behavior that is guided by instruction, modeling others, and direct experience. What a person may do in a specific situation also is a function of stimulus conditions (changes in the environment that signify probable response consequences) and reinforcing conditions (what must be done to increase positive outcomes and avoid negative ones).

Performance is also governed by the meaning a person ascribes to environmental stimuli or reinforcing consequences. Meaning attribution involves three important dimensions. First are *stimulus-outcome* and *behavior-outcome* expectations. These are simply predictions about relationships between certain events and other events-hypotheses about behavior and probable outcomes. Second are *subjective* values. These have to do with the estimated value of a stimulus (stimulus value) and the motivating value of a stimulus (reinforcement value). Third are the *self-regulatory systems*. These are the rules that govern behavior in the absence of external stimuli and reinforcers. Self-regulatory systems include the rules specifying behavior performance levels, self-consequences, and instructions for self-control, as well as organizing rules for sequencing complex behavior. Self-regulatory systems denote the meaning of a stimulus, data gathering procedures, determination of the reinforcement value of a stimulus, response reinforcement value of a stimulus, response reinforcement contingencies, and response aids needed to maintain behavior.

The social-psychological underpinnings of Thoresen's counseling theory (Thoresen and Coates, 1978) help one to understand the basic concepts of behavior change, counseling techniques, and the power of counseling relationships. A more detailed explanation of social learning theory may be found in texts authored by Thoresen and Mahoney (1974) and Bandura (1977).

The Development of the Person

Thoresen has not formulated a comprehensive theory of human development or of personality. In this respect, he is similar to Ellis and Glasser. Thoresen adheres to a social learning theory of human behavior that emphasizes person-environment interaction and cognitive functioning. From this it can be assumed that Thoresen believes the development of human beings is shaped by reinforcers emanating from the external environment (social) and the internal environment (self). Ultimately, human beings can learn to control and shape their own behavior through self-administered behavior change strategies.

Thoresen, in the behavioristic tradition, has little interest in a general theory of human behavior. He, therefore, concentrates his study and efforts on how behavior is learned and the conditions under which it can be modified.

Concepts of Functional and Dysfunctional Behavior

Thoresen (1973b) believes that tremendous harm has been done in psychology by conceptualizing personality in terms of abstract myths and traits rather than individual patterns of behavior. Personality theories that suggest the notion of a healthy personality such as Rogers' person-centered approach make it difficult for counselors to deal realistically with people. Thoresen believes that counselors are more effective with people when they move away from sterile abstraction to useful observation—observing the personal difficulties of people instead of forcing them into a rigid notion of good or bad health.

Given the behavioral humanism of Thoresen, notions such as the healthy personality are supplanted by notions of self-management and self-efficacy. The counselor's task is to arrange the counseling relationship to teach skills of self-awareness, self-understanding, and self-change. This includes helping people assess and alter their thoughts, feelings, behaviors, and situations. Effectively functioning persons, as opposed to healthy personalities, can be viewed as having skills to manage internal and external environments that exert control over their actions. For Thoresen this represents "power to the person" and a way of creating personally competent individuals.

Thoresen (1973b) views effective human functioning as the integration and implementation of a developed set of skills. He emphasizes (1) how persons develop cognitive and behavioral competencies, (2) how personal expectations influence the outcomes of behaviors, and (3) how self-control skills influence behavior. This view of personality functioning eliminates underlying traits or labels such as psychotic, neurotic, introvert, extrovert, and the like as explanatory notions of behavior.

Thoresen (1973b) warns that labelling people with global traits has a pernicious influence in shaping the environment of some people. Others look differently at people who have been so labelled and treat them according to the label. For instance, others may come to expect a person to be "aggressive," and unwittingly encourage and reinforce that behavior. A vicious circle results that confirms for the labeler the existence of a cause (the label) for the behavior in question. Furthermore, people who are labelled may internalize the labels, and thus attribute the causes of their actions to the particular personality label or trait.

When the causes of a behavior are unknown to people, they reach for explanations using scientific inquiry. When the explanations are based on metaphor the next stage is to transform the metaphor to myth. Thoresen argues that it is not so much the use of trait labels as descriptions of behavior that is counterproductive, but rather, the vicious circularity to which the descriptive label can lead (Thoresen, 1973b).

Thoresen views effective or ineffective behavior from an abilities-skills perspective—that is, what can people competently *do* rather than what are they like. In his view, it is performance that counts. Thoresen's perspectives on effective behavior will be further explored in subsequent sections.

Concepts of Behavior Change

We have already seen that Thoresen's theory of counseling and behavior change is based upon a cognitive social learning model. Thoresen, like many of the more contemporary behavioral theorists, stresses the role of cognition in affecting behavior change. He makes a distinction between a strict conditioning model and a self-efficacy model of behavior change in counseling.

The purpose of counseling, from a *strict conditioning model,* is to weaken the bonds between stimuli and unadaptive responses and to replace them with new bonds. For example, one could reasonably expect that pairing a strong electrical shock with cigarette smoking would reduce smoking. The electrical shock would elicit an avoidance of cigarettes and ultimately extinguish the habit (Thoresen and Coates, 1978).

As opposed to the strict conditioning model, the *efficacy model* provides the person with skills to manage problem behaviors in various situational contexts. Training for self-efficacy encompasses a broad spectrum program that uses many specific behavioral techniques as well as social support (social reinforcement) from friends and counselors (Thoresen and Coates, 1978).

Thoresen describes four conceptualizations of the role of reinforcement in producing behavior change. First, reinforcement influences behavior change automatically and without a person's awareness. This idea suggests that behavior is controlled from external sources, that people are aware of the reasons for reinforcement, and that reinforcement must occur immediately following a particular behavior. Second, reinforcement designates appropriate behavior. This notion of reinforcement informs people as to what behavior is desirable and provides information and instruction regarding behavior and the contingencies that produce desired effects. According to this approach, reinforcement is essentially an incentive for appropriate conduct. Third, reinforcement may be viewed as social contracting. This type of reinforcement represents an agreement between two people and depends on the preference of the person being reinforced. Since it can be presented symbolically, it does not need to occur instantly. People can learn to delay reinforcing consequences for desirable behavior. Fourth, reinforcement may be construed as self-regulation. In this model, people set their own personal standards for evaluating their own actions. The notion here is that people can reinforce themselves by developing control over powerful self-statements. Self-reinforcement at times may be more potent than external reinforcement (Thoresen and Coates, 1978). Behavior change that is clinically significant is generalized across many situations, is maintained over time, and probably involves all four models of reinforcement.

Thoresen (1976), acknowledges three basic learning modes. *Instrumental learning* is based upon the assumption that people operate or act on the environment in such a way as to produce desirable or undesirable consequences (operant conditioning). *Associative learning* involves the pairing of a previously neutral stimulus with some emotionally positive or negative reaction (classical conditioning). *Vicarious learning* occurs through modeling or imitating the behavior of others (social modeling).

Going beyond this relatively simple conception of how people learn and change their behavior, Thoresen (1976) proposes a self-efficacy theory of behavior control and change. He defines self-control as learnable cognitive processes that a person uses to develop controlling actions which in turn function to alter factors influencing behavior.

Thoresen and Ewert (1976) note that self-control relates to how much and what kind of self-controlling behaviors a person can exercise in specific situations. Behavior changes through a self-control framework are construed as a series of cognitively mediated actions that people use to regulate and alter significant situations, including the cognitive environment, so they can produce desirable consequences (Thoresen and Ewert, 1976).

Self-control theory implies that a person requires an expanded awareness of overt and covert response-reinforcement contingencies and the ability to assess and evaluate consequences for change. Internal or covert actions include positive and negative self- statements, images, and imaginary rehearsals of external actions (Thoresen, 1976). External or overt actions include a variety of directly observable behaviors such as self-assertion and verbal expression.

In summary, Thoresen's theory of behavior change is primarily a self-control theory. The theory generates specific techniques for changing behavior and methods of assessing and evaluating change.

Assessment of Human Functioning

Thoresen (1978) asserts that research in counseling must rely on the basics of direct observation, careful description, and systematic planned intervention with the individual. This notion translates directly into a need for a structured, well-planned assessment of human functioning in counseling relationships. Recall that Thoresen firmly believes that a counselor researcher is concerned with what happens to individuals. The individual subject, not groups of subjects, becomes the object of inquiry.

Counseling is an intensive experience involving problem discovery, data gathering (assessment), establishing behavioral objectives, selecting and implementing counseling techniques, evaluating change, and arranging for the maintenance of change (Thoresen and Anton, 1973). This section highlights the discovery of problem areas and the gathering of data. More will be said about the total process later (see Figure 8-1).

The first step in behavior assessment is to define the problem. Counselors can discover problems not only through listening to the concern of a client but by reaching out and working outside the concerns of their offices. The counselor may make careful observations of the *frequency, intensity,* and *duration* of problem behavior. For example, if a client is having a problem with low self-esteem, the counselor or the client can simply count the number (frequency) of negative and positive self-thoughts each day. The counselor and client can then monitor behavior and establish baselines (Thoresen and Anton, 1973).

The second step in assessment is the gathering of information or establishing baseline data. A single behavior may be recorded or many behaviors may be observed and recorded (multiple baselines). Since the primary goal of intensive counseling for self-efficacy is to foster behavior change, it is necessary to compare client behavior before and after counseling. For example, the client who has self-esteem problems may also be reticent in social situations. The client may want to record each time he/she starts a conversation with a friend each day for a specified period of time. By making frequent or continuous observations, the counselor can obtain a baseline measure of how often a client does or does not do a certain thing. Frequency counts before and after counseling enable the client and the counselor to estimate the amount of change more accurately.

Thoresen, Telch and Eagleston (1981) and Friedman, Thoresen, and Gill (1981) provide a comprehensive example of a *cognitive-social learning* model to conceptualize Type A (high cardiovascular risk) behavioral patterns. Counselors working with Type A behavioral patterns need to consider the frequency, intensity, and duration of:

- Cognitive Factors (e.g., the belief that one must always win in any kind of competition),

- Behavioral Factors (e.g., angry verbal outbursts, inappropriate expressions of hostility, excessive smoking),
- Physiological Factors (e.g., increases in heart rate during angry outbursts, increases in blood pressure), and
- Environmental Factors (e.g., media depicting hostility as a normal reaction to stress, failure at work).

The intensive assessment design requires that cognitive, behavioral, physiological, and environmental factors be taken together whenever possible. A major feature of this kind of single organism and intensive assessment strategy is that clients serve as their own control. Meaningful data are gathered on the client prior to the experimental intervention of counseling. Repeated measures (taking the same data at several points during the counseling or research process) of relevant behavior establishes whether behavior is stable or changing. Without baseline information, inferences about the effects of counseling are difficult to make. With baseline data the counselor can assess the direction of changes during counseling and after counseling terminates (follow-up).

Behavioral assessment is a continuous process that involves the careful observation and recording of responses before, during, and after counseling. This procedure allows the counselor to make any necessary strategy changes in order to reduce wasted time and effort if a particular treatment is found to be ineffective (Thoresen and Anton, 1974). Thoresen (1978) and Thoresen and Anton (1974) propose several designs that aid in the assessment and evaluation of client behavior. These will be discussed later. However, the reader should recognize that conducting a behavioral assessment, determining counseling goals, choosing appropriate counseling strategies, and implementing and evaluating the strategies characterize the intensive and integrative counseling process used by Thoresen.

Goals and Directions of Counseling

Once problems have been identified, thoroughly assessed, and baselines established, the counselor and client cooperatively establish behavioral objectives or outcomes in order to design the direction of counseling. Without behaviorally stated objectives, it is virtually impossible to know whether a particular counseling technique is appropriate (Thoresen and Anton, 1973).

Thoresen and Anton (1973) assert that behavioral objectives clearly specify the goals of counseling in objectively measurable terms. Identifying criteria for behavioral objectives in counseling are as follows:

Behavioral objectives specify:

- The responses to be performed.
- The extent to which they may be reliably recorded by some observer.
- A criterion level (how much of the behavior is required to meet the objectives).
- The circumstances or conditions under which the behavior is to occur.

An example of a behavioral objective for a client who has difficulty saying "no" to people would be that he/she would say "no" to two persons per day for one week. Once baseline and objectives have been cooperatively established, the counselor is ready to move into the counseling process per se.

The Counseling Process:
Structuring, Facilitating, and Terminating

Thoresen's view of the counseling process is best portrayed as an intensive and systematic attempt on the part of the counselor to facilitate the client to increase commitment and motivation to change behavior. Thoresen believes that the counseling process, designed to foster change, needs to extend beyond the interview to situations outside the interview setting. The counseling process needs to include the implementation of behavioral change programs in outside situations. Specific actions that a client will take outside of the interview must be delineated in operational terms with specific criteria or standards of performance.

Thoresen and Anton (1973) assert that counselors, regardless of their theoretical allegiance, seek to help people change. However, specific changes made by the client need to be maintained after counseling. This is most likely to occur, they believe, when the client understands the process of change and learns specific behavior modifying strategies, thus achieving greater control over self and the environment.

Thoresen and Anton (1973) propose that counseling is an experimental effort designed to treat the individual client. Counseling is therefore a tentative, open-ended process that is data-oriented and empirical, much like the research process. The counselor is guided by data and information gathered on the client. The counselor is actively and directly involved with the client at the beginning and end of the process. The intensive involvement of the counselor demands continuous attention and responsiveness to the client's concerns based on an ongoing and systematic information gathering process.

A part of the intensive counseling process has already been described

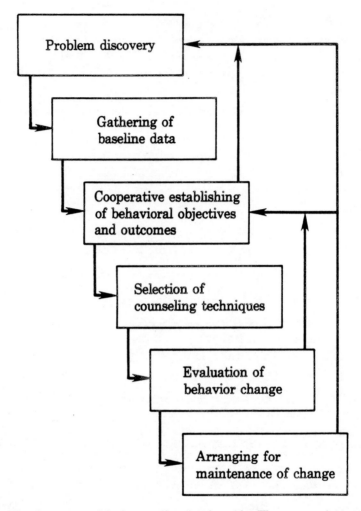

Figure 8-1. The six-stage model of counseling developed by Thoresen and Anton (1973).

in the section on assessment. The specific techniques of counseling and a methodology for evaluating change will be described later. Regarding the overall process of intensive counseling, Thoresen and Anton (1973) offer a model consisting of six stages (see Figure 8-1).

Terminating counseling is a gradual phasing-out process. Termination is based on what data reveals about the client's progress. The systematic recording of relevant behavior will indicate to both the counselor and client the need for either additional help or progress. The intensive counseling strategy provides for data gathering after counseling has terminated. The decision to formally terminate counseling is made on a cooperative basis when specific goals have been achieved.

Thoresen and Anton (1973) warn that counselors are not always successful even with the advantages of an excellent relationship with the client, well-articulated objectives, and a wide variety of methods. Strong environmental influences may serve as barriers to make client change difficult. The intensive model, however, allows for a refinement of objectives based on new material brought to light during the counseling process.

Behaviorally oriented counselors are sometimes accused of being too systematic and too objective in the way they perceive and approach the counseling relationship. This does not seem to be the case with Thoresen. Thoresen does not deemphasize human relationship skills such as active listening and empathic understanding. Intensive counseling acknowledges the importance of positively encouraging the client's self-managed change through an active teaching modality.

Counseling Techniques and Procedures

Thoresen's intensive self-control theory of counseling employs a variety of standard behavior therapy techniques described by Krumboltz and Thoresen (1976), Thoresen (1976) and Thoresen and Ewart (1976) for teaching and learning self-control skills. Some of the most widely used techniques are aversive counter-conditioning, behavioral contracts, cognitive restructuring, covert reinforcement, covert sensitization, feedback, extinction, flooding, imagery, behavioral rehearsal, homework assignments, instruction, paradoxical intention, positive social reinforcements, programmed materials, relaxation, role-playing, self-instruction, self-punishment, self-reinforcement, sharing, simulation, stimulus control, systematic desensitization, thought-stopping, time out, and token reinforcement systems.

Thoresen's (1976) tentative framework for teaching and learning self-efficacy skills consists of four broad strategy areas for self-control: *commitment, awareness, restructuring environments,* and *consequences and standards.*

This dimension of self-control includes people's beliefs, attitudes, self appraisals, and conceptions about changing their behavior. Questions are raised pertaining to (1) attributions of meanings to problems and the avoidance of choices and new experiences; (2) people's beliefs about their abilities and skills to accomplish personal, social, and career tasks; and (3) the extent to which one's self-concept prevents involvement in personal decisions and career selection activities. Commitment implies one's motivation for change. Building commitment behaviors takes time because so many maladaptive beliefs and stereotyped notions about personal competency and performance may serve to inhibit motivation (Thoresen and Ewart, 1976).

Commitment

Commitment skills and techniques that are necessary for developing and sustaining motivation consist of:

- An assessment of factors associated with past and present behavior (i.e., the meanings a person attributes to past and present behavior that have interfered with motivation).
- The exploration of personal beliefs, expectations, one's ability to change and anticipations about possible future consequences.
- Determining the frequency of positive and negative self-statements and the extent of encouragement from others (Thoresen and Ewart, 1976).

Awareness

Awareness implies the ability for self-observation or self-monitoring. Awareness facilitates the development of knowledge of one's actual thoughts, feelings, and behavior in specific situations. As a result people can learn to discriminate, evaluate, and record their activities more accurately. The systematic monitoring of behavior provides people with useful data that fosters motivation, commitment, and more effective management of the environment.

Techniques for developing awareness skills consist of the following:

- Observing self-talk or verbalizations about a situation.
- Observing feelings, bodily responses, and behaviors in the situation.
- Determining the circumstances under which a targeted behavior occurs.
- Observing and estimating the frequency of a behavior (Thoresen and Ewart, 1976).

Restructuring Environments

This technique focuses on changing particular features of the social-psychological environment (stimulus or situational control). Particular features in the environment often hinder a person from making desired changes. Friends, relatives, spouses, siblings, and coworkers, as significant components of the social environment, can provide much encouragement for self-change if they are approached effectively.

Specific techniques for restructuring environments or planning environments are as follows:

- Establishing supportive environments by teaching family, friends, and other significant people how they can assist in particular endeavors.
- Modifying the stimuli that serve as cues for the behavior to be altered. This can be achieved by rearranging the physical environment (external) and by altering undesirable stimuli such as thoughts, feelings, and images (internal) (Thoresen and Ewart, 1976).

Evaluating Consequences and Standards

When a person desires to change a behavior, considerations need to be given to planning and evaluating the consequences of future actions. A variety of pleasant events can be structured that serve to reinforce behavior — that is, increasing the likelihood of a behavior occurring. On the other hand, many negative or aversive experiences can be arranged that may reduce behavior. People can be taught to arrange consequences that support long-term efforts to achieve personal, social, and career goals.

Evaluating the consequences and standards for effective behavior is a continuous effort of assessing and modifying current reinforcement patterns. Techniques to accomplish this are as follows:

- Assess how presently experienced reinforcers or consequences may be maintaining behavior a person may wish to change.
- Assess long-term objectives.
- Reduce and redesign long-term goals to a series of short term subgoals if necessary.
- Provide for self-rewarding experiences by (a) planning positive thoughts to follow successful behavior (covert); and (b) giving yourself a tangible reward for successful behavior (playing golf, a gift).
- Employ self-punishing experiences by (a) planning negative thoughts following immediately undesirable actions (covert); and (b) withholding pleasant activities (e.g., eating your favorite meal and playing golf). (Thoresen and Ewart, 1976)

Cognitive Restructuring and Self-Efficacy

Thoresen's Intensive Counseling for Self-Efficacy gives priority to techniques for restructuring cognitive processes. Cognitive restructuring of irrational beliefs plays a very important part in the modification of behavior. Cognitive restructuring in Thoresen's model consists of (1) the identification of positive and negative self-statements and (2) the substitution of more positive self-statements for negative ones. Positive self-statements increase the feeling of self-efficacy and lead people to eventually believe that they have the ability to perform a task or cope with a situation. The cognitive restructuring technique, then, is employed to undermine distorted expectations that minimize perceived self-efficacy and increase the motivation to function ineffectively.

Reinforcement Techniques

Reinforcement strategies most often employed within the Intensive Counseling framework are *social reinforcement, model reinforcement, covert reinforcement,* and *covert punishment.* Social reinforcement techniques are externally applied by the counselor and occur in the form of encouraging phrases such as "that's good," "that's great," and "tell me more." These phases are contingent upon the client's performing various appropriate behaviors that successively approximate goals. Model reinforcement occurs when a client has an opportunity to observe someone else perform a given task with some degree of success. Models may be live (real people) or symbolic (films, recordings).

Covert reinforcement (positive self-statements) and punishment (negative self-statements) techniques usually make up self-instructional or cognitive self-reinforcement systems. At a covert level, vis-a-vis thinking and imagining, people can, through positive self-statements or positive imagery, learn and reinforce more adaptive beliefs, emotions, and behaviors. The use of covert negative self-statements (i.e., smoking is bad for me) help people to audit potentially harmful situations.

Self-instructional techniques that promote self-efficacy and effective behavior can override external environmental contingencies and are also potent reinforcers. Such reinforcers enhance the power of people to regulate their own behavior.

Evaluation of Counseling Outcomes

Once appropriate counseling techniques have been implemented, the evaluation of their effectiveness in terms of specific behavioral objectives begins. Thoresen and Anton (1973) suggest that evaluation helps the counselor decide (1) if a particular technique is appropriate to the achievement of behavioral objectives, and (2) if the technique is working. If it is not it should be discontinued or augmented with other techniques.

Since counseling is an experimental process, techniques are implemented and evaluated until the clients' objectives are reached.

Thoresen (1976) believes that a counselor should be acquainted with single organism research designs to test the efficacy of counseling. Several designs have been described by Thoresen and Anton (1974). The first, and most simple, is the *AB design*. The AB design has two phases, the "baseline" or "before treatment" (A) and a treatment phase (B). The frequency of response prior to treatment taken over a specified period of time (i.e., each day for two weeks) may be compared to the frequency of responses during the treatment phase (i.e., each day for a two-week period).

A second technique for measuring changes in behavior is the *ABA design*. Measures are taken before, during, and after treatment. A third method is the *ABAB design*. This is a reversal design where the counseling treatment is used a second time (off-on-off-on). The reversal design, while able to demonstrate that behavioral changes are a function of counseling treatment, is typically inappropriate for use in a counseling relationship. Some changes in client behavior may not be reversible and most problem behavior should not be reinstated.

Multiple baseline designs allow for the observation and recording of two or more client behaviors simultaneously, while treatment is applied to one behavior at a time. For example, systematic desensitization may be used to reduce test anxiety and increase assertiveness, and cognitive restructuring may be used to decrease negative self-statements and increase positive self-statements.

Thoresen and Anton (1974) believe that intensive designs afford the counselor a very simple way of assessing the efficacy of intervention. In intensive designs, one is not limited to static estimates of observation represented by means or averages. Thoresen and Anton (1974) suggest that the slope (or drift) of data over time is a better way of assessing change. To estimate trends accurately, frequent and repeated observations over time, using variables that can be easily observed and recorded are necessary. Examples of behaviors that are easily observed and recorded by the client or others are cigarettes smoked, positive self-statements, assertive responses, depressive thoughts, anxiety states, dating behavior, headaches, stomachaches, tardiness, attendance at class, and weight.

COUNSELING APPLICATION

This section describes a case of intensive counseling for self-efficacy with a 43-year-old male who was having sleep disturbances and symptoms of depression. The case illustrates the use of simple as well as complex behavioral interventions ranging from self-monitoring through cue-controlled relaxation and cognitive restructuring. The figures depict the observations, data collection, and the effect of the interventions.

Intensive Self-Efficacy Counseling in a Health Care Setting

Bill R. was a 43-year-old construction worker who claimed to have suffered from insomnia for 15 years. Bill also suffered from symptoms of depression and anxiety periodically. He was recently divorced from his wife. Following a complete physical examination, it was concluded that there was no organic basis for Bill's sleep disturbance. Behavioral counseling was recommended by the physician. Bill was at first reluctant to seek counseling because for years he thought that the cause of his problem was physical.

The first session consisted of identifying Bill's problems, gathering baseline information, formulating goals, and determining counseling techniques. Certainly the counselor wanted Bill to be more comfortable with the counseling relationship and, therefore, spent some time dealing with Bill's misconceptions about it.

The interview already in progress:

Counselor: Now that we have reviewed your record, I sense that you are uncomfortable being here.

Bill: Look, I'm not crazy or mentally ill.

Counselor: Bill, you do have some symptoms that interfere with your personal functioning, and I assume you want to do something about them.

Bill: That's right, but what are you going to do to me? I don't believe in psychoanalysis.

Counselor: You are not here for psychoanalysis. Let's say you are here to learn some basic skills to help you relax more and sleep better.

Bill: What skills do I have to learn?

Counselor: Since your sleep disturbance may be tension related, I believe a simple procedure called cue-controlled relaxation could be helpful with that problem.

In the first session, the counselor determined that Bill awoke on the average of five to six times each night after he fell asleep. Bill would stay awake for an average of 10 to 20 minutes. During the time Bill was awake, he felt quite depressed and ruminated on negative thoughts about himself (i.e., I am no good at all; I am a failure). Bill was then asked to keep a record of the frequency of sleep arousal, minutes of awake time, and number of negative self-statements, and the frequency of depressed symptoms.

The first session continues.

Bill: That sounds okay to me. When do we begin?
Counselor: Before we start the procedure, I would like to make another point. There seems to be another aspect to the problem — that is the negative view you have of yourself and the symptoms of depression. To deal with these, we could teach you a simple cognitive restructuring technique. Let me explain just what that involves.

The second session:

Counselor: Bill, we will begin today's session with cue-controlled relaxation, okay?
Bill: Okay. Let's begin.
Counselor: Good. There are two basic dimensions to cue-controlled relaxation. First, you will learn how to relax. Second, you will associate certain words (cues) with the relaxation response. So, in time these words or cues may serve to activate the relaxation response.
Bill: Will this help me sleep?
Counselor: That is what we want to find out experimentally. You see, Bill, counseling is like a scientific experiment.

The counselor introduced Bill to a standard relaxation procedure involving the tensing and loosening of various muscle groups and deep diaphragmatic breathing. When a relaxed state was achieved the counselor asked Bill to concentrate his attention to two words — "relax" and "sleep." The counselor suggested that Bill should not at this time really fall asleep, but only to concentrate on pairing the cue words with the relaxation response. It was also suggested to Bill while he was in a deep state of relaxation that he might find both the relax and sleep cue words very helpful in falling asleep and remaining asleep. Bill became quite relaxed.

Counselor: If you are relaxed, Bill, signal by raising your right index finger, (Bill responds). Now, concentrate on the word "relax." I will repeat it several times . . . relax . . . (pause) . . . relax (pause) . . . relax (pause). Simply connect the cue word with the sensation of relaxation.

The entire procedure takes about 10 to 20 minutes. If the client becomes upset at any time, the counselor can stop the exercise.

The cue-controlled relaxation process continued over the next two sessions. The counselor, during this time, helped Bill restructure his negative thoughts about himself via positive self-statements. These positive self-efficacy statements were rehearsed while Bill was in a state of relaxation. The last three counseling sessions involved more of the same with the addition of introducing the cue "relax-sleep." Bill was assigned the task of using the cue-controlled technique each night before falling asleep.

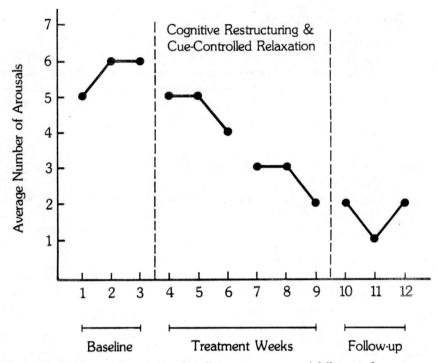

Figure 8-2. Self-report data during baseline, treatment, and follow-up for average number of arousals for each week.

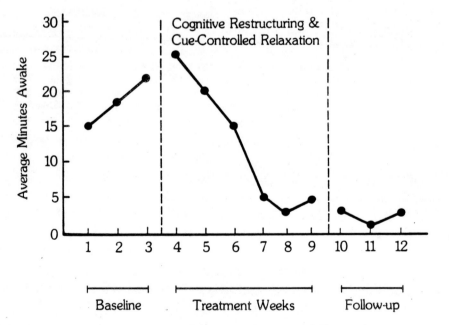

Figure 8-3. Self-report data during baseline, treatment, and follow-up for average number of minutes awake following arousals for each week.

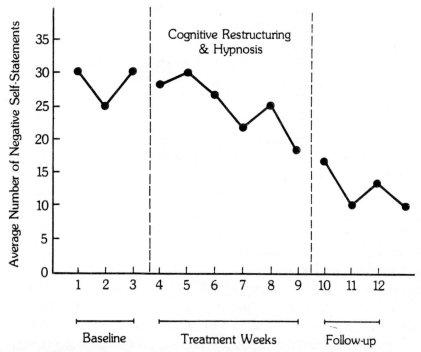

Figure 8-4. Self-report data during baseline, treatment and follow-up for average number of negative self-statements.

Bill's progress in counseling is provided in Figures 8-2, 8-3, and 8-4. These charts show Bill's performance on sleep arousal, awake time, and negative self-statements at baseline, during treatment, and after treatment.

Critical Comments

Of all the cognitive-behavior theories of counseling described in this session, Intensive Self-Efficacy theory conforms most to a scientific model of behavior change and counseling. Thoresen adheres most stringently to the notion that the concepts and procedures of counseling must be stated explicitly, tested empirically, and revised continually. The conviction that "research is treatment" and "treatment is research" is firm in Thoresen's theory of counseling. Thoresen's theory of counseling would rate moderately high in comprehensiveness, very high on specificity, correspondence to fact, researchability, and practicality.

Thoresen effectively operationalizes the concepts of behavior change, thus contributing to the utility of the theory. Intensive counseling is based largely upon controlled experimental studies of the single case.

Thoresen has refined the methods of investigation and treatment of a variety of behavioral problems ranging from vocational and career decision-making to modifying behavior associated with Type A cardiovascular risk factors. Obviously, Thoresen has depended heavily on Albert Bandura's social learning theory for many of the concepts of intensive self-efficacy counseling, especially self-efficacy theory.

Given the strong behavioral leanings of Thoresen, one would not expect to find a comprehensive theory of personality or behavior underlying his approach to counseling. His orientation attempts to bring precision to the study of personality and behavior change through the application of the scientific method. Realizing that an overly strict application of technique can lead to fragmentation and narrowness of perspective, Thoresen incorporates an empirically-derived holistic view of the person and of the counseling process.

A weakness in Thoresen's theory is that it minimizes the role that unconscious factors play in human behavior. He circumvents this to some extent by introducing the notion of covert influences. Moreover, Thoresen has little to say about the role of behavioral dynamics, that is, how thoughts, feelings, bodily responses, and behavior interact as integrative systems and change over time. His more recent writings, however, suggest that he may be moving in this direction with his recognition of imagery and hypnosis as viable treatment and investigative modalities.

Thoresen's notion of cognitive restructuring appears to be a bit superficial. Rather than basic cognitive restructuring on the use of logical-empirical methods to confront belief systems and related behavior in the environment, he talks of substituting positive self-statements for negative self-statements—a touch of Norman Vincent Peale. However, in fairness to Thoresen, he is trying to operationalize a problem construct for behavior theorists, that of "Cognition and Reason." One gets the impression that when behaviorists mention "reason and rationality" they see themselves committing the Cartesian sin of mind-body dualism.

REFERENCES

Bandura, A. (1977). *Social learning theory.* Englewood Cliffs, NJ: Prentice-Hall.

Friedman, M., Thoresen, C., & Gill, J. (1981). Type A behavior: Its possible role, detection, and lateralization in patients with ischemic heart disease. In J. Hurst (Ed.), *Heart update V* (pp. 88-99). New York: McGraw-Hill.

Krumboltz, J., & Thoresen, C. (1969). *Behavioral counseling: Cases and techniques.* New York: Holt, Rinehart and Winston.

Krumboltz, J., & Thoresen, C. (1976). *Counseling methods.* New York: Holt, Rinehart and Winston.

Thoresen, C. (1973a). Behavioral humanism. In C.E. Thoresen (Ed.), *Behavior modification in education, seventy-second yearbook of the national society for the study of education* (pp. 385-421). Chicago: University of Chicago Press.

Thoresen, C. (1973b). The healthy personality as a sick trait. *The Counseling Psychologist, 4*, 51-55.

Thoresen, C. (1976). *Self-control: Learning how to C.A.R.E. for yourself.* Madison, WI: Counseling Films, Box 1047 (Film).

Thoresen, C. (1978). Making better science, intensively. *Personnel and Guidance Journal, 56*, 279-282.

Thoresen, C., & Anton, J. (1973). Intensive counseling. *Focus on Guidance, 6*, 1-11.

Thoresen, C., & Anton, J. (1974). Intensive experimental research in counseling. *Journal of Counseling Psychology, 21*, 6, 553-559.

Thoresen, C., & Coates, T. (1978). What does it mean to be a behavior therapist? *The Counseling Psychologist, 1* (3), 3-20.

Thoresen, C., & Coates, T. (1980). *The behavior therapist.* Monterey, CA: Brooks/Cole.

Thoresen, C., & Ewert, C. (1976). Behavioral self-control and career development. *The Counseling Psychologist, 6* (3), 29-42.

Thoresen, C., & Mahoney, M. (1974). *Behavioral self-control.* New York: Holt, Rinehart and Winston.

Thoresen, C., & Mahoney, M. (1974). *Self-control: Power to the person.* Monterey, CA: Brooks/Cole.

Thoresen, C., Telch, M., & Eagleston, J. (1981). Approaches to altering the type A behavior pattern. *Psychosomatics, 22* (b), 472-482.

CHAPTER 9

ALBERT ELLIS'
RATIONAL EMOTIVE THERAPY

FOUNDATIONS AND STRUCTURE

Historical Foundations

ALBERT ELLIS earned his Ph.D. from Columbia University. He has served on the faculties of Rutgers and New York Universities and is the founder and current director of the Institute for Advanced Study in Rational Emotive Psychotherapy. His original training was in the fields of marriage, family and sex counseling, where he went on to become one of the world's foremost experts on human sexuality and marriage. Having observed that dysfunctional marriages and families are comprised of disturbed individuals, Ellis concluded that there were limitations in any approach to counseling that did not address the problem of individual people. He therefore embarked on a course of training in-depth psychoanalysis, undergoing classical psychoanalysis with a training analyst affiliated with Karen Horney.

During the late 1940's Ellis practiced classical psychoanalysis. Although he considered himself a relatively competent analyst, he found major shortcomings with many analytic techniques, such as free association, dream interpretation, and the nondirective passivity expected of an analyst. He began to suspect that his patients were partly correct when they complained that he wasn't doing his job.

He noted that while his patients gained considerable insight into the origins of their emotional disturbance, they continued to remain disturbed in their daily lives. Becoming somewhat frustrated with this recurring observation, Ellis moved away from classic psychoanalysis into the neo-analytic approaches of Ferenczi, Rank, Horney and Sullivan.

The combined influence of these theorists led him to consider the importance of interpersonal relationship techniques, such as the use of empathy and dealing with the "here and now."

While retaining for a time most of the basic tenets of psychoanalysis, Ellis nevertheless became increasingly active and directive with his clients. By the early 1950's his doubts about many aspects of psychoanalysis were too serious to be ignored any longer. In particular, he believed the system to be too abstract, and too difficult to operationalize for research purposes.

Ellis began to draw upon his training in philosophy to seek answers to the questions he had raised. In 1954 he started to integrate his views of philosophy and psychology in a unique way — the result being the beginnings of a rational theory of human personality and counseling. Ellis is a prolific writer, having authored hundreds of papers on the theory and practice of rational emotive therapy, as well as several books. Among his most noteworthy books are *Reason and Emotion in Psychotherapy* (1962); *Growth Through Reason* (1971); *A New Guide to Rational Living* (1975) (with R. Harper); *Brief Psychotherapy in Medical and Health Practice* (1978) (with E. Abrahams); *Humanistic Psychotherapy* (1973); *Rational-Emotive Therapy: A Handbook of Theory and Practice* (1978) (with R. Grieger); and *Executive Leadership* (1972).

Philosophical Foundations

Rational Emotive Therapy is largely based on certain principles espoused by the ancient Greek and Roman Stoic philosophers, such as Epictitus and Marcus Aurelius, as well as later rational philosophers such as Spinoza and Russell, semanticists such as Korzybski, and logical empiricists such as Hume. These philosophies tend to view humans as highly symbolic beings, capable of using reason to best serve their personal and communal interests.

The principal foundation for Ellis' theory of emotions can be found in Epictitus: "Men are disturbed not by things, but by the views they take of them." This Stoic philosophy suggests that human beings are better off emotionally when they accept or treat with philosophical indifference that which cannot be changed.

The Stoics gave priority to the practice of calm rational thought, which they believed was a beneficial influence to one's emotions and behavior. This view is reinforced by the later philosophy of Bertrand Russell. Russell (1950) states that, "When you have looked for some time steadily at the worst possibility and have said to yourself with real conviction, 'Well after all, that would not matter so much,' you will find that your worry diminishes to a quite extraordinary extent" (p. 47). Russell also maintained that the way to minimize every kind of fear is to think about it calmly, to concentrate on the feared object until the fear becomes familiar.

Korzybski (1933), a general semanticist, has had a significant influence on RET. Ellis believes RET is a truly semantic therapy in that priority is given to the *meanings* of words that people use to describe their thoughts, feelings and behavior. In his most recent writings, Ellis has emphasized a form of language developed by Bourland (1968), called E-Prime. E-Prime eliminates all forms of the verb *to be* (i.e., is, am, are, were). For example, "I am a fallible human being," translates into "I behave fallibly;" "This is awful or catastrophic," translates into "This situation causes me a lot of inconvenience." Verbal statements such as "I am worthless" or "I am wonderful" reflect overgeneralizations that cannot be proven or demonstrated empirically. Such beliefs, in the form of statements made to the self, become the root of most emotional disturbances. The use of E-Prime language generates more precise ways of communication with oneself and others.

One of the major philosophical concepts in Ellis' theory of personality is that of *self-acceptance*. He argues that notions about the inherent goodness or badness of humankind are confusing and unverifiable. At best they are erroneous overgeneralizations. If human beings have any worth, it is because they exist and (most likely) value their existence. Scientifically, human beings cannot be rated as "good" or "bad," although specific thoughts or behaviors may be rated for appropriateness or effectiveness.

These philosophical views are fundamental to and inextricably interwoven into RET, the main aspects of which will be presented in the next section.

Social-Psychological Foundations

The ABC Theory in RET

According to the ABC Theory of human functioning, thinking and emotion overlap. Thinking, a cognitive process, represents a mediation operation between some stimulus event and a response. One's emotional response to a situation, therefore, is not due to the situation itself, but to the thoughts, beliefs and attitudes the person *holds* about the situation. For example, an event or stimulus, which we call (A), does not directly cause one to become emotionally upset (C). It is (B), the beliefs or ideas about (A), that more directly contributes to (C) (Ellis, 1977).

Semantic processes in the form of self-statements or beliefs significantly affect people's emotions, and serve to motivate their behavior. When people talk to themselves in ways that suggest optimism, hope, and joy, they tend to have more positive emotions. However, when their self-talk is pessimistic, hopeless, or derogatory, they tend to feel sad, upset, anxious, and depressed. Semantic labeling and self-talk do not necessarily operate at a conscious level. Often people are unaware of the meanings or values they attribute to themselves, or to other significant people, places and things.

RET hypothesizes that when people do become emotionally upset at point (C) about a situation (A), they have both rational beliefs (rB's) and irrational beliefs (iB's) about (A). Rational beliefs take the form of wishes, preferences, desires and wants. Examples are: "I prefer to have others approve of things I do;" "I don't like to have people disapprove of me for things that I don't do well." These beliefs are more likely to lead to appropriate responses at (C), such as mild frustration, hope, sorrow, or regret, as opposed to depression, loss of self-esteem, and great anxiety (Ellis, 1979). We term the former set of responses appropriate, because they are much more likely to bring about constructive, goal-oriented behavior than are the latter responses.

When people hold rational beliefs they are less likely to experience excessive, counter-productive emotional stress. However, human beings have a tendency that is largely learned, but partially innate, to have both rational and irrational beliefs about the same event. Irrational beliefs (iB's) generally take the form of unquestioned absolutes, musts, shoulds, oughts, commands and demands. Examples are: "I must not fail;" "I should be perfect;" "I can't stand things not to be my way;" "I am worthless if I don't have everyone's approval." Such irrational ideas can produce rather unpleasant emotional and behavioral consequences at (C).

Ellis (1979) asserts that the RET Theory of Personality gives full consideration to multiple origins and influences of personality. While he gives priority to psychological functions, he by no means de-emphasizes cultural, social, physiological and hereditary influences. Several major factors that Ellis (1979) believes contribute to the development of the personality are:

- Interpersonal relationships
- Direct teachings by parents, teachers, relatives
- Clergy, peers and mass media
- Social class
- Social, political and religious organizations
- Biological desires
- Physical and psychological stress and pain
- Poverty
- Self-rating
- Social modeling and identification with others
- Formulating goals
- Superstitions and suggestibility
- Desire for freedom

According to Ellis (1979), these influences have innate as well as socially acquired (learned) aspects. In many instances these influences contradict one another. For example, some interpersonal relationships may be in direct competition with personal, business, and academic interests. Because of the many contradictory forces emanating from the inside as well as the outside, human behavior is often inconsistent and confused.

In a paper entitled "The Biological Basis of Human Irrationality" Ellis (1976) made several points:

- Irrationalities to some extent exist in all of us — no one is exempted.
- Irrational behavior has been observed in just about all societies and cultures.
- Humans tend to be rebellious and are inclined to go against authority.
- High intelligence does not preclude irrationality.
- Insight into one's irrationality rarely eliminates it.
- No matter how hard people work to overcome their irrational tendencies, they find great difficulty in doing so.
- Making overgeneralizations seems to be a characteristic human behavior.
- Humans tend to be naturally hedonistic (pleasure seeking).

At the same time, Ellis believes humans have a countervailing biological disposition to act in a rational, self-fulfilling, and self-actualizing manner. It is these capacities that RET attempts to develop and use.

The Development of the Person

Rational Emotive Therapy has not yet been developed to the point of fully addressing the entire life cycle of human development. While Ellis does provide a framework for understanding people of all ages, the emphasis has been on children and adults (Ellis, 1979), and on adolescents (Tosi, 1974), with little attention given to the elderly.

In his earlier work, Ellis leaned heavily on social-learning theory, the biological sciences, and the cognitive-developmental theories of Piaget and Luria to form a foundation for his theory of counseling and psychotherapy. More recently, however, he and some of his associates seem to be moving toward a more comprehensive social-psychological model of development.

Although Ellis alludes to the notion of unconscious processes in human functioning, he does not assign them priority in RET. What he believes is that most of the irrational prejudices that people hold are due mainly to biological factors, with some measure of cultural influence. Beginning with biologically determined needs for survival, self-protection, and the like, cultures have developed certain structures and rules for meeting these needs. Starting at a very early age, and continuing throughout the life span, human beings internalize these useful cultural standards and sensible cultural rules, and they irrationally turn them into absolutistic shoulds and musts. These irrational beliefs become so ingrained that people are often not even fully aware that they hold them, nor do they understand how they come to arise.

Ellis (1977) also asserts that humans have innate and acquired tendencies to imitate or model themselves after others. People frequently learn and unlearn healthy as well as unhealthy thoughts, feelings, and behaviors through conscious and unconscious modeling. To a great extent, "model reinforcement" and "social reinforcement" serve to shape one's cognitive, affective, physiological, and behavioral response tendencies. He is quick to point out, however, the role of powerful cognitive mediating factors in learning through social modeling processes.

Concepts of Functional and Dysfunctional Behavior

Given the assumption that human beings have innate biological as well as culturally acquired tendencies to function both rationally and irrationally, the question that arises is "What constitutes rationality"? Maultsby (1984) postulates five criteria for determining rationality or rational well-being. These criteria have applications for effective personal, social, and career development. People who are more rational (1) tend to accept what actually exists in the real world, (2) try to live effectively in social groups, (3) relate intimately to a few members of the social group or community, (4) engage in productive and enjoyable work, and (5) participate in chosen recreational pursuits (art, music, sports).

Ellis by no means views rationality as an absolute. If anything, he refers to himself as a "relative rationalist." Therefore, he views people who approximate or move toward meeting those five criteria as being more likely to exhibit rationality. Irrationality consists of interfering with one's own life, needlessly harming oneself, and sabotaging one's personal, social, and career goals.

Ellis accepts a humanistic existential philosophy in at least one major way. While acknowledging the many biological and cultural factors which influence human functioning, he believes that individuals are capable of overcoming many of them. Because humans do possess the ability to be conscious of themselves and their behavior, they can become aware of their limitations and so something about some of them. People can, to some extent, define their own freedom and individuality, choose the way they will live in relation to others, accept their personal experience, live in the "here and now," and accept their own fallibility (Ellis, 1979). Psychologically effective people, according to Ellis, experience a high degree of self-acceptance. People don't need to rate or evaluate their total selves or being, but only their acts, deeds, and performances.

Concepts of Behavior Change

Ellis (1979) admits that RET is not interested so much in constructing a theory of personality change. He makes several assumptions about the conditions that foster behavioral change, most of which stress the importance of modifying the way people think as well as how they behave. The most fundamental assumption underlying RET is that human thinking and emotions are interrelated. People create most of their feeling by the way they think and, conversely, create some of their thoughts by the way they feel or emote. To change negative emotions such as anxiety, guilt, or hostility requires that an individual identifies and challenges the ideas and misconceptions that most likely underlie them. RET helps people recognize and challenge the values and beliefs that encourage the absolutistic and overgeneralized demands they place on themselves and others, and to replace them with ones that help them behave in less self-defeating ways. The ABC method of problem analysis and assessment permits individuals to become aware of the cognitive sources of personal disturbance, and also provides a method to dispute those self-defeating cognitions.

Emotionally disturbed people often attribute causes to external situations. Such attributions may tend to distort reality. When people assume responsibility for their own attributions, ideas, motivations, emotions, and behaviors, they frequently feel better and deal more effectively with others. Ellis (1979) has summarized ten basic irrational ideas and their rational counterparts as follows:

IRRATIONAL IDEAS	*RATIONAL COUNTERPARTS*
• I must be loved and approved by others.	• I desire the approval of others for the things I do.
• I must be perfect and achieving in all possible respects.	• I desire to behave competently and achieve the things that are important to me.
• Many people are evil and wicked and they should be severely punished and reprimanded;	• Some people do act in stupid or bad ways and it is desirable to respond to them appropriately.
• Life is horrible and catastrophic when it is not exactly the way I want it.	• Certain life situations may not be the way I would like them to be, but that doesn't make all of life horrible and catastrophic.
• Events external to me cause me to become emotionally upset.	• I most probably cause most of my own emotional upsets by the manner in which I appraise those events.
• I should be overly preoccupied with fear and anxiety over future events that are potentially dangerous and uncertain.	• Being concerned over potential dangers does not mean that I need to be overly preoccupied.
• It is easier to avoid life's difficulties than to face them.	• In the long run it is better to face one's responsibilities than to avoid them.
• I must have someone stronger than myself.	• I am better off depending on my own resources.
• The past influences almost everything I do now or will do in the future.	• My present behavior is largely due to the meanings I presently ascribe to the past and future.
• I can achieve happiness by inertia, passivity, and inaction.	• Human happiness results from activity and involvement with people, places and things.

Rational Insight

Insight into the nature of one's own personal sources of emotional disturbance is important in RET. RET does not assume that insight will provoke spontaneous changes in behavior. Ellis (1975) recognizes three variations of insight. The first type of insight is the discovery that one's emotional or behavioral responses to a situation do have antecedent causes but not necessarily ones that arc deeply rooted in the past. A person's existing system of beliefs often constitutes the most potent antecedent of most behavior. Meaningful changes in behavior are largely a function of one's awareness of how present beliefs and ideas influence emotional and behavioral tendencies. A second type of insight suggests that when people become upset it is because they continue to reindoctrinate themselves with irrational or distorted ideas that may have originated in the past. In effect, they keep reinforcing themselves. The third type of insight suggests that people change as a result of rational efforts, including actively practicing rational thinking and behaving over an extended period. This is probably the most important one of the three mentioned.

Philosophic Restructuring Via Logico-Empirical Methods

With cognitive awareness gained from rational insights, people are better positioned to identify their dogmatic and rigidly held irrational beliefs that produce emotionally disturbing consequences, and then solidly interrupt them with strong counterbeliefs that lead to more appropriate emotional responses and desirable behavioral changes. People can learn the habit of working against dysfunctional patterns and at the same time accept the fact that perfect solutions to one's problems do not exist (Ellis, 1977).

In Ellis' system, counseling is essentially a realistic vehicle through which people can be educated to restructure their dysfunctional patterns of thinking. Cognitive restructuring makes heavy use of logico-empirical methods. Clients learn to apply logic (to ask if this idea makes sense), empirical observation, and testing (to ask if what I *think* might happen *really* will happen) for the purpose of achieving a more productive life.

Another aspect of philosophic or cognitive restructuring techniques used in RET is semantic reconditioning. This involves learning to think in E-Prime language. As you recall, E-Prime eliminates the verb *to be* (am, is, are, was, were, be, been, and being). For example, instead of saying that "I am an idiot," I could say "I acted like an idiot." In this sense one does not rate the entire being but only one element of behavior. Semantic reconditioning tends to foster attitudes of self-acceptance. RET counselors are very sensitive to the nature of language in the counseling relationship. They, therefore, try to model E-Prime language with their clients.

Assessment of Human Functioning

RET counselors use a variety of clinical and objective methods for assessing human functioning in counseling. The clinical use of the ABC method of problem analysis allows the counselor to identify important situational events, irrational and rational beliefs, and their emotional and behavioral consequences (see Forms 1 and 2).

RET counselors carefully observe the semantic systems of their clients—how they verbalize about themselves and their problems. The counselor listens for statements such as "I am a bad person," "I am no good," "Others cause me to be upset," and "I must be perfect." Careful attention is given to how these statements tend to overlap with or are associated with self-defeating emotions and behavior. The counselor also listens for the more functional elements of the client's semantic system, which are then encouraged and reinforced.

RET counselors try to identify other self statements that have negative emotional implications in the formulation of diagnostic hypotheses. Examples of such self statements are "I become so upset before an examination that I break out into hives." The counselor could hypothesize that a client may be saying: "I must not fail an examination, for that would mean that I am a failure as a human being, and that would be awful."

The counselor then estimates the frequency, intensity and duration of such irrational self-verbalizations, negative emotions and behaviors. The client may then be shown how to engage in rational self-analysis using the five criteria for rational thinking and behavior. RET counselors are eager to share their diagnostic hypotheses with their clients for the sake of minimizing the ambiguity so often characterizing counseling relationships.

Objective measures or irrationality/rationality are also employed in RET. These may include the *Personal Belief Inventory* (PBI) (Hartman, 1968), the *Common Beliefs Survey III* (Bessai, 1976). RET plays down the role of traditional psychiatric classification systems and deemphasizes the importance of earlier life experiences. As a "here and now" approach to counseling and psychotherapy, RET is primarily interested in the client's present functioning.

Goals and Directions of Counseling

Ellis (1962, 1971, 1979), in several of his works, provides goal statements for RET counselors. These goals are quite consistent with his theory about human effectiveness and are as follows:

- *Self-Interest.* Healthy people are primarily interested in and true to themselves, and secondarily in others. However, the RET view of self-interest does not preclude social interest. Rational people enjoy freedom from needless restriction and suffering and want the same for others. They may even be more likely to become involved in community projects that benefit the common good.

- *Self-Direction.* Healthy people tend to be inner-directed. They seek motivation mostly from within rather than without. While they are cooperative at times seek help from others, they most often work out their problems independently.

- *Tolerance.* Healthy people do not condemn other human beings. They refrain from rating or making judgments on the total worth of others, and allow others the right to be wrong. On the other hand, healthy people do discriminate between appropriate and inappropriate behavior.

- *Flexibility.* Flexibility implies open-mindedness. Healthy people are receptive to new ideas.

- *Acceptance of Uncertainty.* Psychologically healthy people have a greater tolerance for uncertainty and ambiguity. They tend to think more in terms of probability and possibility rather than absolute certainty.

- *Scientific Thinking.* People who function well tend toward objectivity, and the use of reason. These people are able to apply the laws of logic and the scientific method to internal as well as external events.

- *Commitment.* Healthy people are involved in other people, places and things. They have strong interests in some field of endeavor, either vocational or avocational.

- *Risk-Taking.* Psychologically mature people take reasonable risks. They are adventurous and are not easily bored. These people strive to accomplish many of their goals even at the risk of failure.

- *Self-Acceptance.* Healthy people tend to like themselves and value their existence, even if they don't always like everyone or their behaviors.

- *Non-Utopianism.* Healthy people do not expect perfection in this world. While they may expect to achieve a certain excellence in personal performance, they do not believe this will make them perfect people.

The Counseling Process:
Structuring, Facilitating and Terminating

Rational emotive counseling is highly structured and highly directive. Counselors who use RET tend to be problem-oriented and practical. Typically, time limits are set for each session, often shorter than in some other counseling approaches. Half-hour sessions, as opposed to the traditional "50-minute hour," are not uncommon among RET practitioners. The basic principles of RET are laid out early in the course of counseling. The client may be assigned various readings (bibliotherapy) covering these principles to reinforce the learnings derived from the counseling sessions. Homework assignments are given regularly. Some counselors tape record sessions and permit clients to review the tapes during the session or at home.

During the counseling process, clients are taught the major techniques of philosophic and cognitive restructuring. Counselors actively confront distorted ideas and maladaptive behaviors, and literally show their clients how to do the same. Each time clients engage in more rational thinking and behavior they are positively reinforced. Of paramount importance is that clients attribute the changes being made in their cognitive, emotional, and behavioral states to *themselves* — to what they are doing for themselves and not to the "magic" of the counselor.

Counseling terminates when the counselor and client both agree that specific goals have been met. Most often this is when the client exhibits more rational ways of thinking and behaving, shows a good grasp of basic RET principles, and is able to apply RET principles to life situations.

The criteria for success in rational emotive counseling are that clients can and do:

(1) assume more responsibility for their thoughts and actions;
(2) accept themselves more fully;
(3) demonstrate more scientific thinking and independence;
(4) increase reasonable risk-taking;
(5) minimize personal and environmental stress (Ellis and Abrahams, 1978).

The last few sessions are devoted primarily to reviewing what has been learned in counseling and gaining a sense of perspective that will enable clients to go out into the world and apply their new learning in whatever situations they meet. Most counselors do leave the door open for future sessions if the client desires.

Counseling Techniques and Procedures

Cognitive Restructuring

As you have seen, Ellis gives priority to cognitive counseling techniques. The major cognitive techniques employed by RET counselors are cognitive restructuring— the Disputing of Irrational Beliefs (DIBS), cognitive homework, Rational Emotive Imagery (REI), and bibliotherapy. Each of these techniques will be presented.

Disputing Irrational Beliefs (DIBS). Ellis (1977) asserts that DIBS, known as direct cognitive restructuring or the ABC technique, is the most fundamental method in RET. DIBS begins with an ABC problem analysis, as we have seen earlier, but then adds two new steps—points (D) and (E). Cognitive restructuring in general, and DIBS in particular, involves the philosophical and logical analysis of irrational thinking. Once clients realize, via the ABC process, that their thoughts, beliefs, etc., at (B) result in certain emotional consequences (C), they are taught at (D) to vigorously *dispute* their irrational beliefs, and replace them with more rational ones. Point (E), then, refers to the effects of this behavior, where clients can observe what happens as a result. The entire ABCDE sequence, showing the DIBS technique, is presented on the following charts developed by Ellis. (See Forms 1 and 2, pp. 210, 211.)

Rational Emotive Imagery (REI). This is a technique that incorporates both mental imagery and cognitive restructuring. It is extremely

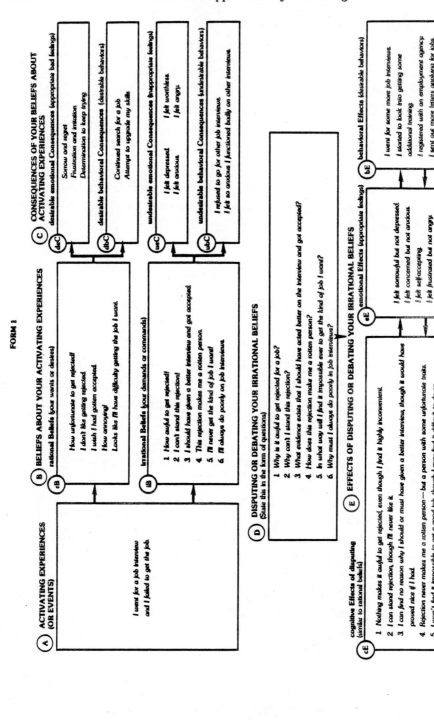

FORM 1

A ACTIVATING EXPERIENCES (OR EVENTS)

I went for a job interview and I failed to get the job.

B BELIEFS ABOUT YOUR ACTIVATING EXPERIENCES

rB rational Beliefs (your wants or desires)

How unfortunate to get rejected!
I don't like getting rejected.
I wish I had gotten accepted.
How annoying!
Looks like I'll have difficulty getting the job I want.

iB Irrational Beliefs (your demands or commands)

1 How awful to get rejected!
2 I can't stand this rejection!
3 I should have given a better interview and got accepted.
4 This rejection makes me a rotten person.
5 I'll never get the kind of job I want.
6 I'll always do poorly on job interviews.

C CONSEQUENCES OF YOUR BELIEFS ABOUT ACTIVATING EXPERIENCES

deC desirable emotional Consequences (appropriate bad feelings)

Sorrow and regret
Frustration and irritation
Determination to keep trying

dbC desirable behavioral Consequences (desirable behaviors)

Continued search for a job
Attempt to upgrade my skills

ueC undesirable emotional Consequences (inappropriate feelings)

I felt depressed.   I felt worthless.
I felt anxious.   I felt angry.

ubC undesirable behavioral Consequences (undesirable behaviors)

I refused to go for other job interviews.
I felt so anxious I functioned badly on other interviews.

D DISPUTING OR DEBATING YOUR IRRATIONAL BELIEFS
(State this in the form of questions)

1 Why is it awful to get rejected for a job?
2 Why can't I stand this rejection?
3 What evidence exists that I should have acted better on the interview and got accepted?
4 How does this rejection make me a rotten person?
5 In what way will I find it impossible ever to get the kind of job I want?
6 Why must I always do poorly in job interviews?

E EFFECTS OF DISPUTING OR DEBATING YOUR IRRATIONAL BELIEFS

cE cognitive Effects of disputing (similar to rational beliefs)

1 Nothing makes it awful to get rejected, even though I find it highly inconvenient.
2 I can stand rejection, though I'll never like it.
3 I can find no reason why I should or must have given a better interview, though it would have proved nice if I had.
4 Rejection never makes me a rotten person—but a person with some unfortunate traits.
5 I won't find it impossible to get a good job, though I may find it difficult to do so.
6 I don't have to do poorly on job interviews always, especially if I try to learn from my errors.

eE emotional Effects (appropriate feelings)

I felt sorrowful but not depressed.
I felt concerned but not anxious.
I felt self-accepting.
I felt frustrated but not angry.

bE behavioral Effects (desirable behaviors)

I went for some more job interviews.
I started to look into getting some additional training.
I registered with an employment agency.
I sent out more letters applying for jobs.

Sample Rational Self-Help Form. ©1976 by the Institute for Rational Living, Inc., 45 East 65th Street, New York, N.Y. 10021

FORM 2

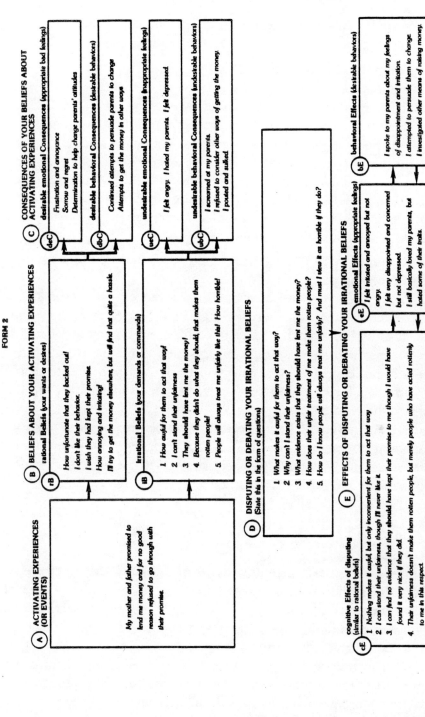

A ACTIVATING EXPERIENCES (OR EVENTS)

My mother and father promised to lend me money and for no good reason refused to go through with their promise.

B BELIEFS ABOUT YOUR ACTIVATING EXPERIENCES

rB rational Beliefs (your wants or desires)

How unfortunate that they backed out!
I don't like their behavior.
I wish they had kept their promise.
How annoying and irritating!
I'll try to get the money elsewhere, but will find that quite a hassle.

iB Irrational Beliefs (your demands or commands)

1 How awful for them to act that way!
2 I can't stand their unfairness
3 They should have lent me the money!
4 Because they didn't do what they should, that makes them rotten people!
5 People will always treat me unfairly like this! How horrible!

C CONSEQUENCES OF YOUR BELIEFS ABOUT ACTIVATING EXPERIENCES

deC desirable emotional Consequences (appropriate bad feelings)

Frustration and annoyance
Sorrow and regret
Determination to help change parents' attitudes

dbC desirable behavioral Consequences (desirable behaviors)

Continued attempts to persuade parents to change
Attempts to get the money in other ways

ueC undesirable emotional Consequences (inappropriate feelings)

I felt angry. I hated my parents. I felt depressed.

ubC undesirable behavioral Consequences (undesirable behaviors)

I screamed at my parents.
I refused to consider other ways of getting the money.
I pouted and sulked.

D DISPUTING OR DEBATING YOUR IRRATIONAL BELIEFS
(State this in the form of questions)

1 What makes it awful for them to act that way?
2 Why can't I stand their unfairness?
3 What evidence exists that they should have lent me the money?
4 How does their unfair treatment of me make them rotten people?
5 How do I know people will always treat me unfairly? And must I view it as horrible if they do?

E EFFECTS OF DISPUTING OR DEBATING YOUR IRRATIONAL BELIEFS

cE cognitive Effects of disputing (similar to rational beliefs)

1 Nothing makes it awful, but only inconvenient for them to act that way
2 I can stand their unfairness, though I'll never like it.
3 I can find no evidence that they should have kept their promise to me though I would have found it very nice if they did.
4 Their unfairness doesn't make them rotten people, but merely people who have acted rottenly to me in this respect.
5 People won't always treat me fairly—though they may often do so. And if they do, tough!
It won't kill me!

eE emotional Effects of disputing (appropriate feelings)

I felt irritated and annoyed but not angry.
I felt very disappointed and concerned but not depressed.
I still basically loved my parents, but hated some of their traits.
I felt determined to find other ways of raising the money.

bE behavioral Effects (desirable behaviors)

I spoke to my parents about my feelings of disappointment and irritation.
I attempted to persuade them to change.
I investigated other means of raising money.

Sample Rational Self-Help Form. ©1976 by the Institute for Rational Living, Inc., 45 East 65th Street, New York, N.Y. 10021.

useful because it can be applied by the client outside of the counseling session. The technique involves the following four steps:

- The client is to complete the ABCDE exercise.
- The client is then to decide what emotional response she or he desires to have, relative to some activating event.
- The client is then instructed to imagine some situation (A) in which he or she became emotionally upset (C). He or she is then to practice more rational self-statements (B) about the event (A), and imagine experiencing more positive emotions (C). While engaging in REI, the client is instructed to remain as calm as possible.
- The exercise can be repeated as often as necessary both inside and outside of the counseling room.

If a client becomes upset during an REI exercise, the experience should be discontinued and discussed with the counselor.

Bibliotherapy. Clients can also be encouraged or even directed to read selected books and other written material in order to further reinforce the learning that is taking place in counseling. Counselors can discuss the readings with clients or encourage them to discuss it with other clients in a group context. Some counselors ask that their clients keep a written journal of their responses—cognitive, emotional, and even behavioral—to the readings.

Cognitive Homework. Clients need to practice the cognitive restructuring methods outside of the counseling situation. Ellis developed cognitive homework—rational self-help sheets—that clients may use at home to practice the ABCDE technique of disputing irrational ideas. (See Forms 1, 2, 3 and 4.)

Evaluation of Counseling Outcomes

Ellis does not propose formal methods of assessing the outcomes of counseling. RET, however, does lend itself to behavioral analyses of clinical outcomes. RET counselors, as indicated in previous sections, do depend on observation for making determinations as to whether a client successfully completed counseling.

In a more formal sense, Ellis' theory of counseling has stimulated many outcome studies of its overall effectiveness. To date, the results of research show quite positive effects. On the other hand, research on the process of RET is noticeably lacking.

FORM 3

INSTRUCTIONS: Please fill out the ueC section (undesirable emotional Consequences) and the ubC section (undesirable behavioral Consequences) first. Then fill out all the A-B-C-D-E's. PLEASE PRINT LEGIBLY. BE BRIEF.

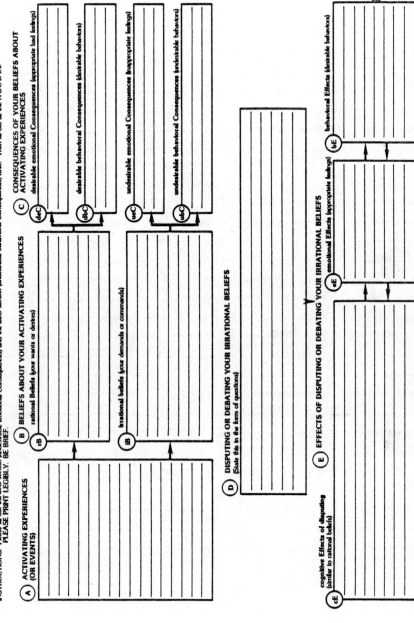

(A) ACTIVATING EXPERIENCES (OR EVENTS)

(B) BELIEFS ABOUT YOUR ACTIVATING EXPERIENCES
rational Beliefs (your wants or desires)

(rB)

Irrational beliefs (your demands or commands)

(iB)

(C) CONSEQUENCES OF YOUR BELIEFS ABOUT ACTIVATING EXPERIENCES
desirable emotional Consequences (appropriate bad feelings)

(deC)

desirable behavioral Consequences (desirable behaviors)

(dbC)

undesirable emotional Consequences (inappropriate feelings)

(ueC)

undesirable behavioral Consequences (undesirable behaviors)

(ubC)

(D) DISPUTING OR DEBATING YOUR IRRATIONAL BELIEFS
(State this in the form of questions)

(E) EFFECTS OF DISPUTING OR DEBATING YOUR IRRATIONAL BELIEFS
cognitive Effects of disputing (similar to rational beliefs)

(cE)

emotional Effects (appropriate feelings)

(eE)

behavioral Effects (desirable behaviors)

(bE)

Sample Rational Self-Help Form. ©1976 by the Institute for Rational Living, Inc., 45 East 65th Street, New York, N.Y. 10021.

FORM 4

1. FOLLOW-UP. What new GOALS would I now like to work on? _____

_____

_____

What specific ACTIONS would I now like to take? _____

_____

2. How soon after feeling or noting your undesirable emotional CONSEQUENCES (ueC's) or your undesirable behavioral CONSEQUENCES (ubC's) of your irrational BELIEFS (iB's) did you look for these iB's and DISPUTE them? _____

_____

How vigorously did you dispute them? _____

_____

If you didn't dispute them, why did you not do so? _____

_____

3. Specific HOMEWORK ASSIGNMENT(S) given you by your therapist, your group or yourself. _____

_____

4. What did you actually do to carry out the assignment(s)? _____

5. How many times have you actually worked at your homework assignments during the past week? _____

6. How many times have you actually worked at DISPUTING your irrational BELIEFS during the past week? _____

7. Things you would now like to discuss with your therapist or group _____

_____

COUNSELING APPLICATION

This case illustrates the use of RET with a 37-year old female executive with mild depressive symptoms. The case dialogue is typical of those counselors and therapists who use RET. The RET counselor quickly intervenes and educates the client about her irrational thoughts and resulting self-defeating emotions and behavior. Rational insight is encouraged through the use of cognitive restructuring and awareness of undesirable thoughts, feelings, and behaviors.

Rational Emotive Therapy in a Health Care Setting

Mary, a 37-year-old executive vice president of a major west coast corporation, completed a routine physical examination with her physician. Her complaints were nervousness, fatigue, insomnia, and weight loss. The physical examination revealed no organic basis for her symptoms. The physician discussed her findings with Mary and recommended that she might see a counselor. Mary was given the name of a woman staff counselor who specializes in executive stress and women's issues.

Counselor: Hello, Mary. I understand Dr. Smith provided you with my name. How can I be of help?

Mary: Dr. Smith suggested that I have symptoms of mild depression. Frankly, I thought it was physical.

Counselor: You do have physical symptoms that have been a source of irritation. It may be quite likely that some stressful events may be associated with these symptoms.

Mary: Not really . . . my life is going fine.

Counselor: How about the job?

Mary: Well, I have been worried about my performance. I just had a recent evaluation by the president of the company.

Counselor: How did that go?

Mary: Well, he said that my performance as an executive vice president was fine as such, but that my division profits did not exceed last year's level. Of course, that was the case for the entire company.

Counselor: Did you become personally upset with the president's feedback?

Mary: Yes, I did. The economy has affected our company, and even so, the corporation is making money . . . but for some reason I am upset with myself. It's like I am not living up to their expectations.

Counselor: You mean you are telling yourself that, "If I don't meet some perfect standard of excellence then I am a worthless person."

Mary: Yes. For me to feel like a worthwhile person I must achieve the highest level of performance—the best. You know that as a woman you must far exceed normal expectations if you want the recognition, rewards, and success in the corporation.

Counselor:	And if you fall short of perfectly achieving in all respects, you somehow seem less desirable.
Mary:	Well, that is how I feel many times.
Counselor:	Do you think the philosophy that you must be the *best* executive, otherwise you're a personal failure, has something to do with the way you feel these days.
Mary:	I never made that connection.

This is an excellent example of how a person does not associate activating events (A), their beliefs about the event (B), and the resultant affective state (C). The counselor wastes little time in directing the clients' focus of attention to some of the perfectionistic and absolutistic demands Mary makes on herself, and how these might provoke the symptoms of mild depression. Obviously, Mary is quite intelligent and may quickly make those connections and gain a certain level of intellectual insight. However, it may take some time before she internalizes a set of rational beliefs that would minimize her negative feelings. In the next segment Mary asks the counselor for a definition of depression.

Mary:	If I am "mildly depressed," just what is it, from your perspective?
Counselor:	In your case, you appear mildly depressed to me. Mild depression often results when one negatively and dogmatically condemns oneself, and the world around them. Moreover, one usually takes a negative view of the future and believes oneself to be virtually helpless. For example, if your boss judged your performance to be inadequate, and fired you, you might erroneously conclude that you were totally inadequate as a human being, as well as inadequate with respect to doing anything to rectify the situation. In effect, you might see yourself as a total failure. And that would be just awful. And in addition, you would most likely ignore many of your fine achievements, assets and abilities.
Mary:	Wow! That's a bit much.
Counselor:	Well, Mary, consider these ideas as hypotheses . . . as tentative rather than absolute.
Mary:	Come to think of it, I seem very rational most of the time, but at some other level I think irrationally and feel that I might lose control—make a fool out of myself.
Counselor:	Like there are two levels at which you are operating at the same time?
Mary:	Yes. But that is so illogical.
Counselor:	Yes. Unfortunately human beings generally operate both rationally and irrationally.
Mary:	I was taught very early that I could not be irrational—that I must be perfect—otherwise I would never be a success.
Counselor:	And a worthwhile human being?
Mary:	Yes.
Counselor:	Do you know any perfect humans?
Mary:	No.

Counselor:	Do you know many effective human beings—people who do certain things well?
Mary:	Yes.
Counselor:	Would you consider yourself a relatively effective human being?
Mary:	Yes. I would.
Counselor:	Could we reasonably assume you value personal effectiveness and will continually strive for it with a great measure of success?
Mary:	Yes.
Counselor:	Consider this question. What does perfectionism do for you?
Mary:	Well, I believed striving for perfection was necessary for success.
Counselor:	But you were striving toward *total* human perfection rather than excellence with respect to your areas of interest.
Mary:	Maybe that's true . . . if you are perfect no one will reject you. You won't have to worry about rejections.
Counselor:	I am not too sure about that. If, for the sake of argument, you arrive at a perfect state of being, you cannot be assured (1) that people will recognize it, (2) that some people won't be jealous and (3) that you won't worry constantly about maintaining that perfect state.
Mary:	Well, that is a thought. I just never made those connections before. I never believed that emotions were connected to thinking. I thought emotions were automatic and the best way to deal with them was to ignore them.
Counselor:	That works for a while—but rarely in the long run.
Mary:	Yes. Well how long will it take for me to learn more about myself?
Counselor:	I think we might try about six to eight sessions.

Notice how the RET counselor questions Mary, engages her in Socratic dialogue, yet at the same time concentrates on the core elements of her problems. Counseling continues in much the same way over a period of several weeks. Since Mary tends to over-intellectualize many of her feelings, the counselor makes sure that she pays attention to how events are affecting her emotionally and behaviorally as well as cognitively. For homework, Mary was assigned *A New Guide to Rational Living* (Ellis & Harper, 1975) and *Executive Leadership* (Ellis, 1972).

The counselor also took note of Mary's natural tendency to be perfectionistic, even in counseling. Counselors using RET need to recognize this tendency in some people and not play into it by overstructuring the relationship. The counselor needs to exhibit flexibility. In one of the later sessions the counselor made an issue of this point.

Mary:	I liked the readings by Ellis—I think I found a new bible.
Counselor:	I am glad you found the material interesting. However, it's not intended as a bible.
Mary:	If I follow the RET philosophy, I should be super-rational
Counselor:	Ellis doesn't see reason as an absolute, or an end in itself, but as a means to accomplish certain personal goals in life.

Mary: Yes. I remember that point. But counselor, many of my symptoms have
               abated! I keep telling myself that *"I am most probably of value to myself be-*
               cause I exist."

Mary continued to make improvements. She exhibited greater insight into the role of cognitive factors and their effect upon emotions and
bodily processes. She became more aware of feelings and was able to use
cognitive restructuring effectively, especially through Rational Emotive
Imagery. The counseling sessions were terminated after ten visits.

Critical Comments

Ellis' Rational Emotive Therapy is primarily a theory of counseling
and psychotherapy. As Ellis himself notes, RET does not reflect a complete theory of personality. For this reason, it is difficult to formulate hypotheses about the types of personalities that may be more or less
responsive to RET. However, RET is presented in such a manner that
many of its concepts can be translated into testable hypotheses (Tosi,
1977; Ellis, 1977).

It may be argued that the theory of RET is too static and does not
pay explicit or sufficient attention to the various stages of human development. However, as one reads the many books and articles written by
Ellis and his colleagues and followers, one can begin to piece together a
developmental perspective that takes into account the natural cycle of
human growth and change.

We believe that Ellis has influenced just about all contemporary
cognitive behavioral approaches to counseling. Certainly, RET has
shown wide applicability to problems of children and youth, marital and
sexual dysfunction, assertiveness training, executive leadership, as well
as to a wide range of clinical problems. The approach is relatively concrete and minimizes excessive abstraction.

Some counselors may not be uncomfortable with RET's heavy emphasis on rationality in that it takes too narrow a view of the problems
presented by many people, or that it does not "fit" equally well with
every personality type. On the other hand, some counselors may become oversold and begin to proselytize for RET, viewing the theory as a
panacea for any and all problems. Such thinking may lead to ignoring
certain facts of individual differences and foster the belief that RET will
affect everyone similarly.

Another potential difficulty with RET is that it tends to downplay a
number of important factors that characterize the counseling relationship. Little mention is made of non-verbal communication and empathy.

Nor does there seem to be an appreciation for the fact that counselors need to be sensitive to different needs of the client at different points in the course of treatment.

While these are serious objections, they have been recognized by Ellis (1977). He has continued to develop the theory and practice of RET and believes that in its present state, it better addresses some of the problems mentioned above. In particular, while he continues to deemphasize the role of unconscious factors in influencing human behavior, he does state that people are often unaware of their irrational beliefs. Thus, he is open to the need for counselors to go beyond a superficial assessment and treatment of just what appears on the surface. Whether one terms the underlying thought processes that disturb people as unconscious or below the threshold of awareness, it is still essential to make them known to clients so that they can better understand their own behavior and what is necessary to change it.

In summation, we would agree that Ellis' theory satisfies most criteria for a theory. It is "specific," logical, corresponds to facts, researchable, and practical. However, it suffers somewhat because of its lack of comprehensiveness.

REFERENCES

Bessai, J. (1976). Self-rating scales of rationality: An update. *Rational Living, 11* (1), 28-30.

Bourland, D. (1968). The semantics of a non-aristotelian language. *General Semantic Bulletin, 35,* 60-63.

Ellis, A. (1962). *Reason and emotion in psychotherapy.* New York: Lyle Stuart, Inc.

Ellis, A. (1971). *Growth through reason.* Palo Alto: Sciences and Behavior Books and Hollywood: Wilshire Books.

Ellis, A. (1972). *Executive leadership: A rational approach.* New York: Citadel Press.

Ellis, A. (1973). *Humanistic psychotherapy: The rational emotive approach.* New York: Julian Press and McGraw Hill Paperbacks.

Ellis, A. (1976). The biological basis of human irrationality. *Journal of Individual Psychology, 32,* 145-168.

Ellis, A. (1977). Rational emotive therapy: Research data that supports the clinical and personality therapy. *Counseling Psychologist, 7* (1), 2-42.

Ellis, A. (1979). The theory of rational emotive therapy. In A. Ellis & J. Whiteley (Eds.), *Theoretical and empirical foundations of rational emotive therapy.* Monteray, CA: Brooks/Cole.

Ellis, A. (1979). Toward a new theory of personality. In A. Ellis & J. Whiteley (Eds.), *Theoretical and empirical foundations of rational emotive therapy.* Monteray, CA: Brooks/Cole.

Ellis, A., & Abrahams, E. (1978). *Brief psychotherapy in medical and health practice.* New York: Springer Publishing Co.

Ellis, A., & Grieger, R. (1978). *Rational emotive therapy: A handbook of theory and practice.* New York: Springer Publishing Co.

Ellis, A., & Harper, R.H. (1975). *A new guide to rational living.* Englewood Cliffs, NJ: Prentice Hall, Inc.

Epictetus. (1967). *The Enchiridion.* Chicago, IL: Henry Regonery.

Hartman, B. (1968). Sixty revealing questions for twenty minutes. *Rational Living, 3,* 7-8.

Korzybski, A. (1933). *Science and sanity.* Lancaster, PA: Lancaster Press.

Maultsby, M. (1984). *Rational behavior therapy.* Englewood Cliffs, NJ: Prentice Hall, Inc.

Russell, B. (1950). *The conquest of happiness.* New York: Pocket Books.

Tosi, D. (1977). Personal reaction with some emphasis on new directions, applications and research. *Counseling Psychologist, 7,* 46-49.

Tosi, D. (1974). *Youth toward personal growth: A rational emotive approach.* Columbus, OH: Charles Merrill Publishing Co.

CHAPTER 10

WILLIAM GLASSER'S
REALITY THERAPY

FOUNDATIONS AND STRUCTURE

Historical Foundations

WILLIAM GLASSER was born in Cleveland, Ohio. He received a degree in chemical engineering from Case Institute of Technology at 19 years of age. At age 23, Glasser became a clinical psychologist and then he attended Western Reserve University School of Medicine where he received an M.D. His psychiatric training was completed at the Veterans Administration Center and UCLA.

The basic concepts of Reality Therapy are found in Glasser's first book, *Mental Health or Mental Illness* (1960). In 1965, he published *Reality Therapy* which put forth a more refined version of his model of human behavior and counseling. Other works include *Schools Without Failure* (1969), *Positive Addiction* (1976), and *Stations of the Mind* (1981).

Late in his psychiatric training, Glasser became disenchanted with psychoanalysis as a theory and a treatment. Toward the end of his psychiatric training he began to doubt much of what he had been taught. He then embarked on a path that broke course with the more nondirective therapies while paralleling some newer developments exposited by O.H. Mowrer. The result was the formulation of Reality Therapy, a system which was radically antithetical to psychoanalysis.

O.H. Mowrer, known for his work in experimental psychology, developed Integrity Therapy. Integrity Therapy gave special emphasis to the role of morality in mental health, which translates further into responsible, realistic, and rational behavior. The central credo was that irresponsible behavior was due to a lack of "temporal integration" or delay of gratification. A new wave of psychologists and psychiatrists, represented by Mowrer and Glasser, were rejecting the classical psychoanalytic and psychiatric medical model of behavior as well as other systems that did not include morality in theories of counseling and behavior change.

Philosophical Foundations

Reality Therapy is firmly rooted in a philosophy of rational-realism — but not a scientific realism that divorces itself from moral and ethical considerations. The view is held that human happiness depends upon sound reason, good judgment, self-control, and living within the rules of society. Human beings are personally responsible for their actions and accountable to society. Freedom does not exist without responsibility. In effect, human beings are defined by what they *do* as opposed to some preexisting essential nature. There is a certain existential quality to Glasser's philosophy in that one's personal identity is based upon personal decision and actions. Glasser's belief in the primacy of reason would lead us to conclude that he is a rational-realist in the tradition of Aristotle and Thomas Aquinas. The realism of Aristotle and Aquinas gives a special priority to reason, ethics, and morality as shapers of the good life.

For Glasser, the physical world is a relatively stable and unchanging fact. People, however, change as a result of their activity in the world or because of their interaction with others. If human beings are to develop themselves fully, they need to understand the world as it is.

Glasser, a rationalist, does not concern himself with unconscious determinants of behavior. His position is extreme on this point. For Glasser, right and wrong exist, and human beings have no excuses for not knowing the difference and choosing incorrect ways of behaving. As will be seen later, Glasser rejects the notion of mental illness as an excuse for maladaptive behavior.

Glasser's early writings on Reality Therapy played down theoretical conceptions of human functioning above and beyond what could be empirically observable and understandable. Thus, while there are apparent threads of existentialism, pragmatism, and logical positivism woven throughout Reality Therapy, these are never developed into strong theoretical and philosophical themes that address human nature. Glasser's later writings, however, exhibit trends toward a stronger theoretical orientation. His focus on behavior and rational choice allies him closely with the cognitive-behavioral systems.

Social-Psychological Foundations

Glasser (1981), in *Stations of the Mind,* describes a model of human functioning that makes extensive use of cybernetics. In brief, he suggests that all humans are internally motivated toward survival, worthwhile-ness, freedom, joy, and belongingness. An individual constructs a complex system for organizing the world based upon these motivational forces or needs. The brain serves as an input control system to manage and manipulate images of the real world so that it approximates one's inner personal satisfaction. One's internal world consists of perceptions of needs while overt behaviors are attempts at satisfying these needs.

Basic Needs

In *Reality Therapy* (1965), Glasser suggests that there are two basic, psychological needs that are shared across all cultures. These are the needs to love and to be loved, and the need to feel worthwhile to ourselves and to others. People who's needs are satisfied in this respect are rarely candidates for counseling or psychotherapy. Human beings all have the same needs, but may vary in their ability to fulfill them.

The need to love and be loved motivates people to continuous activity in the search for satisfaction through relationships with others. When these needs are not satisfied, psychological symptoms such as anxiety and depression may result.

The satisfaction of fundamental physiological needs provides physical comfort, but people also want to belong, to be important, to love, to be loved, and to be free. Because these psychological needs operate at the same time, they often create internal conflict (Glasser, 1981). People are rarely satisfied with what they have as they seem to always want more.

The Brain

Glasser (1981) proposes the existence of two brains — interrelated but with different functions. These are the old brain and new brain. The old brain functions to keep us alive and reproducing; the new brain helps to satisfy needs for food and shelter in the external world. The new brain became more efficient as humans acquired the use of language. As a result, human beings became more social and at the same time, more competitive with one another. Conflicts arose between the need to belong and relate, and the need to compete. Thus, human beings became a highly social-competitive animal with conflict built into the very fabric of personality. As people struggle to satisfy their needs and also try to get along with others, they experience significant frustration, anger, and anxiety. The initial survival needs of people have been extended far beyond their original purpose. The increased demands they have made upon themselves contribute to poor physical health (i.e., heart disease, high blood pressure) and adjustment to the environment.

Human happiness and health depend on how well the new brain functions. Glasser (1981) suggests that the new brain works much like a very complex thermostat, controlling for input or what is sensed. When a difference between what we want to sense and what we do sense is experienced, this serves as a signal that stimulates behavior. Output includes voluntary and involuntary physical activity, mental activity such as thinking or imagining, and feeling states such as joyfulness, depression and so on. Glasser refers to these as feeling behaviors. Therefore, what we sense is called input or perceptions and what the brain produces in an attempt to control the outside world is called output (or behavior).

Glasser (1981) asserts that we are internally motivated to behave in ways that increase pleasure and/or reduce pain. People have ideas, pictures or perceptions of what they want and control behavior (thinking, acting, feeling) in order to satisfy perceived needs in the real world. Perceptions of what we want are stored in the new brain, and are constantly changing in light of new experiences. The Internal World is housed in the cerebral cortex. The diagram illustrates how the new brain or cerebral cortex operates in the External World (see Figure 10-1). When something is desired, the new brain sends the perception to an "active comparing station." Through our senses, perceptions of the outside world are formed, and are then compared to the perceptions of one's needs in the Internal World. Immediate needs or desires are called reference perceptions because they set the standards for what one wants. When the comparing station produces an exact match between the Internal World and a sensory perception, "a controlled perception" is returned to the Internal World. The Internal World is created in this way. Human beings deal with conflicting needs by expanding their Internal World, and controlled perceptions in the Internal World lead to satisfaction. When incoming sensations which are not matched by internal perceptions arrive at a comparing station, errors may result. To a large extent, most behavior is initiated by the error signals. When errors are detected in any comparing station, they cannot be ignored.

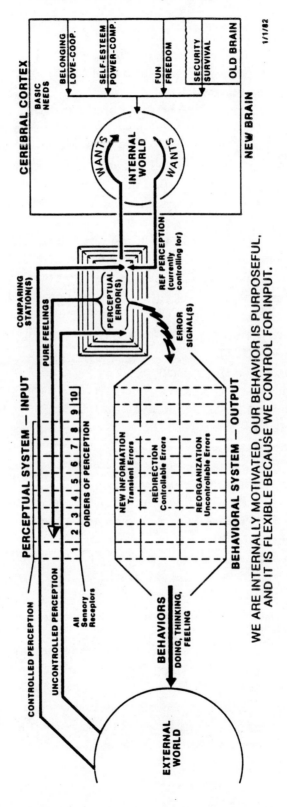

Figure 10-1. A diagram of the brain as a control system.

The BCP Model

Glasser refers to the control system function of the brain as BCP: B-behavior, C-control, and P-perception. Behavior is an attempt to control perceptions. (See Figure 10-1.)

Feeling or emotional behaviors come from two sources. The first source is from increases or decreases in errors in an active comparing station. The second source of emotional behavior is from perceptions of a behavior we are using to reduce errors. Error perceptions produce "feeling behaviors" such as depression, guilt, anxiety, and anger. Errors are usually caused by conflicts that cannot be resolved by existing behaviors. In such instances, a person needs to learn new behavior which would reduce perceived errors. Long-term desirable feeling behavior, such as confidence, self-respect, and self-love, results when perceptions of one's own behavior system are adequate to correct any large or small errors. Undesirable feeling behavior results because of conflicts that go unresolved, occurring when what one perceives is unattainable. As a result, one may behave self-destructively in a futile attempt to reduce errors (Glasser, 1981).

A Behavior System consists of three parts that provide the learned behaviors that one uses to satisfy needs. The two major systems are *Reorganization* and *Redirection* while a minor system also exists to deal with *New Information* (Glasser, 1981).

The Reorganization System, the most complex, separates us from machines. Only living creatures are able to reorganize. According to Glasser, this system is a random system. It motivates random behavior to reduce errors. However, without it people would not be able to learn new things. The System is activated by error signals.

The Redirection System, on the other hand, consists of learned behaviors and logical strategies that can reduce perceived errors. When the Redirection System does not work, one often returns to the Reorganization System. The Redirection System is an efficient system that can logically reduce errors, has access to memory, and can predict outcomes of future behavior.

The New Information System is the connection to the outside world. It is controlled by the Redirection System and is designed to reduce or eliminate small errors. The Redirection System is open to reality and constantly searches for new information to reduce errors. Formal education, for instance, is a blend of new and redirected information.

Another important element of BCP is the *Perceptual System*. Glasser

(1981) asserts that the world is perceived in terms of individual needs. Humans are incapable of perceiving the world as it actually is. While needs for basic survival are universal, the specific needs from which the Internal World is created differ from person to person. Stimuli from the outside world impact the sensory receptors that influence the perceptual system. The real world is constituted of one's own perceptions of it. People constantly try to change these perceptions so they are consistent with the Internal World. For Glasser, what matters is the world as perceived, because energy is changed from the outside world, via input, into a very complex, multi-ordered input which is a person's perception of the world. The external world is experienced through an "orderly hierarchy of perceptions, low to high or simple to complex" (Glasser, 1981). Without this perceptual order a person's life would be disorganized.

Ten Orders of Perception — Perceptions are interpreted by the brain through ten orders. When the brain interprets through any order higher than one, the perceptions include all the orders below it (Glasser, 1981).

- *Intensity.* Intensity perceptions are our only contact with the external world. Examples of intensity perceptions are pressure, taste, odors, and sounds.
- *Sensation.* Meanings are attached to intensity perception. Labels, such as red, bitter, or bright are ascribed to perceived intensity. The most common sensations are emotions. Emotions consist of various combinations of intensity signals which arise both from within our body and from the outside world.
- *Configurations.* Objects have names and shapes so they can be distinguished from each other. They may also be grouped and classified. Every form is recognized as unique.
- *Control of Transition.* The new brain perceives the movement and changes of configurations (i.e., catching a baseball).
- *Control of Sequence.* Sequential activity such as talking and walking are third and fourth order perceptions, but occur in series or sequences. Sequential activity helps to shape our existence and is of a higher order.
- *Control of Relationships.* Relationships are the way things operate together. Perceptions of how sequences, transitions, configurations, sensations, and intensities are related to one another help people to predict and to organize their experiences in the world.
- *Program Control.* This refers to controlling for perceptions of task completion. Rationality, logic, supersitition, and irrationality define

this order. Programs may be simulated in the new brain and tested for workability. Both adaptive as well as maladaptive programs are described.

- *Control of Principles.* Humans are able to perceive beyond the seventh order and deal with morality, values, and responsibility. Controlling the lower orders of perception enable people to belong or get along with others. The eighth order allows for the use of concepts of right and wrong, good and bad, to reduce conflicts. However, concepts of right and wrong may change in the outer world. If beliefs about perceptions do change, the individual suffers a large, painful error. Glasser (1981) notes that the ability to make value judgments, to perceive at the eighth order, determines how the comparing stations are controlled for or kept open. Conflict occurs when a person has difficulty to stop controlling for conflicting needs. If one continues to control for both needs, the conflict could last forever, unless the conflict is resolved in the ninth order.

- *Control of Systems Concepts.* This order refers to a highly personal state of perceptual control — a form of an organizing "rule of thumb" such as "Love Conquers All." People may also choose to resolve personal conflicts through religious cults, specialized groups, or organized rituals.

- *Universal Oneness — Meditation.* This order refers to a mystical higher order in which all perceptions appear unified into one. The tenth order is a state where there is no error. Therefore, we are not redirecting or controlling for new information. In this errorless state, we become aware of our reorganization system, experience a creative sense, and feel a oneness with ourselves and the universe.

The Development of the Person

Basic Needs

We have already discussed the universal psychological needs of love and feelings of worth. Actually, Glasser theorizes that each person has three types of basic needs that must be satisfied in the real world in which the person lives. The most basic need is the striving for identity. This need is intrinsic and the driving force for all behavior (Glasser, 1975). The need for identity, however, depends on physiological and psychological needs. Physiological needs, necessary for sustaining life, include food, water and shelter. The psychological needs, in addition to the need to love and to be loved and the need to feel worthwhile, also include the need for friendship, sexual relations, attention from others, achievement, and living in an orderly world. The satisfaction of these needs must take place in the world of reality.

Human beings operate in a social context—a social world that consists of people, places, and things. This social world has rules, regulations, and standards that prescribe correct behavior. If people are to satisfy each of their basic needs they must learn to abide by the rules of society. When people do not learn to satisfy their needs in the world, significant social and behavioral problems result.

People have the same basic needs, they vary in their ability to fulfill those needs. It is the ego which mediates between the person and the world, and which affects the ability of the individual to satisfy needs. According to Glasser (1965), personality is the sum total of all ego operations including the ego functions, the ego reaction, and the ego defenses.

The Ego Functions

The ego functions are of a general and specific nature. *General ego functions* direct people so that they can fulfill their needs in the world and protect themselves from harm.

Glasser postulates three *specific ego functions* consisting of *identity, judgment,* and *aggressiveness*. Identity is defined as the integration into the ego of a strong, positive "I am I." A strong ego identity means that an individual has a profound awareness of his/her distinctiveness from every other human being. Awareness of uniqueness brings with it an enormous responsibility for what one is to make of oneself (Glasser, 1960, 1975).

To develop a success identity, people need an understanding of the world and of how to fulfill their needs within its system of rules. This means that people must take responsibility for their actions and respond to reality as it is. A failure identity results when this does not occur (Glasser, 1975) (see Table 10-1).

The ego function of *judgment* involves the ability to explore and study the world and to approach those aspects of it which best satisfy one's needs. This ego function includes an understanding of social rules. The ego must fulfill its needs within the rules of the world (Glasser, 1960).

The third ego function, *aggressiveness,* refers to the activity or work efforts to satisfy our needs. People are active, not passive.

Ego Reactions and Ego Defenses

The ego reactions are the feelings which accompany the activities of the basic ego functions. Emotions are important in ego functioning because they provide the reward of pleasant feelings when the ego is operating effectively.

The ego defenses are largely unconscious operations. They protect people from real or perceived dangers and aid in regulating the ego functions. Poor ego defenses result in dysfunctional behavior. In later writings, Glasser plays down the ego defenses as major factors in behavior.

Differences in ego functioning, ego reactions, and ego defenses account for variations in personality and behavior. According to Glasser (1960) needs and environmental factors are not as influential in accounting for individual differences as are the ego functions.

Glasser's formulations on personality development do not include a developmental or dynamic psychology of human behavior. In this respect he does not differ from other cognitive/behavioral theorists described in this section.

Concepts of Functional and Dysfunctional Behavior

In *Mental Health or Mental Illness,* Glasser (1960) describes dysfunctional or abnormal behavior in terms of defective ego functioning. However, in a later work (*Reality Therapy* (1965)), Glasser translates the concept of poor ego functioning into irresponsibility to account for people diagnosed as having behavioral disorders. Various types of ego malfunctioning are operationalized as irresponsible behavior.

Dysfunctional or abnormal behavior results because some people lack the ability to fulfill their basic needs in the (common) world. Glasser's earlier work on abnormal behavior employed terms such as ego functions, ego reactions, and ego defenses. Because of their similarity to psychoanalytic concepts, he began substituting the more practical notion of "irresponsibility." Moreover, the term "irresponsibility" tends to play down the ideas of abnormality and mental illness. To say that people are irresponsible is to say that they do not have the ability to fulfill basic needs, not that they are abnormal. People are not naturally endowed with the ability to fulfill basic needs. The ability must be acquired. Those who have not learned to do this are "irresponsible" (Glasser, 1965).

In earlier works, Glasser discussed dysfunctional behavior in terms of broader ego development. The ego function of judgment is given priority over the others in Glasser's later system.

Table 10-1

BASIC CONCEPTS OF REALITY THERAPY

Failure Identity (Weakness-Irresponsibility)	Success Identity (Strength-Responsibility)
Rigid, Ineffective Behavior	Flexible, Effective Behavior

• Negatively Addicted Person
    Drugs
    Food
    Gambling
	• Fulfilled Person/Positively Addicted
	    Person
	        Loves
	        Belongs
	        Competent

• Symptom Person
    Acting Out
    Emotional Upset
    Psychotic
    Psychosomatic
	Powerful
	        Fun-Loving
	        Free
	        Healthy
	        Confident
	        Involved

• Give Up Person
    Denial of Failure
    Avoidance of Pain
    Passive
    Detached
	• Large Internal World

• Small Internal World	

Role of Morality

Psychoanalysis and behaviorism minimize the role human values and morality play as a motivator of effective behavior. Glasser (1965) asserts that most people who become psychologically disturbed do so not because they have too much super-ego or because they are too moral, but because they have acted irresponsibly. Mowrer (1965) states, "Conventional psychiatry and clinical psychology hypothesize that neuroses arise because the 'afflicted individual's' moral standards are unrealistically high, that he has not been bad but too good, and that the therapeutic task is to counteract and neutralize conscience, soften the demands of a presumably too severe superego, and thus free the person from inhibitions and blocks which stand in the way of normal gratification of his instincts" (p. xiii).

Glasser (1965) asserts a radical position that neurotic and psychotic persons suffer not so much from the effects of thwarted past efforts, experiences, traumas, and too many restrictions, but from character and conduct deficiencies. People are emotionally ill because they have acted irresponsibly. Glasser believes that all psychiatric and emotional problems are alike and that treatment involves reeducation so a person can become more responsible. He further notes that responsible behavior is characterized by the ability to fulfill one's needs and at the same time not to deprive others of the same satisfaction. Responsibility equals self-worth and a responsible person is one who is motivated to endure privation and to delay immediate gratification for long-term gain. Counseling, therefore, helps people to move in the direction of greater maturity, conscientiousness, and responsibility.

For a more theoretical understanding of one of Glasser's most basic concepts, we once again turn to Mowrer, who flatly rejected Freud's theory of the origin of neurotic anxiety. According to Mowrer (1965), Freudians assume that anxiety arises when the ego senses some danger or threat. In neurotic anxiety, the greatest threat to the ego is that some repressed impulse of a sexual or aggressive nature will overwhelm it. Given the fear of punishment, the child learns that such impulses are evil and should not be expressed. The impulses associated and fantasized are then repressed. Anxiety is a signal that something unacceptable is approaching conscious awareness. According to Freud, neurotics have unrealistically rigid moral standards which force them to suppress or repress unacceptable impulses.

Long before Glasser, Mowrer (1950) proposed that anxiety comes not from repression of unacceptable desires and impulses to act, but from actions which people have committed but wished they had not. For Mowrer, the *conscience* is characterized by repressed, not instinctual, urges. The neurotic acts irresponsibly and hurts others. If the neurotic feels emotional distress it is because of wrongdoing. Guilt is a natural consequence of irresponsible behavior. The neurotic tends to give into impulses and act for short-term rather than long-term gain.

Reality Therapy is the psychiatric version of the three R's — Reality, Responsibility and Right and Wrong (Mowrer, 1965). Traditional therapy contributed to a generation of parent-hating children. Psychoanalysis does not help children become mature and responsible, but fosters defiance and rejection of authority. Further, emotionally disturbed people do not need insight, understanding and freedom as much as they need commitment (Glasser, 1965). Glasser's system of counseling, unlike other contemporary systems, stresses traditional notions of morality in mental health.

Concepts of Behavior Change

Reality Therapy teaches that people suffer psychologically when they are unable to fulfill their needs realistically and have resorted to less realistic attempts to do so. The counseling relationship is a special kind of training or teaching situation where more irresponsible people can learn about acceptable responsible behavior (Glasser, 1965). The therapeutic condition that fosters change in people consists of three separate but related procedures. The counselor must be involved, reject unrealistic behavior, and educate the client to fulfill needs in more acceptable ways.

Involvement is the first condition for behavioral change. Glasser (1965) asserts that the counselor must establish a firm but caring relationship with the client. A relationship of this type may be the first ever experienced by the client. When people are distressed they look for someone who cares enough to convince them that there are better ways of fulfilling needs. However, many clients resist involvement because they have been so often disappointed.

The ability of the counselor to "get involved" may be the major skill a counselor needs to practice Reality Therapy. Certain counselor behaviors and characteristics related to the counselor's level of involvement with the client are (1) personal responsibility; (2) tough-mindedness; (3) sensitive and caring interest in people; (4) ability to fulfill their own needs; (5) willingness to self-disclose; (6) ability to withstand intense criticism; (7) willingness to admit imperfections; (8) willingness to watch clients suffer difficulty if it helps them toward responsibility; (9) ability to withstand requests for sympathy; and (10) ability to "accept" clients uncritically and understand client's behavior (Glasser, 1965). Once involvement is established, a client is expected to either behave more responsibly or leave counseling. Involvement increases the likelihood that a client will remain in counseling and eventually give up many irresponsible behaviors. Glasser uses the illustration of Annie Sullivan's contribution to the dramatic success of Helen Keller.

Glasser (1965) believes that attitude change follows behavior change. He rejects maladaptive behavior in clients and forces them to consider new patterns of behavior, regardless of any excuses they offer to the contrary. Responsibility for change is placed squarely on the shoulders of the client.

Behavior change is accomplished through hard work and effort on both the counselor's and client's parts. Counseling is an educational process where the counselor serves as a teacher and model for responsible behavior.

Assessment of Human Functioning

Reality therapists place little value on traditional diagnostic categories and psychiatric classifications of abnormal behavior. Glasser does not offer a formal behavioral assessment system as those in other behaviorally-oriented approaches (i.e., Thoresen). However, Shearn, and Randolph (1978) used behavioral assessment procedures similar to those described by Thoresen to determine the effectiveness of Reality Therapy in a classroom situation involving discipline behavior.

Glasser appears to support clinical behavior assessment procedures. It appears that behavior suggestive of greater involvement, client evaluation of problem behavior, and planning and commitment to responsible behavior should be observed and evaluated by the counselor.

Goals and Directions of Counseling

The ultimate goal of Reality Therapy is to assist people who have failure identities to achieve success identities. This means that people give up their self-critical and irresponsible tendencies and replace them with self-accepting and rational ones. In effect, people can move from personal weakness and irresponsiblity to strength, responsibility and self-discipline. People who are fulfilled have a sense of love and belongingness, self-worth, fun, and freedom. Moreover, their behavior is responsible, flexible and effective. Glasser believes that "we are what we do." Acquiring a "success identity" depends on implementing effective actions and giving up ineffective ones (Glasser, 1975, 1981).

The more immediate goals of Reality Therapy have to do with the recognition of rigid and ineffective behavior and making commitments to change them. The counseling relationship provides clients with the opportunity to become more involved with other people and to gain a sense of reality.

Glasser's more recent theoretical concepts account for the development of orders of perception. Therefore, the counselor would attempt to make some determination of whether the client was functioning at one level or another. To date there are no formal assessment procedures for the "orders of perception." These orders have to be inferred through the formulation of clinical hypotheses.

The Counseling Process:
Structuring, Facilitating, and Terminating

Glasser views counseling as an educational endeavor. The counseling relationship is a context in which people with dysfunctional behavior patterns learn to become more reality oriented and responsible. People are instructed in the basic three R's—Responsibility, Reality, and Right and Wrong. This process is characterized by a high level of counselor involvement with the client.

Counseling is a special kind of teaching or training in that it serves a remedial function. Reality Therapy tries to accomplish in a relatively brief but intense period what should have been established during normal growing up (Glasser, 1965). Glasser (1975) proposes seven principles of reality counseling. These are summarized as follows:

- **Involvement.** The counselor must develop a relationship with the client that is warm, personal, and friendly. This relationship satisfies the need for involvement which Glasser claims each person has. Involvement is a precondition for the implementation of other steps and procedures which come later.

- **Focus on Current Behavior.** The client is to realize that irresponsible behavior is not only the focus of counseling but that which creates the *need* for counseling in the first place. The counselor wastes no time informing the client that he or she choose to behave irresponsibly and that it is within one's power to change what one is doing.

- **Evaluating Present Behavior.** The evaluation of behavior considers what the client already believes to be socially acceptable. Clients are persuaded to evaluate their own behavior on the basis of whether or not it was based on sound judgment or choices. This step involves a value judgment on the client's part. Making sound value judgments is central to the learning of responsibility.

- **Planning Responsible Behavior.** The client is encouraged to make a plan for more responsible behavior based on value judgments made in step three. The counselor cooperates with the client in determining a feasible plan. The plan needs to be feasible and realistic so that the chances of failure are reduced. Alternative plans should also be developed in case the first plan does not work. The counselor helps the client to acquire the skills needed to carry out the plan and evaluate it.

- **Written and Verbal Commitment of the Client.** Commitment, according to Glasser, helps to motivate the client and reinforces positively his/her sense of identity. This step provides the groundwork for evaluating plans and for determining success.

- **No Excuses for Failure to Meet Commitments.** Constructive action is a result of the client's judgment and commitment. The client gains the experience of fulfilling a commitment to a responsible plan. The counselor accepts no excuses for this not happening.

- **No Punishment.** Punishment is another way of letting people off the hook. Punishing people can make them feel free of responsibility. This does not imply, however, that there are no consequences for failure to do something. The client and counselor should come to an agreement regarding appropriate consequences beforehand.
- **Working with Clients on Specific Behaviors and Problems.** Glasser intends to teach the client a variety of skills (abilities, as Glasser refers to them) to change other behaviors.

Such skills include the ability to make judgments, the ability to make plans, and the ability to make commitments.

Reality Therapy is terminated when the client exhibits stabilized patterns of responsible behavior. As with most systems of counseling, termination is a joint decision between the counselor and client. A reality-oriented counselor, however, takes pains to procure sufficient evidence from various sources that the client's behavioral changes are genuine.

Counseling Techniques and Procedures

It is very difficult to separate the process of Reality Therapy from its technique because they are effectively interwoven. Some of the most obvious techniques employed by Glasser are similar to those used by other theorists whose work is discussed in this section. He makes extensive use of educational methods involving direct teaching of the concepts of Reality Therapy to his clients. Some of these techniques are described below (Glasser, 1965, 1975).

Reality Therapy Techniques

Direct Teaching. The counselor serves an education function. The more people act irresponsibly, the more they need to learn what is and is not responsible and realistic behavior. The counselor uses persuasive methods of communication based on clear reasoning principles.

Confrontation and Challenge. The counselor directly and forcefully confronts irresponsible behavior until clients admit they have acted irresponsibly (Bratter, 1972). One aspect of challenging the client is to ask "what" questions as opposed to "why" questions. What are you doing, not why you are doing it (Glasser, 1965)? The counselor's task is to confront the reality of what a client is doing.

Positive Reinforcement. Clients are positively reinforced for responsible behavior throughout their sessions. Irresponsible behavior is ignored or directly confronted and challenged.

Rational Problem Solving. The client is taught to approach problem areas with logical reasoning. The counselor demonstrates the use of reason as a means of teaching clients to delay immediate gratification for longer term gains and to consider the consequences of behavior before engaging in it.

Support. The counselor provides an accepting and encouraging environment as the client attempts to change behavior. The client needs to feel that the counselor cares.

Planning. Clients are forced to construct action plans for responsible behavior. This leads the client to think about present and future behavior.

Modeling. The reality counselor serves as a model of responsible behavior throughout the counseling process. The modeling effect serves as a reinforcer of constructive behavior change.

Evaluation of Counseling Outcomes

As indicated earlier, Glasser's assessment of human functioning is based on making observations of behavior that are consistent with this theory. Because of its strong emphasis on behavior, standard behavioral assessment of outcomes of counseling with single individuals is possible. There are some controlled studies on the effectiveness of Reality Therapy, however, the evaluation of counseling outcomes in Reality Therapy is based more heavily on clinical judgment and observation than experimentation. Glasser (1965) argues that meaningful experimental studies of therapeutic effectiveness are too difficult to conduct.

COUNSELING APPLICATION

Reality Therapy has been used in institutional settings for adolescent delinquent boys and girls, neuropsychiatric hospitals, public schools, and private practice. Despite the many differences in these settings with regard to the ages and background of the people treated, the basic method of Reality Therapy varies little.

This section provides an example of Reality Therapy in a case involving a young adult male on probation from prison. This case highlights the counselor's use of involvement, dealing with reality, and rejection of client irresponsibility.

Reality Therapy in a Substance Abuse Treatment Setting

Tom S. was indicted for grand theft, found guilty, sent to prison. Tom was 24 years old, a high school graduate, a frequent user of marijuana, and had a cocaine habit costing him $300 to $500 a week. His parents were both professional people with a combined income of well over $150,000 a year.

Tom was an only child who was considered by many to be a model child throughout elementary and secondary school. His parents expected him to enter a prestigious private university. After one year at the university, Tom suddenly dropped out, left the state, and turned up one year later in a Mexican jail, until his parents were able to use some political connections to arrange for his release. He came back to the States, moved into his parents' home, and took a job in a gasoline station. Over a three year period Tom saw six different psychiatrists and psychologists. His response to treatment was poor. He continued to take drugs, moved from job to job, and lived at his parents' expense until his indictment, trial, and sentencing.

Tom spent six months in a penitentiary, then was released on shock probation. He agreed to participate in a substance abuse program for an extended time. During the probation period Tom was assigned to a counseling psychologist who was trained in Reality Therapy. The following are excerpts of several sessions beginning with the later part of the first session.

Tom: I am very happy that you are my counselor, Dr. Jones. I had four psychiatrists and a psychologist before you and none of them helped me. My mental condition is so complex that none of my previous shrinks could help me. One psychologist said I was a psychopath and had no moral conscience and no control of myself and my actions.

Dr. Jones: I am not interested in what your previous psychologists had to say about your personality diagnosis. I am interested in you right now—what you are doing, what you want to achieve in life, and whether or not you are really satisfying your needs.

Tom: Hey, I'm mentally ill. That causes me to take drugs and to get into trouble with the law.

Dr. Jones: You are not mentally ill—that's no excuse for your actions—you are simply acting irresponsibly. You believe you can achieve your goals in life the easy way without considering others, only yourself. If you have any problem, it's that you are selfish. That's right—preoccupied with yourself.

Tom: That's what my parents tell me. Are you giving me that same parental rap?

Dr. Jones:	If you want to put it that way. Are they wrong?
Tom:	You people don't understand me. By the way, what is this shit?! You are no supposed to say anything! My other doctors just sat back. They didn't pass judgment on me.
Dr. Jones:	Look, Tom, I'm not passing judgment on *you*—I'm passing judgment on your thinking and behavior. I'm passing judgment on your lack of caring for others. I'm passing judgment on your sense of judgment. You see, Tom, you are in this fix because you decided to act in ways that were in opposition with the rules of this society. You knew the rules—you made a choice and you are angry because you are experiencing the consequences of your actions.
Tom:	You sound like my old minister and my parole officer.
Dr. Jones:	So what! Have they ever mistreated you or done you harm? I would bet they do nothing more than question some of your behavior.
Tom:	Look—if you keep this crap up I am going to ask for another counselor.
Dr. Jones:	Our policy here is that we don't permit clients to change counselors on a whim. The counselors here reach a consensus on who will work with a particular client. You will be working with me, Tom.
Tom:	OK—who cares?
Dr. Jones:	How are you doing these days?
Tom:	Good. I'm staying out of trouble—Don't want any more hassles with the law.
Dr. Jones:	How are you doing with drugs?
Tom:	Oh. I'm straight.
Dr. Jones:	Good.
Tom:	There is one thing. Could you talk to my parole officer? He is constantly checking on me. He bothers me. I don't think he trusts me.
Dr. Jones:	No. If you want to talk to your parole officer that's your business—not mine.
Tom:	You're supposed to help me. Why can't you do that for me?
Dr. Jones:	That's not my job.
Tom:	Why not?
Dr. Jones:	My job is to try to persuade you to behave in more personally productive ways.
Tom:	OK, so what *can* you do for me?
Dr. Jones:	What can you do for yourself? Or what *will* you do for yourself? You have the ability to accomplish many things for yourself—good and bad. Over the past few years you seemed more interested in sabotaging the very things that would make you a more effective person. Yes—I said "sabotage."
Tom:	Why would I do that? OK. What can I do, counselor?
Dr. Jones:	I believe you have some ideas. But, I will give you some concrete ideas since you asked. I think you need to become more involved with other people—especially your parents. You have done enough to embarrass them. Have you ever shown them appreciation for the many good things they have done? I grant you they might have made some mistakes, but frankly, I think you owe your parents an apology.

Tom: Are you crazy? I don't apologize to anyone.
Dr. Jones: I'm sure that's true—but I think it's high time you apologize to your parents for the misery you put them through.

It can be seen that the counselor does not reinforce Tom's notions about mental illness, but challenges Tom's use of the psychiatric diagnosis of "psychopath" as an excuse for irresponsible behavior. In this first encounter, she introduces Tom to the three R's—Reality, Responsibility, and Right and Wrong.

In spite of Tom's tendency to try to manipulate the session, Dr. Jones focuses on the three "R's." In a dramatic departure from conventional forms of counseling, she suggests that Tom should apologize to his parents for the problems he caused them. And she was very serious. Tom was taken by surprise but realized that Dr. Jones was not going to be manipulated or intimidated, even by his threat to change counselors.

Dr. Jones sees no logical necessity for counseling to be based upon a theory of "psychopathy." If Tom is psychopathic or sociopathic, he is sick and has excuses for his irresponsible behavior. Over and over again, Dr. Jones identifies Tom's irresponsible behaviors and discusses their consequences. She did permit Tom to express hostility, to argue, and to disagree with her, but she confronted him constantly. She obviously took a vigorous and directive role in the session.

Later in the first session, Dr. Jones gave Tom a homework task. She suggested that he make a list of all his behaviors that were problematic for his parents. He first resisted, but then conceded. Dr. Jones then gave Tom a second assignment in which he was instructed to share this list with his parents and offer an apology for every irresponsible behavior.

In the second session, Tom revealed that he did not carry out the assignment. The counselor did not ask why or preach, but responded as follows:

Dr. Jones: Did you make a list of your irresponsible behaviors?
Tom: No.
Dr. Jones: OK. Do it now. Here is a pencil and some paper.
Tom: (Taken aback) You're kidding?
Dr. Jones: No, I'm not. (Pause for three minutes)
Tom: OK (Tom begins then stops and looks up at the counselor.) Look, I don't know what to say. I can't think of one thing to put on the paper.
Dr. Jones: Give it a try.

Tom expresses a great deal of frustration with this task. The counselor forced him to make a commitment to it. Tom resisted but the counselor did not yield. Twenty-five minutes went by before Tom wrote one item on the list. By the end of the session he listed four items.

Tom: Now what?

Dr. Jones: You know what.

Tom: Do I have to say these things to my parents?

Dr. Jones: Do you want to become a more responsible person?

Tom: Don't give me that garbage.

Dr. Jones: Do you want to become a more responsible person?

Tom: I don't know.

The session ended with the question, "Do you want to become a more responsible person?" Dr. Jones refused to let Tom off the hook. She continually forced him to focus on the issues of responsibility and commitment. The counselor's persistent confrontation of Tom's irresponsible behavior was the beginning of a deeper counseling relationship. Excerpts from the third session revolve around the homework task.

Dr. Jones: How did it go this week?

Tom: I talked to my parents. They were shocked when I apologized to them. My father cried. So did I. We talked for six hours. I never felt so much relief in all my life. My father and mother seemed human to me — real. That's the first time I cried since I was a kid. I'm going back to school, I'm enrolling at State. That pleased my Dad. I also told Dad that I would pay for it. He said I didn't have to, but I insisted. I also got a job with the city — sweeping streets. It pays $5.00 an hour.

Dr. Jones: Those were some achievements. I am impressed.

Dr. Jones and Tom continued weekly counseling sessions during the entire probationary period. Tom obtained a job with the city and worked 40 hours a week, and also attended the state university on a full-time basis. He stayed at his parents' home and paid them room and board, maintained a 2.7 average in school, and volunteered to help adolescent drug abusers in the treatment center. He also became involved in his church, and was especially active with the adolescent groups. Over the course of the year, Tom's relationship with Dr. Jones became very meaningful to him, although he still tested her to the limit many times. She continued to maintain a hard line with him throughout the course of that year. In his striving to establish and maintain limits for himself, he found her firmness supportive.

Critical Comments

Reality Therapy is a practical approach to helping people. The three R's — Reality, Responsibility, and Right and Wrong are very popular among counselors and teachers who share conservative values or who are looking for a directive method of counseling. Glasser's system of counseling offers a no-nonsense approach to human problems.

Glasser's theory of personality is not fully developed, but he does offer some useful theoretical constructs that assist the counselor to understand client behavior. However, many of Glasser's constructs do not lend themselves easily to empirical investigation. Glasser's theory has not stimulated much theoretical or outcome research. For the most part, Glasser emphasizes the single case study method to demonstrate the effectiveness of reality therapy. One problem with this method is that cases that do not respond well to treatment are often excluded in a discussion of the efficacy of an approach.

We believe that Glasser's rejection of psychodynamics and other insight-oriented systems of counseling is unfounded. His conclusions seem to be derived from personal observations, not from experimental evidence. There is a strongly dogmatic flavor running throughout Glasser's system. Recall that Reality Therapy was based primarily on Glasser's work with juvenile offenders who would no doubt benefit from a hard line therapy. However, would this approach benefit other groups of people with different symptoms? How generalizable is Reality Therapy?

Glasser's more recent theoretical views that incorporate cybernetics into his theory of behavior represent a noteworthy development. It adds a certain conceptual elegance to the earlier theory. Though, there is one glaring contradiction in this scheme. It has to do with exactly what reality is. In his early writings he leads one to believe that there is a reality that exists independently of the person, which includes moral and ethical standards of conduct. In his later work, Glasser gives greater emphasis to the individual's perceptions of reality, which are variable and based on need systems. The latter scheme introduces the question of whether reality is indeed objective or subjective in nature. If it is more subjectively determined then how does it become objective?

Glasser is often taken to task by critics for his stance on the role of morality in mental health. They argue that moral issues are subjective and transitory phenomena rather than objective and fixed. Many theoretical systems of counseling avoid moral issues with regard to the counseling relationship and their role in human behavior. Glasser has shown an unusual amount of courage in equating responsible behavior with moral behavior. He addresses the issue rather than ignores it. Although his views on this matter may be somewhat extreme for some, they are indeed provocative.

A more comprehensive theory of behavior that ultimately modifies some of his earlier formulations of counseling and therapy has not been advanced. The BCP model, for instance, places more emphasis on a person becoming more aware of the internal world of perception. Glasser, similar to the other theorists in this section, does not offer a comprehensive theory of behavior change. Especially lacking is a developmental perspective on human behavior.

In summary, Glasser's theory of reality counseling is characterized by "practicality" and "parsimony." We believe that its difficulty lies in the fact that it lacks comprehensiveness and has not stimulated much research interest. We would agree that the theory does show internal consistency. However, without empirical verification of its theoretical concepts and effectiveness, it is difficult to judge in terms of "correspondence to facts" and "comprehensiveness."

REFERENCES

Bratter, T.E. (1972). Group therapy with affluent, alienated, adolescent drug abusers: A reality therapy and confrontation approach. *Psychotherapy: Theory, Research & Practice, 9* (4), 308-313.

Glasser, W. (1960). *Mental health or mental illness?* New York: Harper and Row.

Glasser, W. (1965). *Reality therapy: A new approach to psychiatry.* New York: Harper and Row.

Glasser, W. (1969). *Schools without failure.* New York: Harper and Row.

Glasser, W. (1975). *The identity society.* New York: Harper and Row.

Glasser, W. (1976). *Positive addiction.* New York: Harper and Row.

Glasser, W. (1981). *Stations of the mind.* New York: Harper and Row.

Mowrer, O.H. (1950). *Learning theory and personality dynamics.* New York: Ronald Press.

Mowrer, O.H. (1965). In W. Glasser, *Reality therapy: A new approach to psychiatry* (pp. xi-xxiv). New York: Harper and Row.

Shearn, D.F., & Randolph, D.L. (1978). Effects of reality therapy methods applied in the classroom. *Psychology in the Schools, 15* (1), 79-83.

PART IV

SYSTEMS AND FAMILY PERSPECTIVES

THE FOLLOWING section entitled "Systems and Family Perspectives," includes discussions of the family and individual counseling theories and techniques of Virginia Satir, Paul Watzlawick, and Salvador Minuchin. A common thread that is found among the works of these authors is the General Systems model of human functioning theorized by Ludwig von Bertalanffy (1968). The work of Satir, Watzlawick, and Minuchin was chosen for this volume for two reasons: (1) they are well known and respected in the family and individual counseling field, and (2) they represent three consistent yet different models of adapting a General Systems Theory approach for use in counseling environments. The reader should be reminded that a systems approach is only one of the many models involved in the delivery of effective family counseling services. In essence, this section of the book is dedicated to an examination of General Systems Theory as it can be used in the counseling process and is not meant to be a complete presentation of family counseling theories and techniques. A family orientation was chosen as the major vehicle to illustrate these approaches because most applications of systems theory have been developed and implemented within this context.

Before we continue with the presentation of the three functional styles, the authors feel that a discussion of General Systems Theory would be appropriate and helpful for the reader. In the next few pages we present a description of the model, selected applications, and a short introduction to the varying interpretations of General Systems Theory as they are applied to counseling.

General Systems Theory

Ludwig von Bertalanffy (1968) pioneered an interactionist perspective of human functioning which portrays the organism as an entity that is self-regulating and intrinsically active. An organism interacts with the environment, exchanging matter and energy, while its behavior is constantly motivated by internal activity and processes. In other words, the organism acts as a result of both environmental stimulation and an internal dynamic structure. Von Bertalanffy's definition of an organism was a life form "composed of mutually dependent parts and processes standing in mutual interaction" (1968, p. 33).

As a biologist, most of Bertalanffy's early work concentrated on the growth of organisms and philosophical issues in biology (Bertalanffy, 1968). As his work continued he found more and more applicability of his General Systems Theory to a variety of natural and synthetic processes, including sociology, economics, engineering, business administration, agricultural development, etc. Based upon his studies, he concluded that all open systems share the same principles of organization and function.

Open and Closed Systems

One important differentiation that must be made when discussing the properties of systems is that of open vs. closed systems. It is this differentiation which holds significant importance for counseling theorists and practitioners. A closed system is one which is considered to be "isolated from the environment" (Bertalanffy, 1968, p. 39). In other words, no transactions occur between the system and elements outside of that system. Any changes which take place must rely upon those characteristics and processes in the system itself, and not upon any impact from outside stimulation. The only systems which can be considered closed are those involving inanimate structures and, even then, certain conditions must apply. Living organisms, however, are all open systems in that they continually interact and transact with the environment and other systems. A basic premise upon which the use of systems theory in counseling is based is that human beings themselves are open systems, although they are not all equally open nor are they as equally well organized at any given point in time.

Certain properties of open systems have been identified by Watzlawick, Beavin, and Jackson (1967) and have received considerable attention by counseling theorists. These properties are wholeness, feedback, equifinality, and homeostasis. Wholeness refers to an active integration resulting in a coherent entity that is greater than the sum of its constituent elements. A change in one part or process within the system may result in a change in any of the subsystems or in the larger whole itself. In some cases, the change in the whole may be greater (or different) from the individual changes involving subsystems. When the changes in the whole cannot be understood by studying the changes occurring in the subsystems, then systems theorists refer to this phenomenon as non-summativity.

Feedback refers to the continuous and circular process whereby the constituent parts of a system communicate with each other. In a feedback loop, the original stimulus may itself become a response to a later-occurring stimulus. For example, when the air becomes too warm in a house that has a central air conditioning system, the thermostat will perceive the change and turn on the cooling element which, in turn, will cool the house to a point where the thermostat will shut off the device, thus completing a feedback loop. A continuous feedback process occurs within the adaptive human system as well, sometimes involving other people and events in the environment.

The feedback system in a house is responsible for maintaining the temperature at a specific level which is comfortable for the inhabitants. The balance and maintenance of such a steady state in an open system is called homeostasis. In an individual or a family, homeostasis is the point at which the system is at its most stable and tension free state, regardless of how "effectively" it may be functioning at that particular level. This homeostasis is constantly threatened by external and internal sources of stress. When an individual or a family has reached a state of homeostasis, an attempted change is encountered by very strong resistance.

Equifinality, the last property of an open system, refers to the fact that in open, circular systems the end state of the interactions within a system are not determined as much by the initial conditions as by the nature of the process and rules (parameters) of the system. The same outcome may arise from different origins as the result of the nature of the organization and process of the system. This leads us to conclude that if we are searching for the answer to the question "How did this system arrive at its present state?", then we must look to the organization and interactional processes within the system.

Communication and Structural Theorists

Systems Theory is used as a general framework within which counselors can operationalize their own philosophical and personal points of view. One way in which theorists have distinguished among different systems perspectives is to concentrate on either the structural qualities of systems or on the communication processes within and between systems. The difference lies in the emphasis they choose within Systems Theory itself.

Ritterman (1976) suggests that the two different perspectives, communication and structural, parallel the distinctions between the Newtonian and Einsteinian world views. Until recently, Newtonian physics, which relied on reductionistic and mechanistic principles, was the basis for the world's understanding of physical science. In this view, matter can ultimately be broken down into all of its constituent parts. Understanding of events could be reached by observing the direct causal relationships between these bits of information. The physical sciences used this view to explain all relationships and reactions between and within bodies of matter. The social sciences largely accepted this same view, and incorporated it into the study of humans and human relations.

Einstein offered a very different way of explaining relationships and events. His notion of reality included the shift to observing whole systems and their structures rather than breaking them down any further. He believed that processes could not be broken down without drastically changing their properties, or "reality." Thus, while the Newtonian universe is one characterized by reductionism, the Einsteinian universe takes a more holistic approach to matter and persons.

A system is composed of its structures, functions, and rules as well as its parts and interactions. The communication theorists prefer to work with the interactions within and between systems, taking a more reductionistic posture. The structural theorists, on the other hand, are more interested in the dynamic structure and parameters of a system, and function more consistently within a holistic framework. While the techniques used may be quite different at times, the communication and structural theorists both accept the underlying concepts of a General Systems Theory approach to describing and explaining human behavior.

The difference between communication and structural positions lies in the specific aspects of a system that each of these styles seeks to impact as well as the particular techniques used in counseling. In the following chapters, discussions of the theories and techniques of Virginia Satir and Paul Watzlawick represent a communications approach, while the discussion of the work of Salvador Minuchin illustrates an approach based upon a structural model of systems.

REFERENCES

Bertalanffy, L. von. (1968). *General systems theory.* New York: George Braziller.

Ritterman, M.K. (1976). Paradigmatic classification of family therapy theories. *Family Process, 14,* 29-46.

Watzlawick, P., Beavin, J.H., & Jackson, D.D. (1967). *Pragmatics of human communication.* New York: W.W. Norton.

CHAPTER 11

VIRGINIA SATIR'S COMMUNICATIONS AND FEELING APPROACH

FOUNDATIONS AND STRUCTURE

Historical Foundations

FRITZ PERLS, in a conversation with Robert Spitzer, once described Virginia Satir as the most nurturing person he had known (Satir, 1972, p. x). As a reknowned consultant, teacher, lecturer, practitioner, and author on family therapy and interpersonal relations, she has stressed a counseling approach concentrating not on sickness but on the roadblocks that impede effective growth and development. Her professional experiences have led her to a wide variety of educational and clinical settings including psychiatric hospitals and clinics, welfare programs, residential treatment centers, community correctional services, family and children's services, university training programs, and private practice. She completed her bachelor's degree at Wisconsin State University in 1936 and received an M.S.W. from the University of Chicago in 1948, specializing in psychiatric social work. Much of her early training was psychoanalytic in nature, reflecting the prominence of that theoretical perpective at the time. As a result of her later experiences the medical model of psychoanalysis developed into a "growth model" which concentrates on experiencing and reaching for one's potential.

Satir's first book, *Conjoint Family Therapy* (1967), is composed of the teaching materials she once used when she instructed classes of psychiatric residents at the Illinois State Psychiatric Institute in the mid 1950's. In this work, she outlines her views of family functioning and development, communications theory, and family therapy goals and techniques. Later writings, including *Peoplemaking* (1972), *Helping Families to Change*

251

(1975) and *Changing with Families* (1976), have helped to elaborate on her model and reflect changes her theory has undergone in recent years.

In 1959, Satir was among the initial staff at the Mental Research Institute in Palo Alto, California, joining Gregory Bateson, Donald Jackson, Jay Haley, Jules Riskin, and John Weakland. It was at this time that many of her theories and treatment techniques were developed. Previously, her early psychoanalytic perspective had evolved to include concepts of communications, homeostasis, and systems. At the Mental Research Institute she began to realize the importance of growth, awareness, and gestalt concepts. This shift in thinking helped her to focus on the family as a developing and growing entity. Her emphasis on personal growth was further developed at the Esalen Institute where she became the director of the residential program in the mid 1960's. Here, working with Fritz Perls, she developed her theories related to experiencing and the integration of those experiences.

As Hanson and L'Abate (1982) note, Satir has been influenced by many different theories and a number of people in the development of her unique style. These authors go on to say that the underlying structure of her perspective is reflected in a strong emphasis on the emotive, affective, and here-and-now.

Philosophical Foundations

While operating within a systems framework, Satir focuses her attention on the communication patterns within and between systems. Foley (1974) notes that Satir brings to the highly cognitive communications approach a strong concentration on the feelings associated with the communication process. For Satir, communication is focused on feelings while the cognitive aspects take on a secondary importance.

Philosophically, Satir represents a modified existential-phenomenological point of view. Feelings and the present experiences of an individual are of prime importance, yet these must be recognized and interpreted within the existing social environment system. A system, for Satir, typically refers to the family and is viewed as a constantly changing entity attempting to continually maintain a delicately balanced steady state, or homeostasis (Satir, Stachowiak, and Taschman, 1975). The concentration on the here-and-now is another point of consistency between Satir's approach and an existential-phenomenological view. This technique, central to the process of experiencing, focuses on increasing the awareness and integration of all the senses so that each individual will be able to express and receive messages as effectively as possible. Accurate perceptions about oneself and others and validation of concepts of reality in the environment are essential to effective communication and decision-making.

Satir's views are growth-oriented in a developmental sense. Being influenced by both Maslow and Rogers, she believes that all individuals are basically good and each has the capacity to grow to one's fullest potential. For Satir, people are a collection of continually changing intellectual, emotional, physical, and psychological processes (reflecting the Gestalt influence). These processes can be shaped, with help, in order to facilitate growth.

Social-Psychological Foundations

A core concept in Satir's theoretical perspective is that of self-esteem. While there are probably as many definitions of this concept as there are social scientists, Satir (1972) uses the term self-worth interchangeably. For her, self-esteem (or self-worth) is the totality of the feelings and ideas one has about oneself. It is the amount of personal resource one has to rely on at a given time. Satir has observed that self-esteem and not the sex drive is the basic motivator in human beings. People with high self-esteem will be able to communicate with others, have faith in their own ability to deal effectively with the rest of the world and their part in it, and simply accept themselves as creatures who will succeed at some life events and fail at others. People with low self-esteem, however, will have a difficult time communicating with others and succeeding in the world because of a lack of confidence and acceptance of themselves. The stresses and strains of everyday living will be felt much more strongly by persons with low self-esteem because of their lack of an anchoring device (self-acceptance) which would help them view the world in a more realistic manner.

A concept which goes hand in hand with self-esteem is the emphasis Satir places on family communication patterns and processes. She states that "communication covers the whole range of ways people pass information back and forth. It includes the information they give and receive and the ways that information is used. Communication covers how people make meaning of this information" (Satir, 1972, p. 30). She believes that all communication is learned and that it reflects the self-esteem. A person with high self-esteem will probably be an effective communicator while a person with low self-esteem will experience difficulties in sending and receiving messages.

Certain elements of communication are discussed by Satir (1972) which are consistent from one person to the next. She says that into any communication situation all people bring their bodies, values, expectations, sense organs, the ability to talk, and their brain. Communication extends a considerable distance beyond a careful choice of words and phrases. It carries everything people are (and think they are) into a situation where judgments and perceptions are instantaneous and sometimes long-lasting.

Satir (1967) describes three basic levels of communication reflecting the many modes of sending and receiving messages. The denotive level refers to the actual content of the words used in an exchange and excludes any other messages being transmitted besides the literal interpretation of content. At this level, both receiver and sender are limited by the words themselves; the meaning of what they are trying to get across is dependent upon choice of words and phrasing.

The second level of communication described by Satir is called the connotive. This level involves the nonverbal aspects of communication including gestures, facial expressions, body postures and movements, as well as the tonal qualities of one's voice. The connotive meaning also includes something called metacommunication, or the message of the message. In Satir's words, metacommunication is a "comment on the literal content as well as on the nature of the relationship between the persons involved" (1967, p. 76). The metacommunication level includes the attitudes, values, feelings, and expectations the communicators have for one another. Even when these aspects may impede the communication process, they are still a part of the message because, as Satir says, humans cannot not metacommunicate.

Context is the last level of communication and refers to the place and time in which the exchange occurs. Miller (1972) called the context of communication the most important aspect of all, in which certain learned protocols must be attended to in order to increase the effectiveness of the interaction. The questions Who, What, Why, and Where all must be processed to understand the meaning behind the situation, and thus the parameters of the communication. Difficulties arise when a style of communication which may be appropriate in another context is used in a situation where it may be uncomfortable for either the sender or the receiver. The context changes over time as other aspects of the system and environment change. What may have been inappropriate a short while ago could be perfectly acceptable now. The ability to recognize changes in the "protocol" (contextual) issues involves a continuous monitoring of interactions. The three levels of communication (denotive, connotive, and context) illustrate the complexity of the seemingly simple task of expressing a message. Each person brings into the interactional and transactional situation their own personal mode of functioning at each of these levels, adding more complexity to the process.

A third basic social-psychological concept for Satir is maturation which she describes as "the most important concept in therapy, because it is a touchstone for all the rest" (1967, p. 91). Maturation, a growth process everyone experiences, leads to two basic goals: (1) mature individuals are fully in charge of themselves and, (2) mature individuals can make accurate decisions based on knowledge of self, others, and the context, and can take responsibility for the outcome of those decisions. Mature people are in touch with their own feelings, values, and expectations; they are able to recognize, appreciate, and grow from the acknowledgement of different-ness; they accept full responsibility for their thoughts, feelings, and actions; and they are knowledgeable of and comfortable with the methods of giving and receiving feedback. This definition of maturation is quite similar to the concept of differentiation of self as theorized by Bowen (1972). Both theorists see the individualized movement of a person away from strict adherence to the rules of a system as a positive step. This differentiation leads to the independence necessary to develop effective levels of self-esteem.

Homeostasis is a fourth important social-psychological concept in Satir's theory. She sees this process as a balance of relationships which is maintained (overtly or covertly) by family members. It is often quite circular and predictable (Satir, 1967). Actually, a more appropriate word to use in describing this dynamic equilibrium may be steady state; the family is at its most "comfortable" position in terms of its ability to deal with threats caused by internal or external stressors.

If something occurs to change the functioning of a single piece of the system, it is possible that this event would change the complexion of the entire system. For example, when there is an identified "problem child" in a family, that family has learned to adapt the system to accommodate the difficulties the child is experiencing, as well as any hardships the other members must endure as a result of the situation. If something happens to abruptly change the behavior of that child the system will experience difficulty in functioning. The steady state has been broken, and there will be strong attempts on the part of other members of the system to continue functioning as if nothing has happened. The steady state balance has thus become dependent upon the problem child's behavior and the system will do whatever is necessary in order to maintain its present status. A quality, therefore, of a steady state or homeostasis is strong resistance to change.

The Development of the Person and Family

While Satir's theoretical formulations focus on the maturation process and the self-esteem of individuals, she has not concentrated much of her writing on the specific developmental stages one goes through to reach these goals. Her ideas tend to focus on people in a more concrete manner than many other theorists. This is also true of her theories of family development. Satir recognizes the importance of developmental issues, yet she tends to concentrate her efforts on the specific processes of communication and one's feelings related to that communication. Maslow's ideas have influenced Satir significantly and her approach tends to operationalize his developmental theories, focusing on their impact upon specific aspects of maturation and the communication process within systems.

There are three aspects of Satir's theory which can be viewed from a developmental perspective in order to glean the most important information about the individual or the family. The development of self-esteem and maturation, the ability to communicate effectively, and the rules a person or a family live by are all aspects of human functioning which can be analyzed along a developmental continuum. There is considerable overlap between and among these three concepts since, in many cases, one's behavior related to one aspect may be highly related to one's ability or developmental level in another.

The level of one's self-esteem, described earlier as Satir's basic human drive, is largely dependent upon the feelings one has developed about oneself and how these feelings impact functioning. High self-esteem is developed in family and social systems where trust, the potential for developing awareness through experience, making new understandings possible and applying those understandings, and putting the model into practice are all a part of the environment (Satir et al., 1975). The key element to this progression of events and experiences is the effective establishment of trust in the system. With trust, the individual and the family have the opportunity and the open climate within which to grow.

The development of self-esteem in a trusting environment assists individuals in separating themselves from the family system. It is important for a mature person to become a differentiated self, able to experience the world as an entity separate from the other members of the family unit. This differentiation is not a breaking off from the family, rather, it is an acknowledgment that people are different and all people must be willing to experience the world in their own unique way. People who have not been exposed to an environment where they could learn to differentiate themselves from the system or who have lacked the motivation to risk such a move, are more bound to that system. Their ability to effectively respond is hampered by the rules of that system.

It is also possible to analyze how communication patterns and styles have been developed, thus shedding considerable light on present behavior. For Satir, the origin of poor communication methods is in the parental relationship. Not only is communication learned behavior, but Satir (1972) feels that even at a very early age our ideas related to communication stabilize and "will become fixed guides for the rest of our lives" (p. 31). Parents illustrate their style and teach (overtly and covertly) their offspring how to relate to the world. By the time the children have reached the point of conversational communication, the patterns of sending and receiving messages are already well established.

Another communication difficulty illustrated by parents which may have a significant effect upon a child is a devaluing or invalidating communication toward the child itself. This inhibits the child in mastering the environment and strongly limits the development of self-esteem. Satir said: "If the parents consistently show that they consider their child a masterful, sexual person, and if they also demonstrate a gratifying functional sexual relationship, the child acquires self-esteem and becomes increasingly independent of his parents" (1967, p. 53). Effective communication skills and patterns will enable the individual to deal appropriately with stress and problem-solving activities. Good communication leads to functional adaptation after a stressful incident because the individual has the ability to receive and send clear messages and acquire the necessary information with which to deal with the situation.

The family system is seen by Satir as a series of two person interactive relationships or dyads. While a member of the family is involved in one dyad, that person also is observing the interaction of other dyads. The most important dyad in a family is the one formed between the parents. If this one is working well and the needs each parent attributes to the marital relationship are being met, they each are free to develop an effective relationship with the child. When the parental dyad is not effective, Satir (1967) says that both parents attempt to satisfy their un-met needs from the parental relationship in their relationship with the child. In these cases, the dyad becomes a triad (or triangle) with all members of the relationship shifting their attention in attempts to develop effective dyads which will meet individual needs. Satir believes there is no such thing as a functional family triad; for her there only exist shifting dyads with one person left out as the observer. When children are frequently left out to be observers they are in a frightening position of low support and guidance and lack the parental attention and concern to help them deal with the ambiguity.

The developmental aspects of the dyads within the greater system are the rules which the members have constructed in order to provide ways to attend to the business of the family. These are the "shoulds" that are sometimes overt and explicit and at other times, or in other family situations, are covert and quite vague. The value system of the family is clearly evident in the rules which have evolved in the system. These rules have been developed to help maintain the family's steady state. Their impact upon individual and family functioning may facilitate growth or impede any further development, depending upon the situation and the specific rule. Satir (1972) mentions that one characteristic of a functional family is the ability to keep current and abreast of its rules.

The most important set of rules a family faces are the rules related to what Satir calls "freedom to comment." These rules limit what one family member can say to another about what is felt, thought, done, heard, etc. Satir (1972) recognizes the following four areas as central to the issue of freedom to comment:

- What can you say about what you're seeing and hearing?
- To whom can you say it?
- How do you go about it if you disagree with or disapprove of someone or something?
- How do you question when you don't understand (or do you)? (p. 2)

These four areas describe the possible limitations evident in the "appropriateness" of different topics and styles of communication within the family. Satir points out that frustrated efforts to communicate may lead to the development of low self-esteem. Other family rules are derived from social taboos, historical family methods of functioning, and individualized rules directed toward the functioning of a particular family.

In all cases, Satir focuses on the feeling aspect of family rules . . .

what they mean to the members and how the members feel about the place these rules hold in the family. The rules which are painful to family members are the most important because they are often the real culprits in the development of family problems. Concentrating on the basic good of humans, Satir believes that "bad" people don't cause the pain experienced in a family, "bad" rules do.

Concepts of Functional and Dysfunctional Behavior

Satir's definitions of "functional vs. dysfunctional" (1971, p. 128) and "troubled vs. untroubled" (1972, p. 3) families are related to the lack of balance evident in the families' homeostasis systems caused by inappropriate or ineffective communication strategies. For Satir, a functional family behaves the way an open system should: feedback lines are in place and effectively used in order to facilitate information flow; the family is a well-integrated whole where a change in one part will cause a change in the total system; a healthy dynamic equilibrium has been established; and the family exhibits equifinality. A dysfunctional family behaves as if it were a closed system, denying its need to change and adapt to the changing needs of either its members or the environment. The degree to which a family is functioning in either an open or closed manner is an indication of its effective or ineffective nature.

In addition to the three levels of communication discussed earlier (denotive, connotive, and context), Satir (1972) proposes that a person can be either congruent or incongruent in sending and receiving messages. Congruence is defined as a condition where "Two or more messages are sent via different levels but none of these messages seriously contradicts any other" (Satir, 1967, p. 82). Satir (1967, 1972) also refers to this style of communication as unilevel or leveling. A leveling response is a flowing one in which the messages sent by the words, voice, and body are consistent and integrated. On the other hand, an incongruent communication message, according to Satir, is "one where two or more messages sent via different levels seriously do contradict each other" (1967, p. 82). Incongruent communication patterns are also referred to as double-level communication, implying that a different message is being sent on two or more levels of communication. Any incongruency among the three levels of communication can lead to a misunderstood message.

Nobody is perfectly congruent at all times and in all situations, nor are they expected to be. Problems arise, however, when a person adopts an incongruent pattern of communicating as the primary way of interacting with others. Satir (1972) says that people with low self-esteem rely upon these dysfunctional styles when they fear rejection, exposure of weaknesses, or judgment by others. Not only are these people illustrating low self-esteem, but they are also sending nonaccepting and invalidating messages to others. Their difficulties related to their inability to differentiate themselves from the family system are evident in four distinct communication patterns.

Satir's first dysfunctional communication pattern is called placating. A placator is always trying to please others in a syrupy, ingratiating manner. These people are continually invalidating their own thoughts, feelings, and behaviors, preferring to receive the approval, guidance, and leadership of others. When this pattern is analyzed for elements of self, context, and other, the self is downplayed or eliminated while the other and the context are held as most important.

The second dysfunctional pattern is called blaming. A blamer consistently finds fault with others, defines problems as being in others, and tends to dominate other members of the family (or at least tries to). The tone of voice of blamers is usually quite accusatory, projected with a shrill strength. This style is typically a show of power without any identified objective other than to gain attention. The self is the only aspect of life that matters to blamers, as they simply use the other and the context in order to accent themselves.

The third dysfunctional pattern is called super reasonable, or computing. A computer is the prototype of an automaton: cool, collected, and always correct. People who use this pattern do not accept the affective sides of either themselves or others. Their responses are made without the input of emotions from any source within the system. Intellectualization is the favorite method computers use to deal with stress. Computers deny both the self and other, leaving only the rather mechanical context within which to live.

The last pattern of dysfunctional communication discussed by Satir is called irrelevant, or distracting. Distractors seem as if they are moving and functioning in many different directions at once. Communication seems totally unrelated to the context or to what other people are saying. The bodies of distractors are constantly in motion, adding to the distraction. Satir notes that a distractor is actually terribly lonely and has feelings of purposelessness, but the constant movement and irrelevant messages help to keep them out of touch with this. The self, others and the context hold little or no relevance to the distractor.

In a functional family, communication is congruent, taking into consideration self, other and the context. On the other hand, dysfunctional families communicate with the use of combinations of the four dysfunctional patterns discussed above. These patterns develop as a result of the style present in the family, and are reinforced and maintained once they are made a part of the everyday style of the members. These patterns become the communication roles of family members and the steady state of the family depends upon their existence. Not only are the patterns a result of the family system, but they also help keep the system functioning as it has been. Any changes in a member's pattern would be extremely threatening to the system because it actually means the loss of a role which is an integral part of that system.

Another aspect of dysfunctional families is the general lack of self-esteem among individual members. Satir (1967) indicates that the self-esteem of an individual is linked to the communication patterns that person has seen modeled and has eventually learned. Difficulties in communication seem at times to be causing the lack of self-esteem, and at other times to be the result of it. Dysfunctional families do not nurture others within a growth facilitating environment. It may be the wish of family members that everyone should grow and reach their potential, but the rules, operationalized by communication patterns, actively impede the members from reaching such goals. The communication patterns are developed to both reinforce the overt rules and to relate to the covert rules. Rules are developed for a particular purpose and, in many cases, rules which were quite adaptive at one time may have lost their usefulness in the present. Such outmoded rules are maintained by dysfunctional families because individual members lack the skills to change them. Flexibility of rules would allow an individual to have the freedom to change within the system and reach a higher level of self-esteem.

In functional families, the self-differentiation process is facilitated by the flexibility of the system to allow each member to leave the system on occasion in order to gain experience in relating to members of other systems. Each person may move in and out of the system, using the familiarity of the family to help process what has been encountered outside. The system not only accepts this behavior as part of the growth process, but it also actively promotes it when the individual is ready to learn from the experience. In this case, the system is open and supportive, helping each member to feel accepted, yet free to experience the world as a separate person.

Concepts of Behavior Change

Satir does not deal with the presenting problem of an individual experiencing some type of uncomfortable or maladaptive thought, feeling, or behavior. Instead, she identifies this problem as a sign that the individual is experiencing the pain caused by membership in a dysfunctional system. In her approach, the therapist is a change agent impacting the entire system, and not just the person identified as the one experiencing or causing the difficulties.

It is Satir's belief that most personal difficulties actually result from dysfunctional communication patterns which have developed within a system. In order to change a person's behavior or to help that individual develop a higher level of self-esteem, one must change or improve upon communication methods. The process of change includes the family's gaining insight into their present communication patterns and why they are not adaptive within the present context, plus an educational process of teaching the system members more effective modes of communicating and having them work through these in the system's environment. Members are taught to monitor themselves in order to watch for and guard against the reappearance of old, dysfunctional communication styles. When the system has changed to become more accepting of new behavior on the part of the person identified as the one with the problem, then that person has the possibility for change. Without a change in the system, a person who has left and undergone successful treatment will come back to the system and probably resume the old problem behaviors. Again, this illustrates Satir's belief in the resistance of a family system to change once it has reached a steady state, regardless of whether that state is functional or dysfunctional.

The actual process of how an individual or a system changes is not delineated within Satir's theory. Since it is the communication which is of prime interest to the change agent, underlying changes in functioning are seen as following a change in the communication patterns. For Satir, change occurs through a process of transacting with others in a supporting and facilitative environment. It is the process of communication that Satir focuses on, because this is the aspect of the system which is dynamic and moving. It is easier to change the path of something already on the move than it is to attempt to change something which is static.

Assessment of Human Functioning

The assessment process in Satir's model involves taking a complete family chronology in order to gain information about the interrelation-ships of the members as well as to structure the first few sessions. This task is designed to help the counselor identify the degree to which the family is behaving in either a functional or dysfunctional manner. This structured form of history taking is a way of not only gaining informa-tion about the family but also takes some of the responsibility for what happens in sessions away from the members in order to reduce any threat they may feel concerning their need for counseling.

The first step in the family chronology is to identify what the family members believe the problem situation in the family system actually is. Satir (1967) views problems in the family as being extensions of prob-lems in the marital relationship. She sees family counseling as focusing largely on the parents because "their marital plan has prevented them from parenting their child according to his growth needs" (1967, p. 114). If the marriage partners can readily acknowledge and discuss the pain which is present in their relationship, then the chance for a relatively fast and successful conclusion to treatment is good. If, however, the parents insist on focusing on a child who is manifesting the most problems (the identified patient) rather than upon themselves and their relationship, then the chance for a quick and effective end to treatment is diminished. After the counselor has listened to the family identify the problem(s) from their perspective, the chronology begins, starting with the marital relationship. Satir sees the parents as the "architects of the family rela-tionship," and feels that it is important for the children to see their parents as a couple who had a relationship before they entered the fam-ily.

When the mates' relationship as a couple has been described and discussed, the counselor then elicits what Satir (1967) calls a cast of characters. During this time, the family is urged to identify and briefly describe all of the people who are presently living within the family, those people who once lived with the family but are now gone, and any-one else who has been a part of the system. Satir stresses that what has happened and will happen in this family is guided by its own process and membership and that no other family will act or could ever act in exactly the same manner.

Further questions are asked in order to accumulate information on how members think and feel about the relationships, communication patterns, rules, and expectations found in the family. This process allows the counselor to see the homeostatic processes at work, as well as the rules in action. Gaining information through the use of the family chro-nology also assists Satir in determining the substance of the dysfunction.

She uses four concepts in her analysis: how each family member handles the presence of differentness (1967, p. 103), what their roles are in the family structure (p. 104), how congruent or incongruent each member is in communicating (p. 105), and what model and expectations have been influencing the members in their own development (p. 105).

Satir uses traditional diagnostic categories only inasmuch as they offer descriptions of behavior manifested by individuals at a particular time. Her suggestion to the professional is:

> "The therapist must say to his patient, in effect: you are behaving now with behavior which I, as a clinician, label 'schizophrenia'. But this label only applies at this time, in this place, and in this context. Future times, places and contexts may show something quite different." (Satir, 1967, p. 103)

Since treatment involves a totally individualized approach to a family system performed within the most objective environment possible, identification of dysfunctional patterns and rules is a more facilitative than a labeling process in the development and implementation of decisions concerning treatment plans. While Satir does use a method of evaluation concentrating on a family's past development, present behavior, and the individuals' expectations for the future, the procedures are not followed in the same manner or even in the same order for every family seeking help. She takes a highly individualized approach to assessment, fitting it into the process of the family's interaction with the counselor in a subtle manner, using the time to enhance the relationship as well.

Goals and Directions of Counseling

Three goals have been identified by Satir (1971) as important components of her growth oriented approach:

- Each member should be able to report congruently, completely, and obviously on what he sees, hears, feels and thinks about himself and others, in the presence of others.
- Each person should be related to his uniqueness so that decisions are made in terms of exploration and negotiation rather than in terms of power.
- Differentness must be openly acknowledged and used for growth. (p. 130)

These goals focus largely on the communication processes which take place among members of a system with the objective of respecting the other members' uniqueness, differences, and right to grow.

There is an obvious lack of problem-focused decision-making in this goal structure. Actually, the identified goals are very abstract and energetic, including such things as the prevention of further distress, growth producing opportunities for all members, as well as the alleviation of the specific pain the system of individuals may be experiencing at that time.

The goals of counseling are operationalized through an increased understanding by all family members of the rules which have been used in the structure, a growth in the ability of each member to use all sensory input systems efficiently, and an increase in the effectiveness of each member and the system itself to interact and transact in an open, clear manner. A focus on the feelings of family members both toward themselves and their communication patterns is Satir's method of engaging the family in a highly empathic and warm relationship. Satir chooses to offer much of herself and engage families in this caring manner because of three primary beliefs she holds about human nature:

- Every individual is geared to survival, growth, and getting close to others and all behavior expresses these aims, no matter how distorted it may look.
- What society calls sick, crazy, stupid, or bad behavior is really an attempt on the part of the afflicted person to signal the presence of trouble and call for help.
- Human beings are limited only by the extent of their knowledge, their ways of understanding themselves, and their ability to "check out" their perceptions with others. (1967, p. 97)

Satir's goal as a counselor, therefore, is to act as both a resource person and a model of communication. She feels strongly that the counselor should only be an observer trained to help the family with the identification of the dysfunctional aspects of patterns and styles of behavior, and not become swept up within the system itself.

The Counseling Process:
Structuring, Facilitating, and Terminating

Satir does not necessarily have a strict "plan" for following the family through counseling. Since her emphasis is on the continually moving process of the family's functioning, she feels that the counselor must be actively involved at all times. We have seen how the counselor can structure the first few sessions by taking the family chronology. With some families, the counselor may immediately become an active observer in the process of family interaction, gaining awareness and sharing this with the members. Although the nature of the counseling process is more circular than linear, there are a few basic procedures she follows.

During the first contact with a family, Satir (1967) makes it a point to find out who makes up the family, learn their ages, briefly introduce them to her approach, and respond in an accepting manner to any discussion of the problem they are experiencing. When the family and the counselor formally meet for the first time, the introductions are made, along with a quick review of who makes up the family and a discussion of the nature of counseling. It is important for the counselor to elicit from the members of the family their needs and expectations of the counseling relationship. This may be a very confusing time for the family, both from the perspective that they are facing difficulties they do not know how to deal with on their own, and from the perspective that they have just entered into a new kind of relationship, one in which they may not be sure what is supposed to happen. The confusion is explained to them as a normal feeling for people in their situation, again trying to relieve some of the pressure they are experiencing.

In many cases, Satir meets with the parents alone for the first few sessions. This says to them that the counselor sees the marital relationship as the foundation of the family, the pivotal force supplying both the structure and movement to the system. If the family is dysfunctional to the point where the marital couple simply cannot deal with their own relationship at this time, then the children are included in the first sessions as well, in order to balance the interaction. Another purpose for meeting with the parents alone for the first session is to prepare them for the inclusion of the children in the counseling relationship. The task is to make the parents feel comfortable with the children's behavior, and not to be embarrassed or feel like "bad" parents.

Even though Satir sees the relationship between the parents as the focus of counseling, it is important to have the whole family present for as many sessions as possible. This is important because the counselor needs to view the complete functioning system in order to observe the patterns of communication and rules (both overt and covert) in action. As the dysfunctional patterns and rules are uncovered and discarded or changed, the entire family must be a part of the process, so that any changes which occur will be integrated effectively into the system.

The setting and atmosphere which is created and maintained by the counselor is one where all family members candidly observe themselves and each of the others in as objective a manner as possible. Satir (1967) indicates that this can be accomplished in the following manner:

- The counselor must concentrate on giving the family confidence, reducing their fears, and making them comfortable and hopeful about the therapy process.
- The counselor must show a direction in counseling, that they are going somewhere.
- Above all, the counselor must show clients that questions can be structured in order to find out what they both need to know. (p. 160)

This process helps to deal with the initial fears of the clients by having the counselor provide support, competence, and direction, thus taking much of the responsibility for early sessions.

The termination of Satir's counseling relationship occurs when the family members have learned effective methods of communication and have created an environment conducive to the development of self-esteem. It is not likely that this will be reached over the course of just a few sessions, so Satir's approach seems to be at least a moderate-length counseling process. Because of the warmth and caring exhibited by the counselor, it can be expected that a close relationship develops between family members and that individual. While this is an issue to deal with upon termination of any counseling relationship, it is believed that the family now has a more effective communication style with which to face the separation.

Counseling Techniques and Procedures

The purpose of any techniques and procedures used in Satir's counseling sessions is to create a climate conducive to the emotional growth of the family and its members, as well as assist the family in the development of more facilitative communication patterns. The family system must become a caring, supportive group or the individuals involved will not reach higher levels of self-esteem and self-differentiation.

The two major tools that Satir (1967) identifies as the building blocks of the counseling process are a family chronology and specific techniques designed to enhance the family's growth process. The family chronology has been outlined in the section on assessment. One thing that can be added to what has already been presented is the idea that Satir believes the chronology can be used to identify exactly what role the counselor will take in the relationship. This is accomplished by studying what the family reveals about its communication weaknesses and rules within the system. In recent years, Satir has concentrated more on the here-and-now of the counseling relationship to gain information concerning the communication patterns. She does not seem to be using the complete family chronology as often, choosing rather to step directly into the present interactions of family members (Hanson & L'Abate, 1982).

Satir (1967) has listed many of the different counseling techniques used in her approach. While some of them are quite broadly defined and may seem more as objectives than techniques, they are worth noting to give the reader a better idea of Satir's methodology. A slightly edited list is presented below:

- The counselor must create a setting within which people can risk experiencing themselves and their actions clearly and objectively.
- The counselor asks questions without fear or suspicion in such a way that the clients become less afraid of the situation.
- The counselor shares with the clients how other people view them.
- When the counselor asks for and gives information, it is done so in a matter-of-fact, nonjudgmental, light, congruent way.
- The counselor builds self-esteem.
- The counselor decreases threat by setting the rules of interaction.
- The counselor decreases threat by structuring the interview.
- The counselor decreases threat by reducing the need for defenses through the use of openness and empathic understanding.
- The counselor decreases threat by handling loaded material at the appropriate times and with care.
- The counselor teaches clients that they are accountable for their actions and they can determine what their behavior will be.
- The counselor helps the clients see how past models influence their present expectations and behavior.
- The counselor helps the clients become aware of their dysfunctional roles and change these patterns into more adaptive ones.
- The counselor completes the gaps in communication and interprets messages.

One of the more broadly defined techniques listed above is the process used to help build the client's self-esteem. Some of the specific suggestions Satir offers to counselors are the following: point out individual strengths of family members with the use of ego-enhancing questions and statements; stress that many difficulties are the result of bad communication rather than some negative quality inherent in the members (reframing); have the counselor be portrayed as someone who is also continually learning and in need of their feedback as well; and promote family members to identify what they can do which brings pleasure to other members so that they are each forced to see themselves as others do.

All of this is done in as unthreatening an atmosphere as possible. It is believed that this self-exploration, concentration on good qualities, and dealing with the universality of feeling uncertain can, with the help of a trusting, warm, and open atmosphere, develop stronger feelings of self-esteem in individuals, and help families see what type of conditions are necessary for the growth of the family and each of its members.

Another broadly defined technique which deserves more explanation here is the process a counselor uses to complete gaps in communication and interpret messages. Satir (1967) indicates that one of the most important counseling tasks is to teach the family the difference which may exist between the content of a message (denotive) and the message itself (connotive). What is happening in many situations involving a dysfunctional family is a confusion between these two levels of communication, leading to confusion and frustration for both the sender and the receiver of messages. The counselor also separates messages about oneself from messages about someone else and actively points out discrepancies and confusing patterns of the family's interactions, both verbal and nonverbal. The purpose of these techniques is to make the family aware of their patterns and educate them in ways of changing. The interactions also allow the counselor to model effective, congruent communication patterns.

Satir's techniques may be nonverbal or verbal, highly active or less active, and continuous or static, depending upon the particular needs of the family she is working with at the time. She often makes use of homework assignments to help all family members learn how others in the system view them and how the communication patterns which have developed are being maintained. She often "prescribes the symptom" in order to set the stage for the family members to experience their role directly. In an attempt to have the members experience their roles, Satir uses touch to physically move people around and position them in ways which portray their own style of dysfunctional communication (placating, blaming, computing, or distracting). She also uses this "sculpting" to place the family members in more effective poses which will enhance their interactions. Other techniques used by Satir include making clients rephrase passive statements into active ones in order to reinforce and accentuate the continuous movement of the family system. They may also be asked to use understatement in relation to problem areas or personal qualities so that people will be motivated to open up in response.

In order to enhance the growth of individuals and families, Satir (1967) has delineated three types of experiential games which concentrate on awareness. The first game, the Simulated Family, is a way to teach families about themselves and how they view each other. Family members are asked to play other members of the family or themselves in some type of simulated situation. They would then review the "game" on video tape and process their feelings and perceptions concerning the experience. The second set of games, called Systems Games, are designed to illustrate to the family the differences in the communication patterns of families who function as closed versus open systems. The last set, the Communication Games, were developed to teach congruency and clarity in communication.

Evaluation of Counseling Outcomes

Since Satir's method of dealing with the communication difficulties of a family is somewhat unique and specific in terms of its focus, an evaluation of outcome may be more clear than with some other approaches. Satir (1967) has presented certain criteria which she uses to identify a time to terminate counseling. Among the criteria presented are the following specific outcomes:

". . . when the adult male and female as husband and wife can:

- *be direct,* using the first person "I" and following with statements or questions which: criticize, evaluate, acknowledge an observation, find fault, report annoyance, and identify being puzzled.
- *be delineated,* by using language which clearly shows "You are you, separate and apart from me, and I acknowledge your attributes as belonging to you."
- *be clear,* by using questions and statements which reflect directness and the capacity to get knowledge of someone else's statements, directions, or intentions, in order to accomplish an outcome. (p. 176-177)

It is the family members' ability to effectively communicate with each other in a congruent manner which is viewed as a successful outcome. These patterns of communication should reflect each person's differentness, and the exchange of information should be done in a manner which is efficient and to-the-point.

These outcome evaluation criteria may not address many of the questions counselors representing other approaches may have, but they do concentrate on the areas Satir has observed as contributing the most to personal and family dysfunction. Whether or not they actually do attend to the most important aspects of human functioning depends largely upon how one views the world.

COUNSELING APPLICATION

The purpose of this section is to present a few examples of Satir's work in counseling sessions. The illustrations were chosen from books either written or edited by Satir and they represent different aspects of her style in use with real or simulated families. A short discussion of each passage is presented following the transcripts.

The first situation is an example of Satir helping clarify a family's interactional process.

Counselor: (To husband) I notice your brow is wrinkled, Ralph. Does that mean you are angry at this moment?

Ralph: I did not know that my brow was wrinkled.

Counselor: Sometimes a person looks or sounds in a way of which he is not aware. As far as you can tell, what were you thinking and feeling just now?

Ralph: I was thinking over what she (his wife) said.

Counselor: What that she said were you thinking about?

Ralph: When she said that when she was talking so loud, she wished I would tell her.

Counselor: What were you thinking about?

Ralph: I never thought about telling her. I thought she would get mad.

Counselor: Ah, then maybe that wrinkle meant you were puzzled because your wife was hoping you would do something, and you did not know she had this hope. Do you suppose that by your wrinkled brow, you were signalling that you were puzzled?

Ralph: Yeah, I guess so.

Counselor: As far as you know, have you ever been in that same spot before, that is, where you were puzzled by something Alice said or did?

Ralph: Hell, yes, lots of times.

Counselor: Have you ever told Alice you were puzzled when you were?

Alice: He never says anything.

Counselor: (Smiling, to Alice) Just a minute, Alice, let me hear what Ralph's idea is of what he does. Ralph, how do you think you have let Alice know when you are puzzled?

Ralph: I think she knows.

Counselor: Well, let's see. Suppose you ask Alice if she knows.

Ralph: This is silly.

Counselor: (Smiling) I suppose it might seem so in this situation, because Alice is right here and certainly has heard what your question is. She knows what it is. I have the suspicion, though, that neither you nor Alice are very sure about what the other expects, and I think you have not developed ways to find out. Alice, let's go back to when I commented on Ralph's wrinkled brow. Did you happen to notice it, too?

Alice: (Complaining) Yes, he always looks like that.

Counselor: What kind of message did you get from that wrinkled brow?

Alice: He don't want to be here. He don't care. He never talks. Just looks at television or he isn't home.

Counselor: I'm curious, do you mean that when Ralph has a wrinkled brow that you take this as Ralph's way of saying, "I don't love you, Alice. I don't care about you, Alice."

Alice: (Exasperated and tearful) I don't know.

Counselor:	Well, maybe the two of you have not yet worked out crystal-clear ways of giving your love and values messages to each other. Everyone needs crystal-clear ways of giving their value messages. (To son) What do you know, Jim, about how you give your value messages to your parents.
Jim:	I don't know what you mean.
Counselor:	Well, how do you let your mother, for instance, know that you like her, when you are feeling that way. Everyone feels different ways at different times. When you are feeling glad your mother is around, how do you let her know?
Jim:	I do what she tells me to do. Work and stuff.
Counselor:	I see, when you do your work at home, you mean this for a message to your mother that you're glad she is around.
Jim:	Not exactly.
Counselor:	You mean you are giving a different message then. Well, Alice, did you take this message from Jim to be a love message? (To Jim) What message do you give your father to tell him that you like him?
Jim:	(After a pause) I can't think of nothing.
Counselor:	Let me put it another way. What do you know crystal-clear that you could do that would bring a smile to your father's face?
Jim:	I could get better grades in school.
Counselor:	Let's check this out and see if you are perceiving clearly. Do you, Alice, get a love message from Jim when he works around the house?
Alice:	I s'pose . . . he doesn't do very much.
Counselor:	So from where you sit, Alice, you don't get many love messages from Jim. Tell me, Alice, does Jim have any other ways that he might not now be thinking about that he has that say to you that he is glad you are around?
Alice:	(Softly) The other day he told me I looked nice.
Counselor:	What about you, Ralph, does Jim perceive correctly that if he got better grades you would smile?
Ralph:	I don't imagine I will be smiling for some time.
Counselor:	I hear that you don't think he is getting good grades but would you smile if he did?
Ralph:	Sure, hell, I would be glad.
Counselor:	As you think about it, how do you suppose you would show it?
Alice:	You never know if you ever please him.
Counselor:	We have already discovered that you and Ralph have not yet developed crystal-clear ways of showing value feelings toward one another. Maybe you, Alice, are not observing this between Jim and Ralph. What do you think, Ralph? Do you suppose it would be hard for Jim to find out when he has pleased you?

(Satir, 1967, p. 97-100)

In this interaction, the counselor modeled, clarified, and reflected so that the family could see how the patterns of communication they have developed are dysfunctional. The family had a change to see how messages they believe they are sending to the other members are often distorted or completely missed in the process of the interaction. The dys-functional communication patterns of the parents serve as models for the child, and have led him to develop a similarly dysfunctional communi-cation style. At this point, Satir is simply allowing the family to see for themselves the problems in the process. Already, however, they are learning some important skills from her modeling a congruent method of interaction with them.

In the next example of Satir's approach she illustrates how a coun-selor can identify and begin to process the ideas children have concern-ing why the family is in counseling. This not only approaches their ideas concerning the "why," but also illustrates the children's perception of the way in which the parents explained counseling to them.

Counselor:	Patty, where did you get your ideas about why you are here?
Patty:	Mother said we were going to talk about family problems.
Counselor:	What about Dad? Did he tell you the same thing?
Patty:	No.
Counselor:	What did Dad say?
Patty:	He said we were going for a ride.
Counselor:	I see. So you got some information from Mother and some information from Dad. What about you, Johnny? Where did you get your informa-tion?
Johnny:	I don't remember.
Counselor:	You don't remember who told you?
Mother:	I don't think I said anything to him, come to think of it. He wasn't around at the time, I guess.
Counselor:	How about you, Dad? Did you say anything to Johnny?
Father:	No, I thought Mary had told him.
Counselor:	(To Johnny) Well, then, how could you remember if nothing was said?
Johnny:	Patty said we were going to see a lady about the family.
Counselor:	I see. So you got your information from your sister, whereas Patty got the clear message from both Mother and Dad.
Johnny:	Daddy told Patty we were going for a ride.
Counselor:	And Mother told Patty you were going to talk to a lady about the fam-ily.
Johnny:	Yeah.
Counselor:	So what did you do with that? Dad is saying one thing and Mother another? You have to figure that one out. What did you make of it?
Johnny:	I figured we would go for a ride. And, uh, we would see a lady or something.
Counselor:	I see. You decided that you would be doing both. So in this case, you were able to fit these things together . . . what Mother and Dad said to Patty.
Johnny:	Uh huh.
Counselor:	How about that Mother? Were you and Dad able to work this out

	together . ... what you would tell the children?
Mother:	Well, you know, I think that this is one of our problems. He does one thing and I do another.
Father:	I think this is a pretty unimportant thing to worry about.
Counselor:	Of course it is, in one sense. But then we can use it, you know, to see how messages get across in the family.

(Satir, 1967, p. 143-144)

Satir helped the family to focus on an example of the inconsistency of the parents and the mixed messages occurring in the family which have placed the children in frustrating and ambiguous situations. While the father correctly points out that this specific instance may not have been extremely important in and of itself, the counselor could see the importance of this interaction as an example of a greater dysfunctional pattern. Again, the counselor used probing clarifications to identify the *process* of the interactions rather than simply discussing the outcomes. In this way, she reinforced the dynamic nature of communication in the family system.

Although some of the unique qualities of Satir's approach do come across in these written examples, it may be useful for the reader to see her in action by viewing some of the videotapes she has made. In these, her warmth and caring come through more strongly, and the videotapes also allow the student to see, hear, and feel her congruent communication style.

Critical Comments

The emphasis of Satir's counseling approach is on emotional awareness and development within the dynamic process of a family system. The points of access she has chosen are the communication styles and patterns which have been developed by each family member. Satir doesn't believe that "bad" people exist, she feels that dysfunction is caused by the rules, roles, and communication patterns family members carry with them. Since the point of origin for the family and thus the key to the development of dysfunction is the two-person marital relationship, Satir's major counseling focus is aimed at dealing with the difficulties encountered by the couple. The process of identification and remediation (through teaching and modeling) of the dysfunctional, incongruent styles of communication experienced by the marital couple becomes a center of the counseling activity. This process occurs regardless of who is identified as the family member with the problems, because of Satir's belief that the problems of any individual are simply symptomatic of problems in the entire family system.

Although Satir's approach is typically seen as an example of communications theory in action, it has roots which extend to many other theoretical positions. Psychoanalytic thought, Transactional Analysis, Client-Centered, and Gestalt Therapy can all be seen as contributing to the development of her formulations. The result (at this stage in its development) is an emphasis on communications within a strongly affective, present-centered framework. Other communications theorists (Watzlawick, Bandler and Grinder, and Haley) tend to concentrate much more on the rational nature of sending and receiving messages. Although Satir does use some techniques which could be described as rational in nature (i.e., analyzing communication patterns), their ultimate purpose is to assist clients in becoming more aware of the feelings they associate with their behaviors.

Many of Satir's perspectives have received initial research validation. Stachowiak (Satir, et al., 1975) studied families over a ten-year period in order to identify any cycles and important decision-points in individual and family development. Family differences were studied in four categories: family productivity, leadership patterns, expression of conflict, and clarity of communication.

Adaptive families illustrated group decision-making skills, a balance between task-oriented and emotional messages, shifting leadership roles depending upon the task at hand, an open atmosphere for the expression and resolution of conflict, and congruent communication styles and patterns. On the other hand, a dysfunctional family was found to be one in which either the task-oriented or emotional needs were typically the rule, leadership was either absolute or totally diffuse, conflict was either avoided or given too much attention, and communication patterns were ineffective in assisting the family to carry out its business. The characteristics of a dysfunctional family support Satir's view that the counseling process is one where the expert takes the role of both a teacher and a model in order to help the family learn more effective ways of interacting and functioning.

Satir herself is an extremely skilled counselor who has the ability to work effectively in various situations with many different family groupings. Her style is very flexible, always adaptive to the needs of the particular family she is working with. Even though she "grew up on the 50-minute hour," she is now able to work with people in many types of physical settings over short periods of time or over the course of several days. She has indicated that the variables of time and place are determined by the availability and accessibility of both her and the family (Satir, et al., 1975). She does not seem to be as tied to the professional "givens" related to the counseling relationship as are many other therapists. She is adamant, however, that no violence or sexual activity occurs within the sessions, although the feelings related to those behaviors are explored and processed.

While these characteristics of Satir's style follow from her personal background and make-up, they don't seem to follow necessarily from her theoretical model. It would be a difficult task for anyone to identify the specific counseling strategies Satir uses by studying her formulations of human and family functioning. Her methodology is so individualized that it may be impossible for anyone to identify a specific pattern beyond openness, warmth, nurturance, and congruent communication.

Another difficulty that some people may experience when studying Satir's theories and methods is the global nature of her goals for the counseling relationship. She describes the relationship as focusing on process and leading to congruent communication, self-differentiation, and acknowledgment of differences as growth-producing. While these goals do cover the major aspects of her theoretical perspective, they do not, for the most part, lend themselves to efficient evaluation. It is not that these goals are necessarily ambiguous, although each may be interpreted differently from varying frameworks, it is the fact that they are so broad that they may not be totally attainable.

In the evaluation section of this chapter, it was said that "an evaluation of outcome may be more clear than with some other approaches." By this, it was meant that accepting Satir's outcome criteria may define a rather clear evaluation task. A question arises, however, concerning how closely the identified outcome criteria actually relate to the proposed goals for counseling. The criteria reflect behaviors which Satir accepts as related to the goals, but other counselors may have very different perceptions, finding her criteria to be extremely limited and too specific. In this light, the counseling process may actually be a significant growth-producing experience for the family, but the measurement and evaluation of that growth may be problematic for some counselors.

Despite the broadness of the goals of counseling and the gap in the detail of explanations of theory and method, Satir's approach has become a respected and highly used style in family counseling. Her use of systems concepts in counseling is unique, as is the contribution she has made to the entire field of family counseling and process.

REFERENCES

Bandler, R., Grinder, J., & Satir, V. (1976). *Changing with families.* Palo Alto, CA: Science and Behavior Books.

Bowen, M. (1972). Toward the differentiation of a self in one's own family. In J. Framo (Ed.), *Family intervention: A dialogue between family researchers and family therapists.* New York: Springer.

Foley, V.D. (1974). *An introduction to family therapy.* New York: Grune and Stratton.

Hanson, J.C., & L'Abate, L. (1982). *Approaches to family therapy.* New York: Macmillan.

Miller, L.A. (1972). Resource-centered counselor-client interactions in rehabilitation settings. In J. Bozarth (Ed.), *Models and functions of counseling for applied settings and rehabilitation workers* (2nd ed.). Fayetteville, AR: Arkansas Rehabilitation Research and Training Center.

Satir, V. (1967). *Conjoint family therapy* (2nd ed.). Palo Alto, CA: Science and Behavior Books.

Satir, V. (1971). The family as a treatment unit. In J. Haley (Ed.), *Changing families: A family therapy reader.* New York: Grune and Stratton.

Satir, V. (1972). *Peoplemaking.* Palo Alto, CA: Science and Behavior Books.

Satir, V., Stachowiak, J., & Taschman, H.A. (1975). *Helping families to change.* New York: Jason Aranson.

CHAPTER 12

PAUL WATZLAWICK'S INTERACTIONAL APPROACH

FOUNDATIONS AND STRUCTURE

Historical Foundations

IN THE FOREWORD to this book, *How Real is Real?* (1976), Watzlawick makes the following statement: ". . . the most dangerous delusion of all is that there is only one reality" (p. xi). This thought summarizes a major thesis in Watzlawick's work, that each person has an individualized concept of reality, and that conceptualization is shaped and maintained by communication styles and patterns. For this theorist, reality is not dependent upon one set of unchanging facts, it is actually a result of the manner in which individuals have created their own modes of how the world functions.

Paul Watzlawick was originally trained in philosophy and modern languages, receiving a Ph.D. from the University of Venice, Italy. He has had professional experience in security work and criminal investigation and has functioned over the past three decades as a psychotherapist, a researcher, a consultant, and a teacher. He has served as a Research Associate and Principal Investigator at the Mental Research Institute in Palo Alto, California (established in 1958) for the past two decades. While in this capacity, his major research undertakings have focused on both the theoretical and practical perspectivesof human communication within social and family contexts. In addition to his research responsibilities, he holds a clinical appointment in the Department of Psychiatry and Behavioral Sciences at the Stanford University Medical Center (Watzlawick, 1976).

In 1966, Watzlawick, along with colleagues Richard Fisch and John Weakland, established the Brief Therapy Center of the Mental Research Institute. Each of the founders had undergone traditional psychotherapy training experiences and had become frustrated with the uncertainty of their methods, the length of treatment, and the paucity of results (Watzlawick, Weakland, & Fisch, 1974). They also were interested in the sometimes surprising successes of the "gimmicky" therapeutic intervention styles when it appeared these strategies ignored the orthodox methods which had received popular validation over time. They decided to investigate the process of change itself in order to identify any basic explanations which could be generalized to various individual styles of therapeutic intervention. As a result of his association with the Center, Watzlawick has published two books delineating the theoretical bases and strategies initiated by the group's investigations, *Change: Principles of Problem Formation and Problem Resolution* (1974) and *The Language of Change: Elements of Therapeutic Communication* (1978).

Watzlawick's writings often freely illustrate the influence other theorists have had upon his work. The communication theory of anthropologist Gregory Bateson provides the theoretical framework within which much of the work at the Mental Research Institute has been accomplished. Of particular influence on Watzlawick was the work of Donald D. Jackson, the Institute's Director until his death in 1968. Both of these individuals helped Watzlawick attend to the process rather than the content of human interaction and regard the here-and-now as the major focal point of therapeutic activity. The work of Milton Erickson has also had a significant impact upon Watzlawick's thinking. Much of the material in *The Language of Change* is a result of the influence Erickson had upon Watzlawick in the areas of language patterns and therapeutic interventions.

The work of Watzlawick is fresh and exciting, carrying with it few of the traditional models accepted as "truths" by therapists using more orthodox approaches. An advantage Watzlawick has is an academic background in areas which are quite different from the norm for psychotherapists. This training has probably allowed him to experience a different "reality" from most therapists, not being bound by learned expectations which may limit one to a fixed view of the therapeutic process.

Philosophical Foundations

It is a rather difficult task to identify the philosophical foundations of Watzlawick's approach because of his concentration on both the behavioral effect of communication in interpersonal situations and the individual meaning attributed to events through each person's own world view. While behavior is the focus of his activity as a therapist (leading us to conclude that he views the world from a realistic, Lockean point of view), he believes that each individual holds his own model for determining reality (supporting more of an existential-phenomenological point of view).

Tentative Axioms

The key to his philosophical orientation may be found in the "tentative axioms" Watzlawick presents in relation to the interpersonal communication process (Watzlawick, Beavin & Jackson, 1967). The first axiom states that one cannot *not* communicate, meaning that any behavior (active or inactive, purposeful or random, verbal or nonverbal) has a message value in interpersonal situations. The implication for this axiom is that even when an individual is trying to not communicate, a message is still being sent to others.

Watzlawick's second axiom is the notion that every bit of communication has a content (report) and a relationship (command) level. The report level is the actual work message of the communication which conveys specific information to the receiver. The command level, or metacommunication, is the information necessary for the receiver to successfully understand the message as sent. Understanding the report level of the message is contingent upon effectively comprehending the rules or parameters one must use in order to interpret the words. Difficulties arise when these levels become ambiguous, leading the communicators to confusion and frustration. Watzlawick, et al., (1967) indicate that the ability to metacommunicate is not only the condition *sine qua non* of successful communication, but is intimately linked with the enormous problem of awareness of self and others (p. 53).

The third axiom of interpersonal communication concentrates on the process of exchanging messages between communicants. The flow of communication-response patterns is called the punctuational sequence, a system of organizing the interaction. Punctuation sequences become "a series of overlapping stimulus-response-reinforcement triads" (Watzlawick & Beavin, 1967, p. 7). The learned punctuations create different views of reality experienced from one person to another. Since punctuations concentrate on the command level of communication, difficulties arise when communicators (either as senders or receivers) are unaware or misinterpret each other's messages.

A fourth property of communication says that the communication may be either digital or analogic. Digital communication refers to the content/report, verbal aspects of communication. This concept is closely related to Satir's definition of denotive communication, or the actual words used in the message. Digital communication is more logical, objective, complex, and precise than analogic communication, which refers to the relationship/command, nonverbal aspects of messages. Analog communication corresponds to Satir's connotive communication level, focusing on the relationship and metamessage being sent. While digital communication concentrates on the objective use of words to convey meaning, analogic communication concentrates on identifying relationships between concepts and synthesizing ideas. In order to communicate effectively, humans must constantly translate back and forth between analogic and digital styles. In making these translations in either direction, certain parts of the message will be lost. Digital communication, while being much more complex and specific, does not have adequate semantics to describe relationships effectively. Analogic communication can effectively express relationship aspects, yet lacks the specificity and complexity to remove any ambiguities that may be present.

The last axiom mentioned by Watzlawick says that all communicational exchanges are either symmetrical (based on equality) or complementary (based on differences). Symmetrical communication is evident in situations where the communicators mirror each other's behavior, while complementary communication describes the situation where the communicators' behaviors complement each others' based upon some concept of opposites. Difficulties arise when there are disagreements as to the degree of symmetry or complementarity which should be displayed in a relationship.

Watzlawick's axioms of communication illustrate the highly individualized way people communicate within their world view. Lives are governed by the meaning attributed to events and that meaning is both developed and can be seen in the communication strategies used. The absence of meaning in one's life is seen by Watzlawick and his colleagues at the Mental Research Institute as the basis for all forms of emotional distress. Existentialism, then, seems to be the major philosophical viewpoint in Watzlawick's world view, even though many techniques and strategies in his therapeutic style may not appear to be totally consistent with that way of thinking.

Social-Psychological Foundations

Since communication is a social phenomenon, much of Watzlawick's work focuses on the individual within the context of the social or family system. The model of viewing a family as a system was originally proposed by Jackson (1957) in discussing the concept of family homeostasis. Jackson discovered that families of people who were facing an emotional difficulty experienced significant repercussions when the "sick" members started to improve. He hypothesized that these behaviors and perhaps the original emotional difficulties as well were homeostatic mechanisms, operating to maintain the system's steady state. These homeostatic mechanisms are central to much of Watzlawick's approach, as are the other properties of open systems.

Properties of Open Systems

The properties of open systems (for Watzlawick, this includes all human relationships) are wholeness, nonsummativity, feedback and homeostasis, and calibration and step functions (Watzlawick, et al., 1967). Wholeness refers to the belief that the behavior of each family member is interrelated with the behavior of all other members. A change in any one member will result in a change in the others, especially in the areas of emotional, social, or physical well-being. The key to this concept of wholeness is its interactional nature, implying that all pieces of an open system can and do interact with each other. The second property, nonsummativity, refers to the notion that in an open system (as in a gestalt) a whole is greater than a simple summing of its parts. In a family, this means that a sum of the analyses of individual members are not equivalent to the analysis of the family taken as a whole. Feedback and homeostasis are the concepts making up Watzlawick's third property of an open system. They imply that communication entering the system (input) is acted upon by the system and modified, if necessary, in order to maintain the delicate balance of functioning which has been established. If the feedback and homeostatic mechanisms are working effectively and the system is functioning purposefully, then these forces help the system adapt to unique situations and stimuli, providing somewhat of a "survival" function. The last property of an open system is the belief in the existence of calibration and step functions. In order to maintain a steady-state, the system must give the elements a range of possible behaviors within which to operate in order to make any necessary adaptations. This range of behaviors (family "rules," for example) is called the calibration of a system. If that range does not include those behaviors which are required in order to effectively adapt, the range must be changed to include behaviors which will satisfy the system's needs. This change in the calibration is called a step-function.

Paradox

In communicational situations, the degree of contradiction, ambiguity, or confusion in the relationships can be quite paradoxical to the participants. Paradox is a basic concept for explaining how problems are developed and in determining how they can be resolved. A paradox is "a contradiction that follows correct deduction from consistent premises" (Watzlawick, et al., 1967, p. 188). He has identified the following three types of paradoxes: logico-mathematical (antinomies), paradoxical definitions (semantic antinomies), and pragmatic paradoxes (paradoxical injunctions and predictions). Antinomies are the most common and can be described as contradictions based upon accepted ways of reasoning and viewing the world. Paradoxical definitions occur when inconsistencies of language create confusion and contradiction in the thought that is being expressed. The phrase "I am lying" is an example of a paradoxical definition because there is nothing in the language itself which can help us understand the message. The third type of paradox, a pragmatic paradox, is illustrated when a thought, value, belief, or expectation leads one to function in a certain way when the context of the situation requires something quite different.

The most crucial type of paradox in Watzlawick's model is the pragmatic paradox because of its importance in regard to behavioral functioning. A pragmatic paradox can be either a paradoxical injunction or a paradoxical prediction. The paradoxical injunction is at the center of the double-bind theory of schizophrenia, one of the major theoretical contributions made by the early Bateson group (Bateson, Jackson, Haley, & Weakland, 1956). In the paper entitled "Toward a Theory of Schizophrenia," these authors outlined three ingredients of a double-bind message: (1) An intense relationship exists between two or more people which has considerable survival value for at least one of the individuals, (2) A message is transmitted which asserts something, and also asserts something about its own assertion, and these two assertions are mutually exclusive, and (3) the recipient of the message is prevented from stepping outside of the frame set by the contradictory message. Since the message is a paradox and recipients have no way of effectively ridding themselves of the paradox, they are left to respond to something that simply cannot be successfully responded to. There is a gap between what "is" and what "should be," or between correct perceptions and the way the sender would like things to be perceived. If the message in the double-bind is an injunction, then the recipient must disobey it in order to obey. Watzlawick, et al., (1974) see the paradox as a logical deduction of a contradictory situation which often leads to a significant impasse in functioning. Paradoxical predictions result from the situation where mutually exclusive predictions are made in the digital and analog levels of communication. In this case, one's words say one thing yet the meta-communication message contained in nonverbal communication or the underlying logic of the situation say the opposite, leaving the communicators no foreseeable way out of the paradox. The more one protests with words, the more the other is convinced of the opposite due to the logical expectations based on the metacommunication.

Language

The focus of Watzlawick's pragmatic approach is on the different world views of the communicants. If the conceptualization of "reality" is similar and each of the individuals is able to effectively communicate within that context, then messages will be sent and received in a fashion which will lead to successful behavioral cues and expectations. If, however, the models are different, or the communication styles used do not lead to an adequate exchange of information, then problems arise.

Watzlawick (1978) believes that language does not reflect reality as much as it creates it. It has already been mentioned that human beings communicate both on digital and analogic levels. Each of these levels of communication contributes uniquely to the meaning of messages. Since the manner in which each of these levels of communication actually expresses messages is so different, each participant is left with a very different world view created by the two styles of language. Watzlawick (1978) offers his idea of a human being's possession of two languages to support the notion that the right and left sides of the brain have different functions and are the focal points in the creation of the two world views. He notes that the dominant hemisphere (usually the left one) has as its major function the role of translating perceptions into logical, semantic, phonetic, and sequential representations of reality and communicating in a digital manner with the outside world. The nondominant hemisphere serves as a system which deals with the gestalts, patterns, and structures of stimuli. The language capability of the nondominant hemisphere is underdeveloped and lacks the semantic specificity which would enable it to communicate its messages in a clear and unambiguous manner. The actual existence of "two brains" functioning in a coordinated yet distinctly independent fashion remains a theoretical proposition, although there has been significant empirical evidence to support this theory in recent years.

In summary, the psychological aspects of Watzlawick's approach center around three important areas. The first is the notion that families are open systems functioning as dynamic units in order to adapt to the environment.

The Second Psychosocial Notion

Important to Watzlawick's stance concentrates on the impact of paradox upon the behaviors of individuals and families. The third psychosocial basis to his theory is the importance that language holds in the development of different world views within and between people. He believes that digital and analogic communication are used in a coordinated yet independent fashion and serve to create different conceptualizations of the world (or, of one's "reality").

The Development of the Person and Family

Watzlawick's theory represents an approach to counseling and not a comprehensive personality theory. This fact makes it difficult to identify a specific theoretical formulation describing the growth and development of families and individuals. In his approach, much of the concentration is on how problems are created, how they are maintained, and how they can be changed. There are however, some human growth and development assumptions which are implicit in his conceptualization of the counseling process which will be discussed in this section.

The first and most obvious conclusion which can be drawn from Watzlawick's theoretical formulations is the belief that the human development process is continually tied to the ability of each individual to clearly send and receive messages. The manner in which people learn to communicate (both on digital and analog levels) will have a strong impact upon the way they view the world and other people around them. Members of a family most often develop characteristic ways of communicating with each other and with people outside of the family. This will not only influence the development of each member's world view, but it will also create a "family world view" which helps to maintain the system's structure and processes. These world views are actually created by the language patterns each member has learned to use within the system. The language style not only creates one's vision of "reality" but also may change and adapt in order to maintain that view.

Watzlawick, et al., (1967) have indicated that existence is "a function of the relationship between the organism and its environment." This proposal has certain implications for the growth and development of both the individual and the family. While the threat of an ominous environment has largely been neutralized in modern, industrial society, one's physical, psychological, and social environments still have a significant impact upon the developmental process. Human beings are dependent upon the environment for adequate information which will help them deal effectively with situations which are not consistent with their own expectations of the "typical sequence" of events. Watzlawick believes that this interactionist perspective is at the center of the growth and development process as an aspect of life which is continually moving, continually changing, and dependent upon both the environment and the individual for input. While Watzlawick does not outline any specific developmental sequence, his interactionist perspective indicates that specific sequences may exist only if the interaction between the person and environment is open to adaptation and change.

Concepts of Functional and Dysfunctional Behavior

The concept of "world view" is at the center of Watzlawick's (1978) definition of individual and family differences. If the world view of an individual or family is inconsistent with universally accepted definitions of "reality," then this contradiction results in pragmatic difficulties. The difference between the way things appear and the way they "should be" affects the individual's or family's ability to adapt their world view and defines the degree of difficulty they face. The world view influences the functioning of the system; as greater discrepancies are identified between what "is" and what "should be" the more the system must adapt to minimize or eliminate that conflict. In this case, the system has the job of adapting while still maintaining its present structure and processes. Many times, the system finds that the change necessary to adapt to the discrepancy is too great and the present course (despite its dysfunctionality) is retained.

Mathematical Logic

A short discussion of mathematical logic may help to illustrate the conflicts faced by some systems which lead to pragmatic difficulties. Watzlawick, et al., (1974) introduce the theory of mathematical groups into the explanation of their theoretical perspective in order to provide an analogous description of conflicting expectations leading to paradoxical situations. The theory of groups proposes that a group has the following four properties:

- A group is composed of members which have at least one common characteristic.
- The members of the group can be combined or sequenced in any way and the outcome will always be the same.
- Each group contains an identity member which, if presented in combination with any other member, maintains the other member's identity or value.
- Every member in a group has an opposite or reciprocal member in the group which, when combined with the original, will give the identity member.

The theory of groups provides Watzlawick, et al., (1974) with a framework for understanding the interdependence between change and persistence. The usefulness of this theory can especially be seen under conditions characterized by "the more things change, the more they stay the same." In some situations, people become trapped within a particular group and lack the options to deal with the environment in a functional manner. In these cases, abnormal behaviors may not be as much a result of active choices, but rather of a paucity of alternative responses which are consistent with the accepted behaviors within the system. Until the frame of reference is changed, the individual or system is locked into one manner of conceptualizing the reality of the situation. If the way out cannot be found in that world view, then a shift must be made.

Watzlawick views the problems experienced by most people to be problems of interaction (Weakland, Fisch, Watzlawick, & Bodin, 1974). Problems often do not arise from the reaction to crisis, but rather from maladaptive ways of dealing with everyday difficulties and normal life changes. In this way, Watzlawick and his colleagues have focused on day-to-day events and each individual's reaction to them. Communication difficulties are the primary ways problems develop because when an individual lacks the skills necessary to negotiate what is happening in the environment, problems are created where they need not exist.

Problem Formation and Solutions

Watzlawick and his colleagues believe that more serious problems can develop out of the various kinds of solutions that are applied to the initial problem. They have identified four such "solutions" that may actually create further problems (Watzlawick, et al., 1974). The first type results when a chosen solution to a particular problem exacerbates the present difficulty and, instead of lessening the uncomfortable situation, intensifies it. Watzlawick calls this process "more of the same," where the over-riding philosophy is "if a little is good, a lot will be better." The "more of the same" type of problem formulation is related to the fourth group property (see above). The intended solution is the opposite or reciprocal member in the particular group. When it is attempted, it does not lead to the alleviation of the problem situation, it actually leads to a state of no change (the identity member).

A second type of problem formation is described by Watzlawick, et al., (1974) as "the terrible simplification." In this case, a problem exists which is simplified or mishandled to the point where its existence is denied. Watzlawick notes two consequences following a terrible simplification: (1) the acknowledgment of the problem is perceived as an admission of badness or madness, and (2) the original problem has become compounded by problems created by its denial or mishandling. The "terrible simplification" type of problem formation is likened to the third number which is applied to the problem situation, thus maintaining the problem as it exists. Watzlawick indicates that human problems often do not remain stable so the simplification may result in a compounded or intensified difficulty.

The concept of utopia is central to Watzlawick's third type of problem formation (Watzlawick, et al., 1974). A utopia is an ideal system where there are either no problems or there are at least solutions to all possible problems. When experience does not conform to the utopian model, people either try to force reality into a more consistent position or they deny that problems actually exist. Some of the specific difficulties experienced by people who view things from a utopian frame of reference include: (1) the belief that solutions exist for every problem situation, which leads to frustration and self-deprecation when they are not found; (2) treating a normal developmental issue or a typical day-to-day difficulty as a problem because of its inconsistency with a utopian model of how things should work; and (3) the denial of the existence of problems in such a "perfect" existence. This type of problem formation relates to the fact that membership in any group is a finite concept. If the true solution to a problem situation cannot be found inside of the group within which the individual is searching for alternatives, then the person will be frustrated as long as the search is limited in that manner.

The fourth type of problem formation proposed by Watzlawick, et al., (1974) concentrates on the pragmatic results of a paradoxical situation. Paradox, as it has already been described, is a contradiction which follows from the correct deduction of consistent premises. Problems are developed when a paradox either inhibits, limits, or defines the way in which an individual must behave within a system. In most cases, the individual is left in the position of having few or no behavioral alternatives. Paradox, as a method of problem formation, is similar to the utopia syndrome due to the fact that actual solutions to the difficulties can be found only outside of the group of logical alternatives. In both cases, the people either have painted themselves or have been painted by others into a corner and must break from their accepted "world views" to gain freedom.

Feedback Loops

Once a problem is developed it is continued, in Watzlawick's perspective, as a result of a feedback loop. When an existing system is faced with a symmetrical element being introduced into its functioning, it will typically react by a "more of the same" style of behavior which will amplify the impact of the element until some stability is reached. This amplification is called a positive feedback loop and is often a component of the development of problem situations. When a point of stability is reached, the system achieves some level of complementarity. A system can be maintained at this level for an indefinite period of time. This level of stability is called a negative feedback loop, leading to no changes in the system's functioning. When a positive feedback loop is in operation, the system is changing or in the position of being ready for change, while a negative feedback loop functions as a mechanism which maintains the status quo.

Watzlawick and his colleagues believe that the chronicity of a problem does not necessarily mean that a basic defect exists in the underlying make-up of the system (Weakland, et al., 1974). They believe that chronicity is simply indicative of a repetitively poorly-handled problem situation. It becomes a question of length rather than seriousness or degree. For example, a personality disorder may be seen as a learned way of responding to the world given the way a person has developed a conceptualization of what "should be," rather than a deep-seated and stable process which is always resistant to change. This concentration on repetition and persistence rather than underlying processes promotes a very different "world view" on the part of the counselor, which may help to open doors which have been seen as somewhat impenetrable by theorists representing other conceptual frameworks.

Concepts of Behavior Change

In the discussion of problem formation, Watzlawick, et al., (1974) borrowed a central theoretical analogy from mathematical logic, called the Theory of Groups. As was mentioned in the last section of this chapter, the Theory of Groups offers a framework for understanding the interdependence between persistence and change within a system. When difficulties arise which cannot be solved from within a specific system or world view, another type of mathematical theory must be studied in order to find answers. The Theory of Logical Types allows us to step back conceptually from the limitations of the group and recreate a more conducive reality. This perspective holds that whatever involves all of the members of a class cannot be one of the members itself (Whitehead & Russell, 1910-1913). The individual components of the whole are called members (as in Group Therapy), but the whole itself is called a class rather than a group. Each class can itself be a member of other classes which include members which have at least one characteristic in common. Watzlawick utilizes the Theory of Logical Types to explain changes which can occur when one transcends a system.

The Theory of Logical Types is not concerned with the relationship between members of a class as much as it enables us to consider the relationship between member and class and the process of shifting to a higher logical level (Watzlawick, et al., 1974). The Theory of Groups enables us to identify changes which may occur within an existing system, based upon a similar world view. These changes will be sufficient to deal with the problem situation if (1) the system itself need not be changed in order to effect or maintain the necessary changes in functioning, and (2) the alternative exists within the system which will lead to a satisfactory outcome. If either of these two stipulations are not present in an existing class, a shift to the next higher level must be made to reach success. Watzlawick, et al., (1974) indicate that the simplest type of change is a change in position, or one involving motion. They say that motion can be changed by acceleration or deceleration which results in a metachange (change of change). A change within an existing system is labeled first-order change while a shift to a higher class level in order to achieve a desired end is labeled second-order change.

One of the characteristics of open systems discussed earlier, calibration and step-functions, has considerable importance in the definition of first-order and second-order change. An automobile with a manual gearshift assembly is an excellent example of first and second order change in action. Within any particular gear, the potential speed of the automobile is limited by the calibration of the machine in terms of revolutions per minute of the drive shaft. A change in speed can be attained by pushing on the gas pedal but is limited by the gear itself. If additional speed potential is desired, the operator must shift to another gear (thus go one level higher on the step-function) and operate the automobile at that level. The use of the gas pedal is a first-order change because it occurs within one class and is limited only by the calibration of that class. A shift to another gear is a second order change because it transcends the initial state and is no longer limited by the constraints of the original class.

Watzlawick, et al., (1974) note four characteristics of second order change:

- Second-order change is applied to what in the first-order change perspective appears to be a solution.
- While first-order change always appears to be based upon common sense, second-order change usually appears weird, unexpected, and uncommonsensical.
- Applying second-order change techniques to the "solution" means that the situation is dealt with in the here and now. These techniques deal with effects and not with their presumed causes.
- The use of second-order change techniques lifts the situation out of the paradox-engineering trap created by the self-reflexiveness of the attempted solution and places it in a different frame. (p. 82-83)

A first-order change is limited to alternatives which are present and available within a specific world view. In order to reach a second-order change, the original world view must be either changed or transcended so that the problem situation can be redefined within a new context which will make it solvable. In later formulations, Watzlawick (1978) has proposed that the world view that any individual has developed is largely formulated and expressed by the nondominant hemisphere of the brain. Since it is not the nondominant but the dominant hemisphere which responds to logic, argument, interpretation, and other cognitively specific activities, then other routes must be used to impact problem situations which have at their center an ineffective world view. Watzlawick proposes that communication be made with the nondominant hemisphere in order to directly influence the world view.

Assessment of Human Functioning

Watzlawick (1966) has said that "one of the basic assumptions of psychotherapy is that human behavior is not a random phenomenon, but that it is patterned" (p. 256). His assessment style involves extensive interviewing so that the counselor actually experiences the family's interaction patterns in action. Since he believes that most problems which occur can be related to basic communication styles and processes, a first-hand view helps the counselor understand the family's world view as well as individual realities. For this purpose, he developed a structured interview format which lasts approximately one hour and serves as a clinical assessment tool.

Watzlawick (1966) mentions that the structured interview format is not only an assessment tool, but it also has implications for treatment. The tasks help the family to start concentrating on themselves as a unit and viewing their own functioning within their roles in the system. It also assists the family to start discussing their problems both with each other and with an "outsider." Watzlawick notes that the structured interview has been found to be most effective if the therapist is not the interviewer but, rather, observes the interaction from behind the one-way mirror and is introduced by the interviewer at the end of the experience.

In later work, Watzlawick discusses a counseling process which has been developed at the Brief Therapy Center in the Mental Research Institute (Weakland, et al., 1974). Two of the steps identified as parts of this process are directly related to the assessment of the status of the system. The first of these, the definition of the problem, is an attempt to identify a well-defined problem which will enable the counselor to start developing appropriate treatment strategies with the family. Watzlawick follows the general principle of "starting where the patient is at." All of the family members are asked to share from their vantage point what they believe the difficulties are that the family is facing at the moment. The counselor's job is to help the family members clarify what is actually happening, what they would like to see changed and how they would like to be functioning in the future. The counselor tries to help the family put the problem into a perspective that makes it seem solvable, as opposed to the apparently insurmountable difficulty they may have been facing up to this time.

The second assessment step proposed at the Brief Therapy Center is the process of estimating what behaviors are maintaining the problem. Again, Watzlawick believes that while problems may have specific causes, in order to persist they must be reinforced in some way. The task in this step is to identify the beliefs, expectations, feelings, and other aspects of the world views of the family members which help to maintain the problem behaviors. The counselor first asks the family members how they have been coping with the problem situation. While this alone may sometime elicit enough information to identify the reinforcers, in many cases the counselor must probe deeper. It is quite possible that the exploration of this issue with the family will allow the counselor to see the maintenance of the problem in action.

Formal diagnosis does not play a very important role in Watzlawick's work. Since human difficulties are identified and treated within the context of a system, individual classification methods are not useful. When he does use diagnostic terminology in his writings, it seems more for the communicative value of these labels for other therapists than as a way of expressing his own beliefs. In the same way, he believes that the counselor must talk with the client in the client's language, he perhaps may feel he must talk with traditional therapists in their own language as well.

Goals and Directions of Counseling

The goals of the counseling process for Watzlawick and his colleagues are based upon two general principles which they apply to most family difficulties (Weakland, et al., 1974). The first principle is the assssumption that the problems people bring to formal counseling persist only if they are maintained by behavior patterns inherent in the system. In other words, the problems are reinforced from within the system itself, setting up a negative feedback loop. The second principle says that if the behaviors which maintain the problem situation within the system are changed or eliminated, then the problem will "be resolved or vanish, regardless of its nature, origin, or duration" (p. 145). If the problem facing an individual or a family can be successfully dealt with from inside the system as it is currently functioning then this first-order change process can often be accomplished without the aid of a trained professional. If, however, a second order change is needed (a change in the structure or pattern of the system itself) then professional intervention is often helpful. The goal of counseling for Watzlawick and his colleagues, therefore, is to facilitate second-order change.

The Brief Therapy Center at the Mental Research Instititue is interested in achieving a resolution of the problem situation. They are primarily involved in the pragmatic aspects of the problems and the clients' attempts to resolve the difficulties themselves. Their chief aim seems to be assisting the individual or family in breaking away from their present behavioral and communication patterns. A specific behavioral goal isn't as important as the goal of simply changing the present patterns because once these patterns have been broken, then the specific direction of the change can be shaped. It is their intention to assist clients in escaping from the trap which is being maintained for them by the system. Once they are released from this circular relationship, they are more free to deal with the problem with a new and more facilitative world view.

In his book entitled *The Language of Change* (1978) Watzlawick says that "the purpose of therapy is seen as a change of the patient's predominantly right-hemisphere world image" (p. 128). In this case, the system has reinforced and maintained some type of problem for the client which is especially evident in that individual's world view and is the point which must be impacted in the counseling process. A change in the world view held by the right hemisphere is what actually happens during the process of second-order change.

The goals in the counseling process for Watzlawick all concentrate on the pragmatic consequences of individual and family world views. Counseling assists the clients in changing this world view, leading to some type of second-order change. Once this freeing effect is completed, then specific behavioral goals can be identified and achieved.

The Counseling Process:
Structuring, Facilitating, and Terminating

Six Stages of Counseling

Weakland, et al., (1974) use a six-stage counseling process at the Brief Therapy Center. They indicate that while each step involves some rather specific activities, overlapping may exist in actual practice. The

first step is an introduction to the setting and organizational requirements of the therapy process. In their facility, no waiting lists are kept,
so when they have no openings the potential clients are referred elsewhere. During the first meeting the clients complete a demographic
questionnaire, are told about the need for recording and observing sessions, and are requested to sign written consent forms for this aspect of
the program. An expectation of rapid change is engendered in the
clients during the introductory session as they learn that treatment consists of one session per week for a maximum of ten weeks.

The next two steps in the counseling process, defining the problem
and estimating the system behaviors which are maintaining the problem
situation, have already been discussed at length in the assessment section of this chapter. One crucial point which should be reiterated here is
the importance that Watzlawick and his colleagues place upon the active
observation of the family during this period of assessment and problem
definition. They believe that the counselor must view directly the structure and patterns of the family in order to effectively identify the processes which have developed in the system.

Setting individualized goals for treatment is the fourth step in the
process. Weakland, et al., (1974) indicate that the act of setting goals
suggests to the client that change is possible within the allocated time
periods, and also provides a measurement tool to be used by both the
counselor and the clients to evaluate the effectiveness of the relationship.
Goals are explicit, relevant, and attainable and should be reestablished
by the end of the second to third sessions. For the most part, the identified goal is not aimed at reshaping the client's entire world but, rather, to
help the client set up a specific goal which will facilitate breaking out of
the patterns established in the non-functional aspects of the system.
Once this is done, the client is then more free to shape other life changes
within the new context.

Once goals are established, the most appropriate interventions must
be selected and implemented. The specific interventions used by Watzlawick and his colleagues will be discussed at length in the following
section of this chapter. To some people, the techniques used in this approach may seem illogical and somewhat radical. Since the intervention
strategies are aimed at creating second-order change, they must impact
upon the clients' logical view of the world. What may be necessary to
modify a person's individual reality will probably appear to be quite "out
of synchrony" and paradoxical to other counseling approaches.

Termination (either at or before the ten session limit) involves a review of the gains made and difficulties left unresolved. The clients are given the credit for any changes actually made during the time of the counseling relationship. In some cases, however, changes made are minimized and skepticism is expressed concerning any future progress. Watzlawick and his colleagues believe that both of these tactics act as "dares" to the client and thus create a situation where the counseling relationship continues beyond the active sessions. Whatever can be done to help the client remember and learn from the changes made during counseling is used during the termination phase.

As is evident from the previous discussion, the counseling process at the Brief Therapy Center is a pragmatic, highly individualized approach which has as its major focus identifiable, manageable problems. The purpose is to help individuals change some aspect of the ineffective structure or patterns in their system. Once the change is made, the clients are given maximal credit for any progress, reinforcing a belief in their ability to continue the change process and that they have acquired more tools which may help them help themselves.

Counseling Techniques and Procedures

The techniques used by the clinicians at the Brief Therapy Center are active, specific to the individual client, and directed at changes in behaviors. The strategies are designed to assist people in doing things which lead them to stop doing whatever is reinforcing and maintaining the problem behaviors. Watzlawick (1978) classifies these specific counseling interventions into the following areas: (1) the use of right hemispheric language patterns; (2) blocking the left hemisphere; and (3) the use of specific behavior prescriptions (p. 47).

Right Hemispheric Language

The *right hemisphere*, as has been discussed earlier, has its own language style and is the seat of an individual's world view. Watzlawick (1978) has discussed numerous examples of the language patterns used by the right hemisphere and believes that direct influence can be made upon the world view through the use of these patterns. The structure of this language is very primitive and is characterized by metaphorical, figurative, and allegorical bits of communication. Watzlawick notes that verbosity and meaning exhibit an inverse relationship.

The longer a statement, a thesis, or the expression of a simple thought becomes, the more the essential meaning may be confused. Some simple utterances of primitive language forms, called condensations, may carry explicit yet truly expressive meaning. What condensations do is offer in one or very few words that which the dominant hemisphere's rational language would need a lengthy explanation to express. Watzlawick (1978) gives the example of biodeplorable foods (in reference to the fare in a health food restaurant) and popollution (combination of population and pollution). Both of these examples present a glimpse of the world view of the speaker. An awareness of condensations developed by clients and the ability to use them in therapeutic communication enables the counselor to access the nondominant hemisphere.

Meaning can be expressed and understood with a minimum of verbal explanation. A second type of right-hemisphere language pattern is the figurative language found in dreams and dreamlike states. Autogenic training and hypnotic techniques have concentrated on this language and experience for quite some time. The language itself is one of images transmitted as visual, auditory, kinesthetic, olfactory, and gustatory perceptions. The explanation of meaning is not a part of the message, it is simply an expression of that person's internal process. Figurative language lacks any concept of negation because it is impossible, for example, to form a picture or a symbol which expresses the meaning that something does not exist. The expression, "The boy throws a ball to the dog" can easily be pictured and that picture can adequately convey the intended meaning. If, however, one tries to picture the expression "The boy does not throw a ball to the dog," then problems occur. What cannot be expressed is a clear message of the negative idea. Negation, then, relies upon logic and is a product of the dominant hemisphere. It is important that the counselor, when trying to communicate with the right hemisphere, does not use negative phrases. As opposed to saying "you will not be anxious when you speak in front of the group," the counselor may say "you will feel calm and comfortable when talking to the group."

The use of figurative language allows the counselor to convey meaning without becoming dependent upon the use of logical syntax (which can be analyzed, argued with, and easily dismissed as being inconsistent with one's world view). The use of imagery can be useful to express meaning within the client's own frame of reference. While a dream is the passive enaction of unconscious or subconscious material, the use of imagery is an active intervention that introduces something into awareness without the use of left hemisphere language.

A style of language called pars-pro-toto involves helping clients evoke a gestalt (a total picture) by presenting to them a part of their world view. Accurate empathy (knowledge of the client's world view) is essential for this technique to work. The purpose is to bring the total picture into focus (quite possibly for the first time) so that change may be facilitated.

Other types of right-hemisphere language patterns used by Watzlawick in the counseling process are aphorism, ambiguities, puns, and allusions. All of these language forms have one thing in common with pars-pro-toto, figurative language, and condensation: they are able to avoid being subjected to the logic and rationality of the left-hemisphere and communicate directly with the right hemisphere. Watzlawick continuously reinforces the importance of an empathic understanding of the client's world view which is essential in being able to speak the client's language. Without this the ability to communicate with the left-hemisphere is severely diminished.

Left Hemispheric Blocking

Certain of Watzlawick's techniques have been developed to block the *logical intrusion* of the *left-hemisphere*. Among these are the use of paradox, symptom prescription, symptom displacement, illusion of alternatives, and reframing. While the paradox has been discussed as one of the ways problems are developed, it is also used in their resolution. Watzlawick (1978) describes paradox as the Achilles heel of an individual's logical world view. The reliance upon any form of dualistic thinking breaks down as one discovers that this type of perspective is inadequate to deal with reality. In the same format that problems are developed by encountering paradoxical situations, the counselor can help to eliminate difficulties by making their existence untenable. Watzlawick, et al., (1974) give an example of the use of paradox in the process of problem resolution. The authors note that many insomniacs place themselves in the "Be spontaneous" paradox by trying to force themselves to sleep. The method counselors at the Brief Therapy Center use to deal with this problem is to approach it in a paradoxical way by telling the client to try to stay awake and not fall asleep. Rather than fighting the symptom, the client is actually placed in the position of actively doing it. Sleep typically is encountered quite soon after this technique is attempted because the clients no longer must fight the symptom and expend their energy in such a useless fashion.

The type of paradox used in the example just presented is called symptom prescription. Watzlawick (1978) believes that persons who either cannot do something they would like to do or have a compulsion to do something they would rather not do both feel as if they are experiencing spontaneous and uncontrolled inhibitions or impulses. His suggestion for these situations is to actually prescribe the inhibition or the impulse so that the client can perform these behaviors in a voluntary and deliberate manner. When control is exerted over behaviors which heretofore have been perceived as outside of the individual's sphere of influence, clients then are able to overcome the problem. In most cases the attempted solutions to the problem have become the problem themselves. These attempted solutions are behaviors controlled by the left hemisphere. When the symptom is prescribed, the left hemisphere influence is blocked and the right hemisphere is allowed to deal with the difficulty on another level (second-order change).

Symptom displacement involves shifting the focus of a symptom rather than attempting to influence it directly. Watzlawick (1978) indicates that his technique has been used in hypnotherapy for some time, shifting symptoms over time and place (concentrating the symptoms on particular days or in specific parts of the body in order to make them more manageable).

The illusion of alternatives is an instance where an individual's behavior has largely been determined by the perception that certain alternatives exist and there is no possible behavior outside of those alternatives. The difficulty often faced is the knowledge that none of the presenting alternatives is appropriate and no others are possible within the given context. What the Theory of Logical Types assists the client in doing is to change the context, thus creating more appropriate behavioral alternatives. For example, many young adults have been somewhat limited in their thinking concerning the types of careers which are available to them. A very bright child is typically reinforced for thinking that a future as some type of professional is the most appropriate direction. By the time the actual career choice is made, most of these people entertain only these types of occupations as alternatives, believing that the other possibilities are simply not within the realm of possibility. What they are doing, then, is eliminating a vast number of gratifying, creative, and productive alternatives because of the illusion of limited alternatives. When the other alternatives are opened to them they may have a greater opportunity to find an effective "fit" for their work life. The illusion of alternatives is a left hemisphere function which can be blocked by changing the context to include the next higher class of alternatives.

The last method Watzlawick uses to block the influence of the left hemisphere is called *reframing*—the process of changing the subjective realities of a client's world view. This is accomplished by changing the context within which a situation is experienced. What actually takes place is a change in the client's perspective to a metalevel where the same facts can be conceptualized in a more facilitative manner. The facts remain the same, only the context has been changed. Watzlawick, et al., (1974) illustrate the "gentle art of reframing" in this story about a police officer who found himself in a rather delicate situation:

> "A police officer was in the process of issuing a citation for a minor traffic violation when a hostile crowd began to gather around him. By the time he had given the offender his ticket, the mood of the crowd was ugly and the sergeant was not certain that he would be able to get back to the relative safety of his patrol car. It occurred to him to announce in a loud voice: 'You have just witnessed the issuance of a traffic ticket by a member of your Oakland Police Department.' And while the bystanders were busy trying to fathom the deeper meaning of this communique, he got into his patrol car and drove off." (p. 109)

Behavior Prescriptions

The use of *specific behavior prescriptions* is the last major intervention technique discussed by Watzlawick. It involves asking a client or family to do something they would not ordinarily have considered. The purpose of such an action is to approximate the phenomenon of spontaneous change which occurs when an individual's experience cannot be integrated into one's world view, making it necessary to change that view at least slightly. Watzlawick (1978) indicates that as long as the disparity is not too great and the change which is being attempted is not too drastic, then the experience can be growth-producing. An example of a behavior prescription can be seen in the following summary.

A single parent and her two teen-age children sought counseling services in order to deal with issues of independence which had surfaced in the family. The children felt that their mother was domineering in the way she constantly controlled their actions, including what time they went to bed, what friends they could associate with, and how they should dress. The children thought that their mother was being unfair and should "loosen up" her controlling influence. The mother, however, indicated that whenever she would loosen up control, the children would take advantage of the situation and abuse their privileges. The counselor noted that the task of working full-time and taking care of a family is a tremendous task for any person and that it would be nice if the mother could have at least a little break from the responsibility. The counselor gave a very simple behavior prescription: The children were to fix their mother's breakfast each morning for a week and serve it to her in bed. After one week, what had occurred was a very different reality than the mother had expected. The children had prepared the breakfast, served it to their mother and had left the kitchen in top shape before the mother came downstairs each morning. With this evidence of maturity, it was difficult for the mother to maintain her image of the children as totally dependent upon her for everything so she began to loosen her rein on other areas as well. The children, happy to be given this vote of confidence, had no need to abuse the privilege. The mother related to the counselor at a later date that it seemed as if the children had literally grown up before her eyes.

Evaluation of Counseling Outcomes

Weakland, et al., (1974) presented a summary of the evaluation methods used at the Brief Therapy Center. In this account, they state that therapists' reports of treatment outcome are typically limited to general clinical impressions, and the results which are presented by the researcher are based upon ideal designs which are rarely implemented in practice. At the Brief Therapy Center, Watzlawick and his colleagues have attempted to accumulate systematic evaluations of their interventions from the beginning of their program. Each client has been followed up and asked the following questions: (1) Have the specific goals of treatment been met? (2) What is the current status of their main complaint? (3) Has therapy been sought elsewhere since the end of therapy at the Center? (4) Have any improvements occurred in areas outside of the focus of treatment? and (5) Have any new problems appeared? Cases were then classified into three outcome groups: complete relief from presenting problem (success), clear and considerable relief (significant improvement), and little or no change (failure). The overall results for 97 cases averaging 7 sessions each are:

Success	39 cases	40%
Significant improvement	31 cases	32%
Failure	28 cases	28%

The authors note that these data are consistent with available statistics on longer-term counseling. In this light, it would seem that Watzlawick's communication approach can be a very efficient method of intervention.

COUNSELING APPLICATION

Watzlawick and his colleagues at the Brief Therapy Center use a short-term, active, individualized form of intervention. Since the specific style of intervention used in each case has been developed for that particular situation, verbatim accounts of actual sessions may not offer the reader a true picture of the counseling process. In addition, the short-term nature of the relationship also limits the amount of information one gains from observing one or two interactions. Because of these limitations, the authors felt that case summarizations would be more appropriate. In this way the reader will be aware of the content, the context, and the rationale for the intervention. The case is a summary of a short-term intervention with a family consisting of a mother and father, two daughters who were 9 and 15, and an 8-year-old son.

The Problem. The family sought counseling due to the recent rise in disruptive, loud, and physically abusive behaviors on the part of the 15-year-old daughter. The parents indicated that their daughter had always experienced minor difficulties in getting along with other people. As a young child at school she found it hard to sit still over extended periods of time, which held her achievement back somewhat during the early years. The family had sought assistance at that time to insure that other aspects of her development would not be hampered by this problem. Within the last two years, their daughter had become much more aggressive in the family — arguing, yelling, and sometimes becoming physically abusive toward both her parents and siblings. The parents have become increasingly concerned about this uncontrollable behavior, which they feel is becoming dangerous and potentially destructive to the health of the family as a unit. The parents note that the difficulties do not seem to be exhibited at school at anywhere near the frequency or intensity as they have been at home.

Attempted Solutions. The parents believe that much of the inappropriate behavior exhibited by the daughter is related to her need for increased independence now that she has entered her teen years. They note that when she is away from the family in social situations, her behavior is always appropriate and, in fact, they have received feedback from others that she is actually quite mature for her age. When their daughter becomes physically abusive or verbally overwhelming at home, the parents see this as a cry for independence and try to discuss the problem with her in a rational, adult manner. At this point, the more the parents apply their solution of rationally discussing with their daughter the crux of the present difficulty, the more she escalates her inappropriate behaviors.

The counselor sees quite a different reality in this situation. While the parents perceive the daughter's behavior as a cry of independence, the counselor observes the daughter expressing a need to remain dependent upon the family unit. The daughter is being thrust into the position of needing to learn how to be independent, while she still feels a strong need to be a child, safe within the family. She does enjoy some aspects of independence, but resents her younger siblings for the care afforded to them by the parents. She fears that the parents no longer love her as much as they do her siblings and feels as if she is being "pushed" out of the nest. Therefore, the more the parents try to treat her as an adult, the more resistant she becomes and actively displays her disagreement.

The Goal. The goal of the intervention is to stop the abusive behaviors by helping the daughter realize that one can learn how to become independent without losing the love of parents and the support of the family. The specific goal chosen by the parents is to hear their daughter say to them, "I am no longer a child, I'd like to take more responsibility for myself."

The Intervention. It appeared that both the parents and their daughter were trapped in a circular pattern of behavior which was based upon two very different views of reality. The counselor decided to help each of the major forces in the problem situation change their view of reality by suggesting a behavior prescription. One of the things the parents had been trying to do was to make sure that they were allowing their daughter to be as independent as possible within a structure of guidance offered by them. The counselor asked the parents to stop treating their daughter as an adult and go to the opposite extreme by eliminating most of her privileges. They were asked to say to their daughter that they had made a mistake in thinking that she was old enough to be more independent and it was obvious that she needed the constant direction given to her siblings. At that point, they were to mention that the freedoms which she had enjoyed for a few years would be cut back or eliminated, because they care about her so much that it hurts them to see her in so much difficulty. At first, the parents were quite confused by this idea because it seemed to be just the opposite of what they thought was best for their daughter at her age. They were at a point, however, where they felt that any approach would be worth a try. The counselor indicated that the parents must follow through on all of the aspects of the intervention in order for it to work.

The parents did carry out the instructions and one week later they reported that the inappropriate behaviors on the part of their daughter had stopped completely. After they had expressed to their daughter all of the new "rules," she was obviously quite confused about the whole situation. A couple of days later she had come back to them and indicated that she knew they were only doing this out of love for her, but that she is old enough to enjoy some independence. The parents reminded her that she would have to earn her independence by showing them how mature she could be. They also told her that they were always available to her for any help she may need.

Analysis. The daughter's inappropriate behaviors were actually demands for attention, limits, and evidence that her parents still cared for her. When the behavior prescription was enacted, she was put into the position of getting what she believed she wanted, then discovering that this new reality was uncomfortable. Both the parents and the daughter had been caught in an illusion of alternatives. The parents felt that their only alternative was to give her more independence when she exhibited the outbursts or she would become even more difficult to handle while, on the other hand, the daughter felt that acting out was the only way to wake her parents up to the fact that she was unhappy with her recent lack of attention from them. The behavior prescription gave each of the parties other ways to look at the situation, both finding effective alternative explanations they could use to slightly change their world view.

Critical Comments

Watzlawick's interactional approach is a distinctive form of counseling focusing on communications within a General Systems Theory framework. It has a behavioral emphasis, concentrating interventions on the pragmatics (behavioral aspects) of communication interaction and transactions. Watzlawick brings into this frame of reference a strong existential view, dealing with the realities of individuals as opposed to a counselor-provided reality. As a result of his strong reliance on individual realities, Watzlawick's approach transcends any specific theoretical perspective and concentrates on the underlying dynamics of change itself. Three major themes which characterize his framework are (1) an anti-causal/anti-historical frame of reference to problem formation and resolution; (2) a concentration on communication processes as a way to understand an individual's world view; and (3) seemingly unorthodox intervention techniques.

Instead of relying on a study of the past to identify specific causal links with existing problems, Watzlawick is more interested in investigating how a problem is being maintained in an individual's present mode of functioning. This is not to say that he ignores all historical perspectives, but that he only uses this information as it relates to the perpetuation of inappropriate interpersonal behaviors. The past, then, is used to assist clients in changing their views of reality and to deal more effectively with the demands of the environment. When Watzlawick asks the family to relate to him the important aspects of their past development, he is actually asking them to show him how they function in the present. He will observe them in the interview in order to gain information regarding the way they can interrelate and the way the family relates as a whole with someone from outside of the system.

When the intervention strategies are implemented, they are experienced in the present so that clients can directly encounter the disruption to their world view. This creates a situation where the client becomes uncomfortable with the present world view and must change in some way in order to make sense out of the situation. Watzlawick is interested in helping any change to occur in a system which has heretofore been caught in a static, ineffective state. Once the old boundaries are removed, the counselor and client can shape the change within a more adaptive world view. This change process occurs in a here-and-now context because it would be too easy for a client to rely upon intellectualizations and logical, left-hemisphere arguments if the problems were faced in a then-and-there frame of reference. When the clients are faced with a logically untenable situation in the present, they are forced to do something about it immediately.

Watzlawick's theoretical framework proposes that communication creates reality. There exist two different languages, the logical and analytic language of the left brain (digital) and the language of the right brain which uses imagery, metaphor, and patterns in communication (analogic). Each of these languages represents a different world view for the individual, a different set of parameters within which to interact and transact inside and outside of the system. Much of Watzlawick's focus in counseling is to manipulate these two languages in order to change one's ineffective world view. While world views are ultimately the foci for counseling attention, the conduit used by the counselor to make the impact is the client's style of communication.

While this focus on communication is not unique among counselors and theoreticians, the specific manner in which Watzlawick attempts to make changes reflects his own background and experiences. In his 1978 book, *The Language of Change,* he acknowledges that the unorthodox nature of the intervention methods he discusses in his case examples usually raise three skeptical questions. The first question concentrates on the apparent difficulty a therapist would face in choosing the appropriate technique to fit the client's difficulty. In many traditional counseling approaches, the interventions are aimed at dealing with the historical antecedents of the problem — the "whys" of the situation. Within Watzlawick's perspective, the most important aspect of the present situation is the identification of those behaviors which are maintaining the problem — the "hows" of the situation. Once those behaviors are identified, then interventions are chosen which will stop them with little or no attention paid to the set of circumstances which led to the initial difficulty. The clients attempted solutions become the focus of counseling. Watzlawick also notes that some skeptics question the length of effectiveness of these intervention strategies. He indicates that in all aspects of human existence other than classical psychotherapy is the acceptance of the fact that perfect solutions do not exist. The belief that any human difficulty can be totally resolved is a utopian philosophy which simply does not reflect the true state of affairs in human interaction. Watzlawick believes that counseling can only assist clients in increasing their survival skills, not lead them to a problem-free existence.

The third question often posed to Watzlawick is grounded in the perception that the intervention strategies only deal with superficial problems, not the deep-seated difficulties experienced by some clients. To this, Watzlawick says, "the mere fact that a given technique does not fit into the conceptual framework of another theory cannot be taken as a *a priori* evidence for the wrongness or uselessness of that technique" (1978, p. 160). What may appear to be superficial to one person may be seen as "efficient" and "to the point" by another. It is Watzlawick's belief that a time-limited intervention focuses on the specific behaviors which have maintained the problem and is the most effective way to develop an initial change and to prepare the system to deal more successfully with other existing or potential problem areas.

In summary, Watzlawick's counseling approach appears to be an effective method of intervening in and changing systems experiencing a variety of problems. The techniques are specific, and the counseling environment is structured in such a way that both the client and counselor expect a change in behavior to occur. The counselor plays an active role in the process, offering a different world view to the client. The theoretical formulations and intervention strategies are unique, reflecting Watzlawick's nontraditional road to his present profession. This uniqueness is refreshing in that it offers professionals a substantially different world view themselves.

REFERENCES

Bateson, G., Jackson, D.D., Haley, J., & Weakland, J.H. (1956). Toward a theory of schizophrenia. *Behavioral Science, 1,* 251-264.

Jackson, D.D. (1957). The question of family homeostasis. *Psychiatric Quarterly supplement, 31,* 79-90.

Watzlawick, P. (1966). A structured family interview. *Family Process, 5,* 256-271.

Watzlawick, P. (1976). *How real is real? Confusion, disinformation, communication.* New York: Basic Books.

Watzlawick, P. (1978). *The language of change: Elements of therapeutic communication.* New York: Basic Books.

Watzlawick, P., & Beavin, J. (1967). Some formal aspects of communication. *American Behavioral Scientist, 10,* 4-8.

Watzlawick, P., Beavin, J., & Jackson, D.D. (1967). *Pragmatics of human communication.* New York: W.W. Norton.

Watzlawick, P., Weakland, J., & Fisch, R. (1974). *Change: Principles of problem formation and problem resolution.* New York: W.W. Norton.

Weakland, J., Fisch, R., Watzlawick, P., & Bodin, A. (1974). Brief therapy focused problem resolution. *Family Process, 13,* 141-168.

Whitehead, A.N., & Russell, B. (1910-1913). *Principia Mathematica* (2nd ed., Vol. 3). Cambridge: Cambridge University Press.

CHAPTER 13

SALVADOR MINUCHIN'S
STRUCTURAL FAMILY THERAPY

FOUNDATIONS AND STRUCTURE

Historical Foundations

SALVADOR MINUCHIN has developed a highly unique orientation which focuses more on the practical aspects of therapy than on theoretical perspectives and model-building. He calls his approach *Structural Family Therapy,* and attends to the practical question of what works in what kinds of situations. He is truly a student of family therapy, having spent years accumulating various stories and anecdotal incidents on the successes and failures of therapeutic techniques (Minuchin and Fishman, 1981). With the help of this study and dedication he has achieved considerable prominence in the field of Family Therapy.

Trained as a physician at the University of Cordoba in Argentina, Minuchin's early experience includes service in the Israeli army during 1948-1949, postgraduate training in child psychiatry in New York at Bellevue Hospital in 1951, and work as the Director of Psychiatry at Youth Aliyah, Department for Disturbed Children in Israel during the years 1952-1954. Later, in 1954, he joined the William Alonson White Institute in New York as a candidate for a certificate in psychoanalysis. Upon the completion of this program, he joined the staff of the Wiltwyck School for Boys, a private residential treatment center in New York City for delinquent boys between the ages of 8 and 12 years. While at this institution, he became involved in a major research project designed to investigate the organization of disadvantaged families. A book, *Families of the Slums* (1967), summarizes the project and illustrates the format which has become an accepted manner of working with families from this type of background.

In 1965 Minuchin founded the Philadelphia Child Guidance Clinic which, under his directorship until 1975, grew into the largest and most well-known facility of its kind. There, with Jay Haley, he elaborated upon many of his ideas, honing them into what has later become the foundation for his practice. Later, he was the Director of the Family Therapy Training Center at the Clinic, a Professor at the University of Pennsylvania in the Departments of Psychiatry and Pediatrics, and a psychiatrist in private practice. Among his other most popular and important works are *Families and Family Therapy* (1974), *Psychosomatic Families: Anorexia Nervosa in Context* (1978), and *Family Therapy Techniques* (1981).

Minuchin's publications document his belief that all too often psychoanalytic methods are not effective to deal with the complex issues facing families in trouble. His "unorthodox" ideas still reflect a client's trial of facing the issues at hand but he makes the additional assumption that the individual must be studied within the context of the family environment. While both Satir and Watzlawick focus almost exclusively on the communication patterns and styles of the family unit, Minuchin concentrates on the structural components of the family. He goes beyond the bits and pieces of communication and identifies difficulties with subsystem boundaries and interrelationships.

Philosophical Foundations

A basic assumption made by Minuchin is that society is a strong, influential factor in the growth and development of the individual. His formal training and experience in psychoanalysis contributed to an early concentration on a linear, causal model of human behavior. He accepts the notion that the family is the smallest social unit which has as its role the transmission of society's demands and values. This, coupled with his experience in working with families, led him to first question and then reject the concept of linearity. He now views the complex structure of the environment as the major determinant of behavior which is seen and studied within a systems framework. While he does accept more of an environmental position at this time, he still accepts that reality is defined by both internal and external elements (Minuchin, 1974).

Minuchin (1974) believes that human experience is largely determined by membership in social groups. The concept that people belong to and are at least somewhat dependent upon a certain reference group and yet are free to respond in various ways to different environmental stimuli is a central concept in Minuchin's approach. He indicates that this experiencing of both dependency and autonomy is characteristic of all human beings. One's well-being and identity partially depend upon how this complementary relationship has developed within the context of the present system. The family is the crux of the development and maintenance of both dependency and autonomy and has as its major function the task of meeting the psychological growth needs of the individual. Minuchin (1974) says "in all cultures, the family imprints its members with selfhood . . . The laboratory in which these ingredients [dependency and autonomy] are mixed and dispensed is the family, the matrix of identity" (p. 47). He indicates that the family is more than the biopsychodynamics of its individual members. In fact, both the external environment and the internal realities of the members make up the forces and expectations which are defined as the family.

In previous chapters, it has been indicated that both Satir and Watzlawick appear to conceptualize their counseling techniques in a way that is parallel to a behavioral frame of reference, regarding communication as a behavior. Minuchin also concentrates much of his effort on individual and family behaviors but does not focus as much attention as the communication theorists do on the bits and pieces of interpersonal interactions and transactions. Like Watzlawick, there are certain remnants of existential thought in Minuchin's writings, especially as he discusses freedom to respond sometimes within and sometimes beyond the expectations of the family.

Social-Psychological Foundations

The social-psychological aspects of Minuchin's approach are especially important because of his insistence upon studying and working with people within the context of their environment, primarily within the social sphere of the family itself. Since he sees people as social animals, any explanation of his theories must include a strong emphasis on the "person within the context." The following four major topics will be discussed in this section, all being crucial to an understanding of the social-psychological foundations of Structural Family Therapy: (1) the structure of the family as a system, (2) family subsystems, (3) subsystem boundaries, and (4) individual and family adaptation to stress.

The Structure of the Family as a System

Minuchin (1974) views the family as a system which operates through an established set of transactional patterns developed in response to functional demands which have been placed upon the system by the environment. These patterns help to define how, when, and to whom to relate and they give the family members feelings of security in their ability to negotiate day-to-day life tasks. These patterns are learned by the repetition and acceptance of behavioral exchanges developed and used in reaction to everyday occurrences. Transactional patterns are maintained by two systems of constraint, generic and idiosyncratic. Generic constraint involves the acceptance of universally accepted rules which govern family behavior including the power hierarchy for controlling purposes, the function of the parents and grandparents to pass on ethnic and cultural knowledge and information, the complementarity of the husband-wife team, and the provision of care and safety to the children by the parents. Idiosyncratic constraint involves the family members' mutual expectations which have developed in response to the interaction between this specific family and the demands of their environment. The negotiations which have occurred throughout the years of the relationship have led to "accepted" ways of responding and interacting. These unwritten rules are the idiosyncratic constraints and typically are maintained because of their effectiveness and family support.

The system, made up of these transactional patterns and interpersonal influence, maintains itself. While it allows for the freedom to vary behavioral responses to certain stimuli, the variation is limited to a specified, accepted range of alternatives. The extent of this range determines how flexible and adaptable the family will be to changes within and from outside of the system. Minuchin (1974) indicates that "the continued existence of the family as a system depends on a sufficient range of patterns, the availability of alternative transactional patterns, and the flexibility to mobilize them when necessary" (p. 52). This change must be accomplished without breaking the continuity relied upon by the family members which provides them with a common frame of reference.

Family Subsystems (Holons)

The system relies upon its subsystems to carry the bulk of the responsibility in accomplishing the necessary tasks of maintaining everyday functioning and promoting individual differentiation. Minuchin identifies subsystems as individuals, dyads, or small groups which may be partitioned based upon role, sex, age, or interest. In his later writing, he has referred to subsystems as *holons,* borrowing a term from Arthur Kestler (Minuchin and Fishman, 1981). This word is chosen because it reflects the true nature of the subsystem: both a whole and a part simultaneously. Each system member belongs to multiple subsystems, or holons, at any given point in time. Different relationships exist between people (as do different roles) from one subsystem to another. There exist at least four major subsystems within the family: the individual holon, the spouse holon, the parental holon, and the sibling holon.

The *individual holon* represents the unique qualities of each person. While all members of a family are influenced by a similar social context, each person's interpretation and experience is different, leading to unique development. In the early developmental stages of the family, the *spouse holon* is the first formed and is responsible for developing the first set of transactions in response to the demands of daily living. The patterns generated from the early stage of this relationship form the basis for the family's future development. The couple must learn not only how to become interdependent and complementary, they also must learn how to effectively separate from their families of origin and from other family systems. The second subsystem formed in the majority of families is the *parental holon.* At the birth of the first child, new expectations and demands are imposed upon the couple. The spouse subsystem must differentiate and satisfactorily perform the tasks necessary for the child's upbringing without jeopardizing the mutuality developed earlier. A renegotiation of old patterns and the initiation of a new set of transactions occurs each time a child is born into the family. The exact roles of the parental subsystem will differ depending upon the dominant culture, environmental demands, and the developmental level of the children. The *sibling holon* is described by Minuchin as "the first social laboratory in which children can experiment with peer relationships" (1974, p. 59). This is a subsystem which is much more prone to change than either the spouse or parental subsystems. The children are constantly learning how to negotiate, cooperate, and compete with each other and try out this knowledge on their peers outside of the family. When some transactional pattern has been established within the sibling subsystem and it is found that it is not effective in the "outside" world, then this information is brought back to the siblings and either incorporated into their learning or ignored (as in the case of subsystems which are particularly rigid).

Subsystem Boundaries

In each subsystem rules exist concerning who shall participate in it and how this participation will take place. These rules are called the *subsystem boundaries,* clearly defined so that the functions of the subsystem will be accomplished yet flexible enough so that open communication is maintained between subsystem members and others. Minuchin believes that the clarity of the boundaries is more important for effective family functioning than is the definition of who shall be included in the subsystem. There are three basic types of boundaries found along a continuum: (1) *enmeshed boundaries,* where a lack of clear boundaries exist and the differentiation of family subsystems becomes diffuse; (2) *disengaged boundaries,* where a rigid set of rules exists, leading to a distancing of subsystems and an isolation of individuals; and (3) *clear boundaries,* characterized by flexible yet clear lines of responsibility and membership. Minuchin tries to make it clear that disengagement and enmeshment do not necessarily mean that the subsystem is ineffective or maladaptive, they simply refer to the relationship style of the members within the subsystem and between these people and those outside of the subsystem. He indicates that most families have subsystems which are either presently enmeshed or disengaged or have been so in the past.

Individual and Family Adaptation to Stress

Minuchin believes that there are four major sources of stress imposed upon a family and that each family develops characteristic ways of adapting and responding. The first source, contact of an individual member with stressful extrafamilial forces, requires accommodation on the part of the family as a whole to help the single member through this time of stress. The second source involves contact of the whole family with stressful extrafamilial forces. The overall coping mechanisms of the family are challenged and, again, the whole family must accommodate wherever necessary in order to deal effectively with the stress. The third source of stress is associated with the transitional points in the family structure and/or lifestyle. The key to the transitional period is the maintenance of effective patterns and adaptation to new demands placed upon the subsystems. Idiosyncratic problems make up the fourth source of stress among individuals and families. A parent who is in an automobile accident and becomes disabled may be the focus of a unique type of stress within the system. The family must learn how to accommodate this new variable into its system in order to deal with the stress involved.

The social-psychology of Minuchin's approach includes the assumption that people are social animals, responding to environmental demands based upon some flexible yet well-defined set of rules. The family, while serving as the major source of rules and transactional patterns, is transformed over time, adapting to different functional requirements. We are able to study the structure of the family only through its movement in reaction to changes and through developmental stages.

The Development of the Person and Family

In Minuchin's framework the concept of development is linked with the change and adaptation of the holons. As the family and its members progress through the developmental process, they are continually faced with the tasks of negotiating and modifying subsystem boundaries in order to meet the needs of daily living. These structural changes force the family to remain flexible and open to feedback from within the system and from the outside.

In the early development of children, Minuchin (1974) believes that the "self" is defined through the context provided by the family. With increased social interaction outside of the family, the children begin to develop skills and areas of competence which were not a part of their initial experiencing. He says that an individual's potential is enhanced and limited simultaneously in the process of learning new behaviors. By this he means that children learn many behaviors in response to various new situations but are limited to a certain degree by the range of behaviors which are available to them at any given time. The transactional patterns which have been learned and developed define the self while other behaviors remain outside of the child's awareness of alternatives. Those behaviors which are used more frequently and are reinforced by the context of the family system shape the definition of self. Feelings of dependency and belonging are fostered by an acceptance of those transactional patterns which form the family structure. The opportunity to interact with other family subsystems and with persons outside of the family helps to create a sense of autonomy. While the intrafamilial transactional patterns offer continuity of values, behaviors, and viewpoints; the ability to communicate outside of a system or subsystem helps the individual gain feedback concerning the adaptability of the acceptable range of behaviors.

As the system progresses, it becomes differentiated enough to satisfactorily accomplish its major daily living tasks but not differentiated to the point where it is needlessly disjointed and distant. The development of each of the four primary holons (individual, spouse, parent, and sibling) calls for a reorganization of the family system as a whole and is often accompanied by necessary changes in function by individual members. With each status change of existing members, each addition or deletion of a member, and each change in functional requirements, the family faces both internal and external pressures to make accommodations. The preferred transactional patterns are quite resistant to change beyond a certain range but the family must be willing and able to adapt to new pressures and situations.

Certain developmental tasks are associated with the growth of each of the primary subsystems. The development of the self-concept and other aspects of the individual holon have been discussed earlier in this section. During the initial stages of the spouse holon's development, the couple must learn that they each bring into the relationship specific rules and expectations of human behavior (Minuchin, et al., 1978). In order to maintain the sense of self which flows from these expectations, the rules for the spouse holon must be developed from a reconciled version of the originals. The reconciliation and negotiation that takes place in developing the common set of rules lays the groundwork for future accommodations. In time, the new set of transactions will be chosen as the preferred way of responding and the marital partners will be able to differentiate themselves from their family of origin and other past subsystems.

The development of the parental holon is defined by the developmental level of the children involved. Different demands are placed upon the parents throughout the child's development so a constant process of adaptation is necessary. An important task facing the parents is the attention which must be paid to the children's development while, at the same time, being sure to exclude the children from the spouse functions. As has been mentioned before, the sibling holon provides an experimental laboratory for the children to try out behaviors and learn from each other in a relatively safe environment. The developmental process assists them in forming their self-concept and provides them with a common frame of reference and problem-solving strategies.

While the developmental process should be characterized by an open, flexible system of clear rules, in some cases the family becomes rigid to the point where it inhibits any form of adaptation to internal and external demands, or it becomes so ambiguous that it fails to provide a common frame of reference and facilitative definitions of the self. In the next section, factors will be explored which differentiate between adaptive and maladaptive family systems.

Concepts of Functional and Dysfunctional Behavior

An effectively functioning family is characterized by Minuchin as a system which is "moving in stages that follow a progression of increasing complexity" (Minuchin and Fishman, 1981, p. 22). There is evidence of balance and adaptation as well as disequilibrium. Both of these are the result of the family's encounter with stressful events. The resolution of each stressful situation leads to a level of functioning which is a step more complex than the one previous to it. In functional families, when new tasks are faced, the system has the flexibility to either change its present modes of behavior or incorporate new ones so that more functional behaviors can be learned and emitted. The effectiveness of a family actually addresses its flexibility to adapt to new pressures coming either from the outside or from within the system itself. As the family matures, it will face new complexes of demands to which it must attend. Effectiveness is defined by the degree to which the family can learn new, more adaptive skills while still retaining the basic rules which supply a foundation for the system's identity.

Minuchin believes that the simple incidence of a family problem does not necessarily indicate a need for restructuring. He recognizes that today's society is full of problems and the stress felt by families is quite understandable. Many families are seen as undergoing a difficult transition while still possessing the skills which are necessary to negotiate this process without major structural changes. When the environmental pressures change or the family can slow down to focus on the difficulty, then the problem situation may be resolved with a minimum of effort.

When family members reach the point where they have exhausted the available adaptive and coping mechanisms, then they are in need of counseling services. On an individual basis, Minuchin (1974) said that "pathology may be inside the patient, in his social context, or in the feedback between them" (p. 9). Both the communication process within and between holons and the structure of the system may be involved in this problem-formation process.

Studying the movement of the family through the development process and in reaction to the four major sources of stress illustrates the initiation and maintenance of many problem areas. If the set of transactional patterns developed in each of the holons lacks the flexibility or range to adapt to the complexities of family development, then problems occur. There not only may be a lack of effective transactional patterns, but the family may also lack the skills to develop more adaptive ones when they must.

Although enmeshed and disengaged boundaries are found even in functional families in reaction to specific types of situations or at certain times in the development process, dysfunctional families may experience strong and consistent patterns of enmeshment or disengagement. In certain dysfunctional families, holon boundaries may be enmeshed, leading to overly involved, intertwined and overintrusive relationships which are unable to effectively promote the differentiation of the individual. As a result of his observations of several disadvantaged families, Minuchin (1967) said that an enmeshed family is characterized by a "tight interlocking" of the members. "Their quality of connectedness is such that attempts on the part of one member to change elicit fast complementary resistance on the part of others" (p. 358). The primary tool used by the members to deal with stress is control and power. When the organization of the family is threatened, they are prone to centrality, concentrating their efforts as a unit, not allowing the stressful event to change their existing structure or transactional patterns.

In other families, the boundaries may be disengaged, resulting in both a rigid separation between the members and ineffective behavioral patterns. Uninvolvement of the members with respect to "family business" characterizes this family. Disinterested or emotionally absent parents are often at the center of a disengaged family. A significant degree of individual variability is allowed in a disengaged system, but this independence does not lead to an effective differentiation of the self due to the lack of support and guidance by the family.

An example of a dysfunctional family pattern which has been identified by Minuchin, Baker, Rosman, Liebman, Milman, and Todd (1975) is that of the psychosomatic family. They found that bronchial asthma, certain forms of childhood diabetes, and anorexia nervosa have a higher probability of occurrence in families that exhibit the following transactional patterns: (1) enmeshment (poorly differentiated holon boundaries), (2) overprotectiveness (overnurturance and a heightened sensitivity to each others' distress), (3) rigidity (holding on to ineffective behaviors simply because they serve to maintain the system), and (4) lack of conflict resolution (leaving problems unresolved, setting up the reappearance of the symptoms). Minuchin and his colleagues believe that the symptom or "illness" actually becomes a mode of communication which assists the family to avoid the true problems.

The degree of family dysfunction is directly related to the effectiveness of the family and its holon to adapt to the stresses of the changing environment. Both the transactional patterns and the boundaries established by individuals, subsystems, and the family as a whole are studied to make certain they are flexible and complex enough to meet the needs of the members.

Concepts of Behavior Change

Minuchin and Fishman (1981) make the following statement: "The structural approach sees the family as an organism: a complex system that is underfunctioning" (p. 67). Change is concentrated on both the family's organization and its accepted view of reality. Structural Family Therapy recognizes the strategic therapist's concern for "cure" and an existentialist's concern for the growth of the system and its members. Minuchin and Fishman use the term *challenge* in order to accent the reality of the dialectic between the counselor and the family.

What actually happens in the process of change is quite similar to the concept of second-order change proposed by Watzlawick, Weakland, and Fisch (1974). The family is functioning as if it is in a circular, closed system, allowing little or no feedback from the environment to modify ineffective behavioral patterns. What the counselor does is help restructure the family's organization and beliefs to open the possibility for new learning to occur. The context of the family changes so that the subjective experience for each member is also changed. This allows the feedback to be sent and received in a new light, one which allows family members to act upon it effectively. The specific aspects which are changed by the counselor are the transactional patterns developed within the holons. The counselor places the family in a position where they must explore alternative ways of transacting. In doing so, the counselor initiates the development of new transactional patterns which will be used, reinforced, and finally, accepted by the family members as the preferred way of behaving.

Assessment of Human Functioning

Minuchin (1974) does not believe that a full assessment of the development of dysfunctional transactional patterns is necessary in most families. He feels that the problems facing the family are manifest in the present so the most effective way to complete a workable assessment is for the counselor to become involved within the family system during the counseling process. He links the assessment process with intervention, calling it interactional diagnosis.

The information necessary to develop appropriate hypotheses is not immediately available to the counselor. Even though "hunches" will be based upon early interactions with family members, the step of joining with the family initiates the process of intervention. During this stage the counselor concentrates on gaining information relative to six current intrafamilial dynamics:

1. The structure of the family, including the holons and their transactional patterns.
2. The flexibility, adaptability, and capacity for restructuring as evidenced by the responses of alliances, coalitions, and holons to change.
3. The degree to which the family is sensitive to the needs of individual members.
4. The context of the family, including the resources and obstacles facing the members.
5. The developmental stage of the family and its effectiveness in completing the tasks facing it.
6. The manner in which the system uses the identified patient's symptoms to maintain the present transactional patterns.

The counselor would not be able to gain this information unless he or she was actually a part of the family system. The stress and mini-crisis set up by the entrance of the counselor into the family structure helps to illustrate how the family reacts to a new variable entering their system. Their style of assimilation, accommodation, and restructuring can be observed in a real life situation.

This diagnostic picture developed by the counselor may take the form of a family map. After the initial assessment data has been accumulated, the counselor identifies holon boundaries, transactional patterns, and develops hypotheses concerning the functionality of the present structure. Minuchin (1974) discusses three specific pitfalls in the use of structural analysis (mapping) in the identification of counseling goals and strategies. First, there is the possibility that the counselor may forget that a map is only a static phenomenon while the true structure of the family is continually changing in reaction to different life events. The second pitfall is the possibility that the counselor may ignore some of the holons, thereby splitting coalitions among holons, placing an unnecessary amount of stress upon selected holons, or escalating symptoms which may have initially been misdiagnosed. The last pitfall is the possibility of the counselor identifying with one of the holons to the exclusion of the others. In this type of a situation, the counselor joins a holon and becomes blind to the workings of the others.

Minuchin (1974) has indicated that "any type of diagnosis is merely a way of arranging data. The family therapist has the advantage of working with the concept of a system of interconnected people who influence each other. Therefore, if his arrangement of data leads him to an insoluable problem, he searches for a different angle on the same complex phenomena" (p. 131-132). The assessment process gathers enough data and provides enough openings for the counselor to identify alternative transactional patterns and points of flexibility which will enhance the intervention process. If used correctly, maps can be a way to organize the counselor's ideas about the family, formulate counseling goals, and assist in monitoring the outcome of the interventions.

Goals and Directions of Counseling

As has been discussed previously in this chapter, Minuchin recognizes that the family is an open sociocultural system which continually needs to adapt to changing internal and external environments. The dysfunctional family has not developed the capacity to make these adaptations and falls into a stereotypic pattern of behavior which has as its sole purpose the maintenance of the system. Alternative behaviors are seen as a threat to the structure of the family so they are not accepted.

Minuchin (1974) feels that the overall goal of family counseling is to "help the identified patient and the family by facilitating the transformation of the family system" (p. 110-111). This transformation takes place in the form of changing the family organization, thus the social context in which an individual's symptoms may develop. A change in the family structure will cause changes in both the members' positions relative to each other and their perceptions of the social context, freeing each person to try alternative behaviors and facilitate their own growth and development. While individual growth does occur, the target of interventions is always the family. The family system is the primary focus because individual behavior and adjustment are dependent upon their social context. The family, then, is seen as both the *matrix of identity* and the *matrix of healing and growth* of its members.

The direction that therapy takes is often determined by the specific circumstances which bring the family into counseling. Most often, the counselor and family share a common set of functional goals which become the focus of the activities of the partnership. Since the majority of families seeking counseling services have concentrated most of the responsibility for the problem on an identified patient, the first functional goal is to free this individual of symptoms. The counselor's task is to challenge the family's definition of the problem in either an implicit or explicit fashion and change the context so they must search for other explanations. A second functional goal is to reduce conflict and stress for the whole family. This involves the task of reorganizing the family structure so that members are free to try more adaptive alternative behaviors and feel open to new experiences for growth. The third functional goal concentrates on the need to learn new and more effective ways of coping. Both the family as a whole and its individual members go through a process which helps them become more flexible in the face of future change.

Each of the functional goals is accomplished by an integrated process involving the transformation of the family system by specific challenges of three dynamics: the symptom, the family structure, and the family reality. The importance of each of the challenges and counseling techniques associated with them will be explored more fully in the section addressing counseling techniques and procedures.

The Counseling Process:
Structuring, Facilitating, and Terminating

Minuchin (1974) discusses three steps in Structural Family Therapy. The counselor first joins the family as a leader, accommodating to the dysfunctional system. Then, the counselor identifies the underlying structure of the family and evaluates its functional and dysfunctional qualities. Once the counselor has identified both the resources and obstacles to individual and family growth, circumstances are created that will allow for the transformation of the structure. In more recent writings, Minuchin and Fishman (1981) have identified these three steps as joining, planning, and change.

Joining

The first step in the family counseling process, *joining,* focuses on the formation of the therapeutic system. Minuchin believes that the counselor must take a leadership position within the family system because, in most cases, the family and the therapist have different levels of understanding concerning the treatment process and the etiology and location of the pain. Initially, the counselor is interested in removing as much of the distance which exists between him and the family. This is done by accommodating to the very structures that must later be changed in order to blend in with the family and experience the transactional patterns as they do. Minuchin describes three styles of accommodating to the family structure. The counselor may provide *maintainence* of the family's existing structure by offering planned support and active confirmation of selected transactional patterns of the holons. This confirmation is said to validate the reality of holons joined by the counselor as well as provide a source of self-esteem for family members by reinforcing the positive aspects of the system. The second style of accommodation, *tracking* (following the content of family communication and behavioral patterns), is designed to gain information about the family rather than challenge existing structures or transactions. Minuchin also calls this being in the median position, both following and sometimes gently directing the interactions and behaviors of family members. In the third transactional style, *mimesis,* the counselor joins in with the family in a spontaneous manner, providing to the family members a feeling of common experience.

During the process of joining, counselors must be aware of their own background and experiences so that the most effective link will be made. Counselors must be flexible in their attitudes and in their ability to pursue different levels of involvement with the family. Minuchin and Fishman (1981) say "At times the therapist will want to disengage from the family . . . At other times he will take a median position . . . At other times he will throw himself into the fray, . . . taking one member's place in the system, allying strongly with a family underdog, or using whatever fits his therapeutic goal and his reading of the family" (p. 31). The levels of self involved in the joining process and the types of techniques used are determined by an interaction among the type of participants, the problems in the system, and the social context.

Planning

After a family has been "joined" by the counselor the second step in the counseling process, that of *planning,* begins. While Minuchin feels that every family counselor develops initial hypotheses about the structure and transactional patterns of each family in treatment, he believes that the process of joining is essential so that these ideas can be tested and either validated or modified. Minuchin and Fishman (1981) present a discussion of certain types of family groupings which may offer a further explanation of the importance of this step. In their thinking, families may vary in terms of shape, adaptation to unique developmental events, and structural arrangements. Families representing different shapes include the Pas De Deux Family, consisting of only two people; three-generational families, with a very close proximity between various generations in an extended family; the "shoe" family, characterizing a family with many children; an accordion family where there is an extended absence of at least one family member on a regular basis; and the foster family which has at least one foster child and often is impacted by the presence of a controlling agency. Families which have as a major characteristic the adaptation to some unique life event are represented by the step-parent family where one parent has been added and is going through an integration process; families with a ghost where a member is missing because of death or desertion; and the disabled family where one family member has become disabled, leading to role and duty changes. Examples of families that differ in terms of structural arrangements include the psychosomatic family, discussed earlier in this chapter, and the out-of-control family, characterized by problems in one or all of the following areas: the hierarchical structure of the family, the implementation of parent functions, and the proximity of individual family members and holons. Each of these family groupings must be approached in a different, individualized manner, a process which can be identified with the help of effective diagnosis and planning on the part of the counselor.

Change

At this point, the family has been joined by the counselor, the initial hypothesis has been either validated or modified (keeping in mind that any hypothesis is static and should always be modified as the family moves and develops), and the definition of the problem areas have been broadened to open the way for system change. Minuchin feels that a contract now must be established between the counselor and the family. This contract makes the promise of help to the family and specifies what will happen during counseling. In addition, it accents the accountability of the relationship by delineating the frequency of sessions and the length of the whole process. Anything that is developed in the contract can be changed as the relationship changes over time.

The process of change, as has been mentioned before, involves the

The process of change, as has been mentioned before, involves the restructuring of the family system. Structural Family Therapy is a very confrontive, challenging style of family intervention. Minuchin's style has been described as "innovative, unconventional, and deliberately manipulative in his calculated interventions" (Goldenberg and Goldenberg, 1980, p. 180). The counselor adds both stress and involvement to a family, helping them to mobilize alternative transactional patterns. The specific restructuring techniques used in Minuchin's approach will be discussed in detail in the next section.

The relationship is terminated when the contract has been met or when both the family and counselor feel that the structure now operating in the family can effectively adapt and cope with stress in the future. The counselor is satisfied that the counseling goals have been reached and the family members feel more secure in their ability to solve problems and make decisions. While Minuchin does note the importance of maintaining the change achieved in counseling, he does not mention how this will be accomplished other than saying that the self-perpetuating properties of the family will preserve the change through the more effective context which was developed in the relationship.

Counseling Techniques and Procedures

Minuchin and Fishman (1981) outline and describe three major strategies used in Structural Family Therapy and identify the specific techniques serving each. The strategies include challenging the symptom, challenging the family structure, and challenging the family reality.

Challenging the Symptom

By challenging the symptom, Minuchin is referring to a counseling process aimed at broadening the definition of the problem away from the identified patient and onto the dysfunctional family system. A structural family therapist sees identified patients as sacrificing themselves to defend their family's steady state. In actuality, this sacrifice is not attending to the problem at all, it is simply accepting the responsibility for the situation and providing the family with a maladaptive way to lessen the stress. Minuchin says that the family is framing reality in such a way that the transactional patterns will reinforce and maintain the system just as it is. The counselor's task is to change the context of the problem so that the family members are free to see the difficulty in another light.

This reframing process involves the specific techniques of *enactment, focusing,* and *achieving intensity.*

Enactment is the process of getting the family members to interact with each other, illustrating the dysfunctional transactional patterns in use. This is one way of gaining information that the family members feel may be neither relevant nor available. The counselor realizes that any observation must be made from a participant-observer frame of reference, because family behavior is influenced by the act of observation itself. A scenario is created by the counselor which spurs the dysfunctional patterns into action. During the enactment, the counselor can test the system's rules, engage quickly with the family (thus enhancing the development of the relationship), and begin to challenge the family's reality. Enactment may be a rather large scale intervention as in the case of Minuchin and Fishman's "dance in three movements" (observing spontaneous transactions, eliciting dysfunctional transactions, and suggesting more effective ways of transacting), or it may be a very spontaneous event, often related to the counselor's need to experience the family's patterns rather than just hear about them.

After the basic information about the family is accumulated and an initial evaluation has been made, the counselor must organize this information into a schema which will facilitate the change process. One method of accomplishing this involves the process of *focusing* which serves to organize the family transaction around relevant themes thus offering the members new meaning for old behaviors. Focusing constitutes the development of a plot which helps to guide the counselor through the counseling process. The assumption is made that knowledge of the transactional patterns in one, specific life area will be generalizable to other areas due to the isomorphic nature of families. Minuchin warns, however, that focusing may lead to a "tunnel vision" which could impede the sensitivity of the counselor to new bits of information.

Since all families are limited to a certain range of available behaviors and tend to filter and distort incoming messages because of this, many messages sent by the counselor may never be received clearly by the family. A third method of challenging the symptom is to raise the *intensity,* thus the impact of the therapeutic message. Some messages will need to be expressed in a more intense fashion because of the meaning of the proposed change to the family, while others will not require this special push. Methods of increasing the intensity of a message include simple repetition, repetition of isomorphic transactions (those which are similar to others at a deeper level), encouraging the family to continue transactions regardless of a system's habit (or implicit order) to stop, altering the "accepted" psychological or physical distance between the counselor and family members, and resisting the family's pull exerted upon the therapist to follow their rules. Minuchin and Fishman say, "Enactment is like a conversation, in which therapist and family try to make each other see the world as they see it. Intensity can be likened to a shouting match between the therapist and a hard-of-hearing family" (1981, p. 141). In Minuchin's perspective, the counselors cannot assume that their messages have been received properly just because they were sent.

Challenging the Family Structure

In the second major strategy, challenging the family structure, the counselor attempts to change the overaffiliation or underaffiliation exhibited in the family holons. The ability of members to function as differentiated beings is inhibited by the rules of the holons. Counselors can use their positions of being "outsiders" within the system and create coalitions, conflicts, and affiliations which can assist in restructuring the ineffective system. The specific techniques used include *boundary making, unbalancing,* and *teaching complementarity.*

The purpose of boundary making is to regulate and reorganize the boundaries separating family holons. Minuchin makes the assumption that alternative transactional patterns can be learned and adopted if the individual can try them out in another subsystem or if there is a change in the rules of the existing subsystem. He indicates that boundary making can be focused on the psychological distance existing among family members and on the duration of interactions within significant holons. Manipulating the psychological distance is one way of changing affiliations or altering conflicts in the family. The counselor can introduce new members to holons by physically structuring the environment in the session, reinforce and strengthen an existing but ineffective holon by paying special attention to it, and separate destructive affiliations by pointing out the dysfunctional patterns thereby making all of the family members aware of them. The other way to make boundaries, manipulating the duration of subsystem interactions, is also used to reinforce specific holons or separate others. The counselor sets up a task or an interaction which allows the subsystem to practice unfamiliar transactions. In cases where the assignment takes the family outside of the session, Minuchin and Fishman (1981) say that the counselor's "ghost then carries the therapeutic task. Practicing unaccustomed transactions in a natural setting facilitates structural change" (p. 154).

The unbalancing technique focuses on the hierarchical relationship among family members. When the counselor enters the family system as the undisputed therapeutic leader, the hierarchy shifts to make this accommodation. The counselor is then in position to challenge the family's power system. Typically, the counselor will affiliate with a low power individual, empowering this family member with the ability to behave in new, unfamiliar ways. The purpose of the technique is to help the family reach the point where they are no longer tied down by the existing power hierarchy and are free to try more effective behaviors. Minuchin says that the counselor can also ignore individuals who tend to drain from the others the freedom to choose alternative behaviors and participate as a coalition member against one or more family members. Typically, a number of unbalancing techniques are used in succession, changing style or content upon the demands of therapeutic need.

With the use of unbalancing, the counselor proposes to change the existing family hierarchy. The last technique designed to challenge the family structure, complementarity, challenges the very notion that a hierarchy exists in the family. The purpose of this technique is to help the family understand that the system functions as a whole and any difficulty is a result of the behavior and interrelationships within the system. The counselor challenges the family's beliefs that the problem exists and was developed outside of the family context, that one family member can control the others, and that individual behavior is not part of a larger whole. Minuchin feels that "I" messages should be expressed, but they should be done so within the context of the family. Individuals must expand their focus of attention beyond the bits and pieces of relationships and interactions to the matrix supporting them. "They must experience not action, response, and counterresponse, but the whole pattern" (Minuchin and Fishman, 1981, p. 206).

Challenging the Family Reality

The third set of techniques are all designed to challenge the family reality, or the world view held by that system. When a family seeks counseling, in many cases they have developed a world view which reinforces and maintains the problem areas. A change in family structure will lead to a corresponding change in world view and, conversely, a change in world view will lead to a change in structure. The specific techniques used in Structural Family Therapy to challenge the family reality are *constructions, paradoxes,* and *searching for strengths.*

Each family has developed realities, or cognitive constructs, which provide an organizing schema which helps members relate to the world around them. This schema, while offering a simplified version of the world upon which family members can act, sometimes limits behaviors to the point where individuals cannot effectively negotiate the demands of daily living. The counselor's task is to change the family's reality in such a way that members will be free to respond and interact in a more diverse manner. This task can be accomplished by the introduction of new constructs to the family which will offer them more freedom for movement. The first type of construction is called the universal symbol, referring to realities which are supported by "an institution or a consensus larger than the family." The counselor relies on statements such as "In this culture . . ." or "Everyone knows . . ." in order to introduce these concepts in a more acceptable way. The use of family truths is the next type of construction. Here, the counselor captures the style and content of accepted intrafamilial concepts and uses them in the therapeutic contact with the family. In the third construction, expert advice, the counselor presents an alternative view of reality, relying on experience, wisdom, and leadership position to carry influence with the family.

In contrast to constructions, a paradox serves as an *indirect* challenge to family reality. It is designed to eliminate the symptom, thereby eliminating the role of the symptom as the self-regulating mechanism for the system and exposing the true context of the problem. If a family does not take the advice of the counselor and try new behaviors as prescribed, there may be some sort of a hidden rule in the family which is actually doing the defying. This hidden rule or interaction becomes the target of the paradoxical intervention. For a paradox to be efficient it must redefine the problem, the dysfunctional rule must be prescribed (to make it explicit, thus losing its power), and the counselor must regulate the pace of change by restraining the family's press for change in reaction to the behavioral prescription. Once the paradox has had its initial effect of challenging the family reality, the counselor reinforces the message so they will not have the opportunity to place it aside in some manner.

The third technique involved in challenging the family reality is the process of accenting and mobilizing family and cultural strengths in the struggle for family and individual growth. This includes the acknowledgment of strengths in both the family and the identified patient. What the counselor does by pointing out these strengths (either directly or indirectly by interacting as if they obviously were a part of the system) is challenge the accepted impotence on the part of the family concerning their ability to adapt and problem-solve. In many dysfunctional families, the alternative transactional patterns have become fewer and fewer, leading to increased ineffectiveness in accomplishing daily living tasks. The counselor should interact with the family as if they are not limited so severely (as they actually are not) in order to accent forgotten or displaced strengths.

Minuchin and Fishman (1981) note that the counselor's choice of techniques will vary depending upon that individual's training and background, the therapeutic setting, and the needs of the specific family. They warn against the use of any technique as "the answer" to all families' needs. They say that "beyond technique, there is the wisdom which is the knowledge of the interconnectedness of things . . . When techniques are guided by such wisdom, then therapy becomes healing" (p. 289-290).

Evaluation of Counseling Outcomes

Structural Family Therapy has been developed and modified based upon various investigations carried out by Minuchin and his colleagues during the past three decades. Based upon his studies at the Wiltwyck School, where he worked with many disorganized, disadvantaged, multiproblem families, he developed his theories concerning the need for dealing with the whole family in a concrete, present-centered manner (Minuchin, Montalvo, Guerney, Rosman, and Schumer, 1967). In this experience, he identified characteristics of family process and structure which could be generalized to a variety of therapeutic contacts.

Minuchin's work with families of persons who have anorexia nervosa (Minuchin, Rosman, and Baker, 1978) and bronchial asthma (Minuchin, Liebman, and Baker, 1974; and Liebman, Minuchin, Baker, and Rosman, 1976) allowed him to further define his theories concerning family structure and test the efficacy of a structural therapy approach. A major study on the structure and treatment of families with anorectic children was reported by Minuchin, Rosman, and Baker in 1978. Not only did the authors want to verify the characteristics of a psychosomatic family (enmeshment, overprotectiveness, rigidity, and poor resolution of conflicts) but they also wanted to test the long-term responses of this group to treatment. Upon follow-up investigation it was found that 86 percent of the identified patients no longer exhibited anorectic symptoms and had achieved a satisfactory adjustment in their social context. Unfortunately, no control groups were used and, in addition to structural family therapy, the treatment strategies in the study included a variety of behavioral and medical techniques administered by individuals from a wide variety of backgrounds.

While the effectiveness of Structural Family Therapy has not been unequivocally documented in well-controlled experimental investigations, the studies which have been performed and a number of truly impressive case studies which have been reported in the literature lend considerable credence to the model. It is distinctly possible that complexities of family structure may preclude the possibility of tightly designed studies due to the inadequacies of research design technologies at this point in time.

COUNSELING APPLICATION

In this section, the authors attempt to show the dynamic style of a Structural Family Therapist in action. A verbatim account is presented from a case chosen because of its appropriateness for structural intervention. Throughout the case, the authors will offer comments both to help clarify the purpose and use of techniques as well as to describe the context of the family problem and the counseling relationship.

Structural Family Therapy in a Mental Health Setting

The Bakers are seeking family counseling at a local Community Mental Health Center due to the fact that the father, Jim, is experiencing a recurrence of a depressed state for which he has been hospitalized in the past. His wife, Donna, initiated contact with the family counselor in order to pursue the possibility of another type of intervention. They have all noticed a slow deterioration of many family functions and feel that Jim's depression is impacting the family quite heavily.

As was mentioned before, Jim has been hospitalized in the past due to his depressive episodes. The first time was for six weeks and the second time for three months. He was involved with aftercare services at this mental health center for approximately four months following his release 18 months ago. For the last 14 months he has been back on his old sales job which takes him out of town for weeks at a time. Jim had his present sales job when the couple married 13 years ago. He was absent when their first child (Debbie, now 12) was born during the first year of their marriage. The couple also has a son, Jeff, age nine. Donna works as a lab technician at a local hospital and serves as the main parent to the children. We will start off with a segment from the initial interview and then jump to a later encounter.

Counselor: Jim, the aftercare counselor who worked with you before and referred you to me has very briefly told me about you and your family. I really know very little about why you have come in today. Why don't you tell me something about it.

Jim: (Very softly) I've been feeling very down lately and Donna thought that we should all come in to talk about it.

Donna: Yes, you see we've all been going through quite a bit lately and want to be able to help Jim get through this thing.

Counselor: So what is this "thing" your family wants to help you get through, Jim?

Jim: I just get depressed a lot. Especially when I'm on the road.

Counselor: From my own experience I know that it's hard when you have to do a lot of traveling that takes you away from your family. Do these feelings occur at other times as well?

Jim: What do you mean?

Counselor: Are you ever depressed when you are at home with your family?

Jim: I have been lately.

Counselor: What's been happening lately in the family?

Donna: Nothing out of the ordinary, really. He's just been getting more and more distant from all of us. Jim's depression is really tearing us up.

Counselor: So the problem in the family lately has been Jim's depression. Is that it?

Donna: Oh, yes, definitely.

Counselor: I'm not so sure about that. Why don't we see what else is happening. Jeff, what do you think is going on in your family?

Jeff: (Quietly) I don't know, I guess my father doesn't feel too well.

Counselor: So that's the problem, that your father doesn't feel well?

Jeff: Yeah, and he's never around.

Counselor: Jeff, what's it like when your father is at home?

Jeff: It's kind of funny, in a way.

Counselor: What do you mean by "kind of funny"?

Jeff: Well, even when he's home, it's like he isn't there. He never does anything with us.

Donna: Now, Jeff, that's just not true. Your father goes out with you a lot when he's home. You two are great friends.

Jeff: (Softly) Yeah, I guess that's true.

Counselor: Jeff, who disciplines you when you do something you aren't supposed to?

Jeff: Mom does.

Counselor: Who do you go to when you need to ask permission to do something?

Jeff: I go to Mom.

Counselor: Even when your Dad is at home with you?

Jeff: Yeah.

Counselor: How about you, Debbie, we haven't heard anything from you today. What do you think is happening in the family.

Debbie: I think we're different from other families.

Counselor:	How do you feel you are different?
Debbie:	Well, a lot of other families have two parents who are there all the time. Mom and my father aren't divorced or anything but its like they are.
Counselor:	Could you explain that a little bit? What do you mean by "its like they are divorced"?
Debbie:	Well, even when my father is at home, they never talk. Jeff and I always have to go to Mom for anything we need.
Counselor:	Would you like to be closer to your father?
Debbie:	(Emphatically) Sure I would. Of course!
Counselor:	(Holding his arms out, motioning for the parents to face each other) Jim and Donna, how do you react to what Jeff and Debbie have just said?
Donna:	I guess it kind of takes me by surprise. I had no idea they felt that way.
Jim:	Me neither.
Counselor:	You seem to be in the same boat right now. Speak to each other about what seems to be happening.

In this exchange the counselor actively questioned and challenged the family's definition of the problem. They had centered the full responsibility for the problem on Jim's shoulders and the counselor explored the context of the difficulty within the family. The personal remark by the counselor regarding "being on the road" was done to develop a kinship between him and Jim, thus facilitating the joining process. The counselor now believes that the family functions in a similar manner to an "accordion family," characterized by one parent being away for extended periods of time while the other takes on the responsibility of all parenting functions. They have developed into a one-parent family, leaving Jim in an uncertain position. The counselor also hypothesizes that Jim and Donna have not developed an effective couple holon, considering they have never had an extended time together and they tend to approach family tasks separately. At the end of the exchange the counselor has asked Jim and Donna to start working on that subsystem by conversing with each other.

This second segment has been taken from the fifth counseling session with this family. Much success has been reached in working with the couple holon and the counselor has turned the attention to the parent holon. We continue . . .

Counselor:	Jim, it's good to see you looking so happy. Things must be going well.
Jim:	I have been feeling better lately.
Donna:	I think things are going along a little more smoothly, also.
Counselor:	How about you, Jeff, what's been going on with you?
Jeff:	It's about the same.
Counselor:	What's about the same, Jeff?

Jeff:	Everything. Dad's feeling better but it's still the same.
Donna:	(Annoyed) What do you mean by that? We haven't been this happy for years! Why, your father is really doing well.
Counselor:	Jim, why don't you talk with Jeff about his ideas. We'll listen, but you speak with your son.
Donna:	It's really no use. Nothing can get through to Jeff when his mind is made up.
Counselor:	Jim, here, turn your chair so that it is facing Jeff and talk with him. (Jim does as the counselor asks. Debbie giggles and Donna sighs.)
Jim:	Jeff, what's going on? I don't understand why you're feeling the way you are.
Jeff:	Nothing is going on. Absolutely nothing!
Donna:	(Triumphantly) See! I told you!
Counselor:	Please. Let them talk.
Jim:	You know, son, I guess I don't really know you too well, being on the road as much as I have been. Maybe we can try to do a little better.
Jeff:	Yeah, maybe.
Jim:	(Physically turning to Debbie) I feel the same way about you, Debbie. Do you think we can do a better job talking and getting to know each other?
Debbie:	Sure, Dad.

This exchange went on for a few minutes, with Jim talking to the two children as a father for the first time in quite a while. This was a first step in the restructuring of the parent holon. Jim and Donna were now more secure in their relationship (with a lot of work still ahead) so it was time to restructure another source of ambiguity in the family, Jim's lack of a clear, yet flexible parental role. You will notice the boundary-making operations conducted by the counselor in this encounter. His physical structuring of the environment to get Jim and Jeff to talk with each other as parent and child, his refocusing on them after Donna steps in, and his affiliating with the father and his two children are all examples of boundary-making. At the end, Jim created a boundary himself by physically attending to Debbie. Later on, Jim gained more confidence in the parent role, Donna became more flexible and adaptive in letting him follow through on parenting tasks, and the children no longer felt he was an "outsider" in the family. Jim's symptom has not returned because it serves no function in the restructured family system.

Critical Comments

Structural Family Therapy is currently one of the most popular styles of family intervention practiced by mental health professionals. It offers a wide appeal because it appears to be adaptable and at least moderately effective with families from many different backgrounds. This approach, while very practical in its orientation, is grounded in a rather solid theoretical base. Minuchin's work reflects an understanding and acceptance of many General Systems Theory principles which serve to provide the underpinnings of his approach. His specific extension of these principles is somewhat simplistic due to the fact that he has concentrated less of his efforts on theory building and more on the identification of what type of intervention works with what family in what context.

The structural approach involves an acknowledgment and a general comprehension of the context of family interactions. Minuchin sees the family as a whole unit operating within a unique social structure. Any intervention must at least attend to this social context or it will be limited to superficial impact. Since the reality of the family (thus, the individual members) is created by the social context and the family is the smallest of the major social units, a change in the reality of the family will create a corresponding change in the reality of individual members. The linear concept of causality accepted by many theorists is therefore rejected by Minuchin in favor of a more holistic view which does not concentrate on single causes for events. His acceptance of the General Systems Theory concept of wholeness may be taken to an extreme if one would try to generalize it to all family problems.

In a similar manner to most family counseling theorists, Minuchin's approach grew out of early theoretical concepts which were later validated in his clinical practice and empirical research. This "follow-back" type of development may have led Minuchin and his associates to apply their own reality to the process. They may have labeled certain occurrences in ways which could be quite different if this would have been done by another person who accepts a very different world view. This perspective may be one reason why people from varying professional and personal backgrounds are able to use this approach in an equally successful fashion.

Although Minuchin himself functions as a highly dynamic, compelling, and persistent counselor, others have been very successful in adopting his approach and practicing it within their own personal styles. If a professional counselor is able to affiliate well with the family, has ample sensitivity to the internal dynamics of the family structure, understands the nonlinear framework of problem development and resolution, and has the creativity to develop behavioral prescriptions and alternative transactional patterns then that person will probably be effective.

After a lengthy discussion of each of the major Structural Family

Therapy techniques, Minuchin and Fishman (1981) make the following statement: "There are, of course, many other techniques that we do not use but which serve well in the hands of experienced therapists. But technique is not the goal. The goal can be achieved only by putting aside technique" (p. 285). That is a forceful sentiment for a person who is typically seen as a technique-oriented family therapist. It is also a key to much of his work because it accentuates his feeling that the relationship and the wisdom of the counselor to capitalize on the techniques which have been put into action are the true "healers." In the same way that he studies the context of the family for the causes and solutions to their problems, he sees the context of the family counseling relationship as the essential guide for the intervention.

REFERENCES

Goldenberg, I., & Goldenberg, H. (1980). *Family therapy: An overview.* Monterey, CA: Brooks/Cole.

Liebman, R., Minuchin, S., Baker, L., & Rosman, B. (1976). The role of the family in the treatment of chronic asthma. In P. Guerin (Ed.), *Family therapy: Theory and practice* (pp. 312-319). New York: Gardner Press.

Minuchin, S. (1974). *Families and family therapy.* Cambridge, MA: Harvard University Press.

Minuchin, S., Baker, L., Rosman, B., Liebman, R., Milman, L., & Todd, T. (1975). A conceptual model of psychosomatic illness in children. *Archives of General Psychiatry, 32,* 1031-1038.

Minuchin, S., & Fishman, H.C. (1981). *Family therapy techniques.* Cambridge, MA: Harvard University Press.

Minuchin, S., Liebman, R., & Baker, L. (1974). The use of structural family therapy in the treatment of intractable asthma. *American Journal of Psychiatry, 131,* 535-539.

Minuchin, S., Montalvo, B., Guerney, B., Rosman, L., & Shumer, F. (1967). *Families of the slums.* New York: Basic Books.

Minuchin, S., Rosman, B., & Baker, L. (1978). *Psychosomatic families: Anorexia nervosa in context.* Cambridge, MA: Harvard University Press.

Watzlawick, P., Weakland, J., & Fisch, R. (1974). *Change: Principles of problem formation and problem resolution.* New York: W.W. Norton.

CHAPTER 14

ISSUES RELATED TO THE RESEARCH, EVALUATION, AND PRACTICE OF COUNSELING

Introduction

I N THE PREVIOUS chapters the authors have presented discussions of twelve systems of counseling representing psychodynamic, existential-humanistic, cognitive-behavioral, and systems and family orientations. An attempt has been made to acquaint the reader with the basic theoretical tenets of each approach as well as offer examples of their practice. The concentration has been on individual theories and not a discussion of the efficacy of counseling as an overall intervention method designed to assist clients in either their personal growth and development or in the remediation of their problems.

The question: *How effective is counseling and psychotherapy in assisting people in eliminating or lessening problems?* has been the focus of numerous research studies over the past decades. No true answers have been found and, for the most part, the conclusion has been reached that researchers may have been asking a severely limited question. Rather than attending to the effectiveness of "counseling and psychotherapy," Kielser (1966) insists that a more appropriate question might be: *What kind of therapy* works best with *what kind of client* with *what kind of problem* in *what kind of setting?* While the methodology available at this time may not be able to investigate this complex question with clear accuracy, certain inferences have been drawn concerning specific components of this issue. The first section of this chapter will present a short review of major counseling and psychotherapy outcome studies, focusing on specific issues related to the efficacy of counseling.

While it is important to investigate the effectiveness of counseling approaches on a large scale, it is probably more important for the individual professional counselor to be well versed in evaluation methods which will allow that person to judge personal effectiveness. Of course, the specific goals espoused by different counseling perspectives are taken into consideration by any evaluation process, but there are common systems which can be used by many counseling professionals in order to make them more accountable to client needs and help them identify areas in themselves which are in need of attention. In the second section of this chapter, the authors will present a few guidelines and suggestions related to the evaluation of the counseling process. Particular attention is paid to methods of monitoring different aspects of the relationship.

The image, visibility, and style of counseling have all gone through some rather significant changes in recent years. Each of these changes has offered something new to the profession and to society. In the last section of this chapter, the authors discuss a few of the issues which have prompted these changes. While this is certainly not a comprehensive discussion of the counseling profession, it is meant to assist in providing the reader with a context within which to view the practice of counseling.

The Effectiveness of Counseling and Psychotherapy

Counseling has been defined in this text as an interactive process between a professionally trained human service professional and a client who collaborate in order to facilitate learning and enhance the growth and development of the client. The specific goals of the relationship differ depending upon the theoretical framework of the counselor and the needs of the client but certain similarities have been pointed out by Mahrer (1967) which cross settings and situations. The first broad goal is to decrease the level of psychological distress experienced by the client. This can include such difficulties as anxiety, depression, anger, hopelessness, confusion, and grief. The second goal is to heighten the individual's feelings of satisfaction and ability to feel pleasure. An awareness and acceptance of the self and the environment is the third goal, while the fourth is enhancing the ability to improve and further develop interpersonal relationships. If one is investigating the effectiveness of such a broad concept as "counseling and psychotherapy," then these goals, or approximations of them, are the focus of study.

Overall Effectiveness

Even with the use of Mahrer's goals there has been considerable controversy related to the question of effectiveness. When Eyesenck (1952) published his first summary of outcome studies and concluded that the effectiveness of counseling and psychotherapy could not be substantiated based on these data, the battle began. Rosenweig (1954) was one of the first to criticize Eyesenck's work, saying that the equivalency of comparison groups and outcome measures in the original studies was questionable and that the untreated control groups may have received attention (thereby raising a placebo effect) since they were drawn largely from hospitalized groups. Luborsky (1954) also criticized Eyesenck's conclusions by pointing out that the historical effects of time may have impacted upon the results as well. Eyesenck (1961, 1966) reported on the results of two other investigations which added four and eight studies respectively, to his initial group and arrived at similar conclusions. While the studies chosen for these investigations included those with control-group designs, threats to internal validity still existed in the form of outcome criterion inconsistencies.

Other authors have found empirical support for the effectiveness of counseling and psychotherapy. Meltzoff and Kornreich (1970) reviewed 101 studies on therapeutic effectiveness and reached an 80 percent positive change rate among those investigations. They used randomization in the selection of the studies but did not impeach (or eliminate) studies based upon ex post facto decisions about the quality of the research design. They did review each study in order to decide if it had an adequate vs. questionable design, then grouped the studies accordingly. The outcome criterion used in their investigation was the statistical significance found by the original researchers.

Luborsky, Singer, and Luborsky (1975) reviewed studies which were performed with the use of "real clients," those people who were actually seeking services and not simply volunteering to be research participants. This strict inclusion criterion limited the final sample of studies to only 33, but out of that number they concluded that 20, or approximately 61 percent, showed positive results. Smith and Glass (1977) and Smith, Glass, and Miller (1980) built upon this work and reviewed 375 studies in the first investigation and 475 in the second. The research design used was a meta-analysis, where the effect size (the mean difference between the treatment and control groups divided by the standard deviation of the control group) was used as the measure of therapeutic effect. Since the effect size is a standardized statistic, it was possible to compare outcomes across studies regardless of the scale of the specific criterion measure used in the original study. They reported an average effect size of .67 in the first study and .85 in the latter. The authors feel that both of these figures support the conclusion that counseling and psychotherapy lead to a positive behavioral change. More discussion of the work of both Luborsky, Singer, and Luborsky and Smith, Glass, and Miller will be presented·later in this chapter during the discussion of comparative outcome research.

Rachman (1971), in support of Eyesenck's skeptical view of therapeutic effectiveness, said that satisfactory evidence did not exist to support the claim that psychotherapy is effective (at the time of that writing). He still finds fault with studies which have led to positive conclusions as easily as his rivals have criticized Eyesenck's work. He uses strict, "by-the-book" criteria to make ex post facto decisions about the quality of research designs used in studies chosen for a variety of outcome study reviews, leading to the nullification of many claims of effectiveness. He has more recently indicated that although modest evidence exists to support the claim of beneficial changes related to psychotherapeutic intervention, he still finds that negative outcomes dominate the positive and inconclusive results are the most common of all (Rachman and Wilson, 1980).

The argument related to the effectiveness of counseling and psychotherapy appears to be a circular one at this time. As new evidence is shared which supports *any* claim, evidence to the contrary soon appears in the literature. Three possibilities exist which may explain this situation: (1) methodological problems may exist which limit our ability to adequately measure therapeutic outcome; (2) a conceptual problem may exist in attempting to investigate the outcome of something as broad as the full range of counseling and psychotherapy services; and (3) the assumption of the human services may be wrong, perhaps psychotherapeutic interventions are not as effective as we take for granted. In an attempt to deal with these issues, many investigators have undertaken the task of studying the differential effects of specific approaches. In these studies, they are looking at the overall effectiveness of all interventions used as well as the strengths and weaknesses of specific styles in different settings. Among the most notable of these are studies by Sloane, Staples, Cristol, Yorkston, and Whipple (1975); Luborsky, Singer, and Luborsky (1975); and Smith, Glass, and Miller (1980) which will all be discussed in the next section.

Comparative Effectiveness

Differences in effectiveness do exist between and among different types of counseling approaches. In most instances, these differences are related to an intervention's applicability to specific problem areas or its "fit" with background characteristics of the client. Rachman and Wilson (1980) fear that most comparative outcome research is premature. They feel that the primary questions (Is therapeutic intervention effective? and, Are specific approaches effective?) must be answered before one can contrast and compare various styles in the same study. Smith, Glass, and Miller (1980) acknowledge the difficulty and the probable impossibility (for the time being) of arriving at any conclusions relative to the "effectiveness of therapeutic intervention controversy," so they feel that studying the comparative effects of counseling and psychotherapy approaches is appropriate and warranted.

Sloane, et al., (1975) compared the relative efficacy of behavior therapy and short-term analytically oriented psychotherapy in the hospital-based outpatient treatment of clients with neuroses and personality problems. Bergin and Lambert (1978) call this study "probably the best comparative study of psychotherapy yet carried out" (p. 164). Both of the treatment groups improved more than the waiting control group, although all groups improved significantly on the target symptoms. In terms of global outcome, 80 percent of the clients in the two treatment groups were judged to have improved as opposed to 48 percent of the waiting control. On general adjustment, 93 percent of the clients in the behaviorally-oriented groups were seen as improved while that number was 77 percent for the analytically-oriented groups. The authors suggest that behavioral interventions may be effective for a wider range of clients or analytic styles may be more variable in their effect upon different people. Luborsky, Singer, and Luborsky, in their 1975 review of selected studies investigating the effectiveness of a variety of counseling approaches concluded that the results of comparative studies were equivocal. They found that although psychotherapeutic intervention was effective, no differences existed between individual and group, time-limited and time unlimited, and behavior therapy and psychotherapy.

Smith and Glass (1977) and Smith, Glass, and Miller (1980), in meta-analyses of 375 and 475 studies respectively, increased the scope of the work accomplished by Luborsky, Singer, and Luborsky. In their first study they found insignificant differences between the major types of counseling and psychotherapy. One interesting finding, however, was that behavioral styles (systematic desensitization, implosion therapy, behavior modification, and Gestalt) were found to be slightly more effective than nonbehavioral ones (analytic therapy, Adlerian, Rogerian, RET, eclectic, and TA). In the second study, the authors added 100 studies in order to expand the range of the investigation. The results showed even greater support for the overall effect of counseling and psychotherapy and did reveal differences between the effects of some major types. Without controlling for type of client or types of outcome observed, the authors conclude that among the 16 major theoretical perspectives studied (18, including "Undifferentiated Counseling" and "Placebo treatment"), the most effective appeared to be cognitive, cognitive-behavioral, hypnotherapy, and systematic desensitization. Those included in the "average effectiveness" designation were psychodynamic, dynamic-eclectic, Adlerian, client-centered, Gestalt, RET, TA, implosive therapy, behavior modification, eclectic-behavioral, and vocational-personal development therapy. Reality therapy, undifferentiated counseling, and placebo treatment ranked lower than all others in effect size. Based upon their studies on therapeutic effectiveness the authors reach the following three conclusions:

- Counseling and psychotherapy is beneficial.
- Different types of counseling do not yield significantly different results.
- The modality of counseling (group vs. individual), its duration, and the experience level of the counselor have very little effect upon outcome.

These conclusions may be questioned by other authors (as indeed they have), but this was the most comprehensive study of its kind ever undertaken. It has served as a model to others, assisting them in taking the step to try out new methodological techniques. While it has been criticized for flaws in its own design, it has broken the mold of traditional outcome research.

Other types of comparative research which have been quite actively pursued in the past three decades are studies concentrating on client variables, counselor variables, counseling process variables, and placebo and expectation effects. The investigations of client variables have focused on the relationship between a client's background, personality, and demographic characteristics and continuation and outcome in counseling. The counselor's background, personality, demographic, and professional characteristics have been related to counseling process and outcome. These are typically assessed as independent elements but, in a growing number of studies, they are being investigated in interaction with client variables. Quite consistent results have been reached in these studies looking at the relationships between very specific variables having a bearing on the counseling relationship. The results certainly are more consistent than those found in relation to the major questions of effectiveness. For an excellent review of client, counselor, process, and expectation variables the reader can consult the *Handbook of Psychotherapy and Behavior Change,* (1978) by Sol L. Garfield and Allen E. Bergin.

Evaluating the Practice of Counseling

A thorough knowledge of the complexities of research design strategies is not something that many counselors recognize as an integral part of the counseling process. While most professionals are cognizant of the results of major outcome studies, they may lack the sophistication to apply the concepts learned as a result of these investigations to their own practice. Granted, there are very few practitioners who are actively involved in large group research, but all professional helpers use some form of evaluation in determining if they have achieved a desired outcome. In this section, the authors will present a discussion of evaluation as an integral part of the counseling process. The specific topics addressed will be: the similarities of formal research and individualized evaluation methods, the purposes of evaluation, selected problems associated with evaluating counseling services, and designing and analyzing evaluation efforts.

Similarities of Research and Evaluation

Today's society is a research-oriented society. New technological achievements are directly related to the development of knowledge from scientific investigations. Kerlinger (1973) said that "the basic aim of science is not the betterment of mankind, it is theory" (p. 9). These theories are applied to real-world problems and solutions are developed through the use of technology. The practical side of the newly developed technology is then evaluated in order to "fine tune" the implementation of the research efforts. Research is a standardized, integrated process designed to develop theories and the underlying structure of techniques, intervention processes, and whole counseling services programs. Evaluation, on the other hand, is a similarly standardized, integrated program which is designed to assess the efficacy of a particular technique, counseling process, or counseling program within a specific context. The processes of research and evaluation are quite consistent, both concentrating on the development of knowledge, but differ on the need for and use of the knowledge.

In counseling services, the accepted research process has become one of group design, involving a treatment group and at least one comparison group of some kind (usually a nontreatment control). The process focuses on differences between and among the average performance of the different groups. Individual performance is treated as a part of the whole and, therefore, is not the subject of inquiry. The effect of a treatment upon a particular client is often obscured so no clear conclusions can be drawn about the efficacy of the treatment with *that* person in *that* setting using *that* treatment. The reliance upon this type of research, while contributing much to the "theory and knowledge" of counseling and its general impact, often alienates the practitioner from an interest in keeping up to date on research literature. Without an emphasis on the individual, the message resulting from the results may be a difficult one to send.

Some researchers, in order to relate to the needs of the practitioner, are becoming interested in single-system designs to investigate different aspects of counseling process and outcome. In this method, a particular unit (typically including one person but sometimes extending to one family or one classroom) is the subject of a very intense investigation. The specific aspects of the intervention can be chronicled in a much more detailed manner, enabling the researcher to document the subject's reactions to precise stimuli. In this sense, the methods which are used in single-system research designs present a perfect fit with an individual practitoner's evaluation needs. Bloom and Fischer (1982) indicate that these designs are especially effective in evaluation not only because they are designed to study individuals, but they also can do so without intervening too much in the counseling relationship, they assist the practitioner in monitoring and recording the case-management process, they can serve as treatment tools by assisting in the choice of appropriate methods and techniques, they can be implemented in a theory-free manner, they are easily implemented, and they can help satisfy the accountability needs within agency and community structures.

The accent on research and evaluation in counseling services has grown out of a belief that the most effective practitioners are those who are aware of others' research which can offer answers to their practice and have the ability to apply scientific concepts to their own techniques and models. Bloom and Fischer (1982) indicate that the "scientific practitioner" is a person who approaches counseling as if it were research, monitors the practice in a systematic manner, is grounded in empirical knowledge, and possesses the skills and motivation to continue questioning and learning. The remaining portion of this section will present a discussion of how one is able to put this process into action.

The Purpose of Evaluation

Evaluation can be a somewhat threatening process to some counseling practitioners even though that is certainly not the intention. The ulterior purpose of evaluation is to provide the practitioner with data which will help that person perform at higher levels in the counseling relationship. Ideally, then, evaluation is centered on the needs of the relationship, identifying those things which must be done by the counselor, the client, and the agency administration to enhance the on-going process. Other, more specific, purposes of evaluation in counseling are as follows:

- *Determining the present status of the counseling relationship relative to the goals and objectives identified.* This gives the counselor and the client the opportunity to evaluate progress and maintain a realistic appraisal of what is happening in the relationship.
- *Assessing the appropriateness of the goals and objectives identified early on in the relationship.* A constant monitoring allows the client and the counselor to retain enough flexibility to adapt the process to needs identified throughout the process.
- *Gaining ideas for future directions.* With an effective evaluation, trends can be identified which will offer the practitioner clues for future action.
- *Identification of the training and development needs of the counselor.*
- *Assisting with program administration activities including those related to accountability to outside funding sources and the community, case management activities, and budgetary considerations.*

Problems in Evaluation

Difficulties do exist both in the process of evaluation and in the ability of practitioners to actually use the evaluation results. The first problem that many people face in an attempt to evaluate their practice is a lack of personal experience, knowledge, and ability to perform the necessary tasks. While most counselor training programs include in their curricula an introductory course in research methods, the majority do not concentrate a great deal of effort in teaching evaluation methodology. Therefore, most practitioners are simply not prepared to undertake the rather complex job of evaluation and when they do the results are of little value because of inconsistencies and difficulties in the design.

A second problem which is often noted is the amount of time involved in initiating, monitoring, and analyzing the evaluation data. Bloom and Fischer (1982), in reference to the use of effectively developed single-system designs, say that the greatest amount of time is expended in learning how to use them. In their own experience they have noticed that once evaluation methodology becomes a part of one's regular practice, time is no longer a problem because evaluation is incorporated into standard monitoring procedures.

Measurement problems do exist in evaluating counseling process and outcome. *What* is measured and *how* are both aspects which tend to be individualized to the particular client within the counselor's theoretical framework. In some cases, the goals of a particular theoretical stance cannot be operationalized clearly leading to ambiguity and uncertainty of measurement. The ability to measure the pertinent variables in a way that does not interfere with the actual counseling process has also been noted as a difficulty. Bloom and Fischer (1982) note that involving the client in the evaluation process may alleviate this concern and can even lead to a more effective relationship. The identification of measurement tools and/or techniques to monitor and assess the process and outcome of the relationship is also a measurement difficulty faced by the practitioner. Since the process is so individualized, it is the counselor's task to identify those tools which will clearly measure its existence and any changes which may occur in its status over time. A battery of perfectly valid and reliable instruments or techniques which can be used across a variety of settings simply does not exist.

When one identifies the problem effectively, is knowledgeable about evaluation methodology, chooses effective measurement tools, and finds a "positive treatment effect," how can that person be certain that the client's change was related to the treatment? The possibility of other experiences impacting the client is always there (usually in a very covert way), making it impossible to ever truly identify direct causal relationships. Even when group research is used, the possibility still exists that either (or both) treatment and control groups have been "contaminated." This problem, related to the complexity of human existence, may be something that will continue to baffle researchers and evaluators for generations to come.

Except for the difficulties with contamination, it may be possible to deal with most of the problems noted above. The practitioner can at least minimize these problems by gaining knowledge and developing effective evaluation designs. A clear, focused design can help to gather meaningful information. While this information may not be flawless, it certainly can contribute to the counselor's understanding of both the client and the process.

Designing an Evaluation

There are many directions that the practitioner may take in the design and implementation of an evaluation. These directions are largely defined by the identified purpose of the evaluation and the counseling process and goals. There is no "preferred" method of evaluation (in the same way that there is no "preferred" method of counseling), but there are certain commonalities across evaluation models. In the next paragraphs, the authors will present a summary of one evaluation process presented by Bloom and Fischer (1982).

The first step in the evaluation process, according to Bloom and Fischer, is to identify the problems which will be the focus of the counseling relationship and develop goals and objectives which will guide the process. Contrary to popular belief, one of the most difficult tasks in counseling is the process of problem identification. Some clients may freely present several concerns while others may be a little more covert due either to cautiousness or a lack of self-awareness. Observation, checklists, standardized instruments, survey forms, and referral information may all be sources which can be pursued to make an initial identification of client problems. Once the problems are identified, it is important to put them into some priority order based upon a combination of seriousness, time-relevance, ease of change, and interrelationship with other problems.

When the problems have been identified and prioritized, counseling goals as well as objectives designed to meet those goals must be developed. A goal is a description of the intended outcome of counseling activity. It is the "realistic ideal" that the counselor and client develop and state in clear, observable, measurable terms. Since the goal tends to be a distant projection, objectives are developed which serve as subgoals to be reached along the counseling process. Sanctity of goals is a common problem in counseling. In an effective evaluation procedure (and in counseling), when circumstances change or new information is found then both goals and objectives must be flexible enough to adapt to these circumstances.

Once the problem has been identified and the goals and objectives have been designed, the counselor must attend to the second major step, the development of a recording plan. The recording plan delineates *what* is to be measured, *when* it is to be measured, *how* it is to be measured, and *who* will be measuring it. Bloom and Fischer indicate that a good recording plan can help the practitioner monitor the counseling process and gain information on client progress in order to identify the need for changes in goals and objectives. An important side benefit of a recording plan is that it may help to motivate the counselor by illustrating slow day-to-day progress which may have gone unnoticed.

The identification and selection of measurement tools and techniques is the next step in the evaluation process. In their presentation the authors identified five major classes of measurement methods. Behavioral observation is the most obvious yet, in some cases, one of the most complex ways of assessing process and outcome. The sampling methods, instrumentation, and actual techniques are flexible and can be adapted for use in almost all types of situations. Self-anchored scales and other rating scales are another class of measurement methods used in evaluation. They have the strength of individualization that other methods may lack because they can be chosen for specific clients with specific problems. Client logs also have this individualized nature and they also allow the client to present material from that person's point of view, adding their own perspective to the process. Standardized instruments can be used in many situations if they are chosen effectively, keeping in mind the nature of the client and the goals of the relationship. The last measurement method, unobtrusive measures, are those techniques which gain information without the knowledge and awareness of the client. They are designed to eliminate the client's reacting to the act of being measured. The actual selection of a measurement device is a process which takes into consideration the problem, the client, the counselor and his or her approach, and the technical aspects of the method itself. The authors believe that whenever possible, the counselor should use more than one method in order to "cover the field" more effectively.

Before the intervention begins it is important to collect baseline information on each of the measures chosen for the evaluation. This step gives the counselor a starting point or "anchoring" information about the client and the counseling process. The identification and selection of the most appropriate design is the next step. The specific design chosen will depend upon the number of problems worked on, the number of interventions used per problem, and the number of clients evaluated. There is no single design which meets the needs of any one practitioner so a knowledge of various designs is necessary. An extensive review of various designs is available in Bloom and Fischer's work.

The selection of the method of analysis is sometimes dictated by the design used by some flexibility can be applied depending upon the needs of the practitioner and client. Bloom and Fischer feel that all analyses should start out with a visual inspection of the data in order to identify continuities and unexplained occurrences over the course of counseling. If this method does not give all of the desired information then other, more complex methods can be used.

The last step to an evaluation is integrating the results back into the counseling process. The original purpose of the evaluation steers the integration. In certain cases, some rather definite and obvious suggestions for changes in counseling practice may appear which can be incorporated into that counselor's style immediately. In most instances, however, the evaluation utilization process is one of carefully studying consistencies and inconsistencies among evaluations, identifying trends from relationship to relationship, and working to gain insight into what changes are necessary and how these changes can occur. Evaluation can give the counselor immediate feedback about specific clients as well as offer information which may lead to large scale changes in technique and style.

Issues Affecting the Practice of Counseling

Counseling is a moving, changing, and growing profession. In order to offer the most effective services to clients, the profession must be ever aware of and adapt to societal changes as well as the changing need structures among clientele. Counseling has been forced to broaden some of its images of the "appropriate work role," and it has constricted others. Individual professionals who have been practicing during the past decade or two have certainly undergone significant changes in focus, clientele, and duties, reflecting the structure and needs of the public. In this section, selected issues which reflect changes the counseling profession has recently undergone will be discussed. They will be grouped under four headings: issues related to new target groups for counselors; issues related to the counselor's workplace; issues related to the counselor's professional role; and issues related to the context of society. Complete books could be written about each of these areas so the authors would like to remind the reader that the following presentation is simply for the purpose of initial awareness.

Issues Related to New Target Groups for Counselors

Since the role of many counselors is to assist others in their growth and development, the supply of potential clients will never run out. Everyone at one time or another could benefit from working with a professional helper, whether it is to deal with a problem or simply to work through a developmental task. In recent years the act of going to a counselor has become much more accepted and many new target groups who can take advantage of this service have been identified. Based upon what we know about the roots of most counseling approaches it can be said that most were originally developed for use with the mass public. Very few, if any, were developed with specific groups of people or special issues in mind. Therefore, problems are often encountered when general counseling theories are applied to each person regardless of that person's background and world view.

While women are more likely to enter a counseling relationship than men (Brown and Kosterlitz, 1964; Davidson, 1976), neither the client nor the counselor have historically been aware of the sociocultural dynamics and expectations which are learned and carried even into the relationship itself. The bias in instrumentation also may be clouding assessment attempts both before and during the counseling process. Recently, these issues have received considerable attention due, in part, to the Report of the American Psychological Association Task Force on Sex Bias and Sex Role Stereotyping in Psychotherapeutic Practice (1975). This group suggested that workshops be conducted to sensitize people to the issues, guidelines for nonsexist practice be developed, a statement on sexism be included in the ethical standards, and training standards be developed for psychologists to educate them in the special issues related to counseling women.

Another group of people who have been identified as having needs which require special areas of expertise and awareness are persons with disabilities. A disability often becomes a major impediment to the growth and development process. Whether it is a developmental disability (any disability which occurs during the early developmental process up to the age of 18) or a disability occurring later in life, its very presence is a variable which often affects many other components of the client's life. While the disability may not be *the* problem, it certainly is something which both the client and counselor must always acknowledge. Shontz (1975) proposes that the process of adapting to a disability never ends, the client will always be in situations which will require an accommodation of some kind. This continuous adaptation is central to the unique focus required when working with this population.

A third target group which has been identified recently is the culturally different. Any counseling process must take into consideration the cultural background of the client in order to help generalize the experience back into "reality." When the counselor does not have at least a basic understanding of the client's background, the counseling process lacks an adequate context within which to operate. Not only will the counselor face difficulties in providing a high quality service, but the end result may be a decrease in referrals due to the inadequacy of that person's (or the agency's) ability to gain the target group's trust and cooperation.

The elderly is the last major target group to be mentioned here, representing a group of approximately 25 million people in the United States alone. Even though aging is a normal part of the growth process, the knowledge we have about the specific emotional, cognitive, and perceptual impact of aging is minimal. A commonly held myth about aging noted by Pulvino and Colangelo (1980) is that "many of the behaviors and attitudes of the elderly are natural consequences of the aging process rather than the consequences of social learning" (p. 6). Due to this belief, elderly people tend to be stereotyped in a way that just reinforces the pattern itself. Counselors have found that they can be quite helpful to the elderly by assisting with the unique developmental tasks which they face and facilitating the continuing growth process.

Issues Related to the Counselor's Workplace

In recent years counselors have been in the position of broadening both the work roles within specific organizations and the range of workplaces available to them. In the past, the counselor's realm was much more limited than it is today. Because of an expansion in areas of training and expertise, counselors find themselves able to move away from the traditional roles of school counselor, social/community agency counselor, and employment agency counselor. Recently, counselors have found themselves in hospitals and health care systems, business and industry, private-for-profit human service agencies, and private practice. The counselor is trained to facilitate communication, self-understanding, problem-solving and decision-making among individuals or groups. These same skills can be used in almost every work site imaginable to assist in career, social, family, and personal development of clients and employees.

One type of "counseling" system which presently is enjoying a healthy development is the employee assistance program or EAP. EAP's are designed to coordinate the complete process of identification, intervention, and reintegration with workers who are facing difficulties on the job due to a variety of personal or family problems. The EAP professional assists the employees so that they can return to their jobs, be more productive, and be more aware of the development of any problems in the future. Employers have typically been pleased with the EAP concept partially because of the cost benefit to the company (avoiding the costs of training and "breaking in" new people) and partially because of the positive image it can offer to the company.

Another way in which the counselor's role is changing in the workplace is related to the economics of human services. In most cases, schools, community agencies, and businesses have accepted the fact that the decade of the 1980's will be a belt-tightening time. The funding difficulties have led to a very interesting phenomenon. When a new position is opened, many agencies look for someone who will be able to wear at least two "professional hats" and take on more responsibility within the organization. This also happens with existing positions, where an employee is asked to take on additional roles so that all necessary tasks can be accomplished. While the research on this issue is minimal, it appears that services are continuing at a similar pace as before the financial crunch both in terms of quantity and quality.

Issues Related to the Counselor's Professional Role

The profession of counseling must adhere to a high level of ethical and legal behavior in order to facilitate and maintain public acceptance. Both the American Association for Counseling and Development (AACD) and the American Psychological Association (APA) have developed well-defined ethical codes which explain the obligations that a counselor has to clients and the society at large. A considerable amount of overlap exists between the two codes, but the AACD code may be more relevant for direct service providers because it deals with issues specifically related to the professional duties of counselors.

The AACD code of ethics defines the counseling relationship, clearly describes the clients' rights of privacy and confidentiality, and outlines standards for measurement and evaluation, research and publication, consulting and private practice, personnel administration, and professional preparation standards. The standards are designed to ensure that the integrity and value systems of all clients are respected and their personal welfare is promoted.

The acceptance of counseling as a profession is also dependent upon a belief in the credentialing systems used. Except for a few subgroups in the profession, the certification or licensure of counselors is a relatively new phenomenon. The purposes of credentialing are to help the public identify individuals who have attained a specified level of competence in their respective areas, assist the profession itself in monitoring the activities of the practitioners, and add to the prestige of counseling as a profession.

The two major types of credentials which are used in the counseling profession are outlined by Forster (1977). *Certification* is a process which recognizes the competence of a practitioner by a profession. Since this credential is typically administered by a governmental body or a professional organization, it does not carry the legal sanctions that the other credential, *licensure*, does. Licensure is legislated at the state level and is designed to regulate the practice and title of a profession. There are a variety of bodies who certify school counselors, substance abuse counselors, rehabilitation counselors, family counselors, and "general" counselors and, at this writing, a majority of the 50 states either have passed, submitted, or are developing licensure bills.

Another issue which is certainly not specific to the counseling profession but affects it heavily is burnout. Counselors face the difficulties and frustrations of other human beings each day. The counseling process is typically slow and methodical, often clouding obvious improvement in small incremental changes. In many cases, there will be no improvement in the client's position, possibly due to any of a variety of personal, environmental, or relationship variables. These factors all lead to a degree of stress within which some people cannot work. The most successful counselors are those who can deal with the ambiguities and frustrations of counseling and persist with a realistic frame of reference. Successful counselors also will be able to recognize when they need to work on personal issues and won't hesitate to seek assistance from others. Stress is a universal characteristic of working. It is essential for a counselor to realize this, understand how to survive within this atmosphere, and raise the possibility of growing from the experience.

Issues Related to the Context of Society

Counseling is a relationship between a counselor and a client, but this relationship occurs within the context of a greater society. In many cases, what happens in society can directly or indirectly affect the goals, process and outcome of counseling.

The most important societal change which has recently occurred is a change in the role of the family. For over hundreds of thousands of years, the purpose of the family has been to rear children, provide intimacy, insure safety from the elements and others, and provide for the satisfaction of the basic needs of food, water, and shelter. Since the time of the industrial revolution the family's role has changed significantly. No longer is the family the primary source of safety; the only source of food, water, and shelter; and the only method of rearing children and gaining intimacy. It still may be the best source for many of these but it certainly isn't the sole source.

Almost a million year's of history is difficult to change over the course of a few generations and many individuals and families are experiencing difficulties with the process. What has happened is not the so-called "decline and fall of the family" or "a break-up of the family" but, rather, a change in the conceptualization of the family itself. The family still exists but, in many ways, it's different than it used to be. Most of the family counseling styles at least recognize that this change has taken place, concentrating their efforts on what *is* rather than what *should be* (as can be seen in the chapters on Satir, Watzlawick, and Minuchin in this book). Despite our knowledge of the change, the actual impact it has on the context of counseling is great.

Another contextual issue that is especially important for counseling in the 1980's is the rise of the new conservatism. This movement touches counselors by influencing legislation, funding, credentialing, and the practice of counseling itself. Robinson (1982) notes that counseling has been referred to by some as "secular humanism" and accused of supplying a means to break down authority. Herr (1982), in defense of counseling, said that its roots reach back to the social reform movement of the 1880's and that the practice and goals of counseling are congruent with the values of a democratic society. It is not the conservatism which is necessarily challenging the counseling profession, it is the change from one style of context to another. Counselors are being put in the position of changing accepted service delivery styles in order to adapt to the environment. In the same way that counselors help clients learn how to adapt to changes in society, so must the counselor learn to function within a variety of systems: liberal, moderate, or conservative.

REFERENCES

American Psychological Association Task Force (1975). Report of the task force on sex bias and sex-role stereotyping in psychotherapeutic practice. *American Psychologist, 30,* 1169-1175.

Bergin, A.E., & Lambert, M.J. (1978). The evaluation of therapeutic outcomes. In S.L. Garfield and A.E. Bergin (Eds.), *Handbook of psychotherapy and behavior change* (2nd ed.). New York: Wiley.

Bloom, M., & Fischer, J. (1982). *Evaluating practice: Guidelines for the accountable professional.* Englewood Cliffs, NJ: Prentice-Hall.

Brown, J., & Kosterlitz, N. (1964). Selection and treatment of psychiatric outpatients. *Archives of General Psychiatry, 11,* 425-437.

Davidson, V. (1976). Patient attitudes toward sex of therapist: Implications for psychotherapy. In J.L. Claghorn (Ed.), *Successful psychotherapy.* New York: Brunner/Mazel.

Eyesenck, H.J. (1952). The effects of psychotherapy: An evaluation. *Journal of Consulting Psychology, 16,* 319-324.

Eyesenck, H.J. (1961). The effects of psychotherapy. In H.J. Eyesenck (Ed.), *Handbook of Abnormal Psychology.* New York: Basic Books.

Eyesenck, H.J. (1966). *The effects of psychotherapy.* New York: International Science Press.

Forster, J.R. (1977). What shall we do about credentialing? *Personnel and Guidance Journal, 55,* 573-576.

Garfield, S.L., & Bergin, A.E. (Eds.). (1978). *Handbook of psychotherapy and behavior change* (2nd ed.). New York: Wiley.

Herr, E.L. (1982). Perspectives on the philosophical, empirical, and cost-benefit effects of guidance and counseling: Implications for political action. *Personnel and Guidance Journal, 60,* 594-597.

Kiesler, D.J. (1966). Some myths of psychotherapy research and the search for a paradigm. *Psychological Bulletin, 65,* 110-136.

Kerlinger, F.N. (1973). *Foundation of behavioral research* (2nd ed.). New York: Holt, Rinehart.

Luborsky, L. (1954). A note on Eyesenck's article, "The effects of psychotherapy: An evaluation." *British Journal of Psychology, 45,* 129-131.

Luborsky, L., Singer, B., & Luborsky, L. (1975). Comparative studies of psychotherapies. *Archives of General Psychiatry, 32,* 995-1008.

Mahrer, A.R. (1967). *The goals of psychotherapy.* New York: Appleton-Century-Crofts.

Meltzoff, J., & Kornreich, M. (1970). *Research in Psychotherapy.* Chicago: Aldine.

Pulvino, C.J., & Colangelo, N. (Eds.). (1980). *Counseling for the growing years: 65 and over.* Minneapolis: Educational Media Corporation.

Rachman, S. (1971). *The effects of psychotherapy.* Oxford: Pergamon Press.

Rachman, S., & Wilson, G.T. (1980). *The effects of psychological therapy.* Oxford: Pergamon Press.

Robinson, E.H. (1982). The counselor and the new conservatism: Challenges in the 1980's. *Personnel and Guidance Journal, 60,* 598-602.

Rosenweig, S. (1954). A transvaluation of psychotherapy: A reply to Eyesenck. *Journal of Abnormal Psychology, 49,* 298-304.

Shontz, F. (1975). *The psychological aspects of physical illness and disability.* New York: Macmillan.

Sloane, R.B., Staples, F.R., Cristol, A.H., Yorkston, N.J., & Whipple, K. (1975). *Psychotherapy versus behavior therapy.* Cambridge, MA: Harvard University Press.

Smith, M.L., & Glass, G.V. (1977). Meta-analysis of psychotherapy outcome studies. *American Psychologist, 32,* 752-760.

Smith, M.L., Glass, G.V., & Miller, T.I. (1980). *The benefits of psychotherapy.* Baltimore: Johns Hopkins University Press.

AUTHOR INDEX

357

SUBJECT INDEX